The Adaptive Leader is refreshingly compelling in its honest ⟨barcode: I0032900⟩ than defending Agile dogmatically, Giles directly acknow offers a credible, forward-looking vision for organizations to thrive – no matter what the future brings. By tackling the myths and missteps that have plagued Agile's evolution, he reframes agility as a leadership responsibility and shows how to embed it across strategy, culture, and execution. If your teams are stuck in ceremony without impact or your transformation efforts are losing steam, this book will show you what's missing – and what to do next.

The Adaptive Leader challenges the growing narrative that Agile is obsolete. Giles argues that agility must be led from the top and that adaptive leaders are essential to bridge the gap between intent and impact, enabling organizations to thrive amid volatility. The book explores how leaders can embed agility into organizational DNA using the CLEAR Model® (Culture, Leadership, Execution, Adaptability, Responsiveness), a framework designed to support sustainable business agility across industries and functions.

The Adaptive Leader is a compelling call to action for leaders to move beyond outdated frameworks and instead build truly adaptive, resilient organizations that can respond rapidly to change and deliver lasting value.

Evan Leybourn
Cofounder and Head of Advocacy & Thought-Leadership, Business Agility Institute

As an Agile leader passionate about driving meaningful transformation, I found *The Adaptive Leader* to be a powerful and timely call to action for leaders navigating today's rapidly evolving business world. Giles goes beyond surface-level Agile practices to expose the true barrier to sustained business agility: leadership. This book is essential for anyone ready to lead change, not just manage it.

Through candid reflection and practical insight, Giles addresses the common pitfalls organizations face in traditional Agile transformations and offers a clear path toward truly adaptive, future-ready leadership. *The Adaptive Leader* delivers invaluable guidance for coaches, consultants, practitioners, and executives, especially those who have struggled with Agile adoption or questioned its continued relevance. Even as an experienced leader in this space, I found this book both refreshing and practical, offering compelling strategies that have reinvigorated how I guide organizations through transformational change.

Amy Luethmers
Agile Coach/Consultant, 108 Consulting Group

The Adaptive Leader arrives at precisely the right moment for executives determined to shape the future, not be shaped by it. Giles goes beyond theory, providing pragmatic, actionable guidance for leaders who must drive meaningful, lasting transformation.

Having spent 30 years at the forefront of strategic change, from global enterprises to nimble startups, I recognize the real difference: success is rooted in leadership mindsets that foster empowerment, resilience, and cultural evolution. Giles's roadmap echoes the very lessons I've seen drive sustainable agility in the real world: clarity of purpose, transparent communication, and true adaptability that permeates far beyond the IT department.

This book is an indisposable asset for executives and change leaders ready to move from 'doing' Agile to cultivating adaptive cultures that deliver value, champion innovation, and inspire their people. Giles delivers hard-won insights, tools, and frameworks that help leaders cut through complexity, embrace agility at every level, and position their organizations for long-term success.

If you, like me, have witnessed both the pitfalls and the transformative power of true business agility, *The Adaptive Leader* will resonate deeply. It's the definitive leadership guide for those intent on sparking cultural change, aligning teams, and unlocking enterprise potential.

Neil A. Walker
Organizational Agility Strategist, Change Expert and Enterprise Coach –
Rehumanizing Agile Practice for over 30 Years

The Adaptive Leader is essential reading for leaders across technology, HR, marketing, financial services, and beyond. Giles expertly bridges the gap between Agile's origins and its evolution into a cross-functional leadership philosophy. This book cuts through the noise and delivers practical, forward-thinking strategies for driving agility at scale, whether you're leading software teams or transforming enterprise-wide culture. A vital resource for anyone serious about thriving in complexity.

Femi Odelusi
PCC, Transformation and Executive Coach

Regardless of perspective, Giles demonstrates the authentic and data-informed behaviours he advocates. Instead of automatically defending the techniques that made him successful, he returns to basic principles, gathers evidence, and asks: 'What is the value of business agility in an AI-enabled era?'

Russ Lewis
Doctor of Professional Practice (Digital Transformation)

Let yourself be drawn into the world of *The Adaptive Leader*, where Giles blends refreshing honesty with practical, real-world insight. Drawing on years of experience guiding transformations, he shows how true agility needs leaders who shape the entire organization.

Giles tackles the big questions head-on: Is Agile still relevant in today's volatile, AI-driven world? His answer is clear – yes, more than ever. But this is only possible if leaders across the business are willing to experiment and lead the change. Through candid reflection and actionable steps, *The Adaptive Leader* reveals how to make true agility happen across culture, strategy, and execution.

This isn't about theory, it's about the practical experiences of an Adaptive Leader, a leader who embraces change, seeing it as an exciting opportunity to adapt.

Anneke Panman
Enterprise Agility Coach, John Lewis Partnership

THE ADAPTIVE LEADER

Leading the Future of Business Agility in a Post-Agile World

GILES LINDSAY

Practical Inspiration
Publishing

To my wife, Anneke, who remains my greatest source of support and my constant inspiration. Your belief in me has made all the difference, and for that, I am endlessly grateful. With all my love, I dedicate this book to you.

Agility is not about doing more, faster – it's about doing the right things at the right time, with clarity and purpose.

Table of Contents

Foreword

A Strong Foundation, A Dynamic Future

Great leadership is built on a strong foundation, but it can't stop there. It has to be dynamic, evolving with the times. In *The Adaptive Leader*, Giles Lindsay takes the deep roots of adaptive leadership and extends them into the post-Agile era, showing us what it really takes to lead in a world where change is constant.

The idea of adaptability in leadership isn't new. Ron Heifetz set the stage in *Leadership Without Easy Answers* (1994), challenging leaders to navigate complexity rather than impose rigid control. A few years later, Stephan Haeckel (IBM) built on that with *Adaptive Enterprise* (1999), introducing the 'sense-and-respond' approach that helped shape modern business strategy. His work influenced my own thinking when I wrote *Adaptive Software Development* (2000).

By the time I published *Adaptive Leadership: Accelerating Enterprise Agility* in 2013, it was clear that adaptability wasn't just a nice-to-have – it was a necessity. Agile was already moving beyond its software roots, and organizations needed leaders who could bridge strategy, execution, and culture in real-time. That's exactly where *The Adaptive Leader* picks up the story.

Let's face it: we've all seen our fair share of 'Agile' which is anything but. Frameworks layered on top of old-school hierarchies, endless ceremonies with no real impact – Agile in name only. Giles cuts through the BS and gets to the heart of what really matters. This book isn't about blindly following a methodology; it's about leading with adaptability, fostering real agility, and making an actual impact.

Giles' work with a major fintech company stands out. He helped them transform from a rigid hierarchy to a flexible, customer-focused organization in just 18 months. That kind of real-world transformation doesn't happen by sticking to a script – it happens when leaders understand how to adapt, empower teams, and create a culture where agility actually works.

And if you're expecting another dry leadership tome, think again. Giles has a knack for making complex ideas digestible. His writing is direct, engaging, and – most importantly – useful. The book is not just about theory. Giles gives you tools you can use Monday morning to start shifting your organization's culture.

As someone who's been in the trenches of Agile transformation for decades, I can tell you that he's taken the baton from pioneers like myself and run with it, pushing the boundaries of what adaptive leadership can achieve. He doesn't just study agility – he lives it, helping companies rethink how they operate, how they lead, and how they create value in a rapidly changing world.

A strong foundation matters, but leadership isn't about admiring the old blueprints – it's about dynamic building. *The Adaptive Leader* is for those ready to move beyond static playbooks and construct organizations that don't just survive disruption but thrive because of it.

Don't just read this book – use it. Highlight it, dog-ear it, scribble in the margins. This is a workbook for the future of leadership. The world is changing fast – are you ready to build something that can keep up?

Jim Highsmith, Agile Pioneer and co-author,
The Agile Manifesto

Preface

During the 2010s, I worked at a global firm struggling with Agile adoption. Despite training and frameworks, teams felt frustrated. The missing piece? Leadership. Only when executives shifted from command-and-control to Adaptive Leadership did we see real transformation. This book shares that lesson at scale.

Now, before we begin, assess your organization's agility with these five questions:

1. Do teams make decisions independently, or does leadership dictate most priorities?
2. Are failures seen as learning opportunities or as mistakes to avoid?
3. Do you measure success based on customer impact rather than output?
4. Can teams pivot quickly when priorities shift?
5. Is leadership actively involved in Agile culture, or is it left to teams?

If you answered 'no' to any of these, this book will provide you with the leadership tools to bridge those gaps.

In *The Adaptive Leader*, I confront the misconceptions surrounding Agile, debunking the myths of its supposed demise while exploring what lies ahead for leaders aiming to navigate and lead in the future of work. Born from the Agile Manifesto in 2001, Agile has transformed how teams deliver value for over two decades, pushing boundaries in adaptability and collaboration. But as critics declare it '*dead*', my aim here is to offer a broader perspective: Agile is not ending – it is evolving, and leadership plays a crucial role in this transformation.

Agile is no longer enough. The future belongs to leaders who can think beyond frameworks, challenge outdated rituals, and build adaptability into the DNA of their organizations. This book isn't just about Agile – it's about leading in a world where change is the only certainty. Welcome to the age of the Adaptive Leader.

This is Post-Agile leadership, where agility is no longer a methodology but a mindset embedded in leadership, decision-making, and culture.

This book is a forward-thinking exploration of Agile's future, built on the understanding that while Agile faces critiques, it remains a vital and adaptive force shaping how we work. In this post-Agile world, where traditional practices are being re-examined, leaders must evolve their approach to stay ahead. Through the lens of recent experiences – including key learnings from conferences and industry insights – I share how Agile is adapting to meet these new challenges. From the rise of hybrid work to the need for sustainability and ethical practices, this isn't just a discussion about whether Agile still works; it's about how leaders can harness Agile's evolution to redefine the future of work.

This journey requires a new perspective – one that views Agile not just as a set of practices but as a catalyst for organizational and leadership change. Adaptive leadership is the cornerstone of navigating Agile's future, requiring leaders to foster a culture of continuous learning, embrace change, and empower their teams to thrive amid uncertainty. Adaptive leaders play a pivotal role in this evolution, shaping how Agile principles are embraced and sustained within teams. It calls for leaders to adopt the mindset shift necessary to lead in an environment that demands continuous innovation and adaptability.

At the core of this journey is the transformation of leadership itself – changing how we work, think, and lead, revealing the potential within teams and organizations to adapt and thrive. Throughout the book, I provide specific leadership lessons and strategies to help you become a more adaptive leader, guiding your teams through change and fostering an environment where agility becomes a shared mindset.

I also aim to provide challenging and insightful perspectives – exploring Agile's perceived pitfalls and claims of its 'death'. By unpacking these myths, I reveal Agile's core strengths and show how effective leadership can harness its capacity for continuous change to shape the future of work. My goal is to help readers understand that Agile is not a relic of the past; it is a way of working that continues to shape the future, especially as it intersects with emerging technologies and shifting cultural dynamics.

With rapid advancements in Artificial Intelligence (AI) and Internet of Things (IoT), which are characteristics of the Fourth Industrial Revolution, the need for Adaptive Leadership has never been greater. Agile is not just evolving – it provides leaders with answers to help organizations thrive amid these disruptive shifts, promoting resilience and long-term growth amid ongoing changes.

This book is written for Agile practitioners, leaders, and business decision-makers across various industries who are ready to challenge conventional thinking, break through outdated myths, and lead their teams toward a future shaped by true agility. It is as much about embracing action-oriented solutions as it is about understanding Agile's challenges from a leadership perspective.

By sharing successes, criticisms, and pitfalls, the book aims to provide you with a realistic, balanced perspective. Understanding both sides of the debate allows you, as leaders, to align Agile more effectively to the unique needs of your teams and organizations, empowering you to make informed, impactful decisions.

This is more than a guide to frameworks and methodologies – it's about embedding agility as a core leadership strength. The concepts I share go beyond IT and software, reaching into every part of the business – from marketing and HR to finance and legal, and into industries such as healthcare, education, and manufacturing. The book's practical examples and case studies will illustrate how Agile's evolution impacts various sectors, making abstract concepts tangible and relatable for leaders.

I want you to take away practical, actionable insights that help you drive transformation within your organization, making it agile in the truest sense: responsive, empowered, and ready to tackle the complexities of modern business. If you're a leader who's tried Agile and not seen the hype deliver, this book will show you why and what to do differently.

My hope is that this book empowers you to lead with confidence, push boundaries, and continue shaping your organization with agility at its core, truly preparing for the future of work. This book is further evidence of Agile's transition from specialization into mainstream management competency.

Your journey into reimagining Agile starts here. As an adaptive leader, you are key to breaking the myths, embracing true agility, and shaping the future of work. Together, we will explore how to harness Agile's full potential to build resilient, innovative, and future-ready teams. Let's embark on this transformative journey.

Giles Lindsay FIAP FBCS FCMI
CEO, Agile Delta Consulting Limited

How to Use This Book

This book is designed to work in two ways: as a complete read that builds your understanding of leadership in a post-Agile world, and as a toolkit you can use straight away. Every chapter links back to the CLEAR Model® – Culture, Leadership, Execution, Adaptability, Responsiveness – so you can move between sections without losing the thread. Choose the path that best suits your role and current priorities.

Path 1: Executive 90-Minute Skim

For senior leaders who need the essence quickly.

1. **Read the Introduction** (5 min) – understand the case for change.
2. **Scan key CLEAR sections in Chapter 7** (10 min) – review the Business Agility Canvas.
3. **Review Chapter 3 Leadership Moves Map** (10 min).
4. **Jump to Chapter 16 Strategic Roadmap** (15 min) – see the high-level sequence.
5. **Check toolkits in Chapters 3, 6, 7, 10, 13, 14, 16** (15 min).
6. **Finish with Conclusion and Epilogue** (5 min).

Outcome: You'll know the CLEAR Model®, the core leadership moves, and the first steps to take.

Path 2: Transformation Lead 7-Day Plan

For programme directors, transformation leads, or heads of change leading organization-wide agility.

Day 1: Preface, Introduction, Chapters 1–2 (including diagnostic).
Day 2: Chapters 3–4 (adaptive leadership, post-Agile context).
Day 3: Chapters 5–6 (culture and team-centric agility).
Day 4: Chapters 7–9 (business agility, scaling, operational agility).
Day 5: Chapters 10–12 (culture across contexts, outcome-based agility, evolving roles).
Day 6: Chapters 13–14 (tech-enabled agility, future of work).
Day 7: Chapters 15–16 plus toolkits in Chapters 3, 6, 7, 10, 13, 14, 16.

Outcome: You'll gain a complete picture and a plan for embedding CLEAR throughout your organization.

Introduction

> **Progress is impossible without change, and those who cannot change their minds cannot change anything…**
>
> *George Bernard Shaw*

Many leaders sense Agile has stalled, caught in routines that no longer deliver results. Yet Agile isn't fading – it's evolving, and adaptability is at its core.

Picture a 150-year-old manufacturer losing nearly half its production within months. Trusted clients shift to quicker competitors, old processes crumble, and stress builds. While some leaders stick rigidly to outdated methods, others choose to adapt. By creating cross-functional teams, simplifying processes, and rekindling team motivation, they slash delivery times, retain key customers, and secure their future. Their story highlights agility's true strength: organizations that evolve, survive, and thrive.

You might have heard, 'Agile is dead.' Is this claim accurate, or have we misunderstood Agile's role and potential?

For nearly 30 years, Agile has shaped my career as a Software Engineer, Agile Coach/ Instructor, and CIO/CTO/NED. I've led organizations through powerful Agile transformations and seen firsthand its immense impact when implemented effectively. But I've also witnessed organizations struggle due to misconceptions. My experience tells me Agile isn't about following rigid processes – it's about leadership that adapts, empowers, and reshapes organizations for ongoing success.

Agile: Both a Vitamin and Painkiller

Business solutions often fall into two categories: painkillers, which tackle urgent problems like inefficiencies or security gaps, and vitamins, which offer gradual improvements in performance and well-being. Many see Agile as a vitamin – useful but optional, yet it can be both. We don't need great ideas; we need great problems.

Agile provides immediate solutions for sluggish decision-making, rigid processes, and disengaged teams while also laying the foundation for long-term success. Leaders who embrace this dual role gain rapid benefits and lasting resilience.

Systems thinker Mike Burrows (2025) describes this balance as a cycle of delivering, discovering, and renewing. Discovery uncovers new opportunities; renewal updates the ways of working to support them. Most teams focus on delivering, but it's the integration of all three that unlocks true agility. Renewal isn't extra work – it's how agility stays alive.

This book consolidates practical examples, expert advice, and real-world insights, clearly illustrating Agile's ongoing value.

Agile is adapting to the times, and so should we!

Leading Through Adaptability

Today, leadership isn't just about managing tasks – it's about empowering teams to confidently handle uncertainty. Adaptive leaders create an atmosphere where teams can quickly respond to challenges, make informed decisions, and continually improve.

At the heart of this book is the CLEAR Model®, a leadership-first approach that centres on *Culture, Leadership, Execution, Adaptability,* and *Responsiveness.* CLEAR moves beyond rigid processes by guiding organizations through complex transformations, embedding agility directly into their ways of working. Rather than relying on static strategies, CLEAR enables rapid feedback loops, continuous learning, and incremental delivery – helping leaders quickly validate assumptions, reduce risk, and pivot confidently before challenges escalate.

Understanding Agile: Adapt or Decline?

Agile is a mindset focused on flexibility, collaboration, and continuous value. Ask yourself honestly: Are you enabling agility or merely ticking boxes? Your answer will determine your organization's future – adaptation or stagnation.

Organizations such as Tesla and Amazon prove that Agile principles apply far beyond IT, enhancing responsiveness across the business. This book guides leaders beyond checklists and towards genuinely living Agile principles.

N.B. In this book, *mindset* refers to individuals' beliefs, attitudes, and approaches toward work and challenges.

What's in It for You?

This book is not just theory – it is a practical guide for leaders who want to thrive in a setting that demands adaptability.

It provides:

- **Clarity on Agile's Future**: Cutting through the noise of sceptics to show how its principles remain valuable.
- **Practical Leadership Strategies**: Beyond frameworks, it focuses on embedding agility at a leadership level.
- **Actionable Tools and Frameworks**: Templates, self-assessments, and case studies that can be applied straight away.
- **Relevance Beyond IT**: Showing how agility extends across finance, HR, marketing, and other areas.
- **A Balanced Perspective**: Recognizing Agile's limits while presenting real ways it can evolve.

Are you ready to embrace change and lead your organization towards evolution?

Agile thrives on simplicity, yet many organizations complicate it unnecessarily. Leaders must return teams to Agile's core values – iterative improvement, clear communication, and collaboration. They must move beyond superficial adherence, reinforcing transparency and adaptability rather than slipping back into comfortable but ineffective routines.

Are you prepared to rethink how Agile principles can drive success in your organization?

Addressing the Critics

Critics of Agile are partly correct – poor implementation and misunderstood principles cause failures. However, these failures result from superficial approaches, not inherent flaws in Agile itself. That said, Agile is not a panacea. Some practices may not fit all projects, teams, or organizational cultures. Effective leaders must adapt thoughtfully, not apply it blindly.

This book tackles these criticisms head on. It demonstrates how Agile, when executed thoughtfully, becomes a flexible philosophy tailored to specific organizational needs. Adaptive leaders ensure Agile becomes a source of genuine, lasting value rather than another bureaucratic exercise.

The Journey Ahead

Agile isn't a final goal – it's continuous learning, adaptation, and refinement. This book breaks down key strategies, exploring how Agile principles evolve from team practices to organization-wide agility.

In 2024, I chaired the first Business Agility Conference UK, reinforcing Agile's evolving relevance. Insights from industry experts and practical case studies provide actionable leadership strategies for navigating complexity.

The future requires leaders who champion resilience, innovation, and confident change. Are you ready to lead boldly, inspiring your teams to embrace agility authentically? This book equips you to embed agility deeply into your organization's approach.

What Solution Is the Book Offering?

This book offers practical approaches, particularly the CLEAR Model®, helping leaders foster genuine agility. Whether scaling Agile, embracing new work models, or sparking innovation, these tools and strategies deliver lasting results.

Adopting Agile is urgent. Organizations that hesitate risk irrelevance amid economic shifts, technological disruption, and workforce anxieties. Agile empowers leaders to future-proof organizations, building responsive and resilient workplaces.

Can your organization afford to wait while others adapt and thrive?

Who Should Read This Book?

This book serves anyone driving organizational change – executives, managers, change agents, consultants, and Agile practitioners across diverse industries. It provides strategies to overcome barriers and achieve lasting agility.

Key audiences include:

- **C-suite executives, transformation leads, and Agile coaches**: Leaders managing complex organizational change, guiding teams through technological shifts, and evolving workplace dynamics.
- **Middle managers and team leads**: Vital links between strategy and execution, seeking actionable insights to foster agility within their teams while aligning with organizational goals.
- **Organizational change agents in HR or Learning and Development (L&D)**: Professionals embedding agility into the cultural fabric of companies across functions like finance, marketing, and operations.
- **Consultants and Agile coaches**: Those guiding businesses through Agile adoption and maturity, looking for enhanced methodologies and refined practices.
- **Non-technical executives**: Leaders in finance, marketing, and other areas who want to understand how Agile can deliver improved outcomes and support organization-wide change.
- **Academic leaders, educators, and students**: Individuals studying business management, organizational behaviour, or project management, seeking real-world perspectives on Agile's evolution and applications.

How Is This Book Organized?

Across six parts and 16 chapters, this book uses the CLEAR Model® to structure and embed agility in your organization's DNA. Each section delivers practical leadership strategies, frameworks, and real-world examples.

Part 1: Understanding the Evolution of Agile (Adaptability and Responsiveness)

This part explores Agile's journey, dispels myths, and affirms its relevance, laying the foundation for how Agile practices must evolve to stay effective. Adaptability is at the core of this evolution, requiring organizations to respond to change with agility and foresight.

Part 2: Reframing Adaptive Leadership (Leadership)

This part focuses on leadership's role in overcoming Agile challenges and creating the right environment for agility to thrive. Leadership is the foundation that ensures Agile moves beyond a process and becomes a strategic enabler.

Part 3: Empowering Teams and Culture for Sustainable Agility (Culture)

This part focuses on building environments that enable sustainable agility – ones that support Agile practices and empower teams for long-term success.

Part 4: The Key Elements for Business Agility (Culture, Leadership, Execution, Adaptability, and Responsiveness)

This part covers how these five elements combine to embed agility beyond IT, uniting strategy, leadership, and delivery for impactful results.

Part 5: The Evolving Agile Organization (Adaptability and Responsiveness)

This part examines how Agile must evolve to remain relevant in modern organizations, covering cultural shifts, measurement, roles, and technology.

Part 6: Continuous Learning and the Future of Agile (Adaptability and Culture)

Agile is not a fixed system – it is a mindset of continuous learning, adaptation, and cultural evolution.

Key Features of the Book

A Journey Through Agile's Evolution
From its earliest roots to its future possibilities, this book charts how Agile has grown – and how it must keep growing.

Courageous and Honest
The book faces Agile's toughest questions head on. No sugar-coating. These are just real insights that help leaders do better.

Built for Action
The book is packed with practical tools, real stories, and the CLEAR Model® to help you lead with purpose and precision.

Leadership at the Centre
It puts people first. Because without strong, adaptive leadership, no framework can deliver lasting change.

Ready for What's Next
It looks ahead to AI, hybrid work, and the changing shape of teams – so you can lead what's coming, not just what's current.

Diversity That Drives Agility
The book shows how inclusion, equity, and belonging aren't side notes – they're the foundation of resilient, creative teams.

Lessons From the Real World
Case studies bring the ideas to life. Successes and failures alike offer lessons that stick.

Agility with Integrity

It highlights how ethical leadership – privacy, sustainability, fairness – is essential to long-term agility.

Designed for Today's Complexity

It offers clear strategies to help you thrive in complexity and not get lost in it. Practical. Tested. Human.

Agile for a Global Stage

It explores how agility works across borders, cultures, and industries – because leadership knows no boundaries.

This Isn't Just a Book About Agile

It's a rallying cry for bold, human leadership in a world that refuses to stand still.

Agile isn't a destination – it's a continuous journey of adaptation. As you read this book, consider what adaptability means for you, your teams, and your organization. The CLEAR Model® provides the framework; your leadership makes the difference.

Are you ready to lead boldly, break outdated myths, and fully harness Agile's potential? The path ahead may twist, but the possibilities for adaptive leaders are enormous.

Let's begin.

Part 1

Understanding the Evolution of Agile

CLEAR Focus: Adaptability and Responsiveness

Agility is not static – it evolves. This section explores Agile's journey, dispels myths, and affirms its relevance. Adaptability is crucial, as organizations must respond to change with agility and foresight. Responsiveness ensures that Agile is not just a trend but a meaningful approach to evolving business challenges.

1

Is Agile Really Dead?

The reports of my death are greatly exaggerated.

Mark Twain

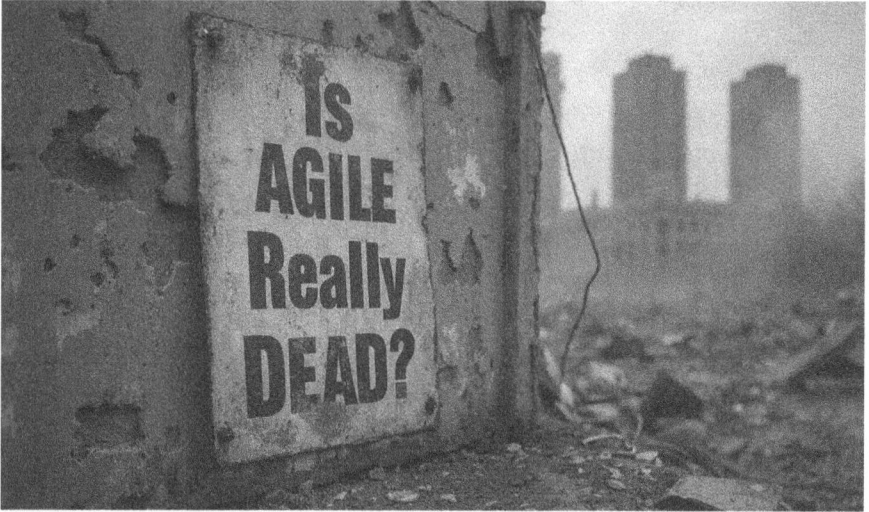

What You'll Gain

- **For Senior Leaders and Executives**: Learn why Agile's reported demise is exaggerated and how strategic leadership can keep Agile relevant.
- **For Mid-Level Leaders**: See how to guide teams through Agile's evolution, avoiding rigid frameworks and focusing on genuine results.
- **For Students or Early-Career Professionals**: Understand Agile's origins and adaptations so you can apply its core values in emerging roles.

Agile's Funeral Has Been Announced – But Who Sent the Invite?

Over the past few years, a dramatic claim has been circulating in conference talks, LinkedIn debates, and boardroom discussions: *'Agile is dead.'*

Agile's success has led to its over-commercialization. Some critics argue it has been diluted by consultants selling frameworks rather than fostering real adaptability. Others believe Agile has become too process-heavy, with rituals taking priority over outcomes.

Now, there is some truth to these criticisms. Many organizations have struggled to implement Agile in a way that truly delivers adaptability, often treating it as a checklist rather than a mindset. In other cases, Agile has been misapplied and forced into rigid corporate structures that contradict its principles.

But does that mean Agile is truly dead? Or is it simply misunderstood, misapplied, and ready for its next evolution?

The reality is that Agile is not dead – it is adapting. And the companies and leaders who recognize this shift will be the ones who thrive in the next decade of business transformation.

Debating Agile's Future: End or Evolution?

Some businesses have since abandoned Agile, only to adopt its principles later under a new name. Others embarked on ambitious changes that faltered – not because Agile was flawed, but because leaders misunderstood it.

Some Agile Manifesto principles – such as 'deliver working software frequently' – were revolutionary in 2001, but in an era of continuous deployment, they require a fresh perspective. Adaptive leaders now prioritize value streams and continuous flow, integrating Lean principles and shifting from project-based to product-based structures. Agility today is about leadership-driven adaptability, not just faster sprints.

Personal Reflection

I remember a pivotal moment in my career when a major Agile transformation was on the verge of failure. Leadership hesitated, fearing it was just another passing trend. Yet, by reframing the conversation – focusing on adaptability rather than rigid adherence to frameworks – we shifted the mindset. The outcome? Higher engagement, shorter delivery cycles, and an organization that continued to evolve well beyond initial expectations. This moment reinforced a key lesson for me: Agile isn't dying; it's adapting.

For executives, this debate isn't just about terminology – how Agile is perceived directly influences their transformation strategies. A flexible mindset underpins modern work practices, so Agile continues to matter. Detractors may dismiss its constant reinvention, yet that trait keeps Agile relevant. Every advance in technology sparks a shift in how people work, and Agile evolves alongside these shifts.

Agile itself is evolving. Leaders should accept that Agile's classic practices now reach into broader areas. People call this 'post-Agile', but it doesn't mean abandoning Agile. Instead, it blends adaptability, customer value, and innovation into daily routines. This chapter explores why Agile keeps evolving and why that matters for staying competitive.

Stepping into this fresh stage means adjusting long-held Agile values such as teamwork, adaptability, and a focus on results to handle the latest hurdles. Watching Agile move from frameworks to a holistic mindset confirms its maturity. Leaders who embrace 'post-Agile' methods encourage ongoing experimentation, embed Agile values into their leadership style, and keep building resilience through the CLEAR Model®, using its five dimensions to equip their teams to quickly adapt, respond effectively to challenges, and sustain high performance.

After coaching many companies, I've seen how Agile's deeper values surpass the surface-level ceremonies. They help teams navigate complexity while staying focused. Chapter 4 digs deeper into 'post-Agile' thinking, showing how modern leadership thrives by evolving these core ideas.

Understanding Agile's Origins

As someone who has followed Agile's journey since the Agile Manifesto of 2001, I've seen the power of putting people first, cultivating collaboration, and embracing flexibility, transforming how organizations handle change. These aren't just lofty ideals; they are the building blocks of resilience. Even before the Manifesto, frameworks like Scrum, Extreme Programming (XP), and Dynamic Systems Development Method (DSDM) steered teams toward iterative, adaptable ways of working. They laid the groundwork for what became Agile, which has evolved in parallel with shifting business environments, making it a cornerstone of modern work. Just as these early frameworks propelled Agile, similarly, adaptive methods will persist, even if the name 'Agile' evolves. Agile's adaptability also extends beyond software development, reinforcing its broad, lasting value across multiple industries.

One lesser-known but influential work from 1990, *Wicked Problems, Righteous Solutions*, by Peter DeGrace and Leslie Hulet Stahl, described many elements that helped shape Scrum. It drew on the rugby metaphor introduced by Ikujiro Nonaka and Hirotaka Takeuchi in their 1987 *Harvard Business Review* article, 'The New New Product Development Game'. Both references showcased cross-functional teamwork, seamless collaboration, and short iterations. Those concepts paved the way for Agile principles years before the Agile Manifesto was written.

Despite these successes, Agile sometimes becomes an all-purpose cure rather than one of many ways to address organizational problems. It was originally a flexible alternative to heavy documentation and rigid planning, never meant to cover every situation. When leaders adopt Agile without checking if it suits their context, disappointment can arise if expectations aren't met. A wiser route is to see how Agile ideas can work alongside other strategies rather than replace them.

Agile's well-known contributions – delivering work in small chunks and building through Minimum Viable Products (MVPs) – come from Lean Manufacturing. These ideas transformed not only software but also the broader business space. Yet, they are not the only option. When Agile is promoted as a 'one true method', hype overshadows its real value: applying relevant principles and adapting them to the team's reality.

So, is Agile truly finished? No. It's one major phase in an ongoing shift in how we work. Moving from frameworks to an organizational mindset, Agile influences how people operate at all levels. Reflecting on its roots highlights its staying power and clarifies the debate about its modern relevance.

Agile, while transformative, does not solve every problem. Critics who label it 'dead' often fail to propose anything more productive. The real question is not whether Agile is finished but how it should advance. Many organizations are ditching cluttered steps, like complicated estimation, opting for simpler processes. This change refines Agile's application to fit current technologies and team habits rather than throwing it out.

My goal in this book is to share both critical and supportive viewpoints, explaining why Agile still thrives as a catalyst for real change. Studying Agile's background helps us interpret current trends, fresh ideas, and expert opinions that shape conversations about its relevance. Observing how Scrum and XP emerged reveals a universal cycle: new concepts challenge tradition, meet resistance, and adapt over time.

With that historical lens in mind, let's see where Agile stands today, including radical approaches such as 'Extreme Agile', to understand how far it can stretch beyond its original boundaries.

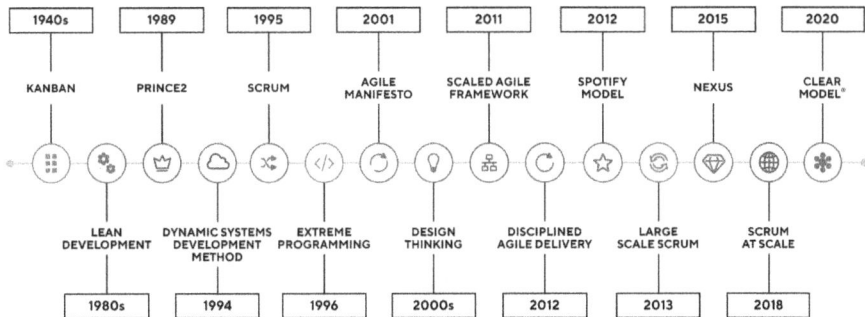

1940s	1989	1995	2001	2011	2012	2015	2020
KANBAN	PRINCE2	SCRUM	AGILE MANIFESTO	SCALED AGILE FRAMEWORK	SPOTIFY MODEL	NEXUS	CLEAR MODEL®

LEAN DEVELOPMENT	DYNAMIC SYSTEMS DEVELOPMENT METHOD	EXTREME PROGRAMMING	DESIGN THINKING	DISCIPLINED AGILE DELIVERY	LARGE SCALE SCRUM	SCRUM AT SCALE
1980s	1994	1996	2000s	2012	2013	2018

Timeline of Agile's evolution

Extreme Approaches and Paradigm Shifts

Agile has matured over the years through incremental improvements and bold experiments. Jeff Sutherland, co-creator of Scrum, introduced *Extreme Agile* – wedding AI with Agile workflows to supercharge productivity. While promising, it demands caution. AI and automation can certainly improve results but also bring pitfalls – overdependence, ethical dilemmas, or diminished human inventiveness. Leaders must ensure tools augment rather than replace critical thinking. Agile should incorporate these tools responsibly, with leadership offering strategic judgment that machines alone can't match.

Renowned coach Tobias Mayer has cautioned that code is like poetry: AI alone can't replicate a seasoned developer's elegant solutions. This insight highlights that Agile's evolution must prioritize merging innovation with human skills.

Agile's progression aligns with Thomas Kuhn's theory of scientific revolutions. Initially, software development was chaotic (pre-paradigm). The Waterfall model brought structure – 'normal science'. Over time, cracks in Waterfall led to rising failure rates, sparking a crisis resolved by the Agile Manifesto and its iterative ethos. This transformation reshaped collaboration, innovation, and how teams deliver value.

Kuhn's lens reminds us that true shifts are rarely linear or universally accepted. They involve conflict, experimentation, and navigating turbulence, with visionary leaders guiding teams through the unknown.

That style of leadership – Adaptive Leadership – is fundamental to furthering Agile, ensuring it morphs to address new complexities and remains a trusted pillar of success.

Why Adaptive Leadership Is Essential for Agile Evolution

Adaptive leadership equips organizations to keep Agile up to date. Leaders who use it connect Agile's conceptual promise with day-to-day outcomes by focusing on constant learning and flexibility. This approach ensures Agile remains influential. It helps businesses stay imaginative and aligned with emerging priorities.

Personal Reflection

At a tech company I advised, leaders struggled with virtual teams. They adopted Adaptive Leadership strategies – regular check-ins, online brainstorming, and anonymous feedback – to maintain collaboration. Results improved morale and showed how Adaptive Leadership keeps Agile relevant when team members rarely meet in person.

This chapter highlights how Agile's progress depends on such leadership. Understanding why is easier when you see how frameworks like Scrum and XP first enabled growth. Leaders who show flexibility encourage a culture where Agile evolves from a method to a philosophy that shapes behaviour. By demonstrating that attitude, they highlight continuous experimentation and context-based refinements as part of Agile's core, not a side note. In education, for example, leaders harness this mindset to stay effective in shifting classroom demands.

Some critics refer to an 'Agile Circus', where fixations on frameworks and certificates overshadow genuine outcomes. Agile, like all large-scale shifts, can become watered down if people lose sight of its essence. Tools should remain tools, not the ultimate goal.

Adaptive Leadership in Action: Practical Tips

- **Promote Open Discussion**: Ask teams what obstacles block progress, then address root causes instead of quick fixes.
- **Encourage Smaller Experiments**: Let teams run limited trials with new ideas. Celebrate lessons, whether the result is success or failure.
- **Lead by Example**: Show your willingness to adapt plans when new data emerges.
- **Ask 'Why?' Often**: Revisit the purpose behind processes or meetings. If they don't add value, adjust or remove them.

Agile's Maturity and Ongoing Value

Some people claim Agile has outlived its usefulness. What we see instead is an approach that keeps renewing itself. Critics of Agile may see the clumsy use of outdated Agile methods as proof of irrelevance. Yet evidence suggests that Agile's flexible thinking remains a strong source of creativity. Organizations around the globe still benefit from Agile approaches. Where it was once a set of frameworks, Agile is now a mindset of curiosity and client focus.

To remain significant, companies must address doubts head-on and avoid letting Agile slip into hollow patterns. Mature Agile isn't tied to repetitive processes. One global logistics provider, for example, places real user feedback at the heart of strategic meetings, guiding decisions with genuine data rather than legacy processes. That is Agile in action: learning from each challenge in an ongoing cycle of improvement.

Detractors sometimes call Agile a passing fad, blaming the hype surrounding it or shallow implementation efforts for its perceived failure. To fully explore that, the next chapter takes a closer look at criticisms and how leaders can tackle them. A few remain unconvinced, believing Agile has drifted away from its essence, now entangled in red tape and commercialization.

The Critics' Viewpoint

Some say Agile became too bloated and lost track of its origins. They argue that many have misunderstood it, turning it into a product to sell rather than a mindset. Dave Thomas, an original Manifesto signatory, points out that 'Agile is Dead' often reflects misguided views and commercial distractions that overshadow Agile's emphasis on adaptability and team spirit. Moving away from certificates and back to Agile's core values can correct this.

Others claim Agile has triggered new layers of management, citing scaled frameworks like SAFe that add complexity. That seems opposed to the simplicity Agile once promised. As Dave Thomas notes, Agile has always prioritized a flexible outlook, not processes themselves. If you want genuine Agile, centre on communication, responding swiftly, and delivering true value – never hide behind rituals.

A disconnect between Agile's theory and real implementation is widely acknowledged. Instead of fostering freedom, some organizations reduce Agile to a routine. That robs teams of the adaptability that defines Agile. Going from 'Doing Agile' to 'Being Agile' involves building a culture of trust, shared goals, and everyday learning. Chapter 2 explores these issues in greater depth.

Agile now faces both worldwide challenges – commercial influences and clashing frameworks – and local resistance in traditional company cultures. Leaders must decide whether they champion Agile's real spirit or reduce it to an item on a checklist. By rethinking leadership methods, we can guide teams back to the energy and creativity at Agile's core. Yet criticism alone doesn't capture the entire situation.

A researcher once asked me: *'Is Agile still Agile? Has it lost its core, or is it evolving?'* That sums up the debate. Some believe Agile has strayed too far, while others see that shift as progress. Agile is not rigid. It never was. Its basic principles endure, even if the ways we apply them morph. As conditions shift, Agile's purpose changes. The real concern is whether leaders are fully embracing Agile's potential or just clinging to worn-out routines.

Three Real Reasons People Think Agile Is Dead

Agile is not failing because its principles are flawed. It's failing in organizations that treat it as a process rather than a leadership philosophy.

Here are the three biggest factors behind the 'Agile is dead' narrative.

1. Agile Has Been Hijacked by Frameworks and Certifications

The Agile Manifesto, written in 2001, was meant to be a guiding philosophy for adaptability and customer collaboration. However, in many organizations, Agile has been reduced to a rigid set of frameworks like Scrum, SAFe, and LeSS, which are often enforced without understanding why they exist.

- Companies prioritize compliance over adaptability – focusing on 'doing Scrum' rather than achieving business agility.
- The Agile coaching industry has become over-commercialized, with certifications creating an illusion of expertise.

The problem? Agile was never about blindly following a framework. True agility means adapting to context, not forcing teams into predefined methods.

2. Many Organizations Are 'Doing Agile' but Not 'Being Agile'

A common pattern in large enterprises is performative agility – teams go through the motions of Agile ceremonies, but decision-making remains slow, bureaucratic, and top-down.

- Daily stand-ups exist, but leaders still expect big upfront planning.
- Sprints are scheduled, but there's no real ability to pivot when priorities change.
- Leadership preaches empowerment, but teams still need approval for every minor decision.

The Problem? Agile is not a process to implement – it's a culture shift. Without leadership buy-in and systemic change, Agile collapses into a façade.

3. The Leadership Gap: Agile Without Adaptability Fails

Agile transformations often ignore the most critical factor – leadership.

- Executives expect agility at the team level but still manage with outdated command-and-control tactics.
- Agile transformations are often treated as IT initiatives when they should be enterprise-wide shifts.
- Leaders don't model agility themselves – they want teams to be adaptable but fail to embrace change at the top.

The Problem? If leadership doesn't change, agility never scales beyond isolated teams.

So, Is Agile Dead? No. But Leadership Must Evolve

Agile is not dying – it's evolving into something more holistic, more strategic, and more leadership driven. The future of Agile isn't about better frameworks or more certifications – it's about Adaptive Leadership, and this book helps bring Agile into mainstream management. Organizations that thrive in this post-Agile era will be the ones where leaders embrace agility as a mindset, not just as a methodology. That means:

- Creating a culture where adaptability is expected, not punished.
- Embedding Agile principles into strategy, not just team workflows.
- Measuring success based on value delivered, not process adherence.

Agile's survival isn't about methodologies – it's about how leaders enable agility. The future of Agile belongs to Adaptive Leaders who embrace its principles beyond IT, extending agility into decision-making and organizational culture.

To lead this shift, this book introduces the CLEAR Model® – a leadership-first approach that equips organizations to embed agility across every level. It's not just a tool for delivery teams but a practical framework that aligns culture, leadership behaviours, strategic goals, and team execution.

Why the CLEAR Model® Matters for Sustainable Agility

The CLEAR Model® bridges the gap between Agile implementation and true business agility by focusing on five critical elements: *Culture, Leadership, Execution, Adaptability,* and *Responsiveness*. Organizations often struggle with agility because they optimize Agile frameworks but neglect adaptability at scale. The CLEAR Model® ensures that agility isn't just a team-level practice but an enterprise-wide capability, enabling leadership to make data-driven decisions while empowering teams to act autonomously.

While several approaches exist to broaden agility across an enterprise, the CLEAR Model® offers a structured way to unify these core drivers. In the modern workplace, organizations often struggle to bridge high-level goals with day-to-day realities. Leaders ask, 'How do we truly embed agility across every part of our business, not just inside a handful of teams?' This is where the CLEAR Model® offers practical guidance. More than a mere framework, CLEAR points the way to an organization-wide mindset that promotes ongoing learning and innovation.

The CLEAR Model®

Building on this need for embedded agility, the CLEAR Model®, presented in my first book, *Clearly Agile: A Leadership Guide to Business Agility*, confronts the myth that agility begins and ends with team practices. Instead, it offers a comprehensive approach for modern enterprises navigating complexity and change.

CLEAR brings together the essential pillars of an Agile organization. It's grounded in real observations of leaders grappling with how to align cultural shifts and strategic goals, offering a focused guide from top-level planning through to daily execution.

From Practical to Principled

Evolving from real-world leadership moments, the CLEAR Model® balances tangible practices with Adaptive Leadership principles. Adaptive leaders use CLEAR to make agility a strategic priority, ensuring teams don't just 'do Agile' but integrate the right behaviours into the organization's DNA:

- **C**ulture: Sharing an ethos of psychological safety and agility-focused values.
- **L**eadership: Showing openness, empowerment, and a unifying vision.
- **E**xecution: Converting Agile thinking into measurable, outcome-driven actions.
- **A**daptability: Staying flexible enough to address shifting markets and workplace conditions.
- **R**esponsiveness: Building feedback loops that allow for quick, data-informed decisions.

The CLEAR Model® wasn't developed in isolation; it arose from real leadership pressures – moments when structure had to meet flexibility and urgent decisions had to be made amid uncertainty. Its core purpose is to help leaders align culture, strategy, and execution with adaptability at every level, ensuring agility becomes a strategic organizational advantage rather than a siloed exercise.

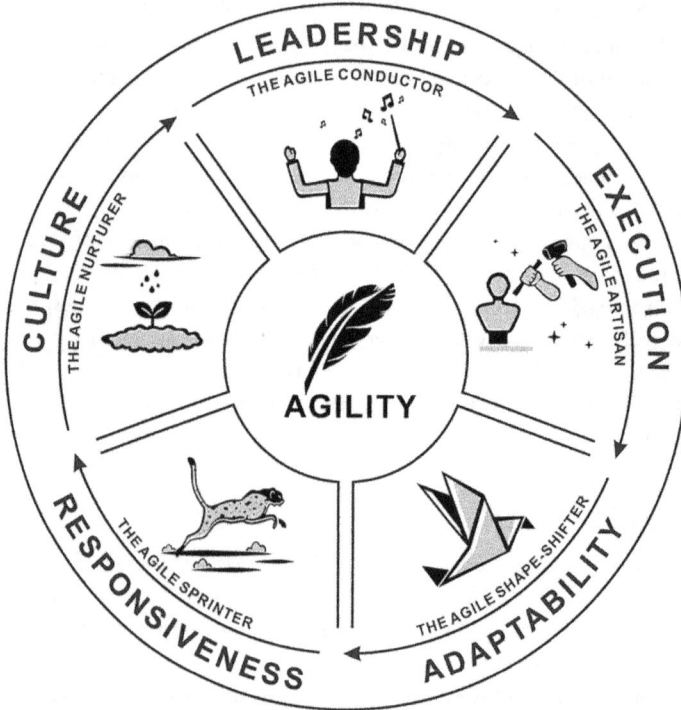

The CLEAR Model® of Business Agility – Each element of the CLEAR Model® supports a sustainable and scalable approach to business agility across all sectors.

Today's Agility Trends

Recent findings, like the 2024 Business Agility Report, classify agility into critical areas for surviving dynamic business environments. The highest-rated capabilities – customer focus, engaged employees, and organizational resilience – mirror CLEAR's emphasis on Culture and Leadership. Acting as one organization demands a blend of values, structures, and behaviours, which CLEAR addresses in each of its pillars.

Designed to solve everyday roadblocks, the CLEAR Model® bridges daily tasks with strategic transformation. It serves as a roadmap to unlock holistic organizational change. Leaders apply its structured yet flexible guidelines to keep agility meaningful and integrated throughout all functions.

Bringing CLEAR into the Real World

With the CLEAR Model® setting the foundation, it's essential to ground the discussion in current evidence. How are organizations actually applying these principles? What results are they seeing? Let's explore the latest data and success stories that show why agility, when supported by strong leadership, still delivers measurable value across sectors.

Supporting Evidence of Agile's Relevance

Various surveys – like the 2023 State of Agile Report – show that 95% of companies have adopted Agile in some capacity, pointing to benefits like improved adaptability to shifting priorities (70%), better project visibility (65%), and higher productivity (64%). Nonetheless, difficulties such as process inconsistency (46%) and cultural barriers (43%) persist. So while widespread adoption is strong, the next step is refining Agile approaches to fit each unique environment.

In the meantime, Forrester's *The State of Agile Development, 2025* also underscores Agile's continuing value: 95% of professionals see Agile as essential, with 58% of leaders focusing on deeper adoption. The biggest hurdles revolve around scaling, championing leadership engagement, and effectively integrating AI to enhance data insights. The conclusion remains that Agile is evolving, not extinct.

Adapting to Change

At the Business Agility Conference UK 2024, transformation consultant Sheetal Thaker quoted Darwin's idea that 'survival belongs to those most able to adjust'. This is the heart of Agile. It remains useful when adapting to new demands. Some schools, for example, are introducing iterative teaching to enhance learning outcomes. Agile's flexibility extends far beyond coding.

Agile never aimed to be rigid. It seeks to help teams deal with complexity and ongoing shifts. As AI, remote working, and varied customer needs evolve, Agile must keep changing while holding on to its original spirit. Success depends on leaders who can guide teams through unknown territory.

Next, we consider the leadership challenges that arise as Agile progresses.

Leadership Challenges in Agile's Ongoing Evolution

Teams adopting Agile sometimes struggle with morale changes, distributed collaboration, and finding a balance between freedom and accountability. Such dilemmas require leaders who admit uncertainty and stay transparent.

Remote teams, in particular, can feel disconnected. Caring leadership steps in to ensure Agile is truly practised rather than simply mandated.

Leadership Challenges

- **Maintaining Agile's Authenticity**: Ensuring that frameworks serve the mindset, not overshadow it.
- **Sustaining Engagement**: Finding new ways to keep distributed or hybrid teams cohesive.
- **Fostering Openness**: Building a culture where sharing ideas and doubts is the norm.

These aspects rely on leaders who understand Agile as an evolving approach. They can accept valid critiques and prepare for the future.

One common example is 'Corporate Theatre', when organizations copy Agile rituals but miss the mindset behind them.

Understanding 'Corporate Theatre'

'Corporate Theatre' or 'Agile Theatre' arises when organizations mimic Agile rituals – like daily stand-ups or retrospectives – without addressing deeper cultural or structural barriers. The result is disillusionment when stand-ups produce no meaningful change, or leadership still imposes commands top-down.

True empowerment requires giving teams genuine access to resources, decision-making authority, and customer insights. Without this, empowerment becomes an illusion – accountability without real autonomy. When teams are expected to deliver outcomes without the levers of influence, Agile practices lose credibility, reinforcing scepticism rather than promoting agility.

How Leaders Can Avoid 'Corporate Theatre'

1. **Focus on Core Values**: Emphasize cooperation, adaptability, and results, not just rituals.
2. **Cultivate Openness**: Admit mistakes, invite honest feedback, and act on team input.
3. **Empower Teams**: Let teams tailor their Agile practices, granting autonomy and accountability.
4. **Measure Actual Outcomes**: Track user satisfaction or speed of delivery rather than compliance with a process.
5. **Provide Education**: Offer coaching so teams truly grasp Agile's essence rather than blindly copying steps.

Personal Reflection

I once visited a major financial firm, and I was impressed by its Agile branding: motivational posters, daily stand-ups, and the works. Observing their actual routines revealed mechanical meetings, ignored feedback, and top leaders still pushing rigid roadmaps. It was corporate theatre on display.

Adaptive leaders must break that cycle. Instead of piling on new ceremonies, they create an environment where teams embrace Agile values. Stand-ups, sprints, and retrospectives become catalysts for connection, not a chore. If teams see Agile as just another box to tick, leadership needs to reset expectations. Agile aims for valuable results, not process compliance.

Have you observed instances of 'Corporate Theatre' in your own organization? How might this be affecting your team's perception of Agile?

Looking Under the Lamppost

A related phenomenon is 'looking under the lamppost', an analogy Edgar Schein used to show how teams focus on easily measurable processes while ignoring deeper-rooted issues. That might involve fine-tuning stand-ups yet neglecting to reform a command-and-control leadership style. Agile leaders need to shed light on these less visible aspects of culture, psychological safety, and mindsets if they want genuine transformation.

Key Insight: Focusing on surface-level rituals but ignoring systemic barriers perpetuates the illusion of agility without achieving meaningful improvements. Real shifts demand confronting cultural and behavioural norms, building trust, and ensuring that each ceremony or practice serves a clear purpose.

Impact of Criticisms

Criticisms of Agile often highlight genuinely dysfunctional patterns. Confronting these head-on leads to stronger, more responsible Agile processes. It also leaves room for new approaches, like building stronger user-feedback loops or refining leadership styles.

'Is Agile Dead in Your Org?' Diagnostic

Agile can look healthy on the surface yet fail to move real outcomes. This self-check helps you spot theatre, weak decision paths, and slow feedback loops. Treat it as a quick mirror, not as a verdict.
How to run it well:

- Invite a small mixed group, e.g. from product, tech, ops, and finance.
- Score on your own first, then compare scores and discuss gaps.
- Pick one weak area to fix now, not three. Depth beats spread.
- Repeat every quarter to see if the score shifts.

What you'll get:

- A clear view of where practice drifts from intent.
- One constraint to remove within the next 30 days.
- A simple way to track progress across teams.

Instructions: Rate each statement 1–5 (1 = strongly disagree, 5 = strongly agree). Add up for a score out of 60.

1. Teams have real autonomy over how they deliver work.
2. Leaders act on feedback from staff and customers quickly.
3. Our Agile practices are tied to measurable business outcomes.
4. Meetings and ceremonies have a clear purpose and value.
5. Priorities are stable enough for teams to finish high-value work.
6. Metrics track outcomes and learning, not just delivery speed.
7. We stop or change initiatives when evidence shows low value.
8. Leaders are visible in supporting Agile ways of working.
9. People feel safe to speak up without negative consequences.
10. Our processes evolve in response to evidence, not fashion.
11. We collaborate easily across departments.
12. We learn from failures and share lessons widely.

Scoring:
- **50–60**: Agile is alive and evolving – protect and refine.
- **35–49**: Agile is at risk – target weak items in the next 90 days.
- **<35**: Agile is theatre – reset with culture and leadership focus first.

Why Agile Still Matters

Core Agile principles – like responding promptly to change, prioritizing customer collaboration, and valuing individuals over rigid processes – are especially relevant in today's fluid markets. Problems occur not because Agile is obsolete but because many teams never adopt its genuine cultural perspective.

Beyond the software domain, Agile's iterative approach enhances marketing campaigns, financial planning, and more. By systematically applying short cycles and constant learning, organizations maintain responsiveness amid fluctuating market and technological contexts.

While some folks boldly proclaim 'Agile is dead', they often conflate the decline of superficial implementations with the real essence of agility. Thus, the next step is to examine these criticisms in detail and explore how leaders can address them successfully. Chapter 2 delves further into the controversies, pinpointing how leaders can convert them into positive reforms.

Agile's resilience stems from the way it merges iterative work with a deeper culture of openness and learning. This synergy fosters continuous adaptation in industries from healthcare to retail. So, the debate about Agile's 'end' might be misreading the natural evolution of a living concept, one that transforms just as markets do.

Agile Evolution in Practice

Below are two examples of Agile's evolution that highlight its value as it matures and shapes modern practices.

Case Study 1: Amazon's Evolution Through Agile Principles

Amazon, a leading e-commerce and technology company, applied Agile principles across its operations.

- **Approach**: Agile ways of working that enable quick pivots, customer-centric experiments, and data-driven learning to adapt seamlessly to customer preferences.
- **Outcome**: Turned agility into a competitive advantage. This illustrates how Agile's evolution underpins its maturity and underscores its critical role in modern organizations.

This example shows how continuous customer focus and adaptation help an organization thrive.

Case Study 2: Toyota's Lean–Agile Synergy

Toyota, a leader in the automotive industry, applied Agile principles to its production system, known as the Toyota Production System (TPS).

- **Approach**: Emphasized continuous improvement (*Kaizen*), respect for people, and just-in-time production.
- **Outcome**: Achieved higher efficiency, reduced waste, and improved product quality, demonstrating Agile's applicability beyond software development.

This case shows how iterative improvement and team empowerment – core Agile values – significantly boost efficiency and quality in manufacturing.

Both examples reinforce how adaptability, customer focus, and iterative thinking can guide diverse industries. Now, let's revisit the essence of Agile's value to see how these guiding principles stay central.

Revisiting Agile's True Value

When the Agile Manifesto launched, it highlighted relative priorities – prioritizing individuals over processes didn't dismiss processes but reminded teams not to become enslaved by them.

Agile was invented to break away from slow, bureaucratic workflows. Its revolutionary achievements can be undermined by misguided attempts or superficial adoptions. The best approach is situational: using Agile's iterative model where it fits, while acknowledging that other approaches might be better for certain projects.

Jim Highsmith (co-author of the Manifesto) points out that 'over' in the Agile principles doesn't exclude items on the right but emphasizes the importance of items on the left. This helps avoid misunderstandings that might cause over-engineered frameworks.

Constantly refreshing the Manifesto's ideals – like frequent collaboration, fast learning, and openness to changing requirements – keeps teams aligned with a real Agile mindset. By re-committing to these elements, we stop bureaucracy from creeping in and overshadowing Agile's value.

Agile's Ongoing Promise

What does the future hold for Agile as AI, machine learning, and broader disruptions arise? Agile must handle these demands while remaining flexible. Each new hurdle can also be a chance to prove Agile's endurance.

At its core, Agile is about continuous learning and iterative change. This concept is vital for organizations dealing with evolving challenges. Teams that adapt will stand out. The pillars that shaped Agile – collaboration, flexibility, and responsiveness – are still essential for progress.

Leaders hold the power to guide teams into this new chapter of agility. Agile's path is also yours. By embracing it, you spark fresh ideas, strengthen collaboration, and build an adaptable culture.

Conclusion

The question 'Is Agile really dead?' matters less than understanding that Agile has matured and changed shape. Critics highlight real flaws when Agile is poorly applied, though their concerns can drive an honest return to Agile's foundational values. True agility comes from a mindset open to new ideas.

Tracing Agile's roots reveals iterative improvement, learning, and collaboration – principles that remain critical in modern business. Adaptive leadership enables these values to flourish by shedding rigid mindsets. Consider how your organization practises Agile. Is it superficial ceremonies or a shared mindset that fosters learning, freedom, and trust?

Some voices insist Agile has run its course. Are they right, or are deeper problems being overlooked? The next chapter explores this discussion, tracing the origins of key criticisms and showing leaders how to address them.

Agile's ongoing worth isn't in doubt – only our ability to apply it effectively. Organizations that cling to mechanical Agile stand-ups risk stagnation, while those that embrace continuous learning will prosper. The real question is not 'Is Agile dead?' but 'Are we evolving swiftly enough to let Agile work for us?'

Call to Action

As someone in a position of influence, reflect on how your organization views Agile. Is it an energizing set of practices or just another process? Which concrete steps will you take to boost trust, enable flexibility, and encourage cooperation? Share thoughts with fellow leaders or write them down – collective ideas can guide real improvement.

Key Takeaways

- **Agile Adjusts, Not Expires**: Despite rumours, it changes form and remains significant.
- **Missteps Come from Misuse**: Criticisms often target rigid or shallow implementations.
- **Leaders Fuel Agile's Next Phase**: Strong leadership aligns with Agile's creative and adaptable essence.
- **Agile Principles Reach Further Than Software**: Finance, healthcare, and education all benefit from its values.
- **From Doing to Being**: Agile transforms culture when it's lived daily, not just followed mechanically.

CLEAR Model® Connection

- **Adaptability**: Agile's survival rests on its ability to evolve.
- **Responsiveness**: Teams must adjust promptly to changing demands.

Key Takeaway: Agile is not dying – it is adapting. Leaders must shift their mindset from rigid frameworks to a flexible, responsive approach that embraces uncertainty and continuous improvement.

Self-Assessment Checklist: Evaluating Your Agile Practice

- **Assess Current Agile Implementation:**
  - o Are Agile practices consistently applied across teams?
  - o Do teams understand the core principles of Agile beyond the methodologies?
- **Identify Signs of Stagnation:**
  - o Is there resistance to change or adaptation within teams?
  - o Are processes becoming rigid or overly bureaucratic?
- **Evaluate Market Alignment:**
  - o Are your Agile practices keeping pace with industry trends?
  - o Do you regularly gather and act on customer feedback?
- **Plan for Evolution:**
  - o Have you identified areas where Agile practices can be adapted or improved?
  - o Is there a strategy for integrating new methodologies or tools?
- **Assess Your Leadership Style:**
  - o What have you done to promote an Agile mindset within your team(s)?
  - o What have you done to encourage adaptability and continuous learning?
- **Identify Barriers:**
  - o Are there organizational policies hindering agility?
  - o Do team members feel empowered to make decisions?

Action Plan Template: Embracing Agile Evolution

1. **Define Objectives**:
   o   Clearly articulate why evolving Agile practices is necessary.
2. **Engage Stakeholders**:
   o   Involve team members, leadership, and customers in discussions about change.
3. **Research Emerging Trends**:
   o   Investigate new Agile frameworks, tools, or practices relevant to your industry.
4. **Pilot New Approaches**:
   o   Implement changes on a small scale to test effectiveness.
5. **Review and Adapt**:
   o   Collect feedback and make adjustments before wider implementation.
6. **Define Leadership Goals**:
   o   Outline how you will embody and promote Agile principles.
7. **Engage Your Team**:
   o   Facilitate open discussions about agility and adaptability.

Chapter Summary

Agile evolved from a software-centric framework to a mindset for meeting challenges in many fields. This chapter showed how its core values still help organizations stay flexible, creative, and focused on continuous learning. Leaders who champion testing, openness, and improvement can preserve these benefits.

Use Agile's roots to adapt it to fresh demands rather than treat it as finished. Agile's future is in your hands. By encouraging a culture of trust and willingness to adjust, you can turn Agile from a routine into a driver of lasting change.

2

Understanding the Critics – What They Get Right and What They Miss

Criticism is something we can avoid easily by saying nothing, doing nothing, and being nothing.

Elbert Hubbard

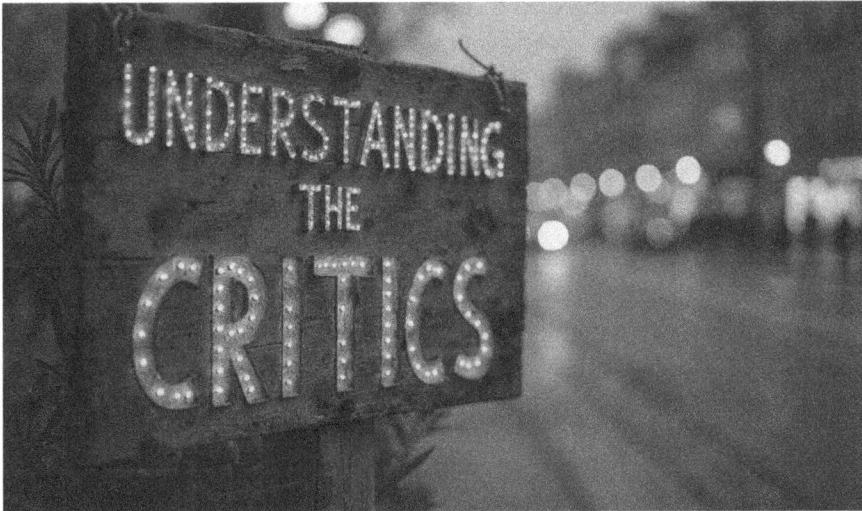

What You'll Gain

- **For Senior Leaders and Executives**: Learn how to respond to Agile's main critics by examining common pitfalls and reorienting frameworks toward genuine cultural shifts.
- **For Mid-Level Leaders**: Gain clarity on typical misunderstandings that lead to rigid application, helping teams evolve rather than get stuck.
- **For Students or Early-Career Professionals**: Discover why Agile sometimes falters in practice and how deeper awareness can spark better results.

Why Agile's Harshest Critics Matter

Agile's critics often speak the loudest when expectations go unmet. Chapter 1 framed the so-called 'death of Agile' as an exaggeration – and it is. But the frustrations behind those headlines aren't baseless. In this chapter, we'll go deeper into what those critics are actually saying. Which complaints are valid? Which stem from misuse or poor leadership? And how should adaptive leaders respond?

True agility doesn't fear critique – it learns from it. Let's unpack the core criticisms and see what they reveal about where Agile breaks down, and where leadership must step up. One executive recently told me, '*Agile teams just create chaos*'. It's a common perception. Without clarity or guidance, Agile can feel disorganized. However, adaptive leadership channels that chaos into experimentation and alignment, turning uncertainty into a strength rather than a liability.

Explaining the Critics' Perspective

Agile has passionate supporters, yet it also faces strong objections from those who find it overhyped or ineffective. Some point to bloated processes, jargon, or transformations that fail to deliver. These detractors may be highlighting real flaws that leaders can correct. Listening to them, rather than dismissing their points, can reveal important insights.

Criticism often arises when Agile strays from its original intent. Identifying these trends helps leaders recalibrate and keep Agile effective. Early in my career, a major Agile rollout sparked anger. Rather than ignoring complaints, leaders integrated feedback to refine their approach, producing better outcomes.

This chapter explores these debates, urging leaders to examine how they themselves adopt Agile. Still, there are moments when agility – done right – can fall short. A former client, despite disciplined sprints and leadership buy-in, struggled to adapt when market conditions shifted dramatically. Agile gave them adaptability, but it couldn't solve a declining market alone. This reinforces that agility isn't magic – it's a powerful tool, not a guarantee.

By understanding the reasons behind each concern, leadership teams can dismantle hidden blockers and unlock Agile's true potential. Some see Agile as a shortcut to predictability, but it actually merges structured iteration with adaptability to address complex challenges. Clearing up confusion about its purpose is vital for keeping Agile relevant and useful.

Critics sometimes claim Agile is merely about minimal oversight or quick fixes. Its true strength lies in an ongoing focus on learning, openness to change, and group collaboration. Leaders who welcome different perspectives often uncover solutions no single individual could develop alone. Being open to scepticism, rather than becoming defensive, keeps Agile valuable. In one large reorganization, clarifying Agile's values during upheaval restored alignment. This reminded me how clarity can be a leader's greatest asset.

Leaders who thoughtfully examine critiques can uncover new ways to shape Agile. By addressing perceived problems, teams develop an Agile system that aligns with modern needs. The section below expands on the main criticisms, exploring their causes to help leaders refine their methods.

The Most Common Criticisms of Agile

Below are five recurring criticisms that appear across industries. These are not flaws in Agile itself – but signs of how it's misunderstood, misapplied, or misled by poor leadership.

1. Process Overload and Framework Fatigue

'Agile was supposed to be simple – but now we're buried in meetings, ceremonies, and certifications.'
  What started as a lightweight alternative has often been overloaded with layers of bureaucracy. Frameworks like SAFe or Scrum were meant to guide, not control – but they're frequently misused as rigid templates.

Leadership Fix

- Simplify where possible. Remove any process that doesn't add value.
- Remember: Agile was designed to reduce bureaucracy, not create more.
- Use frameworks as tools, not rules.

2. Misunderstood and Superficially Applied

'We changed job titles, not mindsets.'
  Too many Agile transformations amount to surface-level rebrands without shifting culture or leadership behaviours. Agile fails not because of the concept but because it's applied as a method instead of a mindset.

Leadership Fix

- Teach Agile as a philosophy, not a checklist.
- Empower teams with autonomy and trust.
- Align cultural change with business outcomes.

3. Lost in Commercialization and Tribalism

'Agile is becoming an industry instead of a mindset.'
  The rise of certifications, expensive consultants, and internal 'Agile bureaucrats' has led some to question whether Agile is about outcomes or appearances. Meanwhile, the community can feel divided by rigid camps: SAFe vs LeSS, Scrum vs Kanban.

Leadership Fix

- Focus on value, not certifications.
- Hire for experience, not just credentials.
- Encourage context-based practices over one-size-fits-all dogma.

4. Misaligned with Strategy and Technical Discipline

'We're delivering quickly – but are we delivering the right things, or building technical debt?'

Agile teams sometimes move fast without clear alignment to broader strategy or long-term quality. Speed without purpose or technical excellence just multiplies problems.

Leadership Fix

- Align Agile delivery with strategic goals.
- Reinforce technical excellence through DevOps, automation, and sustainable engineering.
- Avoid short-term gains that create long-term pain.

5. Fatigue, Disruption, and Resistance

'Agile feels chaotic – it's change without clarity.'

Poor implementation can leave teams burnt out or confused. Constant pivots, unrealistic expectations, or unclear leadership create stress, not agility.

Leadership Fix

- Pace change. Agile should mean controlled, purposeful adaptation – not constant churn.
- Prioritize team health and sustainable delivery.
- Set clear boundaries around what can change, and when.

These criticisms highlight not that Agile is broken, but that the way it's often led is. The real issue lies in leadership gaps – misalignment, misunderstanding, and misapplication. The rest of this book shows how adaptive leadership can restore what Agile was always meant to be.

When Agile Might Not Be the Best Fit

Amid these criticisms, there's also the question of whether Agile is suitable for every type of work. Some environments are so stable or so strictly regulated that short iterative cycles offer limited benefits, or even add unwanted complexity. Others tackle very fixed, one-off projects where requirements rarely change mid-stream.

This doesn't mean Agile is pointless – regular feedback loops and collaboration can still help – but it may not make sense to overhaul a highly regimented project with a full Agile transformation. In heavily regulated sectors, for example, a stage-gate or Waterfall-like approach might be more efficient for certain phases, while Agile techniques can be blended in for smaller parts of the process (like quick user research or pilot testing).

As a leader, it's worth asking: *'Does my project genuinely need continuous iteration, or are we forcing Agile where it doesn't fit?'* Context matters. The key is choosing or adapting methods that enhance outcomes rather than tick boxes. In some settings, combining Agile with other frameworks (like Six Sigma) may achieve better results than purely relying on sprints or ceremonies.

Put simply: Agile isn't a universal solution – it's one powerful way to handle evolving needs. Recognizing when Agile alone isn't optimal can actually reinforce credibility, showing that your leadership is grounded in realism rather than dogma.

Beyond These Five Criticisms: Broader Organizational Challenges

Resistance to Organizational Research

Some teams adopt Agile while ignoring established knowledge about motivation, group dynamics, and change management. This limited approach overlooks proven insights that could strengthen collaboration.

Cultural or Ethical Oversights

A narrow focus on sprint speeds or velocity may eclipse attention to team culture or ethical considerations. One example might be ignoring how an AI-based product affects privacy or certain user groups.

Concluding Observations

Iterative, adaptive ways of working predate the Agile Manifesto. These collaborative responses remain vital for tackling complex goals. Critics often point out where a framework overshadows the mindset. Addressing these points is crucial for preserving Agile's vitality. Leaders must ask if they're contributing to these pitfalls.

Model Drift and Crisis

Model drift describes the moment when a method stops matching the conditions for which it was built. Waterfall once felt suitable, imposing a structure on unclear projects. As complexities grew, it could not adapt, fuelling the rise of Agile. Now, with remote work and new demands, certain Agile frameworks also appear to struggle, as signalled by the popularity of certifications and standardized processes.

However, it's not just external conditions that cause drift – losing sight of Agile's original intent and purpose accelerates it. When frameworks become rigid or prioritize process over principles, Agile is blamed for failure rather than the way it was applied. Critics see trouble unless Agile evolves again.

Leaders should frequently review and update their Agile practices, preserving adaptability, cooperation, and continuous iteration. That stops Agile from becoming a relic. Model drift highlights the deeper mismatch between any method and the behaviours that produce real agility. Solving it calls for less focus on the blueprint and more on the human element behind success.

Frameworks as Distractions from Agility

Another frequent complaint is that frameworks become ends in themselves, diverting teams from the real drivers of agility – behaviours, culture, and leadership. Scrum and SAFe were always intended as flexible frameworks, yet they are often misinterpreted as rigid systems by those who do not fully understand them. This fosters an illusion of agility without the core traits of adaptability and shared ownership.

True agility depends on how people work together, make decisions, and innovate. Leadership is essential: it sets the tone for empowering teams to take risks and solve problems. Instead of forcing compliance with a set process, leaders should cultivate mindsets and behaviours that fulfil Agile's original goal of responding wisely to new situations.

When everyone is scrambling to 'follow the rules', they lose sight of the core values that formed Agile in the first place. Leaders who highlight trust, autonomy, and customer impact restore agility's essence.

Leadership as the Catalyst for Agile Evolution

Critics' frustrations often stem from mismatches between expectations and reality. Leaders who engage with criticism rather than dismiss it can shape Agile's future positively. Adaptive leadership is the missing piece – it bridges the gap between Agile's principles and its real-world execution. Instead of reacting defensively to Agile's shortcomings, strong leaders use them as signals for improvement, fostering experimentation, trust, and continuous learning.

Too often, criticisms of Agile reflect flawed implementations rather than issues with the methodology itself. Many leaders mistakenly impose frameworks without truly absorbing Agile's values, leading to mechanical, process-heavy adoption rather than real agility. Without leadership driving Agile as a mindset, not just a process, teams fall back into familiar patterns, such as 'mini-waterfall' habits. Leaders must create an environment where Agile principles take root, ensuring that iterative ways of working are reinforced and adapted to fit each team's context.

True Agile evolution doesn't come from enforcing methods – it comes from leaders who shape culture. Those who champion Agile's purpose are best positioned to redefine it for modern contexts, ensuring that agility permeates every level of the organization. This requires more than simply rolling out frameworks; it demands continuous refinement, open dialogue, and a willingness to challenge outdated assumptions.

Still, leadership alone isn't enough. Without clear governance and strategic alignment at the executive level, Agile often remains confined to delivery teams. This is where the C-suite's role becomes pivotal – ensuring Agile thinking scales beyond operations and becomes a fundamental driver of business strategy.

How Adaptive Leaders Respond to Agile Criticism

1. Instead of blindly defending Agile, they fix its failures.
2. Instead of enforcing rigid frameworks, they embed agility as a mindset.
3. Instead of viewing Agile as a cost, they use it as a tool for business survival.

Agile's Critics Are Not the Enemy – They're a Mirror

None of these criticisms means Agile is inherently flawed. Instead, they reveal leadership gaps that prevent Agile from working as intended.

As leaders, we can either:

- Dismiss these critiques and defend Agile dogmatically
  or
- Use them as a roadmap to evolve Agile into something better

How Adaptive Leaders Turn Criticism into Action

- Instead of rejecting bureaucracy outright → Find the balance between structure and agility.
- Instead of forcing Agile frameworks → Apply Agile principles where they make sense.
- Instead of chasing certifications → Invest in real-world Agile experience.
- Instead of fearing Agile chaos → Use Agile transparency to increase visibility and control.

Agile's future depends on leaders who embrace adaptability, not those who defend Agile as dogma.

C-Suite Playbook: Governance and Strategy for Agile Enterprises

Transformations often fail when executives treat Agile as the domain of mid-level staff. Organizational agility expands when CEOs and boards embrace iterative thinking in governance and strategic planning.

1. Aligning Agile with Enterprise Strategy

Senior leaders can ensure Agile is more than an IT initiative by integrating it into the company direction. That involves replacing lengthy annual roadmaps with flexible quarterly plans.

Action Steps for Executives

- Update planning cycles to be frequent and adaptable.
- Channel investment into the initiatives that deliver consistent value.
- Form a council or steering group that oversees agility across divisions.
- Use OKRs (Objectives and Key Results) to track and improve on empirical results.

2. Agile Governance at the Board Level

Classic governance often aims at compliance and risk aversion, creating delays. Agile governance values nimble decisions, local accountability, and outcomes focused on customers. Don't apply governance to your agility. Apply agility to your governance.

Board Considerations

- Set performance indicators around the speed of choices and customer benefits.
- Move away from fixed budgets, allowing resources to shift based on value.
- Empower self-leading teams that operate within broad strategic limits.

3. Managing Risk in an Agile Enterprise

Agile acknowledges risk, aiming to manage it through quick learning and small tests. Leaders set a tone where teams feel safe making informed decisions with guardrails in place.

Key Practices

- Keep real-time performance metrics so leaders can spot early signals.
- Plan in short cycles using test-and-learn methods.
- Embrace small-scale 'failures' as valuable lessons that prevent massive setbacks.

When top executives view Agile as more than a method, treating it as a strategic priority, organizations develop genuine adaptability.

Of course, building an Agile organization isn't just about governance and structure. Organizations' development of talent and validation of Agile expertise also play a significant role. This brings us to a common debate: are Agile certifications a meaningful learning tool, or have they become just another career commodity?

From Superficial Adherence (Doing Agile) to True Transformation (Being Agile)

Imagine two companies both calling themselves 'Agile'. Alpha Corp runs daily stand-ups and retrospectives and uses online task boards, yet top managers micromanage, and decisions take far too long. Beta Ltd fosters distributed decision-making, consistent collaboration, and an adaptive culture. The difference: Alpha is 'doing Agile', while Beta is 'being Agile'.

Teams that focus on ceremonies alone might see marginal gains, but they never achieve the broader shift. 'Being Agile' means adopting curiosity, joint ownership, and continuous improvement each day, not only during sprint reviews.

Doing Agile

- Ticks all the boxes (stand-ups, sprints, ceremonies).
- Leaders still micromanage.
- Progress is mostly for show.

Being Agile

- Lives the values of flexibility, customer focus, and iterative learning.
- Leaders empower teams to solve problems.
- Ideas flow freely, fuelling genuine growth.

The differences are massive. Groups stuck in surface-level Agile see mild gains. Those who shift their mindset can see a genuine culture of trust, engagement, and continuous improvement. That cultural pivot also influences ethics and well-being within Agile setups.

The diagram and table below highlight the significant difference between 'Doing Agile' and 'Being Agile':

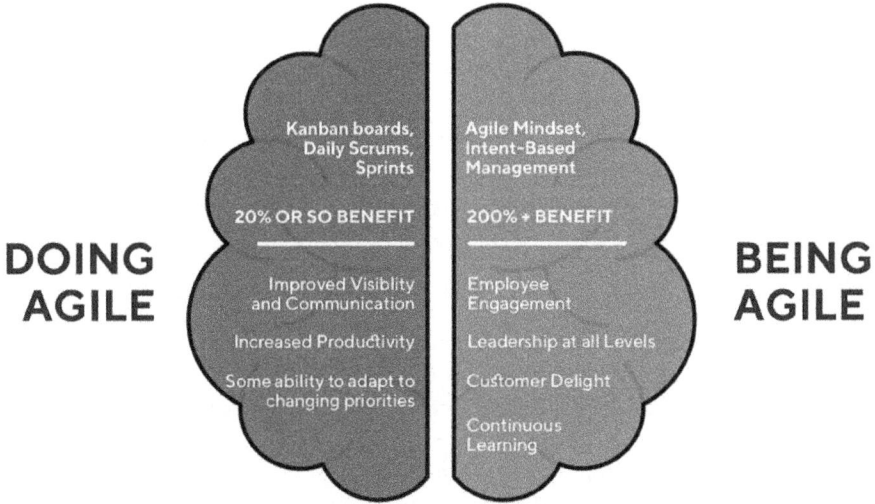

Kanban boards, Daily Scrums, Sprints

Agile Mindset, Intent-Based Management

20% OR SO BENEFIT

200% + BENEFIT

Improved Visiblity and Communication

Employee Engagement

Increased Productivity

Leadership at all Levels

Some ability to adapt to changing priorities

Customer Delight

Continuous Learning

DOING AGILE

BEING AGILE

Doing Agile vs Being Agile

Summary Table: Doing vs Being Agile

Aspect	Doing Agile	Being Agile
Focus	Processes and tools	Mindset and values
Result	Ritual adherence	True adaptability
Team engagement	Compliance with rules	Collaboration and ownership

Teams stuck in 'doing' can realize some positive outcomes, but deeper changes come from 'being', leading to higher engagement, delight for customers, and sustainable improvement. Leaders have a moral duty here as well – protecting the well-being of those adopting Agile.

However, building this kind of culture also raises important ethical questions, such as ensuring that Agile processes don't lead to burnout or disillusionment. Let's explore this ethical dimension of leadership in Agile.

The Ethical Imperative for Leadership

Leaders must ensure Agile does not cause team burnout or degrade trust. Where frameworks become top-down mandates, morale erodes. Some consultancies warn of 'mini-waterfall' setups masked as Agile, highlighting that leaders must safeguard authenticity.

Old patterns of command-and-control can creep back under an Agile label, raising stress and weakening the sense of ownership. Leaders must design iterative improvements that foster psychological safety.

Key Ethical Points

- Protect staff from unhealthy deadlines by pacing sprints realistically.
- Keep ceremonies purposeful, never just box-ticking.
- Maintain open communication about Agile's benefits and limits.

By looking after well-being, leaders preserve Agile's original spirit of adaptability and cooperation. This also means guiding teams to tailor frameworks to their context rather than letting them become rigid instructions.

Misuse and Misinterpretation of Agile Frameworks

As certifications grew popular, certain frameworks also shifted from flexible templates to rigid playbooks. Critics who say 'Agile is dead' often point to misguided applications instead of Agile itself. Methods like SAFe can become rule-heavy if not tailored to the actual context, stifling creativity.

When Agile is poorly implemented, teams may face scapegoating – bearing responsibility without genuine ownership. Leaders must build accountability systems that prevent blame-shifting by aligning responsibility and decision-making power. Without this alignment, team members feel disempowered and unfairly exposed, eroding trust and diminishing Agile's true potential.

Personal Reflection

A group I worked with insisted that all teams adopt uniform two-week sprints. When data analysts asked for a different schedule, management refused, believing 'Agile means standard sprints'. While consistency across teams can help manage dependencies at scale, forcing a rigid cadence without considering team needs risks contradicting the adaptability that Agile stands for.

Dave Snowden, known for the Cynefin sense-making framework, described some large-scale Agile approaches as 'management infantilism'. Processes can become crutches for leaders who avoid real listening or enabling genuine self-organization.

Similar misuse can occur with other popular theories, such as turning Carol Dweck's growth mindset concept into a blame tool for pushing staff. The root cause is the same: leaders latch onto a concept or framework but undercut its essence by applying it in a controlling way. Organizations risk drifting back into command-and-control, losing Agile's real benefit.

Senior leaders can address these pitfalls through adaptation, guided by real input from teams, ongoing reflection, and thoughtful customization of frameworks. If stand-ups become pure status updates or retros produce zero improvements, it signals that the framework has overshadowed the essence.

Have you spotted any rituals in your environment that seem hollow? Which adjustments can shift the focus from procedure to purpose?

Some of the sharpest voices who highlight these issues offer crucial lessons on focusing on value over form.

Agile Certifications: Commodity or Catalyst?

Personal Reflection

When I attended an Agile conference in London last year, I met Sarah, a newly certified Scrum Master. She proudly displayed her fresh SAFe and CSM certifications but confessed, 'I've never actually worked on an Agile team.' This isn't uncommon. In many industries, Agile certifications have become quick career boosters rather than true learning experiences. While certification can be valuable, it risks becoming a business in itself, selling frameworks rather than fostering real agility.

As interest in Agile surged, the industry responded with myriad certification programmes – many emphasizing procedural knowledge over deep understanding. While offering structure, these credentials also risk encouraging superficial adoption. Nigel Thurlow, co-creator of The Flow System, points out that many certifications measure recited knowledge rather than hands-on proficiency.

When teams chase certificates purely as status markers, they sidestep the actual purpose: nurturing adaptability, collaboration, and customer-centric thinking. The best route is to supplement certifications with robust, real-world practice. Mentoring, shadowing seasoned practitioners, and focusing on delivering tangible outcomes all bolster the learning process.

Ultimately, certificates can be a start, but they shouldn't overshadow the cultural and experiential learning Agile needs. Leaders committed to authenticity look beyond the paper credentials, emphasizing meaningful experiences that deepen teams' grasp of Agile's iterative, customer-focused, and collaborative foundations.

Learning from Criticism

Many observers maintain that Agile falters when frameworks are misapplied or incomplete. Misuse of user stories, skimping on planning, or rote sprints feed the narrative that Agile is chaotic. These concerns can be valid where 'Agile' is no more than a rebranded project plan.

Critics Underscore
- Over-simplified user stories that fail to align with real needs.
- Zero upfront preparation, forcing costly rework.
- Rituals devoid of real improvements or reflection.

Action Steps
- Write stories with enough detail to guide teams yet remain open to iteration.
- Combine lightweight planning with feedback loops for better synergy.
- Focus on purposeful outcomes over ceremony.

Tackling these points helps leaders refine and improve Agile so it yields tangible results instead of shallow compliance.

Understanding Agile's Reported Failures

Some reports cite high failure rates for Agile projects – 65% or more in a recent survey by Engprax/JL Partners Research. On closer inspection, incomplete adoption or ignoring fundamental cultural elements often produces these failures, rather than Agile being ineffective.

Implementing Agile reshapes an entire organization, so standard barriers – resistance, complacency, or poor leadership – apply here, too. Shallow buy-in from the top, cultural mismatch, or rushed timelines compound the issue. This reveals that Agile alone cannot fix embedded problems without proper change management.

Key Pitfalls
- Cultural resistance from people used to strict hierarchies.
- Leadership focusing on ceremonies but not empowerment.
- Overemphasis on short increments at the expense of quality.

Ways to Avoid
- Offer staff education to shift mindsets and develop trust.
- Align Agile aims with company-wide direction so people grasp the bigger purpose.
- Integrate thorough testing and incorporate feedback into each cycle.

When Agile fails, it often highlights a deeper leadership or cultural shortcoming. Yet the iterative spirit of Agile allows teams to learn, adapt, and improve. Leaders who view these stumbles as evidence for refinement can realign Agile with its core values.

Personal Reflection

In one transformation I led, a senior stakeholder was convinced Agile couldn't address our compliance demands. Over time, by focusing on iterative learning and transparent communication, scepticism gradually turned into support. This shift taught me that genuine engagement, not mere process steps, overcomes most criticisms.

The Opportunity for Growth

High failure rates, ironically, reaffirm Agile's importance by revealing what happens when it's poorly implemented. Agile's iterative nature allows teams to reflect, adapt, and improve. Leaders who treat criticisms constructively can refine Agile's approach, aligning it more closely with the core principles of iterative learning, collaboration, and flexible response to evolving needs.

Beyond recognizing Agile's reported failures, leaders must also consider structured change management approaches that address resistance, misalignment, and unclear communication. Without these, Agile adoption risks falling into the same traps outlined earlier in this chapter.

Agile and Change Management: Why Many Transformations Fail

Organization-wide Agile transformations often fail not because of flawed methodologies but due to poor change management practice. Resistance, misalignment, and unclear communication can derail even the most well-intended adoption of Agile. Traditional change models can offer useful insights, but their structured, top-down nature often clashes with the emergent, bottom-up character of true transformation.

Two widely recognized models – Kotter's 8-Step Change Model and ADKAR (Awareness, Desire, Knowledge, Ability, Reinforcement) – offer structured approaches often used to support change:

- *Kotter's 8-Step Change Model*: Provides a leadership-driven roadmap for securing buy-in, communicating vision, and embedding change. Steps like 'Creating a Sense of Urgency' and 'Generating Short-Term Wins' echo Agile's iterative rhythm but can fall short when transformation is treated as a linear, controllable sequence rather than an adaptive journey.
- *ADKAR*: Focuses on individual change by ensuring people understand (Awareness) why Agile is necessary, are motivated (Desire) to adopt it, gain the skills (Knowledge and Ability) to work effectively, and sustain (Reinforcement) Agile ways of working. Like Kotter, ADKAR is better suited to planned, predictable changes, such as opening a new office, than to emergent, organization-wide transformation.

Agile leaders should go further. Rather than relying solely on top-down frameworks, they should articulate their own working theory of change – *'I believe if we do X, then Y will happen.'* This invites others to understand the reasoning, engage with the direction, and co-own the path forward.

To lead meaningful transformation, leaders must empower those closest to the work to make decisions. For example, in a university, curriculum teams need the authority to act on student feedback directly, without waiting for top-level approval, so they can respond with relevance and speed.

Successful Agile change isn't just about new processes; it's about shifting mindsets and distributing leadership. It also means addressing cultural blockers – like tribalism within the Agile community itself – that can stall growth from the inside out.

Addressing Tribalism in the Agile Community

Picture a heated debate at an Agile leadership summit. A Lean purist argues that SAFe is 'fake Agile'. A DevOps advocate insists that a culture of measurement and lean management is all that is needed. Meanwhile, a Kanban coach declares that 'Scrum is just waterfall with sticky notes'. Agile has become fragmented – split into ideological camps, each convinced they have the 'true' approach. This tribalism discourages real progress, making Agile feel more like a battle of frameworks than a mindset of adaptability.

This growing tribalism is a troubling development in the Agile world. While Agile should champion openness, some corners of the community cling to insular, dogmatic views. Disputes over 'pure' Agile frameworks or fierce brand loyalty hinder constructive dialogue. This mindset fosters blame and alienation, echoing the critics' claims.

Leaders can help the Agile community overcome tribalism by emphasizing shared values over rigid frameworks, encouraging collaboration among different 'camps', and supporting knowledge exchange. Agile's real strength lies in adaptability, not dogma. By focusing on continuous learning and mutual respect, the community can build on its strengths rather than fracturing into factions.

Another manifestation of misplaced loyalty to old ways is the so-called 'disciplined waterfall' approach, which simply rebrands rigid processes under an Agile label.

'Disciplined Waterfall' Under the Guise of Agile

Nigel Thurlow, co-creator of The Flow System, noted in a post on LinkedIn in October 2023 that many organizations practise a disguised 'disciplined waterfall', applying old methods under new labels. This runs counter to Agile's promise, confusing staff and damaging trust in agility. Some adopt SAFe or similar frameworks but keep the same top-down decision patterns that hamper genuine adaptability.

Teams must recognize the difference between truly iterative, customer-driven improvements and partial rebranding of older processes. Leaders can address this by reevaluating existing structures, removing bottlenecks, and reinforcing the mindset shifts needed for real adaptability. If daily stand-ups remain manager-led status checks or sprints are locked into fixed timelines, the organization might be stuck in 'disciplined waterfall'.

Besides lingering Waterfall patterns, the commodification of Agile roles and practices poses another challenge to authenticity in Agile adoption.

The Commodification of Agile Roles and Practices

Agile's popularity opened the door for a bustling industry of certifications, coaching, and frameworks. This can be helpful, but it also sparks criticism that Agile is just a product to be packaged and sold. Framework-driven transformations risk turning each ceremony into a checkbox.

Some experts, such as Scott Ambler (Disciplined Agile's co-creator), lament that once-radical ideas are diluted by money-making programmes. Many hold fancy job titles but lack true experience or a deeper appreciation of Agile's ethos. Leaders can counteract this by emphasizing real-life problem-solving, outcomes, and a culture of everyday improvement.

Certificates can jumpstart awareness, but they should not overshadow lived practice. Adaptive leaders consider ways to deepen staff skills, like shadowing experienced team members, user-driven pilots, and building on organizational learning. The next step for your teams might involve more than one approach – including design thinking or systems thinking – to foster an Agile mindset that is truly flexible and deeply grounded in understanding customer needs.

Conclusion

Arguments against Agile – whether about bloated frameworks, misunderstanding, or superficial rollouts – reflect legitimate frustrations that leaders should not ignore. Often, the root cause is the partial or incorrect use of Agile rather than Agile itself. Leaders who respond with openness can preserve agility's essence.

When people treat Agile as a box to check, they reduce it to lifeless routines. Authentic Agile emerges from continuous reflection, cultural alignment, and leaders who hold themselves accountable. The approach is not failing, but its execution can falter if leadership becomes complacent or formulaic.

The next chapter takes a step back to weigh both sides of the Agile debate, highlighting where it truly delivers and where it may fall short. A balanced perspective allows leaders to apply Agile's strengths effectively while acknowledging concerns that need attention.

Agility is not about rigid adherence to methods – it is about adaptability. By embracing an iterative approach, organizations can avoid the common pitfalls and ensure Agile remains a source of real value rather than a hollow practice.

Call to Action

Adaptive leaders should evaluate their own setting. Are you simply 'doing Agile' with ceremonies or aiming to 'be Agile' with a genuine shift in culture? Consider which criticisms resonate most with your team. Invite dialogue on any routine that feels empty, and promote fresh thinking to anchor everything in real goals. Share lessons with peers or a leadership circle – collective exploration boosts improvements.

Key Takeaways

- **Misunderstandings Fuel Criticisms**: Many Agile criticisms stem from misapplications rather than flaws in its core principles.
- **Overemphasis on Frameworks**: Strict adherence to frameworks without understanding core values leads to bureaucracy and dilutes agility.
- **Commodification Erodes Authenticity**: Turning Agile into a product of certifications can overshadow its transformative potential.
- **Leadership's Role Is Critical**: Leaders must genuinely adopt Agile mindsets, fostering cultures of collaboration and continuous improvement.
- **Cultural Shifts Are Essential**: Agile transformations need deeper behavioural changes, not just adopting ceremonies or tools.

CLEAR Model® Connection

- **Culture**: An organization's mindset can enable or block true agility.
- **Execution**: Effective execution prevents Agile from turning into surface-level rituals.

Key Takeaway: Agile's biggest challenges are not in the framework but in how it is adopted. Leaders must focus on execution and cultural alignment to ensure agility delivers real business impact.

Reflection Guide: Addressing Common Criticisms

- **Balancing Structure and Flexibility**: Is your current framework too prescriptive? Where could it be streamlined?
- **Leadership Engagement**: Do leaders model Agile principles, or are they reinforcing old, top-down habits?
- **Cultural Alignment**: Are employees empowered to question processes, or is dissent discouraged?
- **Measuring Genuine Value**: Is your team focused on real outcomes (customer satisfaction, team morale) or just fulfilling frameworks?

Workshop agenda: facilitating open discussions

1. **Introduction (10 min):**
   o Present the common criticisms of Agile.
2. **Breakout Sessions (30 min):**
   o Small groups discuss which criticisms resonate with their experience.
3. **Group Sharing (20 min):**
   o Each group shares insights and potential solutions.
4. **Action Planning (30 min):**
   o Develop strategies to address identified issues.
5. **Closing Remarks (10 min):**
   o Summarize key takeaways and next steps.

Chapter Summary

Agile's worst pitfalls – over-engineering, superficial use, chasing badges – can rob it of its capacity to enhance collaboration. This chapter explored why these errors arise and how Adaptive Leadership and cultural alignment preserve Agile's transformative spark. Listening to sceptics can guide leaders to keep Agile genuinely strong.

End of Part 1

You've seen how Agile has evolved and why its critics matter. Yet for Agile to truly flourish, it needs more than frameworks – it demands a fresh style of leadership. In the next part, we'll explore how Adaptive Leadership transforms these insights into lasting change, ensuring Agile isn't just a set of rituals but a mindset that reshapes how people work together.

Part 2

Reframing Adaptive Leadership

CLEAR Focus: Leadership

Agility thrives when leadership evolves beyond frameworks to enable transformation. Leaders drive Agile success by shaping the conditions for trust, empowerment, and continuous progress. This section explores how leadership creates the foundations for sustained agility.

3

Why Adaptive Leadership Is the Future of Agile

The measure of intelligence is the ability to change.

Albert Einstein

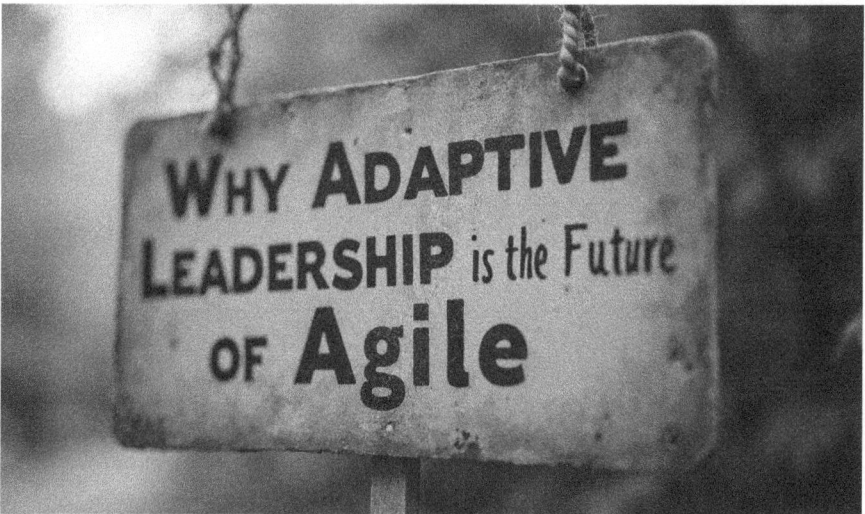

What You'll Gain

- **For Senior Leaders and Executives**: Discover how your leadership approach can make or break Agile success.
- **For Mid-Level Leaders**: Understand the critical balance between Agile pros and cons to drive pragmatic improvement.
- **For Students or Early-Career Professionals**: See how leadership choices can transform Agile from confusion into genuine progress.

Weighing Up the Pros and Cons

Adaptive leaders must recognize that Agile sparks both praise and frustration. Some leaders hail it as the key to revitalizing their organizations, while others find that it unleashes chaos. Why does Agile thrive in certain places yet fail elsewhere? It rarely depends on the framework. Leadership often defines whether Agile becomes a triumph or a hardship. The CLEAR Model® offers a structured way to embed agility beyond frameworks, ensuring adaptability, execution, and responsiveness align with strategic goals.

Part 1 explored critics' concerns and flawed implementations. Now, it's time for a balanced look at Agile's benefits and shortcomings. Sceptical viewpoints often emerge after a painful project collapse or a demoralized team. They're usually driven by high hopes for Agile that went unmet.

Some leaders also worry that too much flexibility can weaken strategic consistency. They fear that constantly adapting might cause teams to lose sight of long-term goals. This is a fair concern. However, adaptive leadership doesn't reject long-term vision – it keeps the vision intact while flexing how you reach it. Done well, adaptation becomes a strength, not a distraction.

This chapter examines how leaders can harness Agile's full promise by addressing frustrations at their source.

Want Agile to succeed? Drop empty rituals. Leaders sometimes impose Agile routines – daily stand-ups, sprint reviews – without adopting a mindset of trust, autonomy, and ongoing learning. Agile's real power comes from collaborative habits, not from rigidly ticking off events. Leaders who free teams to solve problems, remove stumbling blocks, and focus on tangible outcomes convert Agile from a stumbling block into a real asset.

Chapter 5 goes deeper into how leadership sets the tone for genuine cultural change. Meanwhile, the current section weighs Agile's high points against its downsides, pinpointing areas where leaders can strengthen adaptability. It also covers debates, such as the influence of AI on Agile, and ways to refine methods moving forward.

Those who treat Agile as a guide rather than a rulebook will move ahead; those who cling to old frameworks will be left behind. Which type of leader do you want to be?

Leadership Moves Map

Ideas only help when leaders change daily habits. This map turns intent into small, visible acts that staff can see and copy. Start with a few moves, prove they work, then grow from there.

How to use it:

- Choose three moves that fit your context this month.
- Log each move in a shared place so others can see progress.
- Ask one peer to hold you to account each week.
- Review at month end, keep what worked, swap what didn't.

What to watch:

- Fewer approvals and faster unblock.
- Clear links between decisions, reviews, and customer impact.
- More coaching, less status reporting.

Use this list to pick three moves you'll start this week.

C – Culture

1. Create a simple team working agreement; revisit monthly.
2. Run a quarterly psychological safety pulse and act on one hotspot.
3. Tell one 'learning story' in each town hall to normalize smart failure.

L – Leadership

4. Keep a weekly 'decision log' shared with teams (what, why, by when).
5. Remove one rule or approval each fortnight; publish what you cut.
6. Do one Gemba walk per week; fix one impediment within 72 hours.

E – Execution

7. Shift goals to outcome-based OKRs; limit each team to 1–2 active.
8. Limit WIP; make blocked work visible; swarm the top blocker daily.
9. Demo to real users every two weeks; capture one metric from each demo.

A – Adaptability

10. Run short experiments (2–4 weeks) with a clear hypothesis and success signal.
11. Add a monthly scenario drill: 'What would force us to pivot next quarter?'

R – Responsiveness

12. Include live flow metrics (lead time, throughput, ageing WIP) into ops reviews; act when ageing WIP rises.

Tip: Re-select moves each quarter; keep what works, drop what doesn't.

Shifts in technology, especially AI, raise questions about Agile's future. Let's see how these conversations shape what's next for Agile.

Critical Voices on AI and Extreme Agile

Some propose 'Extreme Agile', integrating AI deeply into Agile activities to achieve significant productivity gains. This might involve AI-driven sprint planning, code reviews, and predictions on velocity. Yet many specialists caution that AI tools lack true contextual understanding, requiring careful oversight. They can be helpful 'spike solutions', but they need human involvement and ethical boundaries.

Consider a software team that uses AI to handle code reviews and backlog ranking. Their output initially improves. Overreliance on AI soon leads to missed bugs and major issues that derail the product. Gains vanish, and customers end up disappointed. This highlights why leaders must blend AI efficiency with real-world judgment.

Adaptive leaders introduce these innovations wisely, ensuring that AI bolsters rather than replaces creative thinking. Automation should support decisions, not direct them. Teams remain the drivers of collaboration, guided by a clear ethical framework. While the AI storyline keeps evolving, bigger debates revolve around whether current Agile approaches still uphold core values like ongoing learning and team independence.

Reframing Agile's Shortcomings

Agile sometimes stumbles, but leaders who see these failures as chances to adapt can make Agile stronger.

- **Speed vs Sustainability**
  Many critics say Agile's emphasis on swift releases jeopardizes long-lasting resilience. Leaders should ensure that the pursuit of speed doesn't ignore maintainability or future viability.
- **Unhelpful Rituals**
  Stand-ups and retrospectives lose meaning when leaders let them turn into box-ticking. Refocusing each ritual on learning and goal-setting guards against cynicism.
- **Neglecting Ethical Factors**
  Teams might chase velocity while overlooking data privacy, fairness, or staff well-being. Leaders who embed ethical discussions into Agile cycles keep broader concerns in sight.

Actions for Leaders

- Balance immediate goals with strategic planning to manage technical debt and maintain purpose.
- Remind teams why each Agile ceremony matters, keeping them relevant rather than routine.
- Expand user stories and objectives to include privacy, inclusion, or staff well-being, ensuring a holistic view.

Let's examine these downside factors more concretely in the broader Agile landscape to see what specifically goes wrong and why.

Downsides of the Current Agile Landscape

Agile remains influential, but it isn't perfect. Industry experts like Martin Fowler and Jon Kern note that Agile's problems frequently stem from poor usage, not flaws in the concept. Common issues include ignoring strategic goals or giving too much attention to short-term output. Understanding these pitfalls supports balanced decision-making.

Lack of True Understanding and Application

'Agile in Name Only' occurs when leadership rebrands processes as Agile without nurturing a culture of collaboration or iteration. They may schedule stand-ups and share Kanban boards, yet managers maintain tight control or demand inflexible scopes.

Example: A large consultancy switched to Scrum but forced year-long project scopes. Teams couldn't adapt to changing needs, creativity declined, and deliverables lost relevance.

Leadership Fixes

- **Reinforce Agile fundamentals**: Keep user feedback and adaptation at the core.
- **Shape methods around team realities**: Avoid forcing generic solutions.
- **Provide coaching**: Ensure everyone grasps the purpose behind Agile steps.

Without these fundamentals, rituals devolve into formalities that produce minimal real improvement.

Misuse and Misapplication of Agile Frameworks

As discussed in Chapter 2, many organizations misapply Agile by enforcing rigid frameworks instead of fostering adaptability. Leaders must shift from mandating Agile processes to enabling agility.

Leadership Fixes

- **Empower teams to shape their own Agile approach**: Allow flexibility in sprint length, ceremonies, and team structures rather than forcing a uniform model.
- **Clarify the purpose behind Agile frameworks**: Educate leaders and teams that Agile is about iterative improvement, not strict process compliance.
- **Encourage continuous feedback loops**: If teams feel Agile is restricting rather than enabling them, it's time to reassess the framework's application.

Reflection: Have you observed similar misapplications within your own organization? How might you adjust your approach to ensure that frameworks serve your team's needs rather than constrain them?

Framework Fatigue

Also highlighted in Chapter 2, framework fatigue occurs when organizations cycle through Agile methodologies without mastering any. The key leadership challenge is helping teams cut through complexity and focus on real agility.

Leadership Fixes

- **Prioritize outcomes over frameworks**: Instead of forcing a specific methodology, ask: *'Is this approach helping us deliver value earlier and more effectively?'*
- **Engage teams in framework decisions**: Let teams experiment and adjust methodologies based on their actual workflow needs.
- **Minimize unnecessary complexity**: Reduce excessive governance and framework layering that slows down decision-making and execution.

The Misleading Use of Terminology

Some organizations brand legacy methods as 'Agile' simply to appear current, but they fail to enact real change. Calling traditional status meetings 'daily stand-ups' or rebranding deadlines as 'sprints' without adjusting the underlying structure only causes confusion. If these changes remain superficial, employees become cynical, and stakeholders lose faith in Agile.

Examples

- **Rebranding Project Managers as Scrum Masters** without giving them new responsibilities.
- **Renaming Gantt charts as 'Agile Schedules'**, ignoring iterative development or rapid feedback.

Impacts

- **Creates Confusion**: People don't understand the real purpose behind new terms.
- **Undermines Authentic Adoption**: Misses the principle of empowerment and iterative improvement.
- **Leads to Disillusionment**: When improvements don't materialize, employees blame Agile.

Best Practices

- **Educate teams** on actual Agile values and practices.
- **Realign roles** with Agile's spirit, ensuring responsibilities genuinely shift.
- **Acknowledge that culture change** isn't a simple re-labelling but an ongoing evolution requiring leadership commitment.

Corporate Misalignment with Agile Values

Richard, a Product VP, believed in Agile – until his CFO demanded rigid five-year plans. His executives claimed to 'support Agile' yet resisted real transformation. Mismatched expectations sapped the benefits that Agile brought to development teams.

Agile thrives when it's woven into a culture of accountability, user feedback, and adaptive mindsets. Bureaucratic or command-driven organizations often treat Agile as a superficial fix.

Leadership Fixes

- **Shift decision-making closer to teams**: Encourage autonomy at all levels.
- **Model open-mindedness and risk-taking**: Leaders must embrace adaptability themselves.
- **Align short cycles with broader organizational goals**: Ensure Agile doesn't become disconnected from the company strategy.

Misconceptions About Agile: Speed and Planning

As discussed in Chapter 2, a common misconception is that Agile is just about moving faster. Many leaders expect immediate results without adjusting scope, priorities, or strategic alignment. This misunderstanding leads to rushed work, unrealistic deadlines, and inevitable frustration when Agile doesn't deliver instant success.

The Reality

- Agile is *not about working faster* – it's about working smarter.
- Agile planning is *continuous and adaptive,* not a lack of planning.
- Agile requires *strategic alignment,* ensuring high-value work flows to the right teams, rather than shifting people around like traditional projects, instead of just increasing output.

Leadership Fixes

- **Redefine success beyond speed**: Agile is not about how quickly teams complete work but about whether they're delivering meaningful outcomes and value.
- **Use iterative planning, not rigid roadmaps**: Instead of expecting teams to meet fixed long-term plans, shift to *rolling, flexible roadmaps* that evolve with business needs.
- **Balance short-term execution with long-term strategy**: Encourage leaders to think beyond just sprints – every iteration should connect to a broader vision.

Agile's Role in Cultural Transformation

These downsides often arise when leaders misunderstand Agile's transformative potential. Too much focus on process rather than cultural and organizational shifts leads to missed opportunities for true adaptability.

Key Considerations

- Agile works *only when the culture supports it* – if leadership still rewards predictability over flexibility, Agile will fail.
- Agile should not be treated as a *one-size-fits-all solution.* While Agile principles can be applied broadly, *strict adherence to frameworks is not always suitable* (e.g. in highly regulated industries).
- *Real agility comes from knowing when to apply which approach* rather than enforcing Agile as a universal fix.

Leadership Fixes

- **Encourage adaptive thinking**: Help teams apply Agile principles where they make sense rather than blindly enforcing frameworks.
- **Set realistic expectations**: Agile isn't about making projects magically faster – it's about improving responsiveness and adaptability.

Summary: The Downsides of the Current Agile Setting

- **Misunderstandings and Misapplications**: Surface-level usage spurs disillusionment.
- **Misuse of Frameworks**: A strict or poor application derails progress.
- **Framework Fatigue**: Too many frameworks can confuse teams.
- **Misleading Terminology**: Rebranding old processes kills trust.
- **Corporate Misalignment**: Inflexible cultures clash with Agile's need for collaboration.
- **Misconceptions About Speed**: Agility is about delivering the right solutions, not rushing everything.

Key Takeaway

Overcoming these pitfalls requires focusing on deeper cultural shifts, a genuine understanding of Agile's principles, and flexible leadership approaches rather than rigid processes.

Upsides of the Current Agile Landscape

Despite legitimate criticisms, Agile has transformed how organizations pivot, collaborate, and learn. Its ongoing success shows it's evolving rather than nearing an end. Agile now moves beyond software to marketing, finance, and many other domains, showing its broad adaptability.

Agile Maturity and Integration

Agile is no longer merely a set of processes – it's becoming a company-wide mindset for building flexible operations. The term 'post-Agile' reflects how software-based routines can grow into an overarching philosophy.

Leadership Benefits

- **Embed agility into the organization's DNA**: Agile should extend beyond IT, influencing business strategy, governance, and operations.
- **Foster continuous improvement**: Agile organizations adapt dynamically rather than following rigid transformation roadmaps.
- **Balance structure with adaptability**: Mature Agile enterprises understand when to follow frameworks and when to adjust them.

Simplicity and Value Creation

Real simplicity grows from deep understanding, not from stripping away processes blindly. Large frameworks can limit flexibility, but carefully removing waste can reignite innovation.

Leadership Actions

- **Refine processes without gutting what truly matters**: Cut bureaucracy while preserving high-impact Agile practices.
- **Shift focus from frameworks to outcomes**: Agile should drive value creation, not be a checklist of ceremonies.
- **Encourage experimentation**: Teams should be empowered to explore simpler, more effective ways of working.

Innovation and Collaboration

Short cycles keep teams experimenting, integrating new tools, and adjusting for user feedback. This fosters creativity while mitigating risk. As Agile matures, teams step outside official roles, taking greater ownership and harnessing new technologies to deliver relevant solutions.

Leadership Actions

- **Encourage cross-functional collaboration**: Break down silos and facilitate knowledge-sharing between teams.
- **Integrate Agile with emerging technologies**: AI, automation, and data analytics can enhance decision-making.
- **Create a culture of rapid iteration**: Continuous learning should be an organizational priority.

Adapting to Shifting Demands

Agile isn't just for coding. Many business areas – product innovation, service design, and strategy – use iterative releases and real-time feedback to stay aligned with emerging consumer needs.

Leadership Actions

- **Use data-driven decision-making**: Agile should be informed by analytics, customer insights, and market trends.
- **Enable teams to pivot quickly**: Flexible backlogs and adaptive roadmaps help businesses stay relevant.
- **Validate assumptions continuously**: Testing hypotheses early ensures teams invest in the right solutions.

Integration with Emerging Technologies

Machine learning, AI, and IoT blend neatly with iterative methods, encouraging trial projects and data-led direction. The aim is to feed new insights quickly into the next sprint or release cycle.

Leadership Actions

- **Support technology-driven agility**: AI can assist in backlog prioritization, automation, and predictive analytics.
- **Balance automation with human expertise**: AI should enhance – not replace – collaborative decision-making.
- **Encourage responsible innovation**: Ethical considerations should guide Agile technology adoption.

Enhancing Employee Engagement

Agile encourages team autonomy and open collaboration, leading to stronger morale and retention. Successful organizations refine Agile for flexible or hybrid work setups.

Leadership Actions

- **Adopt digital collaboration tools**: Remote and hybrid teams thrive with asynchronous workflows and shared workspaces.
- **Empower teams with decision-making authority**: Autonomy drives motivation and engagement.

- **Ensure Agile supports – not overwhelms – teams**: Avoid process-heavy Agile that leads to burnout.

Synergy with Other Methods

Agile works well alongside Lean, DevOps, and Design Thinking. Combining these ideas across departments unites a shared goal: delivering high-quality solutions to users.

Leadership Actions

- **Promote adaptability over rigid methodology debates**: Agile isn't in competition with other frameworks – it complements them.
- **Adopt a blended approach**: Hybrid models can integrate Agile with traditional project management where needed.
- **Encourage knowledge-sharing**: Cross-disciplinary teams should leverage best practices from multiple methodologies.

Widespread Adoption

Industry leaders have adapted Agile to fit their unique needs, demonstrating its broad scalability and impact across industries.

- **Spotify's Approach**
  They devised a 'Spotify Model' to tackle scaling while keeping squads autonomous. Though they've evolved away from that original model, the principle remains instructive: design an Agile system, test it, and continue refining it.
- **ING Bank's Transformation**
  They fused Agile with finance-specific needs. Leadership pushed transparency and empowerment, anchoring Agile in the heart of the organization.
- **Netflix's Iterative Innovation**
  Netflix regularly tests features with real users, pivoting swiftly based on feedback. Agile's iterative cycles are key to staying prominent in entertainment services.

Summary: The Upsides of the Current Agile Setting

- **Agile Maturity**: Beyond frameworks, Agile can be a unifying principle.
- **Innovation and Collaboration**: Iterative development nurtures creative problem-solving.
- **Adapting to Shifting Demands**: Rapid feedback loops keep teams aligned with new trends.
- **Integration with Tech**: Data-based experiments mesh neatly with short-release cycles.
- **Employee Engagement**: Empowerment fuels motivation.
- **Success Stories**: Tailored, flexible frameworks yield significant impact.

Key Takeaway

Embracing Agile's core values and supporting principles – and adapting them thoughtfully – can yield significant benefits for innovation, efficiency, and customer satisfaction.

Evaluating Both Sides of the Debate

Aspect	Pros	Cons
Flexibility	Allows quick adjustment to changing requirements, promoting responsiveness.	It can become confusing or lead to scope creep if the direction is unclear.
Customer Focus	Frequent collaboration ensures alignment with user needs, enhancing satisfaction.	Heavy reliance on customer availability or clarity may be challenging if stakeholders are unresponsive or ambiguous.
Team Autonomy	Provides the structure to empower teams to self-organize and find innovative solutions.	Lacking strong leadership can result in unfocused teams or conflicting priorities.
Incremental Progress	Iterative cycles catch issues early, lowering risk and refining deliverables.	Overfocusing on short-term sprints may neglect strategic planning or holistic project vision.
Continuous Improvement	Regular retrospectives improve processes, collaboration, and outcomes.	Meeting fatigue or retrospective stagnation can occur if feedback isn't acted on effectively.
Value Delivery	Emphasizes incremental delivery of features that customers find valuable first.	Rushing features can degrade deeper technical quality or neglect non-functional requirements.
Transparency	Daily stand-ups and reviews keep progress visible, fostering accountability.	Excessive ceremonies may consume time, irritating teams if they don't yield tangible benefits.
Reduced Risk	Frequent review helps detect issues early and promote iterative fixes.	Prolonged decision cycles or incomplete problem analysis can delay solving root issues.
Framework Fatigue	Different frameworks let teams choose what suits them best.	The sheer number of frameworks can frustrate organizations, leading to 'framework hopping' and confusion.

Understanding Both Sides: A Balanced View

The reality is nuanced. Agile isn't monolithic; it can exhibit both pitfalls and triumphs. Instead of viewing Agile as either failing or unstoppable, it's more useful to see it as an evolving system. Adaptive leaders champion Agile's foundational values – collaboration, iteration, and customer-centricity – while continuously refining them to fit their organization's unique reality.

Agile's ongoing evolution is a testament to its strength – its ability to grow alongside changing conditions. Yet, realizing its full potential remains a challenge. According to Forrester's latest report, *The State Of Agile Development, 2025: It's Still Relevant, With Benefits And Challenges*, 71% of organizations report using Agile at scale, but only 44% feel they fully capture its intended benefits. This gap highlights the need for leadership-driven adaptation. The report also emphasizes AI's growing role in enhancing Agile effectiveness, with predictive analytics and automation helping to optimize workflows. Leaders who integrate these advancements can unlock new efficiencies while ensuring Agile remains relevant in a technology-driven world.

The real takeaway is that Agile's continued impact depends on leadership. The ability to move beyond rigid implementations and embrace adaptability is what turns Agile's strengths into meaningful, team-level success. Effective leadership is the key to bridging this gap and ensuring Agile continues to deliver value where it matters most.

Bringing Adaptive Leadership to Life

Leaders must be the glue that joins Agile values with tangible results. When teams face typical adoption challenges – fear of losing control, superficial changes – it's Adaptive Leadership that guides them through. Below are resources to bolster leadership in Agile contexts.

Adaptive leaders clear blockers proactively rather than merely delegating responsibility. They actively share decision-making, ensuring teams have the support required to deliver strategic outcomes. Instead of waiting for obstacles to escalate, adaptive leaders continuously identify and remove barriers, enabling their teams to remain agile and effective.

Framework for Adaptive Leadership

Traditional Agile leadership often focuses on supporting Agile processes, ensuring teams follow Scrum, SAFe, or other frameworks effectively. Adaptive leadership goes further – it enables leaders at all levels to flex their approach based on evolving challenges, team dynamics, and external shifts.

But who is a leader in this context? Leadership isn't tied to a job title – it's defined by influence, decision-making, and the ability to foster agility within an organization. Whether it's a C-suite executive shaping strategic direction, a director mobilizing teams, or a team lead driving day-to-day execution, adaptive leadership applies at every level – but in different ways.

The table below highlights a simple three-step pathway for applying adaptive leadership in Agile settings. Unlike past leadership models that emphasized consistency and adherence to frameworks, this approach prioritizes real-time responsiveness, continuous learning, and strategic influence beyond delivery teams.

Action	Guidance	Example
Diagnose the Environment	Understand the team's agility using retrospectives, surveys, or workshops. Pinpoint gaps between existing methods and desired outcomes. Unlike past leadership models that relied on standardized assessments, this approach embraces real-time sensing and team-led discovery.	A team reports frustration with long, unproductive stand-ups. An investigation uncovers that unclear sprint goals cause confusion, prompting simpler, more goal-focused meetings.
Mobilize the Team	Communicate a vision for change that aligns with organizational objectives. Use storytelling and shared experiences to inspire rather than top-down mandates.	A leader discusses how a global manufacturer cut time-to-market by 30% using Agile methods, motivating the team to embrace similar practices.
Iterate Leadership Practices	Experiment with new leadership behaviours, not just Agile processes – adjust meeting formats, feedback loops, or delegation to discover what works best. Unlike static leadership models, adaptive leaders continuously evolve their role to meet changing demands.	A manager pilots a rotating facilitation approach for retrospectives, boosting team participation by 25% and sparking more creative problem-solving.

Does this apply equally to all leaders? The CLEAR Model® provides a structured way to differentiate leadership roles:

- **C-suite leaders** focus on strategic alignment, ensuring agility scales beyond delivery teams.
- **Directors and senior managers** translate this vision into departmental priorities and remove systemic blockers.
- **Team leads and managers** drive day-to-day Agile execution, creating an environment for adaptability at the team level.

Toolkit: Leadership Action Plan

While the framework above explains what to do at each step, the following table provides a structured plan for how to address specific issues that come up on your team. It helps leaders pinpoint solutions, test new ideas, and measure progress.

Step	Action	Example
Diagnose	Conduct team surveys and retrospectives.	The survey reveals a lack of psychological safety.
Mobilize	Share the vision and create alignment.	Storytelling about Agile success motivates the team.
Iterate	Experiment with leadership behaviours.	New sprint planning process tested for clarity.

By combining the three-step framework with this targeted action plan, organizations can tap into Agile's strengths while addressing the unique challenges leaders face at different levels.

While adaptive leadership can thrive in structured corporate environments, its principles prove especially impactful in unconventional and resource-constrained contexts.

Personal Reflection

Early in my CIO role at a mid-sized tech firm, I noticed how quickly teams reverted to top-down decisions whenever pressure mounted. It wasn't just a process problem – it was a leadership problem. By openly sharing my own uncertainties – and letting teams own their experiments – I saw a surge in both morale and output. This shift proved that being adaptive starts with leadership's willingness to trust teams at every level.

The Real Problem with Agile Isn't Agile – It's Leadership

By now, we've explored why so many critics claim Agile is broken. We've seen how Agile has become over-commercialized, misapplied, bureaucratic, and disconnected from business strategy.

But here's the truth: *The real problem isn't Agile itself – it's how it is being led at different levels of the organization.*

Agile doesn't fail because of frameworks or teams – it fails when leaders don't engage beyond process implementation. Agile can only rise as high in an organization as the leaders who champion it. When C-suite executives treat Agile as an operational tool rather than a business strategy, it stalls. When middle management resists change due to comfort with traditional control structures, it stagnates. And when teams aren't empowered to make decisions, Agile becomes process theatre rather than a driver of adaptability.

While strong leadership is crucial, other factors, such as regulatory constraints or deeply ingrained company habits, can also hinder Agile success. Still, effective leaders are needed to navigate these challenges.

For Agile to evolve beyond the pitfalls outlined in the previous chapter, we need a fundamental shift in leadership.

- Agility doesn't start at the team level – it starts at the top.
- No framework can fix a leadership mindset that refuses to adapt.
- Real agility is about adaptability, not processes.

So, what does the next generation of Adaptive Leadership look like? It looks like this:

Culture → Agility must be embedded in how the organization thinks and operates.
Leadership → Leaders must be the catalysts of change, not barriers to it.
Execution → Agile is not theory – it must deliver real, measurable outcomes.
Adaptability → The only constant is change – leaders must embrace it, not fear it.
Responsiveness → Organizations must react quickly to market shifts, customer needs, and internal feedback.

Yet, none of this will matter if leaders allow their egos and defensive attitudes to get in the way of authentic reflection and meaningful change.

When Ego Blocks Evolution: The Cost of Misplaced Criticism

Adaptive leadership demands authenticity and courage. Leaders must openly accept feedback, even when it challenges their self-perception or status. Yet, a defensive reaction to honest insights can derail meaningful transformation.

During a recent series of leadership workshops, an intriguing dynamic emerged. Leaders were confronted with data clearly demonstrating a wide gap between how they saw themselves (positive and aligned) and how their teams perceived the organizational culture (fragmented, unclear, and negative). Although these findings were revealing, some leaders responded by deflecting, shifting the focus onto minor, irrelevant criticisms rather than addressing the genuine, deep-rooted issues highlighted by the assessments.

One striking example involved criticizing a facilitator for requesting a simple glass of water during room preparation. This trivial request was exaggerated later into an accusation of disrespect as if that facilitator was exerting inappropriate superiority. Though seemingly minor, such reactions speak volumes about underlying attitudes towards hierarchy, status, and openness to feedback. Instead of confronting organizational realities, these leaders amplified trivial incidents to deflect from the uncomfortable truth: their team's perception of organizational culture was deeply misaligned with their own self-image.

Adaptive leaders must reject this defensive stance. Real agility begins when leaders prioritize internal reflection over external deflection. The ability to acknowledge uncomfortable truths without seeking faults in others demonstrates true leadership maturity. Leaders who fail to model this behaviour create environments resistant to change, obstructing the very adaptability their organizations require.

Additionally, adaptive leaders should feel comfortable expressing their expertise without worrying about being misunderstood. Demonstrating knowledge or sharing relevant experiences isn't bragging – it's an important part of credible leadership. Authentic leaders share insights to build trust, provide context, and guide meaningful conversations, not to emphasize their own importance. When adaptive leaders confidently and humbly share their background, experiences, or achievements, listeners – especially fellow leaders – are encouraged to recognize this openness as a genuine effort to drive collective improvement rather than something to react defensively or negatively towards.

Adaptive leadership isn't about fundamentally changing who we are or diluting our authenticity; it's about having the confidence to remain true to ourselves while welcoming feedback and having the courage to act on valuable insights. These qualities are essential if genuine business agility is to thrive.

Organizations intent on real change must abandon ego-driven criticism and embrace reflective openness. Only then can they fully unlock the transformative power of adaptive leadership.

To move beyond these challenges, organizations need a clear, structured framework that explicitly embeds adaptability into leadership behaviours, organizational culture, and execution practices. This framework must address the very barriers we've discussed – ego, defensiveness, resistance to feedback – and shift leadership from being barriers to becoming catalysts of genuine change.

This is precisely what the CLEAR Model® provides – a leadership-first framework designed explicitly to drive real business agility across all organizational levels.

The CLEAR Model® – The Leadership Framework for Agility

Too many organizations try to implement Agile at the team level first, hoping leadership will eventually follow. That approach fails because true agility must be driven from the top down and reinforced from the bottom up.

The CLEAR Model® provides a structured way to embed agility at every level of an organization, ensuring it's not just about IT or software teams – it's about how the business operates as a whole.

Let's break down each component of the CLEAR Model® and how leaders can use it to transform their organizations.

C = Culture – Embedding Agility into the DNA of the Organization
The Problem

Many companies say they're Agile, but their culture still promotes hierarchy, control, and rigid processes.

- 'We want to be Agile, but our performance reviews still reward predictability over adaptability.'
- 'Agile teams are encouraged to experiment, but failure is punished.'
- 'Our leadership team still expects detailed five-year plans with no flexibility.'

The Solution

Agile only works when the culture supports agility at every level.

The Leadership Fix

- Reward adaptability, not just execution. Teams should be recognized for learning and iterating, not just delivering on fixed plans.
- Eliminate fear-based leadership. Agility thrives when people feel safe to challenge the status quo.
- Flatten hierarchies. Encourage decision-making at the point of impact, not through layers of approval.

Agility isn't just about how teams work – it's about how organizations think.

L = Leadership – Moving from Command and Control to Enable and Inspire

The Problem

Traditional leadership is built on predictability, control, and long-term planning – all things that Agile challenges.

- 'Our executives want agility, but they still make all the decisions.'
- 'Leadership supports Agile in words, but their actions contradict it.'
- 'Managers don't know their new role in an Agile organization.'

The Solution

Leaders must transition from commanding to enabling, from controlling to empowering.

The Leadership Fix

- Shift from decision-making to decision-enabling. Leaders should remove roadblocks, not create them.
- Lead by example. If leaders don't model agility, teams won't take it seriously.
- Invest in Agile leadership training. Agile doesn't just transform teams – it transforms leadership itself.

Agile organizations need Adaptive Leaders who create the conditions for agility to thrive.

E = Execution – Agile Must Deliver Real Business Value

The Problem

Too many Agile transformations focus on frameworks rather than results.

- 'We adopted Scrum, but our customers haven't seen any benefits.'
- 'We measure Agile by velocity, but not by business outcomes.'
- 'We're Agile in name only – work is still slow, expensive, and inefficient.'

The Solution

Agile should never be about ceremonies and rituals – it should be about delivering value faster.

The Leadership Fix

- Measure agility by customer impact, not just sprint velocity.
- Ensure teams are focused on delivering outcomes, not just output.
- Reduce waste – make agility about efficiency, not just speed.

Execution matters. Agile that doesn't improve results is just Agile theatre.

A = Adaptability – Leading Through Change, Not Resisting It

The Problem

Even companies that claim to be Agile often struggle with real adaptability.

- 'We use Agile, but we still fear change.'
- 'Our teams are Agile, but leadership still follows fixed, long-term strategies.'
- 'We're stuck in Agile frameworks instead of responding to reality.'

The Solution

Agility means being ready to pivot when the market shifts, customer needs change, or new opportunities arise.

The Leadership Fix

- Create a culture where change is embraced, not feared.
- Use data-driven decision-making to remain flexible and adaptive.
- Teach teams how to be comfortable with uncertainty.

Agility is about thriving in uncertainty, not just managing change.

R = Responsiveness – Making Fast, Informed Decisions at Every Level

The Problem

Many organizations struggle to respond quickly to changes, even when they claim to be Agile.

- 'Our teams are Agile, but decisions still take weeks.'
- 'We wait for permission instead of acting on customer feedback.'
- 'Agile delivery is fast, but leadership decisions are slow.'

The Solution

True agility requires responsiveness at every level – not just in delivery teams.

The Leadership Fix

- Empower teams to make decisions in real-time.
- Shorten decision cycles – eliminate unnecessary approvals.
- Use continuous feedback loops to stay ahead of market shifts.

A fast-moving market requires fast-moving leadership.

The Future of Agile Leadership Starts with CLEAR

The CLEAR Model® isn't just about Agile – it's about Adaptive Leadership. Traditional leaders struggle with uncertainty – Adaptive Leaders thrive in it.

Key Takeaways

- **Agile's biggest failures stem from leadership, not frameworks.**
  Frameworks don't fail – leaders do. When Agile becomes rigid, bureaucratic, or misaligned with strategy, it's usually because leadership hasn't embraced adaptability.
- **The CLEAR Model® provides a leadership-first approach to agility.**
  Instead of focusing on process compliance, it shifts attention to the underlying conditions that make agility stick – embedding it into how organizations think, lead, and deliver at every level.
- **Adaptive Leaders drive agility through culture, decision-making, and responsiveness.**
  Agility isn't just about teams – it's about leadership creating conditions for adaptability, empowering decision-making, and ensuring organizations respond quickly to change.

Developing Yourself as an Adaptive Leader

Change starts with you. Each day, set aside a brief window to consider the biggest challenge you faced and how you handled it. Ask yourself: *'Did I revert to rigid habits, or did I adapt my approach?'* If you find you avoided risks or stifled team input, that's a cue to loosen the reins and encourage more collaboration.

A practical way to begin is to invite honest feedback from those around you – a colleague, mentor, or even a direct report. This can be done informally or using 360-degree feedback tools. Recognize small warning signs where you might be slipping back into top-down patterns, and pinpoint small experiments to foster team autonomy or rapid learning. For example, you might rotate the role of daily stand-up facilitator each week, giving different individuals a chance to lead.

Try Building a Simple 'Personal Agility' Plan

- **Weekly self-check**: Note when you made decisions quickly or welcomed new ideas (and when you didn't).
- **Reading and reflection**: Set aside 15 minutes a day to read a chapter from a leadership book or blog that challenges your thinking.
- **Mentor relationship**: Find a trusted ally or mentor to discuss how you're applying Agile principles in your leadership style.
- **Micro-experiments**: Aim for at least one 'small shift' a week, such as delegating decision-making on a minor issue and seeing how the team responds.

Over time, these little changes become second nature, shaping a leader who adapts swiftly and helps others do the same. Adaptive Leadership is a continuous journey; the more you practise mindful self-reflection, the more naturally you'll embody the agility your organization needs.

Leading with Purpose, Not Just Profit

One thing to note is that Adaptive Leadership goes beyond financial success. In a world where employee engagement and customer trust are paramount, leaders must align decisions with a clear mission. Companies like Patagonia and Unilever have demonstrated how focusing on sustainability and social impact can drive both business success and long-term agility.

Leaders must ask: *Does this decision align with our core values?* By embedding purpose into strategy, teams move beyond short-term gains, fostering resilience and innovation.

Adaptive Leadership in Non-Traditional Settings

While Adaptive Leadership is often explored in corporate or Agile-heavy sectors, its principles can be transformative in resource-constrained, high-impact environments like non-profits, governments, or startups.

For Example: Adaptive Leadership in Non-Profits

In 2022, *CleanWaterKenya*, a non-profit in Kenya, faced a 40% funding cut while supporting 20,000 individuals with clean water access. The leadership team adopted a lean Agile approach. They:

- Broke their goal into weekly sprints to prioritize immediate-impact initiatives.
- Leveraged local partnerships to reduce supply chain costs.
- Introduced digital fundraising campaigns using low-cost social media tools.

Result: They reduced operational costs by around 30% and exceeded their fundraising target, achieving their goal six months early.

Practical Framework for Non-Traditional Contexts

1. **Define Constraints**: Identify limiting factors (e.g. resources, regulatory hurdles).
2. **Simplify Goals**: Break long-term objectives into manageable milestones.
3. **Leverage Partnerships**: Collaborate with stakeholders to amplify impact.
4. **Iterate Rapidly**: Test small initiatives and expand successful ones.
5. **Communicate Clearly**: Maintain transparency with team members and beneficiaries.

By applying these adaptive strategies, leaders in non-traditional settings can achieve remarkable outcomes. Let's now explore how Adaptive Leadership styles align with diverse team dynamics.

When Agile Falls Short: Lessons from Failures

Personal Reflection

Agile isn't a silver bullet. While it has driven remarkable improvements in many organizations, it can also fail spectacularly when leadership isn't truly invested in the transformation. One large-scale Agile transformation I led saw an 800% increase in technical and project deliveries within its first year. It wasn't just about speed – teams were more engaged, cross-functional collaboration flourished, and customer outcomes improved.

Yet, despite these successes, the leadership team wasn't prepared for what Agile exposed. As technology outpaced other parts of the organization, Agile inadvertently made traditional business processes look slow and inefficient. Rather than embracing change, leadership resisted, viewing Agile as a threat rather than an opportunity. The supportive CTO was replaced with a non-Agile 'yes' man, and overnight, the company eliminated Agile entirely, reverting to its old ways of working.

This failure wasn't about Agile itself; it was about leaders unwilling to evolve. The lesson is clear: Agile works only when leaders stay fully engaged, commit to transparency, and challenge legacy habits. Without that effort, even the most successful transformations can unravel. Learn from bad leadership as well as good leadership.

Let's look at some other examples of this:

Case Study 1: Nokia's Failed Agile Transformation

Background: Nokia led mobile phone production, then tried Agile to compete with emerging tech giants. Without a cultural overhaul or adequate leadership coaching, the shift encountered major pushback. Hierarchical structures clashed with iterative ways of working.

   Outcome: Timelines were extended, progress stalled, and Nokia's phone division was sold to Microsoft in 2014. The problem wasn't Agile but mismatched organizational habits.

   Lesson Learned: Cultural readiness and leadership buy-in matter as much as the chosen process. Process changes can't thrive if the culture isn't on board.

Potential Fixes

- Gauge readiness for transparency and collaboration.
- Train all levels in Agile thinking.
- Start small, validate success, then expand.
- Ensure leaders champion iterative learning.

Case Study 2: Electronic Arts' Misapplied Scrum

Background: Electronic Arts (EA) tried Scrum on a major game title while keeping annual marketing-driven releases. There was no freedom to adjust the scope. Teams were forced into a 'crunch' to meet unyielding deadlines.

   Outcome: Developers burned out, and the final product launched with bugs, damaging EA's reputation. The real problem was a refusal to let Agile iteration shape priorities.

   Lesson Learned: For Agile to succeed, scope and timelines must remain flexible. Merely re-labelling tasks as 'Sprints' doesn't solve deeper constraints.

Potential Fixes

- Use flexible backlog planning that ranks features.
- Test game builds early with players or focus groups.
- Ditch 'crunch' cycles for balanced work routines.
- Teach marketing and executive teams how Scrum depends on adaptability.

Key Takeaways

Both Nokia and EA faced challenges due to misalignment between Agile principles and organizational practices. By addressing these issues, they could have achieved better outcomes:

- **Prepare the Culture**: Agile transformations require cultural readiness, leadership alignment, and open communication.
- **Understand the Existing Culture**: While you can't impose a new culture, you can influence a paradigm shift. Acknowledge current norms and build in change management to guide meaningful, lasting change.
- **Educate and Align Stakeholders**: Agile adoption succeeds when all stakeholders understand and support its principles.

- **Embrace Flexibility**: Fixed scopes and rigid deadlines undermine Agile's value. Iterative approaches and sustainable practices must replace traditional workflows.
- **Empower Teams**: Decentralizing decision-making fosters innovation and engagement, ensuring Agile principles are fully realized.

These lessons highlight that Agile is not a one-size-fits-all solution. Success lies in adapting its principles to fit organizational contexts while ensuring leadership and cultural alignment. With these lessons in mind, we can now focus on practical approaches that directly tackle these real-world problems, ensuring Agile's principles inform more adaptive and sustainable solutions.

With these cautionary tales in mind, let's explore some practical ways to tackle the very problems these case studies reveal, ensuring Agile is adapted rather than abandoned.

Practical Approaches to Real Problems

Agile becomes powerful when used as a flexible tool to handle specific challenges rather than an off-the-shelf system. Its success stems from context-driven decisions that keep user value front and centre. For instance, collecting user input every sprint ensures continuous refinement. Meanwhile, teams can adjust sprint lengths and stand-ups to match the work style, preserving relevance.

This pragmatic style helps Agile navigate real pressures. Returning to Agile's original core values (people, collaboration, working outputs, openness to change) reminds leaders why it matters. By re-focusing on those values, you keep Agile genuine and adaptive.

Steps for Conducting Cultural Readiness Assessments

Leaders should confirm that their organization's culture is open to Agile values. This includes evaluating willingness to collaborate, share knowledge, and empower teams.

1. **Ask the Right Questions**: Anonymous surveys reveal staff openness to smaller iterative cycles and direct feedback.
2. **Leadership Interviews**: Check if middle managers and execs are prepared to share control.
3. **Map Decision Paths**: Identify red tape or top-down patterns that impede agility.
4. **Psychological Safety**: Run focus groups to gauge whether people feel safe speaking freely.
5. **Benchmarking**: Compare your readiness with success stories like Spotify or ING. Notice specific areas to fix.

Guidelines for Tailoring Frameworks to Unique Organizational Contexts

No single Agile framework suits all contexts. Customizing is key.

1. **Pilot a Single Team**: Start small to learn what works, gather data, and then expand.

2. **Align with Outcomes**: Choose Scrum or Kanban if it aligns well with strategic goals, or merge them if that's more suitable.
3. **Adapt Ceremonies**: Modify roles, events, and artefacts to match your team's work style.
4. **Focus on Real Impact**: Concentrate on the benefits, like value creation, over strict steps.
5. **Evolve Over Time**: Let teams regularly improve the chosen approach based on new insights.

Staying true to core values, rather than blindly following procedures, draws out Agile's transformative impact.

Returning to Core Values

Some companies are renewing their focus on Agile basics – focusing on user value, open collaboration, and letting teams self-organize. Reducing extraneous processes revives the original power of Agile to deliver incremental, meaningful output. When each department customizes Agile to its unique setting, real adaptability emerges.

Progressive leaders keep it simple by emphasizing user engagement, short releases, and freedom to pivot. This approach helps Agile remain an accelerator of creativity rather than a rigid set of steps.

Evolving Beyond the Challenges

Forward-thinking leaders are simplifying how they apply Agile, removing bureaucracy that creeps in over time. By emphasizing empowered teams, customer-centric thinking, and continuous refinement, they ensure their Agile approach stays flexible, adaptable, and relevant. Building on the renewed focus on principles, the next step involves practical measures that dispel lingering misconceptions, guiding teams toward more value-driven outcomes.

How to Overcome Misconceptions

To move beyond criticisms and strengthen Agile practices, organizations must bridge the gap between the ideals that inspired Agile and how they apply it now. Instead of discarding Agile entirely, the path involves recalibrating: shifting from framework-driven rituals to a meaningful, context-driven interpretation of Agile values.

- **Focus on Real Goals**: Measure success by how well you serve users, not by how flawlessly you follow a framework.
- **Empower Teams**: Grant them leeway to adapt ceremonies or timelines as needed.
- **Encourage Experimentation**: Let teams learn from small risks and share insights promptly.
- **Keep It Simple**: Don't add layers of bureaucracy. Revisit frameworks frequently to cut down on anything that does not add value.

OKRs and Agile Alignment

Allan Kelly, an agility and OKR consultant at the Business Agility Conference UK 2024, emphasized the power of OKRs (Objectives and Key Results) as 'enabling constraints'. OKRs steer Agile teams toward clear objectives while preserving flexibility in how they achieve them. This methodical alignment counters critiques that Agile drifts into bureaucracy, offering a practical tool that zeroes in on value-driven outcomes without stifling innovation.

For example: Teams set monthly OKRs tied to strategic aims. Each sprint cycle is then evaluated against these results, preventing them from getting lost in process-heavy routines and keeping them anchored to business priorities.

However, we must recognize that some criticisms highlight genuine challenges in scaling and sustaining Agile, and leaders must tackle them head-on.

Addressing the Valid Critiques

Plenty of complaints stem from improper usage, but some identify genuine stumbling blocks: scaling Agile across massive organizations can diffuse its focus on autonomy. Overblown coordination efforts hamper the very agility the method promises.

Leaders who want to fix these weaknesses align Agile with local realities. They accept that one blueprint won't work for every challenge. Emphasizing human elements – like trust in teams and freedom to run experiments – anchors Agile in its original spirit.

Approaches like the CLEAR Model® help leaders tackle real challenges by embedding Agile values into the fabric of the organization – not just within project teams.

Adding Nuance to the Debate

Arguments about Agile's fate often become black-and-white. Yet Agile is neither outdated nor static. It has progressed in many respects, but it has also strayed in others. A mature view acknowledges Agile's achievements and shortfalls.

The real query: '*How does Agile stay aligned with its core principles while evolving?*' Sometimes expansions – like wider adoption beyond software – reflect healthy evolution. Other times, ritual overload distracts from genuine collaboration. Embracing nuance helps leaders correct mistakes, not abandon Agile entirely.

By tackling valid critiques, we keep Agile flexible and effective. This includes welcoming the sceptics as key voices, ensuring we don't drift into complacency.

Embracing the Critics as Catalysts for Change

Criticism can trigger vital improvements instead of blame. Naysayers often point out real issues, like bureaucratic overhead or short-term planning, that undermine the Agile mindset. Maintaining dialogue with critics can prompt Agile to shed unnecessary baggage and refocus on delivering tangible value.

Action Step: Hold a feedback session solely to discuss Agile's perceived flaws. Note common frustrations – is bureaucracy creeping in, or do strategic goals lack clarity?

Learning from these complaints stops Agile from becoming stale. By discarding unproductive routines and seeking fresh ideas, Agile remains relevant. Adaptive leaders see critics not as threats but as motivators for ongoing reinvention.

Conclusion

Agile's strength isn't found in frameworks alone – Adaptive Leadership that unites teams around shared objectives encourages openness, and embraces refinements keeps Agile alive. The debate over Agile's supposed decline often masks the reality that its future rests on how well leaders embed and adapt it.

Criticisms of Agile – like complexity, misapplications, or a checklist approach – are valid reminders that Agile falters when done superficially. Yet these cautionary points suggest how we can fine-tune it, upholding iterative principles that still resonate deeply with many teams.

Agile's potential hinges on leaders who promote transparency, shape work around user value, and keep teams motivated to adjust. Addressing concerns about wasted effort or forced frameworks ensures Agile can thrive as a driver of experimentation and quality.

The next chapter examines how Agile's foundational principles – adaptability, team synergy, and continuous improvement – can be embedded across leadership and culture, ensuring its true impact is realized.

Call to Action

Reflect on your organization's Agile critiques. Do daily gatherings feel stale? Does short-term thinking overwhelm strategy? Identify areas needing a course correction. Encourage open conversation with colleagues, unify your efforts, and let genuine Agile principles guide you. Escaping 'Agile in name only' can reignite your teams' ability to work together, keep learning, and deliver real value.

Key Takeaways

- **Balanced Perspective Is Essential**: Understanding both the challenges and benefits of Agile allows for more effective adoption.
- **Cultural Change Drives Success**: Aligning organizational culture with Agile principles is crucial for meaningful transformation.
- **Leaders Must Lead the Change**: Leaders play a pivotal role in modelling Agile behaviours and supporting teams.
- **Practical Solutions Over Rigid Frameworks**: Customizing Agile practices to fit the organization's context leads to better outcomes.
- **Continuous Evolution Is Key**: Embracing Agile's core values and adapting to new challenges ensures ongoing relevance.

CLEAR Model® Connection

- **Leadership**: Strong, Adaptive Leadership elevates Agile from a simple process to real transformation.

Key Takeaway: Agile leadership requires more than just understanding frameworks – it demands an ability to inspire, empower, and navigate change effectively.

Balanced Scorecard Template: Weighing Agile Pros and Cons

- **Strengths:**
  - o List areas where Agile has positively impacted your projects.
- **Weaknesses:**
  - o Identify challenges or drawbacks experienced.
- **Opportunities:**
  - o Recognize opportunities for enhancing Agile practices.
- **Threats:**
  - o Note external factors that may hinder Agile effectiveness.

Decision-Making Framework: Optimizing Agile Use

1. **Data Collection:**
   - o Gather feedback from teams, customers, and stakeholders.
2. **Analysis:**
   - o Use the Balanced Scorecard to assess the current state.
3. **Prioritization:**
   - o Determine which areas need immediate attention.
4. **Strategy Development:**
   - o Plan interventions to amplify strengths and mitigate weaknesses.
5. **Implementation:**
   - o Assign responsibilities and timelines for action items.

Chapter Summary

Agile remains an effective approach if organizations commit to meaningful change rather than shallow ceremonies. This chapter illustrated typical pitfalls (framework overload, half-hearted adoption) and best practices for harnessing Agile's power. Leaders who focus on outcomes, simplify methods, and involve teams in shaping solutions will see Agile flourish.

4

Embracing 'Post-Agile' Realities

It is not the strongest of the species that survives, nor the most intelligent. It is the one that is most adaptable to change.

Charles Darwin

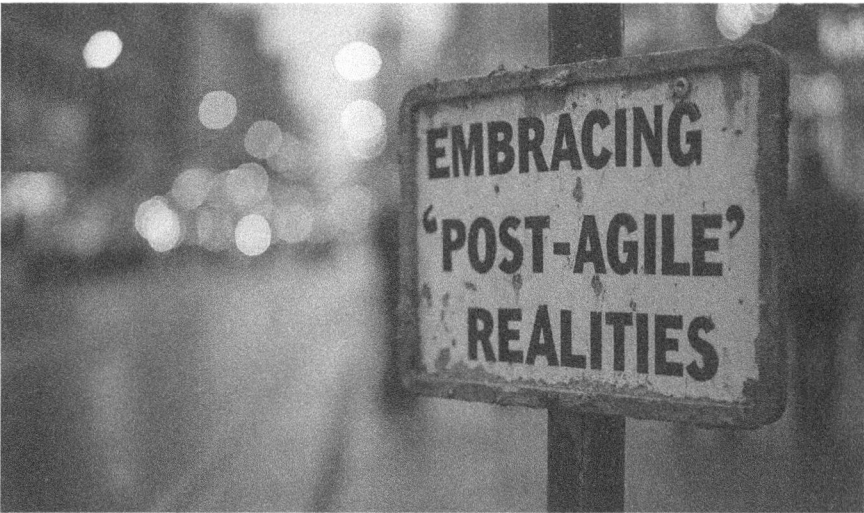

What You'll Gain

- **For Senior Leaders and Executives**: Discover how 'Post-Agile' thinking broadens agility into an organization-wide culture, not just a set of frameworks.
- **For Mid-Level Leaders**: Learn how to embed adaptive mindsets across departments, overcoming rigid rituals or processes.
- **For Students or Early-Career Professionals**: Understand how Agile evolves to meet complex modern demands, with cultural and leadership shifts playing a central role.

Embracing the Evolution

Most transformations fail to meet the expected outcomes of their sponsors. As we move into a 'post-Agile' era, leaders must grow from Agile specialists into adaptive changemakers, ready for rapid disruptions in technology and markets.

'Agile transformed how we deliver, but are we genuinely Agile – or just going through the motions?'

A heated debate was brewing in a boardroom. A senior executive, hands clasped, leaned forward. *'Agile helped us move faster, but we're still struggling with real business agility.'* The room fell silent. The CIO finally spoke. *'We've mastered the stand-ups, the sprints, the retros – but are we truly Agile, or are we just performing rituals?'*

That's the tension in many boardrooms. The stand-ups, sprints, and retros run smoothly, yet real business agility remains elusive. Leaders are now asking whether traditional Agile is sufficient or if a next-level approach is needed.

According to Russ Lewis, a digital transformation leader, Agile gains meaning only when it boosts customer outcomes and staff engagement instead of reducing to box-ticking. His observation captures the essence of post-Agile thinking: genuine progress over ceremonies.

A decade into Agile adoption, some leaders find the initial excitement has faded. Teams yearn to know, 'What's next?' Despite this fatigue, Agile's core – responsiveness, collaboration, and continuous growth – still resonates. However, leaders who see it as a stepping stone rather than an end in itself are the ones successfully reframing agility for today's complexities.

Rather than ditching Agile's core values or piling on frameworks, these leaders anchor agility in their cultural DNA. While some label this shift 'Post-Agile', it isn't about discarding the past. It means evolving Agile's core to face new challenges. Adaptive leaders recognize that change is inevitable. This chapter explores 'Post-Agile' as Agile's natural progression – a pathway requiring foresight and organizational dedication.

Personal Reflection

Many leaders ask if Agile has run its course. I believe it has simply outgrown the methods that once defined it. Now, more than ever, Agile mindsets must evolve to tackle challenges that standard frameworks never imagined. With the right leadership, Agile thrives by shifting in step with these obstacles.

As many enterprises integrate Lean and DevOps or expand digitization, they see agility as a principle woven across teams rather than a single IT initiative. Before diving deeper, let's clarify what 'post-Agile' entails and how it differs from older Agile methods.

Definition: Post-Agile

Post-Agile is a leadership-first, outcome-led way of working that embeds agility as an organization-wide principle, not a team method. It aligns culture, decision rights, funding, and governance with customer value, trims ceremonies to the minimum needed, and blends Lean, DevOps, and product thinking to improve flow, learning, and resilience. Success is tracked through a small set of signals such as lead time, adoption, retention, NPS, and cost-to-serve. The focus shifts from 'doing Agile' to building an adaptive business.

How Post-Agile Differs from Adjacent Ideas

- **Agile 2**: evolves Agile values and balances people and tech. Post-Agile applies that balance **across the enterprise** with changes to funding, controls, and decision paths.

- **Modern Agile**: four simple principles for teams. Post-Agile keeps those principles and adds **executive levers** like strategy, risk, and talent pathways.
- **Product operating model**: structures teams and value streams. Post-Agile provides the **mindset and governance** that make that structure adaptive and outcome-focused.
- **Business Agility**: broad ambition. Post-Agile is the practical route to it, with clear behaviours, measures, and review rhythms.

Post-Agile Leadership – Stepping Forward

Above and Beyond Agile

Agile revolutionized teamwork, adaptation, and user focus. But times have changed – leaders confront shifting work models, fast-moving tech breakthroughs, rising ethical demands, and multigenerational teams. The question is: How do we stay agile in this new complexity?

The answer lies in broadening Agile's principles so they reach every department. This isn't Agile's demise – it's an extension of its mindset and culture.

The Post-Agile Concept

Post-Agile leadership holds onto Agile's core spirit but applies it to more varied demands that need fluid solutions. One important idea is 'holistic agility', which means extending Agile practices across multiple business functions, from marketing to operations. Another aim is lasting practices: rather than focusing on immediate outputs, leaders look toward deeper, long-term goals.

Post-Agile also values context-driven methods, where frameworks are matched to specific needs rather than imposed out of habit. Alongside this sits ethical leadership, based on fairness and inclusion when shaping decisions. By combining these ideas, leaders can adapt to changing forces and create workplaces that learn fast and adjust without losing direction.

Post-Agile leadership is not about abandoning Agile; it's about transcending it.

In the Post-Agile World

- Agile is no longer a framework – it's a leadership mindset.
- Agility is not a team-level method but an organizational principle.
- Frameworks are not the focus – customer impact and speed-to-value are.
- Leaders are not facilitators – they are architects of adaptability.
- Teams don't 'do Agile' – they adapt to fit their specific challenges.
- Rigid Agile roles give way to fluid leadership, where adaptability is the key trait.
- Success is not measured in sprints but in business impact and resilience.
- Post-Agile leaders build businesses that thrive in unpredictability, not just function within existing Agile structures.

The Case for Post-Agile Leadership

Off-the-shelf Agile frameworks sometimes falter in large or diverse contexts. Post-Agile leadership moves beyond procedural checklists, embedding a flexible ethos everywhere. As we adapt to the Fourth Industrial Revolution, it's no longer about how quickly we produce increments but how deeply we integrate adaptability into daily decisions.

Key Insight: Post-Agile leadership fosters a culture where rote processes don't constrain people. Instead, they pivot and innovate at will. Leaders who champion psychological safety, data-driven choices, and constant learning support genuine collaboration at every turn.

In this chapter, you'll find practical examples and tips to steer your organization through this post-Agile environment, clarifying leadership's role in shaping tomorrow's adaptability.

Clarifying the 'Post-Agile' Concept

When Maria, a CTO at a global fintech company, reviewed her Agile transformation reports, she noticed something unsettling. Teams were hitting sprint goals, Jira boards were filled with completed tasks, yet innovation had stalled. The company was 'doing Agile' flawlessly but struggling to evolve. Maria realized that Agile needed to be more than a methodology – it had to be a strategic capability embedded into decision-making, leadership, and organizational culture. This is what 'Post-Agile' thinking is about: not abandoning Agile but evolving it into a deeper, more contextual form of adaptability.

'Post-Agile' represents an era where agility transcends IT or team-level methods, permeating an organization's overall culture and strategic thinking. Instead of fixating on stand-ups or sprint rituals, leaders in a post-Agile world concentrate on adaptability, collaboration, and continuous learning at every level of the business. Classic Agile emphasizes iterative value delivery; post-Agile goes a step further by making responsiveness and rapid learning part of everything from marketing campaigns to customer service processes.

Key Distinction

To see how post-Agile differs, consider the table below:

Aspect	Agile	Post-Agile
Focus	Frameworks (e.g. Scrum, SAFe)	Culture and mindset in every department
Primary Goal	Iterative value delivery	Continual adaptation and joined-up thinking
Leadership Style	Supportive, framework-based	Transformational, championing cultural change
Team Structure	Self-organizing teams	Interlinked, cross-functional groups
Adaptability	Adapting within frameworks	Adapting beyond frameworks, organization-wide

Aspect	Agile	Post-Agile
Measurement of Success	Timely sprint/project delivery	Overall responsiveness and resilience
Cultural Role	Team-level ownership of Agile	An organization-wide embrace of agility

This table highlights how post-Agile fosters a cultural transformation far beyond IT. Surveys indicate that smaller, streamlined firms often see higher success with agility than larger ones, weighted down by complexity. Leaders focusing on enterprise-wide agility create the conditions for faster pivots and robust innovation.

In Practice: A retail giant that seamlessly shifts from in-store to online operations during supply chain turmoil exemplifies post-Agile thinking. Leadership ensures every function, not just software, is ready to adapt.

The core of post-Agile is a cultural foundation, ensuring that Agile principles become instinctive rather than forced. Let's examine how leaders spark this culture. Previously, we explored how culture is vital for Agile. Now, it's more vital in the post-Agile context. Leaders must anchor adaptability within the organizational psyche.

Defining Post-Agile Culture

- **Adaptability as Norm**: Teams pivot smoothly, skipping rigid plan adherence.
- **Collaboration Beyond Silos**: Departments function as interconnected networks.
- **Continuous Learning**: Every slip-up is a chance to improve.
- **Decentralized Decision-Making**: Local authority fosters quick responses.

Leaders build this culture by:

- Running pulse surveys for readiness checks.
- Hosting cross-functional 'problem-solving labs'.
- Celebrating experiments and 'safe' failures.
- Aligning leadership styles through coaching or accountability sessions.

A software firm, for example, found communication bottlenecks in a cultural audit. Enabling cross-team synergy and real autonomy improved speed and product alignment. This shows how cultural shifts let agility flourish at scale.

Practical Steps for Cultural Assessments

1. **Pulse Surveys**: Quick, anonymous questionnaires to measure openness to collaboration, trust, and feedback loops.
2. **Focus Groups**: Small, diverse gatherings to explore cultural strengths and challenges.
3. **Leadership Interviews**: Determine leadership buy-in, exposing conflicting viewpoints or outdated assumptions.

4. **Decision-Mapping**: Identify where bureaucratic layers slow adaptation.
5. **Benchmarking**: Compare internal practices against Agile-friendly exemplars (e.g. ING, Spotify) to spot improvement areas.

Cultivating a post-Agile culture lays the groundwork for truly internalizing Agile mindsets. Rather than just 'doing Agile', teams become Agile – living and breathing adaptability. Once embedded, Agile becomes second nature, freeing leaders and teams to address challenges proactively and continuously.

Embedding a Post-Agile Culture

Leaders guide this cultural shift by consistently demonstrating the behaviours they expect to see:

- **Model Adaptability**: Stay open to shifting plans and pivoting strategies when data or market feedback indicates it.
- **Promote Collaboration**: Break down silos; encourage cross-departmental brainstorming or problem-solving sessions.
- **Emphasize Continuous Learning**: Provide coaching and training, encourage knowledge sharing, and make retrospectives integral to every level of the business.

Such cultural embedding moves organizations beyond framework checklists and fosters genuine agility, enabling them to respond effectively to complex market conditions. In practice, a culture steeped in these values not only transforms how teams deliver products but also redefines how an organization sees itself.

Personal Reflection

Early in my career, I led an Agile transformation at a company that was reluctant to change. We rolled out Agile practices quickly, but leadership wasn't fully on board. Teams followed stand-ups and sprints, yet nothing really changed – approvals still took weeks, and priorities shifted arbitrarily. The problem? Agile had become a surface-level practice rather than a cultural shift.

I had to step back and rethink my approach. Instead of pushing Agile as a process, I refocused on leadership and adaptability. We started with small experiments, proving success before scaling. Leaders began embracing agility themselves, and only then did the transformation take hold.

With a robust cultural base, the next step is to fully internalize these agile values, ensuring that they become a natural element of daily work – an essence of the 'post-Agile' reality.

Internalizing Agility in the Post-Agile Era

The shift to a post-Agile world requires moving beyond critiques and focusing on how Agile principles can mature into deeply embedded organizational values. As organizations evolve, the emphasis shifts from correcting Agile's past misapplications to fully internalizing its principles, creating a culture where adaptability, collaboration, and innovation are second nature. This progression represents a natural evolution from 'Doing Agile' to 'Being Agile', where agility transcends frameworks to become an innate organizational trait.

Building on this foundation, organizations can now focus on operationalizing these deeply embedded principles, ensuring that agility becomes the cornerstone of their resilience and long-term growth.

Recent discourse highlights that Agile principles are not fading but transforming into more integrated and holistic organizational approaches. The post-Agile phase shifts focus to prioritizing principles over processes, outcomes over outputs, and cultivating a culture rooted in adaptability over mere compliance. As such, this next phase involves rethinking and expanding Agile concepts to suit modern, cross-functional teams across industries.

Evan Leybourn, co-founder and Head of Advocacy and thought leadership at the Business Agility Institute, notes declining interest in 'traditional Agile roles' but rising demand for Agile mindsets – a clear sign of Agile's shift from frameworks to culture. This shift from 'Doing Agile' to 'Being Agile' aligns with Systems coach Philippe Guenet's remark that 'post-Agile' doesn't signify the end of Agile. As such, it's a sign that *Agile is growing up*.

To visualize this progression, consider where your organization stands on the Agile spectrum, moving from surface-level methodologies towards deep-rooted cultural agility.

Doing Agile

Focus on processes and tools, rigid adherence to frameworks, superficial adoption without cultural change.

Being Agile

Emphasis on mindset and values, cultural alignment with Agile principles, adaptability and continuous improvement.

Where does your organization stand on the Agile spectrum?

This image illustrates that adopting Agile is not merely about implementing practices (Doing Agile) but about evolving the organization's culture and mindset towards true agility (Being Agile). As organizations evolve and internalize Agile principles, they move along the spectrum, experiencing greater benefits such as enhanced innovation, responsiveness, and team empowerment.

Sustaining Agility Through Authentic Evolution

This transformation directly addresses earlier critiques, like Agile's misapplication or commodification, by helping organizations internalize Agile mindsets. In doing so, they move beyond shallow adoptions or certifications, fostering a deeper agility that permeates their culture. This evolution aligns with my view of Agile as a maturing, adaptable approach that remains vital for navigating complex business challenges. Yet, to sustain this momentum, leaders must curb over-complexity and rekindle the original principles that once made Agile so pioneering.

Leaders must extend beyond processes and truly *embody* agility in decision-making, vision, and strategy.

Adaptive leaders can foster agility by:

- **Delegating decision-making**: Empower teams to drive initiatives at the closest point to the customer or problem.
- **Modelling curiosity and openness**: Embrace change actively, reassuring teams during transitions.
- **Conducting regular retrospectives**: Focus on aligning objectives with strategic goals, ensuring that teams remain both innovative and purpose-driven.

Such Adaptive Leadership spurs environments where agility informs not only *projects* but also long-range vision and cultural change. Building on this foundation, guiding smaller, outcome-driven teams can further enhance organizational nimbleness and creativity.

Next, let's examine how this authentic evolution of Agile principles shapes the broader 'post-Agile' landscape and addresses past misconceptions.

Reframing the 'Post-Agile' Landscape

As Agile matures, we face big questions. Some say 'Agile is dead', but transformation consultant Markus Gärtner sees it as a prompt for leaders to refocus on adaptability and responsiveness. Indeed, organizations dropping standard frameworks might simply be moving on to more context-aware solutions.

Commercial Context: Since late 2023, the market for classic Agile consultancy dipped, partly due to economic pressures and surging AI. Companies reduce external coaching reliance by wanting in-house Agile expertise. Adaptive leaders thus emphasize building internal capacity over costly, one-size-fits-all frameworks.

Simultaneously, smaller firms skip large-scale frameworks in favour of simpler, results-driven approaches, and often succeed more consistently. For them, agility is about freedom from constraints, not memorizing a method.

Agile Is Evolving – Are You?

By now, we've explored the criticisms of Agile and the leadership failures that have caused them. We've also introduced the CLEAR Model® – a leadership-first approach that moves beyond frameworks and into real agility.

But knowing the CLEAR Model® isn't enough – leaders must implement it.

The question is: How do you take CLEAR from theory to practice?

This section provides a step-by-step roadmap for embedding the CLEAR Model® into your organization, helping leaders, teams, and entire businesses become truly adaptive and resilient.

The Five-Step Roadmap for Implementing the CLEAR Model®

Step 1: Culture – Redefining How Agility Is Embedded

The Challenge
Most Agile transformations fail not because of poor frameworks but because of resistance to cultural change.

- 'We say we value agility, but our culture rewards predictability.'
- 'Teams are expected to be flexible, but leadership still punishes failure.'
- 'There's no alignment between company values and Agile principles.'

The Solution
Agility must be woven into the fabric of the organization's culture, not just imposed as a process.

Actionable Steps

- **Align company values with agility**: If adaptability is a core value, make it explicit in company policies and leadership behaviours.
- **Foster a culture of learning and experimentation**: Celebrate small failures as steps toward success.
- **Encourage decentralized decision-making**: Push authority closer to where the work happens.

Real-World Example
Haier (China's Agile Giant) → Haier operates as a network of micro-enterprises, empowering employees to make decisions and respond to market shifts in real-time.

Step 2: Leadership – Moving from Control to Enablement

The Challenge
Even in Agile organizations, leaders often struggle to let go of control.

- 'We want self-organizing teams, but managers still micromanage.'
- 'Leadership supports Agile – but only when things go according to plan.'
- 'Decisions still require multiple layers of approval.'

The Solution

As discussed in Chapter 3, leadership must shift from commanding to enabling. The CLEAR Model® reinforces this shift by providing a structured framework that leaders can follow to embed agility sustainably.

Actionable Steps

- **Redefine the role of leadership**: Leaders should act as coaches and facilitators, not bottlenecks.
- **Empower teams with decision-making authority**: Encourage delegation over escalation.
- **Model Adaptive Leadership**: Leaders must embrace uncertainty and act with agility themselves.

Real-World Example

Spotify's Leadership Model → Spotify's leaders act as coaches, not bosses, creating a culture of autonomy and alignment.

Step 3: Execution – Delivering Value, Not Just Process Compliance

The Challenge

Many organizations measure Agile success by process adherence rather than business impact.

- 'We're doing Agile, but our customer satisfaction hasn't improved.'
- 'Our teams deliver more, but is it the right work?'
- 'Agile has become about velocity, not outcomes.'

The Solution

Agile execution must be focused on value delivery, not rituals.

Actionable Steps

- **Shift from output-based to outcome-based metrics**: Focus on customer satisfaction, revenue impact, and innovation speed.
- **Use Agile to optimize flow, not just structure**: Reduce handovers, wait times, and inefficiencies.
- **Eliminate vanity metrics**: Agile success isn't about how many stand-ups you have – it's about business results.

Real-World Example

Amazon's Two-Pizza Teams → Amazon structures teams to be small, autonomous, and focused on delivering real customer impact.

Step 4: Adaptability – Thriving in Uncertainty

The Challenge

Many organizations embrace Agile but still fear uncertainty.

- 'We use Agile, but leaders still expect fixed long-term roadmaps.'
- 'Our teams struggle with constant change and lack of stability.'
- 'We don't have a framework for managing adaptive decision-making.'

The Solution

Adaptability is the defining trait of future-ready organizations.

Actionable Steps

- **Move from rigid planning to adaptive roadmaps**: Set strategic direction without locking in execution.
- **Embed continuous learning cycles**: Use short feedback loops to course-correct in real-time.
- **Train teams to be comfortable with ambiguity**: Develop scenario-based planning to prepare for multiple possible futures.

Real-World Example

Tesla's Rapid Iteration Model → Tesla constantly refines its manufacturing process based on real-time data, not static plans.

Step 5: Responsiveness – Making Faster, Smarter Decisions

The Challenge

Many organizations claim to be Agile but still operate with slow, bureaucratic decision-making.

- 'Our teams can deliver fast, but leadership takes months to approve changes.'
- 'We're Agile in theory, but we still react too slowly to customer needs.'
- 'Agile development is fast – Agile decision-making is not.'

The Solution

True agility means being able to act fast in response to change.

Actionable Steps

- **Eliminate decision bottlenecks**: Push decision-making closer to the work.
- **Use real-time data for decision-making**: Invest in analytics and automation to improve responsiveness.
- **Foster a test-and-learn mindset**: Encourage teams to experiment quickly and pivot based on insights.

Real-World Example

Netflix's Data-Driven Culture → Netflix constantly analyses customer behaviour to adjust content strategy on the fly.

The CLEAR Model® in Action – Making It Work for You

Implementing the CLEAR Model® isn't just about Agile – it's about creating an organization that can thrive in any environment.

Key Takeaways

- **Agility must be embedded in culture, not just in process.**
  True agility isn't about following a framework – it's about fostering a mindset of adaptability, experimentation, and decentralized decision-making across the entire organization.
- **Leaders must shift from command-and-control to enable-and-inspire.**
  Adaptive leaders don't dictate – they empower. Moving from control to coaching allows teams to take ownership, innovate, and respond effectively to change.
- **Execution must focus on outcomes, not just activities.**
  Agile success isn't measured by ceremonies or velocity – it's measured by business impact. Organizations must shift from tracking tasks to delivering meaningful customer and business value.
- **Adaptive organizations don't fear uncertainty – they embrace it.**
  In a fast-changing world, rigidity is a liability. Future-ready organizations cultivate flexibility, continuously learn from feedback, and adjust strategies in real-time.
- **Responsiveness is the ultimate competitive advantage.**
  Speed alone isn't enough – organizations must be able to sense, decide, and act quickly in response to shifts in the market, customer needs, and emerging opportunities.

Behavioural Agility in Action

At a major pharmaceutical firm, strict regulations stifled standard Agile frameworks. Instead of forcing sprints, leadership taught teams to scan for obstacles, iterate quickly, and engage all relevant stakeholders. A compliance unit introduced weekly 'What's changed?' check-ins instead of classic backlog reviews, improving policy response by nearly 30%. This proves agility thrives on behavioural adaptability, not always formal ceremonies.

Key Lesson: Some of the most Agile companies either apply minimal frameworks or adapt them extensively. They emphasize proactive troubleshooting, cross-departmental collaboration, and swift experimentation. From these come deeper cultural norms that overshadow any single Agile label.

Why Behaviour Matters

- **Team Empowerment**: Emphasizing ownership and autonomy.
- **Cross-Functional Ties**: Integration across finance, marketing, dev, etc.
- **Rapid Learning**: Encouraging small, frequent changes that yield quick insights.

When frameworks become rigid, they often overshadow the flexible spirit of agility. Leaders who focus on norms, like problem-solving attitudes and trust, ignite real results.

Personal Reflection

I once guided a product team that had memorized every sprint ceremony yet still struggled to innovate. Only after we replaced rigid backlog checklists with collaborative roadmapping did they see real customer impact. That moment taught me that 'Post-Agile' means looking beyond rituals and embracing the mindset behind them.

Agile Restoration: Stripping Away the Excess

Authentic evolution demands restoration – shedding needless bureaucracy while retaining Agile's inventive essence. As Dave Thomas (co-author of the Agile Manifesto) notes, the term 'Agile' has been overused, morphing into a 'state religion'. The solution: re-emphasize iterative learning, responsiveness, and collaboration, disengaging from frameworks that suffocate original intent.

Practical Steps

- **Iterative Learning**: Let teams pivot quickly, even without official sprint boards.
- **Responsiveness**: Reduce structural barriers to allow instant adaptation.
- **Empowered Teams**: Let staff make key decisions, fostering buy-in.

The 'Agile Industrial Complex' often pushes certifications over tangible improvement. Leaders must be wary. Real agility doesn't hinge on credentials – it flourishes through consistent, principle-based actions. By reclaiming a simpler, human-focused approach, organizations rebuild the energy that once propelled Agile transformations.

Embedding Agile Mindsets Across the Organization

In a post-Agile setting, external coaches become less necessary because agility is simply 'how we do things'. ING Bank did exactly that, merging agility into squads, 'tribes', and daily work. They moved from measured experiments to full cultural adoption.

Implication: Instead of short-term coaching, agility is permanent and built into the leadership pipeline. This shift – from outside-in to inside-out – confirms maturity and normalizes Agile thinking across finance, operations, sales, and beyond.

Outcome: The role of 'Agile Coach' morphs into broader strategic functions, with leaders championing collaborative, experimental mindsets that define the organization's daily routine.

Context-Driven Agility: Tailoring Methods to Context

Not every environment suits Scrum or SAFe. Real post-Agile leadership starts with questions: *What is our culture? Where are we trying to go?*

- **Tech Startups** might adopt a minimal Scrum model for swift iteration.
- **Global Enterprises** might blend Agile ideas with hierarchy, ensuring scale while preserving flexible squads.
- **Highly Regulated Industries** (e.g. finance, aviation) adapt Agile workflows to complex compliance, mixing them with more structured gating steps.

Key: Avoid forcing frameworks. Align them to existing constraints, letting teams refine or combine approaches. Many complaints about Agile's 'failures' stem from mismatched frameworks in the wrong context.

Leader Guidance

1. **Assess Cultural Norms**: Are teams comfortable with self-management?
2. **Adapt or Blend**: Choose or shape frameworks to address actual problems.
3. **Iterate Over Time**: Revisit processes regularly, adjusting to new lessons.

One transformation lead asked, 'Why isn't productivity improving faster if Agile's so powerful?' The issue typically lies in forced compliance – teams do 'sprints' without removing the deeper bottlenecks. True agility eliminates friction, letting teams pivot fast and harness real-time feedback.

In post-Agile, the question isn't 'Which framework?' but 'How quickly can we flow from idea to outcome?' That leads us to explore the theme of speed-to-value.

Speed-to-Value in the Post-Agile Era

A key differentiator in the post-Agile era is the ability to deliver value rapidly and iteratively. Jim Highsmith refers to this as *Speed-to-Value* – an approach where organizations optimize cycle times to ensure continuous delivery of meaningful business outcomes. Traditional Agile methods emphasize responsiveness, but without a focus on speed-to-value, they risk becoming incremental without impact.

For leaders, this means shifting away from frameworks that emphasize process compliance and instead ensuring that each iteration contributes to tangible results. The focus should not be on how quickly teams complete tasks but on how effectively they meet customer and business needs. These insights suggest that agility should no longer be about speed alone; it should prioritize *the right value at the right time*.

Leaders Can Achieve This by:

- Continuously measuring outcomes rather than outputs.
- Encouraging teams to focus on fast customer feedback loops.
- Embedding a culture where value-based decision-making replaces task-based reporting.

By embedding speed-to-value into leadership practices, organizations ensure that agility remains a strategic advantage rather than just an operational method.

Organizations must focus on behaviours that promote adaptability and responsiveness rather than simply implementing methods or frameworks to achieve business agility.

The Behavioural Core of Business Agility

Business agility thrives when it is anchored in cultural and behavioural norms, not in frameworks. Organizations that excel in agility share a common trait: leaders instil in their teams a mindset of curiosity, accountability, and action. Teams are encouraged to act without waiting for top-down direction, collaborate across silos, and view obstacles as opportunities for innovation.

This behavioural focus drives agility far more effectively than the adoption of any specific framework. Leaders who cultivate this mindset throughout their organization unlock the ability to pivot and adapt at scale, ensuring long-term resilience in a constantly changing environment.

Frameworks are often misused as crutches, overshadowing the behavioural and cultural changes required for true agility. Organizations that succeed in business agility focus on outcomes rather than rituals, integrating diverse methodologies to enhance adaptability. By doing so, they create a system where agility emerges naturally from cultural norms rather than enforced processes.

By embedding these behaviours into their organizations, leaders can transform agility from a set of practices into a way of thinking, ensuring their teams are equipped to handle the challenges of tomorrow.

Adaptive Leadership for Post-Agile Success

Post-Agile leaders do more than facilitate – they create entire systems that foster experimentation and swift adaptation. Command-and-control structures undermine agility; post-Agile leadership demands empowerment and a willingness to pivot.

Core: Post-Agile leadership operationalizes collaboration, continuous learning, and user-centred thinking. Leaders encourage scenario planning, letting teams pivot when needed. They adapt their style to each challenge, ensuring agility remains a flexible mindset rather than a rigid process.

For example: Netflix's 'freedom and responsibility' ethos grants staff autonomy with tight alignment on outcomes. Leaders trust employees to make the right calls, focusing on results, not micromanaging tasks. By removing top-down constraints, Netflix stays innovative.

One effective tactic is fostering smaller, outcome-oriented teams that quickly demonstrate the benefits of post-Agile. Let's explore that tactic next.

Small Teams, Big Outcomes

Agile's power shines in small, empowered units. Research shows smaller, outcome-driven teams deliver higher success rates, partly due to clearer communication and a strong sense of ownership.

Leaders May:

- **Form Decentralized Squads**: Each focuses on a targeted objective or metric.
- **Align on Outcomes**: Rather than uniform frameworks, allow squads autonomy to experiment and adapt.
- **Encourage Rapid Iteration**: Smaller teams pivot faster, respond to feedback sooner, and course-correct as needed.

Yet large enterprises often fixate on compliance-driven transformations with hefty budgets (ranging from $500k to $5 million) and brand-heavy frameworks. This approach typically yields mixed results, emphasizing certifications rather than *capabilities*. The real post-Agile shift demands re-focusing on simplicity, real outcomes, and human-centred collaboration.

Bottom Line: Smaller, focused teams bring agility closer to its essence, fostering efficiency, innovation, and accountability. Meanwhile, integrating with complementary disciplines can further amplify responsiveness and adaptability, broadening agility's impact.

One practical leadership strategy is forming smaller, outcome-driven teams, which can more easily demonstrate the benefits of post-Agile thinking. Let's see why.

Integration with Complementary Disciplines

- **Lean and DevOps**: Post-Agile often merges Agile with Lean or DevOps for maximum flexibility and efficiency. Netflix deploys new code daily, rapidly iterating features while maintaining alignment with user feedback. Combining Lean's waste reduction with iterative sprints ensures every cycle delivers meaningful customer value.
- **Design Thinking**: Marrying Agile with Design Thinking fosters user-centric innovation. IBM's approach exemplifies this synergy – Agile sprints refine prototypes developed via Design Thinking, enabling rapid user feedback and continuous product improvements.
- **OKRs (Objectives and Key Results)**: Aligning objectives via OKRs helps Agile teams ensure daily sprints link directly to long-range strategic aims. Google's example – merging OKRs with Agile practices – illustrates how iterative cycles can be steered by broader goals without stifling responsiveness.
- **Ethical and Responsible AI**: Post-Agile also intersects with emerging tech, like AI or IoT, ensuring that teams incorporate data-driven insights responsibly. Leaders must keep ethical considerations at the forefront so that advanced automation complements, rather than undermines, creativity and accountability.

Merging these disciplines multiplies agility's impact – but how do we measure it effectively? Next, we'll explore meaningful ways to measure agility in the Post-Agile environment.

Measuring Agility in the Post-Agile Era

Post-Agile success isn't about checking compliance boxes; it's about gauging cultural depth, adaptability, and real customer value. Meaningful metrics include:

- **Lead Time/Cycle Time**: How quickly an idea moves from concept to deployment.
- **Employee Engagement**: Do team members feel empowered and adaptive?
- **Customer Satisfaction**: Is the organization meeting or exceeding user needs?
- **Innovation Rates**: Frequency of new ideas tested or implemented.

By regularly measuring these and other relevant metrics, organizations ensure that their agility efforts align with cultural transformation and deliver tangible benefits. By linking these measurements to broader business goals, organizations move from isolated Agile practices toward holistic business agility.

Incorporating visual dashboards or scorecards can help measure these metrics effectively.

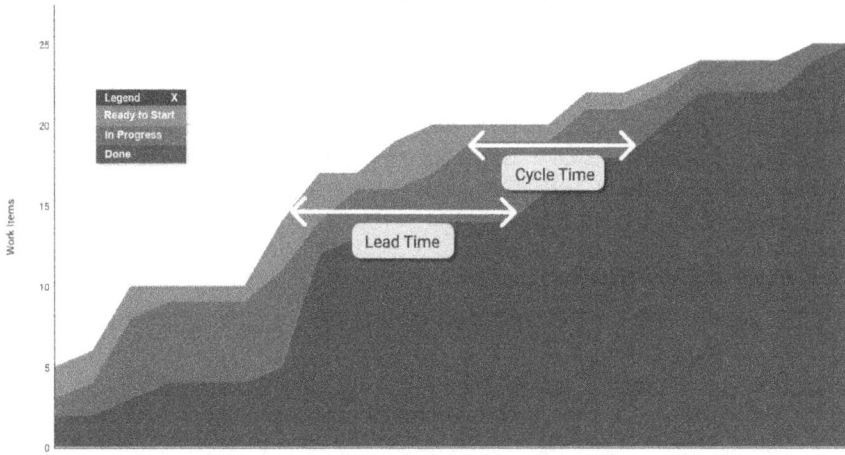

Visual Dashboard Example

Post-Agile as a Business Agility Evolution

Picture two supply chain disruptions: One company keeps rigid sprints but can't adapt outside that cycle. Another – forging 'post-Agile' paths – allows real-time cross-functional decisions, reassigning resources freely. The second firm recovers faster. That's the difference between perfecting a process and perfecting adaptability.

In 'post-Agile', frameworks no longer serve as the end goal. Instead, the organization's entire structure revolves around iterative learning, synergy, and delivering tangible user value.

Key Shifts

- **Outcomes First**: Real-world user or business impact outranks requirements.
- **Culture Everywhere**: Every team embraces iterative feedback.
- **Tight Strategy Links**: Agile goals ladder up to bigger missions, from expansion to ethical considerations.

Thus, agility morphs into a genuine organizational characteristic, surviving market flux. Achieving this demands facing certain structural or cultural challenges head-on.

Overcoming Challenges in the Post-Agile Transition

Moving beyond Agile's legacy frameworks can be daunting. Leaders face hurdles like entrenched silos, misaligned incentives, and established mindsets. Recognizing these obstacles sets the stage for targeted strategies:

- **Resistance to Change**: Employees may cling to familiar processes.
- **Misalignment Among Leaders**: Without executive sponsorship, deeper cultural shifts stall.
- **Skill Gaps**: Teams need training to adapt to a culture prioritizing experimentation and empowerment.

For example: A multinational manufacturer overcame siloed communication by restructuring teams into cross-functional 'pods' with shared KPIs. This repositioning only succeeded after leadership invested in training, built psychological safety, and clarified how everyone's roles aligned with bigger outcomes.

Practical Strategies

1. **Communicate the Vision**: Show how new ways of working benefit both teams and organizational goals.
2. **Provide Ongoing Training**: Whether through mentorship or e-learning, ensure the workforce has the skills and mindset for adaptive work.
3. **Model New Behaviours**: Leaders demonstrate agility by being open to feedback and pivoting when needed.

As organizations grapple with the complexities of moving beyond Agile frameworks, one critical factor often overlooked is the role of the Agile community itself. While Agile was once a movement built on adaptability and collaboration, its evolution has led to contrasting perspectives on what agility should mean in a modern business context. Understanding these shifts is key to ensuring that agility remains a valuable asset rather than a rigid structure that stifles innovation.

The Agile Community at a Crossroads

As Agile extends beyond its original foundations, the community that shaped it is shifting. What was once a space for experimentation and continuous learning has, in many cases, become focused on structured methodologies, certifications, and commercial models. Some see this as natural growth; others argue it has moved away from its original intent.

For years, Agile practitioners focused on adaptability, learning, and collaboration. Over time, structured training courses, enterprise-scale models, and a strong certification culture took centre stage. While these provided credibility, they also led to concerns about rigid implementations that overlook the practical needs of businesses.

There is now a divide. Some advocate for reducing complexity, arguing that Agile should focus on simple, effective ways of working. Others believe scalability requires standardization and structure. The outcome of this debate will shape Agile's future.

A Growing Scepticism

Many leaders now question whether Agile delivers the benefits it once promised. Years of rigid, process-heavy approaches have left teams disengaged. In some organizations, Agile has become a compliance exercise rather than a driver of adaptability.

To stay relevant, the community must focus on results rather than rules. Agility should support innovation and customer value rather than serve as a box-ticking exercise. This means reassessing what Agile truly means in practice and ensuring that it remains a driver of progress, not just a label.

The Role of Agile Leaders in This Shift

The expectations placed on Scrum Masters, Agile Coaches, and transformation leaders are changing. The most effective professionals no longer focus only on frameworks – they influence strategy, coach senior leaders, and shape company-wide ways of working.

For organizations, this means hiring leaders who can bring agility into decision-making, not just within IT or delivery teams. Those who adapt will continue to shape modern businesses; those who rely on rigid interpretations of Agile risk being left behind.

Staying Ahead of the Shift

1. **Focus on Practical Agility**: Move beyond frameworks and focus on real business outcomes.
2. **Challenge Ineffective Practices**: If Agile methods do not add value, adjust them.
3. **Expand Leadership Skills**: Agile professionals should develop coaching and strategy skills.
4. **Engage with Experienced Thinkers**: Follow those who challenge ideas rather than promote trends.
5. **Tailor Agility to the Organization**: Avoid one-size-fits-all models.

The Agile community is moving into a new phase. Those who recognize these shifts and adapt will remain relevant. The key is to make Agile a tool for impact, not just a set of practices.

These tensions within the Agile community are not just theoretical – they play out in real-world scenarios where organizations either embrace or push back against mainstream Agile thinking. In the next section, we examine how different companies have navigated these challenges, showcasing both the pitfalls and the successes of organizations redefining agility on their own terms.

Case Studies of Agile Rebellion

Numerous organizations are intentionally stepping away from traditional enterprise Agile frameworks, choosing instead to forge tailored approaches that align with their unique contexts and objectives.

For instance, Bosch and Haier abandoned costly consulting-driven transformations in favour of lightweight, team-driven processes focused directly on business outcomes. To illustrate how organizations are taking a different route – eschewing heavily commercialized frameworks – let's look at two prominent examples:

Case Study 1: Bosch – Moving Beyond Certification for Sustainable Agility

Company: Bosch (Germany)

    Context: Global engineering/electronics giant. They launched an Agile drive but avoided big-name frameworks or mandated certifications.

    Background: By 2018, Bosch wanted to handle complex product demands in automotive and consumer electronics. Rather than SAFe or LeSS, they built a custom, outcomes-focused model.

Approach:

- **Tailored Agile**: Cross-functional 'Agile Release Teams' replaced standard frameworks.
- **Internal Coaching**: Home-grown coaches who understood Bosch's challenges.
- **Autonomy and Experimentation**: Teams set their own goals, measuring real outcomes.

Outcome: Within two years, Bosch saw faster releases, fewer defects, and higher staff engagement. One automotive electronics line slashed release cycle time by 30%.

Actionable Conclusion

- Develop in-house coaching.
- Value real metrics (cycle times, quality) over certifications.
- Give teams space to design local solutions.
- Track defect rates, productivity, and morale.
- Prioritize multi-disciplinary squads.

Case Study 2: Haier – Creating Agile Micro-Enterprises for Innovation

Company: Haier Group (China)

    Context: A household appliance leader that spurned standard, scaled frameworks, instead forming small, entrepreneurial 'micro-enterprises'.

    Background: By 2012, CEO Zhang Ruimin wanted staff to think like entrepreneurs. This meant micro-units, each agile in user engagement. No mainstream frameworks like SAFe or LeSS.

Approach:

- **Micro-Enterprises**: Teams ran independently, pivoting swiftly.
- **Entrepreneurial Autonomy**: Staff pitched and developed ideas without waiting for top-down approvals.
- **Customer-Centric**: The only measure was delivering real user solutions.

Outcome: Haier gained agility, releasing products faster and energizing employees with genuine ownership. They became a global success known for their responsiveness.

Actionable conclusion

- Start small with a handful of micro-enterprises.
- Give them authority over resources and goals.
- Let them pivot fast on user feedback.
- Encourage knowledge sharing across teams.
- Measure progress on actual user outcomes.

These companies illustrate the power of small, deliberate changes over grand, top-down transformations – emphasizing authenticity, true team empowerment, and the value of learning by doing rather than learning-by-certification. Their journeys prove that rejecting the Agile circus does not mean abandoning agility; instead, it means embracing its most authentic, effective form. These examples underscore that embracing post-Agile realities often means redefining agility on an organization's own terms, setting the stage for a more authentic and enduring transformation.

Conclusion

In the post-Agile world, agility transcends frameworks and rituals, evolving into a cultural ethos. Freed from rigid ceremonies, organizations rediscover collaboration, experimentation, and responsiveness. The core values that once propelled Agile remain potent when stripped of superficial trappings and fully embraced.

Leaders who embrace this transformation focus on cultural shifts: fostering trust, aligning with genuine outcomes, and making data-driven, real-time decisions. They see Agile's past as a stepping stone, not an endpoint.

'Post-Agile' doesn't reject Agile – it evolves it. The pivot from procedural compliance to strategic adaptability marks agility's next stage. Leaders must ensure that agility reaches decision-making, culture, and leadership behaviour.

The next chapter explores how leadership and culture truly shape sustainable agility. Genuine adaptability arises not from processes but from leaders who create the conditions for agility to flourish.

Call to Action

As an adaptive leader, reflect on whether your organization's Agile approach has become mechanical. Which frameworks or processes could you simplify or redesign to align with deeper collaboration and learning? Talk with your teams to identify one area you can streamline or experiment with over the coming quarter.

Key Takeaways

- **'Post-Agile' Reflects Maturity**: It's an evolution embedding agility into organizational culture, not discarding it.

- **Culture and Leadership Matter**: A supportive culture and leaders who model Agile behaviours sustain meaningful agility.
- **Integration with Other Methodologies**: Combining Agile with Lean, DevOps, and Design Thinking broadens and deepens agility.
- **Being Agile vs Doing Agile**: Real success lies in a mindset shift, not in mechanical framework adoption.
- **Continuous Metrics**: Regular, meaningful measures ensure that agility evolves alongside organizational growth.

CLEAR Model® Connection

- **Culture**: Agile must be woven into the organization's cultural fabric.
- **Adaptability**: Maturing Agile calls for continuous learning and readiness to pivot.

Key Takeaway: The future of Agile is not about methodologies – it's about embedding adaptability into every aspect of leadership and culture.

Exploration Guide: Investigating Next-Generation Methodologies

- **Research New Frameworks**:
  o Lean Startup, DevOps, Design Thinking, etc.
- **Assess Compatibility**:
  o How do these methodologies align with your organizational goals?
- **Identify Integration Points**:
  o Where can new practices enhance existing Agile processes?

Transition Plan Template: Evolving from Agile to Post-Agile

1. **Vision Setting**:
   o Define what 'Post-Agile' means for your organization.
2. **Stakeholder Engagement**:
   o Communicate the vision and gather input.
3. **Capability Assessment**:
   o Evaluate current skills and identify gaps.
4. **Roadmap Development**:
   o Outline steps for integrating new methodologies.
5. **Pilot Programmes**:
   o Start with small projects to test and learn.
6. **Scaling Up**:
   o Gradually expand successful practices organization-wide.

Chapter Summary

This chapter introduced 'Post-Agile', showing how transcending rigid frameworks in favour of an authenticity-driven, highly adaptive culture renews agility. Bosch and Haier demonstrated how focusing on empowerment and real outcomes rejuvenates organizations, underscoring the vitality of evolving agility on one's own terms.

End of Part 2

We've explored the crucial role of leadership in guiding Agile beyond superficial adoption. Now, let's turn our attention to the environments in which these leaders operate. In Part 3, we'll see how culture and team dynamics can either turbocharge or undermine Agile progress – and what you can do to foster a workplace that thrives on adaptability.

Part 3

Empowering Teams and Culture for Sustainable Agility

CLEAR Focus: Culture

Agility is sustainable only when teams are empowered, and the culture supports adaptive ways of working. A strong culture fosters psychological safety, autonomy, and collaboration, enabling teams to perform at their best. This section explores how culture shapes agility and long-term success.

5

Culture-Driven Agility – Creating an Organization That Thrives on Change

Culture eats strategy for breakfast.

Peter Drucker

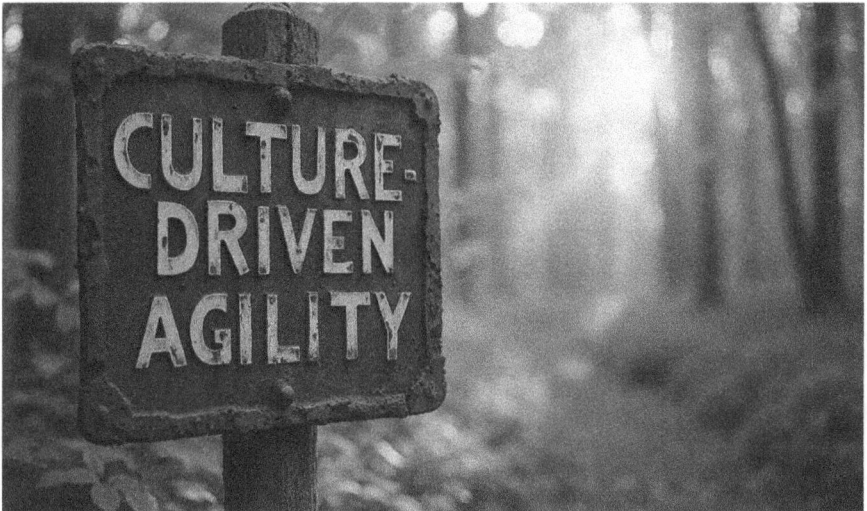

What You'll Gain

- **For Senior Leaders and Executives**: See why culture and leadership form the backbone of any agile shift – and how to align them for real results.
- **For Mid-Level Leaders**: Understand the key leadership behaviours that foster adaptive, collaborative teams.
- **For Students or Early-Career Professionals**: Learn how leadership styles and cultural values drive agility far beyond processes or frameworks.

Agility Isn't a Process – It's a Cultural Shift

Sarah, the newly appointed CTO, scanned the boardroom. The company had invested heavily in Agile training, adopted a leading framework, and even hired transformation consultants. Yet, real agility remained out of reach.

Teams followed Agile ceremonies, but decision-making was still slow. Stand-ups were happening, but collaboration remained siloed. Leaders encouraged teams to 'be Agile' while simultaneously punishing failure. Agile was being done, but it wasn't being lived.

This is why most Agile transformations fail – not because teams lack the right tools, but because organizations fail to change their culture.

Too often, leaders focus on installing systems, tools, and frameworks – hoping they'll force transformation. But culture must come first. Agility grows when people are trusted, teams are empowered, and decision-making is decentralized. If the culture isn't ready, even the best system will fail.

A company can implement every Agile framework in existence, but if the culture resists change, fears failure, and prioritizes control over autonomy, agility will remain superficial and ineffective. One aspect often missed in these efforts is personalization.

Personalization is another often overlooked yet powerful element of cultural transformation. Teams thrive when they feel known, not just managed. Leaders should explore ways to tailor the employee experience, whether through development pathways, feedback preferences, or recognition styles.

Personal Reflection

In one Agile transformation, we introduced team-led retrospectives where individuals could vote on their preferred working norms. The effect was immediate: engagement rose, and team cohesion improved. Adaptive leaders treat personalization not as a luxury but as a lever for belonging.

This chapter explores the barriers that prevent culture-driven agility, the key characteristics of an adaptive culture, and practical strategies for embedding agility into an organization's DNA.

Why Most Agile Transformations Fail

Agility cannot thrive in an organization where the culture contradicts its core principles. Below are the most common cultural barriers preventing true agility:

1. The Illusion of Agility – Process Without Mindset

- Companies claim to be Agile but still operate with command-and-control leadership.

- Leaders encourage teams to 'be Agile' but punish failure, reinforcing risk aversion.
- Agility is seen as an IT practice, not a business-wide mindset.

Fix It: Agility must be modelled at every level, not just in teams. Leadership must embrace learning, experimentation, and adaptability.

2. Fear of Failure – The Biggest Blocker of Agility

- Organizations want innovation but penalize employees for making mistakes.
- Employees avoid experimentation because the cost of failure is too high.
- Agile thrives on rapid iteration, but cultures of fear prevent risk-taking.

Fix It: Create a psychologically safe environment where failure is seen as a learning opportunity, not a career risk.

3. Bureaucracy Over Autonomy – The Culture of Micromanagement

- Teams are expected to self-organize, but still need multiple layers of approval to make decisions.
- Managers resist Agile because they fear losing control.
- Traditional performance reviews reward compliance over innovation.

Fix It: Shift decision-making to where the work happens – empower teams to own their processes and outcomes.

4. Misaligned Incentives – Rewarding the Wrong Behaviours

- Many companies still measure success by hours worked instead of value delivered.
- Leaders promote agility but reward predictability and rigid execution.
- Bonus structures encourage individual performance over team collaboration.

Fix It: Align incentives with adaptive behaviours – reward learning, collaboration, and value creation, not just execution.

Beyond these specific patterns, a broader leadership mindset often holds agility back. One common leadership mistake is treating culture as a function of HR or the people team, rather than a strategic responsibility. While HR plays a supporting role in shaping people processes, culture is forged in daily decisions, leadership tone, and organizational behaviour. When executives delegate culture to a department, they risk disconnecting it from business outcomes. Adaptive leaders understand that culture is embedded through example – how meetings are run, how trust is built, how failure is handled. It is not a task to be assigned but a leadership behaviour to be lived.

A Key Characteristic: The Growth Mindset

Adaptive leaders who adopt a growth mindset – learning from failures, delaying final commitments, and refining continuously – transition from command-and-control to servant leadership. In martial arts, the concept of *Shu Ha Ri* explains this growth:

- **Shu** (守): Start by following established rules and best practices.
- **Ha** (破): Adapt and evolve beyond rigid guidelines.
- **Ri** (離): Master agility and innovate freely, guided by context.

Leaders on this path energize teams to experiment, learn, and push beyond limitations. When leaders themselves adopt iterative improvement, agility takes hold more effectively throughout the organization.

What an Agile Culture Looks Like – The 5 Key Traits of Adaptive Organizations

True agility isn't just about frameworks – it's about building a culture that enables adaptability, innovation, and resilience in uncertainty.

The best Agile cultures share these five key traits:

1. Psychological Safety – The Foundation of Agility

What It Means: Teams must feel safe to speak up, challenge ideas, and experiment without fear of punishment.
Why It Matters: Google's *Project Aristotle* found that psychological safety is the #1 predictor of high-performing teams.
How to Build It:

- **Encourage constructive debate**: Dissenting opinions should be welcomed, not silenced.
- **Normalize failure as part of learning**: Leaders should openly share their own failures.
- **Stop blaming individuals**: Focus on improving the system, not punishing mistakes.

Case Study: Google's *Project Aristotle* – Google discovered that teams with high psychological safety outperformed others in innovation, execution, and team satisfaction.

2. Growth Mindset – Shifting from Fixed Thinking to Continuous Learning

What It Means: Employees and leaders believe that skills and intelligence can be developed through effort and learning.

Why It Matters: Companies with a growth mindset are more innovative, adaptable, and resilient. A fixed mindset leads to risk aversion and stagnation, while a growth mindset encourages experimentation and improvement.

How to Build It:

- **Encourage lifelong learning**: Offer continuous upskilling opportunities through training, coaching, and mentoring.
- **Reward progress, not just results**: Recognize learning efforts, even when they don't immediately pay off.
- **Make feedback a two-way conversation**: Leaders should seek feedback from teams, not just give it.

Case Study: Microsoft's Cultural Transformation – Under Satya Nadella, Microsoft shifted from a fixed mindset ('know-it-all') to a growth mindset ('learn-it-all'), leading to record innovation and financial success.

3. Decentralized Decision-Making – Pushing Authority to the Edges

What It Means: Teams are trusted to make decisions without waiting for executive approval.

Why It Matters: The faster an organization can make decisions, the more adaptable it becomes. Bureaucratic bottlenecks slow down innovation, while autonomy empowers teams to take ownership.

How to Build It:

- **Remove unnecessary approval layers**: Give teams ownership over decisions that impact their work.
- **Create guardrails, not roadblocks**: Define boundaries where autonomy is encouraged.
- **Encourage self-organizing teams**: Empower employees to solve problems without escalation.

Case Study: Haier's Micro-Enterprise Model – Haier reorganized into self-managed micro-enterprises, where small teams act as independent businesses, making their own strategic decisions.

4. Transparency and Open Communication – Breaking Down Silos

What It Means: Information is freely shared across all levels of the organization, ensuring alignment, trust, and speed in decision-making.

Why It Matters: Lack of transparency leads to slow decision-making, misalignment, and disengagement. When teams don't have access to the right information, they can't respond quickly or effectively.

How to Build It:

- **Make leadership decisions visible to everyone**: Share key business insights openly, including financial performance, strategy updates, and organizational priorities.
- **Encourage radical candour**: Honest, respectful feedback should be the norm.
- **Eliminate unnecessary secrecy**: Most company information should be accessible, not restricted.

Case Study: Buffer's Open Salaries Policy – Buffer publishes all salaries transparently, increasing trust, fairness, and employee satisfaction.

5. Bias for Action – Moving from Endless Planning to Fast Execution

What It Means: Agile cultures prioritize action over excessive planning. They test, learn, and iterate quickly rather than waiting for perfect conditions before making a move.

Why It Matters: The world moves too fast for rigid long-term planning. Organizations that take small, rapid steps forward are more resilient and innovative than those stuck in over-analysis.

How to Build It:

- **Minimize over-planning**: Use lightweight planning methods like adaptive roadmaps and OKRs (Objectives and Key Results).
- **Encourage experimentation**: Teams should run small tests before scaling big initiatives.
- **Speed up decision-making**: Cut down on unnecessary meetings, reports, and approvals that slow progress.

Case Study: Amazon's Two-Pizza Teams – Amazon structures teams to be small, autonomous, and laser-focused on delivering real customer impact, allowing rapid experimentation and iteration.

Key Takeaways

- **Agility is a cultural shift, not just a process change.**
  True agility isn't about following a framework – it's about shifting mindsets, leadership behaviours, and organizational culture to embrace adaptability, learning, and decentralized decision-making.
- **The biggest barriers to agility are fear, bureaucracy, and misaligned incentives.**
  Agile transformations fail when organizations resist change, fear failure, or prioritize control over autonomy. Removing these blockers is essential for agility to take root.

- **Psychological safety, transparency, and decentralized decision-making fuel agility.**
  Teams thrive when they feel safe to experiment, have open access to information, and are empowered to make decisions – these cultural traits are the foundation of lasting agility.
- **Leaders must model adaptability and create an environment where agility thrives.**
  Agile cultures don't emerge by chance. Leaders who embrace uncertainty, encourage continuous learning, and remove barriers create organizations that can evolve and succeed in a fast-changing world.

Tip: Alternate short tactical tweaks with scheduled horizon scans to balance reaction and prevention.

The Pitfalls of Psychological Safety: What Leaders Must Avoid

One thing to note here is that psychological safety is often cited as a key enabler of agility, innovation, and collaboration. While the concept itself is essential, there is a concern that it has become a buzzword in some organizations – something leaders talk about but fail to cultivate in practice.

The truth is, psychological safety cannot exist in name alone. If employees are told they are in a safe space but then are punished for honest feedback, transparency, or challenging assumptions, the term becomes meaningless. Many organizations claim to embrace it, but their behaviours tell a different story. If leaders say they welcome risk-taking but penalize failure, or encourage open dialogue but retaliate against criticism, psychological safety becomes an illusion.

A psychologically safe environment is not about eliminating all discomfort or ensuring a consequence-free workplace – it is about creating an environment where individuals can raise concerns, challenge ideas, and make mistakes without fear of unfair retribution. True safety fosters accountability, not complacency.

Key Considerations

- **Beware of performative safety**: If an organization talks about psychological safety but does not back it with action, trust erodes rather than grows.
- **Trust and psychological safety are not the same**: Trust is interpersonal, while psychological safety is about group norms and leadership behaviour. One does not automatically create the other.
- **Psychological safety is earned, not declared**: It is the result of consistent leadership behaviour, not a policy or a workshop.
- **Encouraging psychological safety is not about removing accountability**: It is about ensuring that feedback, challenge, and risk-taking are met with constructive engagement rather than punishment.

To truly foster psychological safety, leaders must go beyond the label and focus on the everyday actions that create it: transparency, vulnerability, fair treatment, and a culture where learning from failure is normalized.

Adaptive Leadership as the Linchpin of Agile Success

Shared values and practices	Organizational Culture
Moral principles guiding actions	Ethics
Guiding framework for goals	Strategy
Central role in Agile success	Adaptive Leadership

Adaptive Leadership and Agile Success

An adaptive culture combines strategy, ethics, and collaboration, ensuring that Agile can flourish. A climate of transparency and accountability aligns decisions with Agile values. For instance, weaving ethics into retrospectives cements the idea that improvement is continuous, not merely for technical tasks but also for how teams treat each other and serve stakeholders.

Adaptive leaders also excel at asking the right questions: *How do we measure customer happiness? Where can we remove friction? Which behaviours most shape a culture of learning?* These questions invite teams to tailor creative solutions. Through such curiosity, leaders unify strategy with everyday execution, which is the heart of genuine agility.

Setting the Strategic Tone

Adaptive leaders know that frameworks alone don't yield meaningful results. They offer a clear sense of why changes matter and trust teams to devise how. One company replaced time-consuming approvals with simpler goal-setting sessions, cutting bureaucratic overheads by 20% and raising ownership.

When leaders nurture a trust-based delegation model, teams can tackle complexity confidently, fuelling agility at every tier. Leadership's job shifts from micromanaging to orchestrating an environment for flexible collaboration. Freed from constant oversight, leaders can focus on strategic decisions and amplify their own contributions – a win for everyone involved.

Leadership as Context Setter

Instead of commanding from the top, leaders set conditions for success. They provide vision, clarifying *why* a goal matters, and allow teams to define *how*. This includes regularly revisiting policies based on real-time feedback and harnessing tech tools (e.g. AI dashboards) to make informed pivots. In short, leaders shape the environment that lets Agile principles thrive.

Shaping Culture Through Policy, Vision, and Structures

Leaders don't merely coordinate tasks; they sculpt the culture that underpins Agile success. They achieve this by embedding Agile principles – collaboration, continuous learning, and adaptability – into the organization's standard operating procedures and day-to-day decisions. Examples include:

- **Policy Implementation**: Adjust processes and rules to enhance productivity and transparency (e.g. flexible work policies and collaborative tools).
- **Vision Crafting**: Unite teams under a shared mission. For instance, a healthcare provider that reframed its vision around 'patient well-being first' saw sharper innovation and stronger commitment.
- **Structural Design**: Shift from hierarchical chains of command to more flexible networks. An automotive firm, for example, reorganized separate teams into cross-functional product squads, accelerating design cycles.

However, policies and structures alone don't create agility – culture does. If cultural barriers remain, agility will be superficial. Leaders must proactively shape culture to reinforce agility at every level.

Fixing Cultural Barriers: Lessons from Leading Companies

Even when Agile frameworks are in place, cultural resistance can block agility. Leaders must align incentives, behaviours, and systems to reinforce agility across the organization.

Case Study: Microsoft's Growth Mindset Transformation

The shift from a fixed mindset to a growth mindset led to:

- A cultural transformation that encouraged continuous learning at all levels.
- Increased collaboration and psychological safety across teams.
- Microsoft's resurgence as an innovation leader has surpassed $2 trillion in market value.

Key Insight: Leaders must model adaptability and create psychological safety for agility to thrive.

Case Study: Buffer's Open Salaries Policy

The impact of making all employee wages public was:

- Increased trust between employees and leadership.
- Greater fairness and clarity around pay decisions.
- Improved engagement and retention, as employees felt valued.

Key Insight: Transparency fuels agility – when employees trust leadership, they take more risks and adapt faster.

Policies, vision, and structures lay the foundation, but agility succeeds when culture aligns. Leaders must ensure that learning, trust, and empowerment are built into daily operations, not just stated in strategy documents.

Keeping It Simple: A Leadership Imperative

Simplicity remains key in Agile. Over time, well-meaning teams can bloat processes with extra tasks. Leaders must counter by consistently guiding everyone back to core goals.

For example, a global finance firm replaced mandated Scrum events with 'value-driven stand-ups' and 'short retros' that boosted satisfaction and output. This reaffirms that the best frameworks are those light enough to be supportive, not stifling.

Simplicity also comes from knowing the difference between coordinating and organizing. Coordination handles the day-to-day scheduling, handoffs, and dependencies. Organizing focuses teams in a useful direction, tied to purpose and outcomes. When leaders try to address both needs in one meeting or process, things slow down. Separate them, and teams move faster with more clarity.

Clarity is equally important. If staff can't see how daily tasks connect to higher-level aims, they may cling to rote routines. Leaders must set clear priorities so autonomy flourishes in a meaningful context. Emotional intelligence underpins this approach.

Emotional Intelligence: The Heart of Adaptive Leadership

During a heated sprint review, the product and engineering teams collided, deadlines were missed, and frustration spiked. Michael, the Agile lead, paused to address the tension head-on. By validating concerns and asking what the real friction was, the blame game dissolved into constructive dialogue. This exemplifies emotional intelligence (EI): leaders shaping psychological safety so teams collaborate effectively.

Teams in Agile settings rely on strong EI to foster trust and handle conflicts smoothly. Leaders who listen, empathize, and respond calmly can steer heated discussions toward solutions, improving morale and ensuring a healthier environment for innovation.

Building Resilience Through Emotional Intelligence

Resilience sets top-tier teams apart, and EI cultivates that resilience. By embracing open dialogue, normalizing risk-taking, and converting setbacks into lessons, leaders promote adaptability. During a supply chain meltdown, a psychologically safe Agile team might pivot daily, limiting productivity losses and seizing unforeseen opportunities.

Such resilience emerges from consistent retrospectives, iterative planning, and supportive leadership that frames challenges as growth moments. As leaders embody these qualities, they project the confidence teams need to stay adaptable under stress.

The Role of Psychological Safety in Resilience

Psychological safety – the collective sense that speaking up won't incur negative consequences – forms the bedrock of resilience. Leaders should ensure employees feel comfortable sharing new ideas or concerns without fear of blame. Treating failures as learning opportunities further cements trust and prepares teams to handle the unknown.

Practical Ways to Build Psychological Safety

1. **Encourage Open Dialogue**: Seek honest feedback without judgment.
2. **Respond Constructively to Feedback**: Welcome new ideas, addressing challenges with transparency and positivity.
3. **Normalize Failure**: Leaders can share personal stories of mistakes to remove the stigma around errors.

When leaders uphold these practices, they create conditions for 'team intelligence' to flourish, harnessing the full collective capability. This synergy of emotional and collective intelligence fosters deeper resilience and the agility needed in rapidly shifting contexts.

Agility Under Pressure

At the 2024 Business Agility Conference, Peter Coesmans, Chief Agility Officer, reminded us that resilience is not just a helpful trait – it's fundamental to agility. Resilience under pressure isn't about endurance alone. It's the ability to stay adaptive when conditions shift without warning. Agile organizations are built for this. They don't wait to be told how to respond – they assess, adapt, and move forward, often faster than their traditional counterparts.

Coesmans' point reframed a common misunderstanding: Agile is not a fragile framework reliant on stability. It's a mindset equipped to handle instability. Practices like retrospectives and adaptive planning are designed to help teams respond constructively when things don't go as expected. Rather than fearing disruption, Agile teams treat it as part of the process.

This mindset helps distinguish organizations that talk about agility from those that live it. When teams are used to reflecting often, adjusting course quickly, and learning from missteps, they don't just bounce back – they move forward with greater clarity. That's real resilience.

Stronger Emphasis on Humility as a Leadership Trait

Humility is an underrated leadership skill. In an Agile organization, it's also an essential one.

Leaders who believe they have all the answers often end up making rigid, top-down decisions that stifle agility. Conversely, leaders who openly admit what they don't know create an environment where teams feel safe to experiment, challenge ideas, and drive real innovation.

Consider two types of leaders:

- **The Directive Leader** who insists on controlling outcomes discourages dissent and sees failure as a weakness.
- **The Adaptive Leader** who listens, evolves based on feedback, and views failure as a source of learning.

One of these leaders enables agility. The other kills it.

Agile doesn't thrive in command-and-control environments. It flourishes where adaptive leaders have the humility to trust their teams, accept mistakes as part of growth, and continuously learn alongside those they lead.

Influencing Culture Through Policy, Vision, and Organizational Structures

When a European bank struggled with Agile adoption, leadership realized the issue wasn't tools or processes – it was culture. Decision-making was centralized, and teams feared taking risks. The solution? Leadership changed meeting formats, replacing lengthy executive approvals with cross-functional decision-making forums. Within six months, employee engagement rose, and Agile adoption felt natural instead of forced. This shift underscores how leaders influence culture through everyday actions, not just policies.

Empowerment must be systematically embedded in the organization's structure. Teams require consistent access to users, real influence over data interpretation, and a shared role in problem definition. Without these structural elements, empowerment risks becoming superficial and unable to drive true cultural transformation.

A recent McKinsey study revealed that organizations fostering inclusive leadership are 1.8 times more likely to capture new markets. How inclusive is your leadership style? Leaders directly influence organizational culture by embedding Agile values into policies, crafting a shared vision, and designing supportive structures. These actions ensure Agile principles are not just theoretical but become the foundation of the organization's identity.

For an integrated perspective on leadership's role in shaping culture, see '**Adaptive Leadership as the Linchpin of Agile Success**' (page 95).

Practical Examples

Area	Example
Policy Implementation	A global tech firm introduced remote-friendly policies, allowing flexible hours and resource-sharing. Morale soared, and productivity rose because employees could align work with peak personal energy times.
Vision Crafting	A healthcare organization emphasized patient-centred care as its mission. Regular alignment meetings kept teams focused, driving stronger collaboration and innovative solutions for patients.
Structural Design	A digital marketing agency broke away from vertical departments, creating squads that directly tackled client pain points. Freed from excessive hierarchy, they iterated quickly on campaigns and met client needs promptly.

By strategically shaping policies, articulating a compelling vision, and designing supportive organizational structures, leaders embed Agile principles into the organization's DNA. This strategic alignment ensures that Agile is not just a methodology but a fundamental aspect of the organization's identity and operations. Yet, even with strong policies and structures, effective leadership also depends on the personal qualities of leaders, including their emotional and collective intelligence.

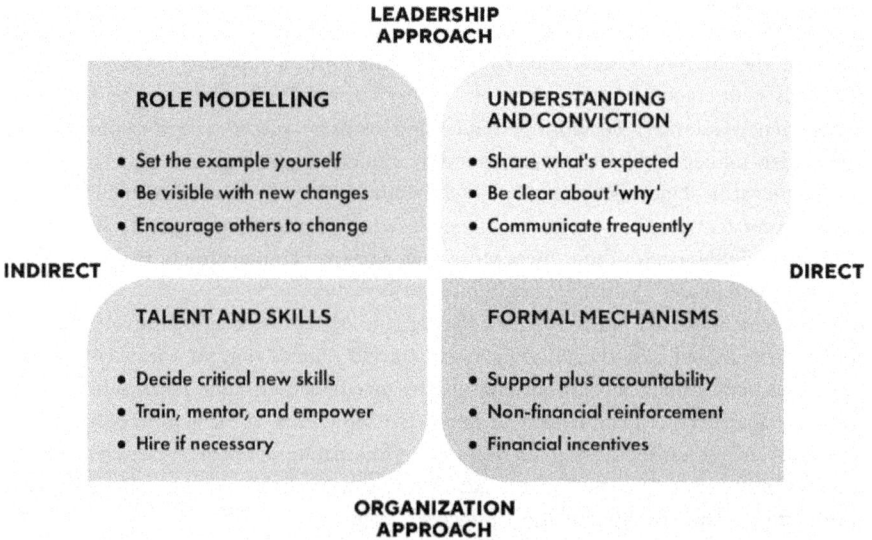

LEADERSHIP APPROACH

ROLE MODELLING
- Set the example yourself
- Be visible with new changes
- Encourage others to change

UNDERSTANDING AND CONVICTION
- Share what's expected
- Be clear about 'why'
- Communicate frequently

INDIRECT ← → **DIRECT**

TALENT AND SKILLS
- Decide critical new skills
- Train, mentor, and empower
- Hire if necessary

FORMAL MECHANISMS
- Support plus accountability
- Non-financial reinforcement
- Financial incentives

ORGANIZATION APPROACH

The Leadership Influence Model

Consider how your current policies and organizational structures support or hinder the adoption of Agile principles. What changes can you implement to foster a culture of adaptability and collaboration?

Vision and structures lay the foundation for cultural alignment, but their success depends on leaders' ability to adapt strategies to the organization's unique context. This alignment bridges strategy with day-to-day team dynamics, enabling lasting transformation. Leaders must not only influence culture but also ensure that their strategies and methods are contextually relevant to drive lasting transformation.

Aligning Agility with Organizational Context

Context matters. Blindly applying Agile frameworks can produce superficial or burdensome outcomes. Leaders must tailor Agile to each environment, from regulated industries demanding specific guardrails to software startups craving minimal process overhead.

Such context-driven agility also means leaders adapt their style. Dave Snowden cautions against chasing 'bright new things' – leaders must see that agility isn't an end but a means to align real-world strategy with user needs. If compliance is essential, build the right checks. If speed is crucial, lighten processes. This is how you craft an Agile approach that truly fits.

Collective Intelligence and Team Empowerment

High-level synergy occurs when leaders empower teams to combine varied expertise and experiences, generating solutions stronger than any individual effort. Cross-functional collaboration plus iterative learning often sparks unique insights.

Such an environment boosts emotional intelligence as well. When trust and open dialogue are standard, teams tackle challenges collectively and bounce back from difficulties with minimal friction. Building that collaborative spirit depends on leaders ensuring autonomy, shared accountability, and transparent communication.

Understanding the Iceberg: Leadership Beyond the Surface

Leadership can be compared to an iceberg: visible actions represent only the tip, while underlying cultural mindsets and systemic patterns drive lasting change. Agile transformations stumble if leaders tackle only surface-level tasks – like scheduling daily stand-ups – ignoring deeper cultural and behavioural norms.

The iceberg model suggests leaders ask questions such as:

- Which behaviours drive visible results?
- How do organizational structures support or hinder agility?
- What assumptions do people hold regarding collaboration and adaptability?

Addressing hidden layers (ingrained mindsets, unspoken values, and systemic habits) is essential for ensuring Agile is more than a performance, creating real, enduring change.

Practical Leadership Practices for Agile Alignment

To successfully align leadership with Agile principles, leaders must engage in deliberate actions that reinforce agility as a core value across the organization. The following practical leadership practices are essential for creating a culture where agility can thrive:

1. **Encouraging Regular Feedback**: Use brief retros or quarterly 360 reviews to keep improvements aligned with strategy.
2. **Promoting Psychological Safety**: Let leaders openly acknowledge mistakes, inviting honest reflections that spark trust.
3. **Providing Space for Experimentation**: 'Innovation Days' or hackathons push iterative improvement and creativity.
4. **Aligning Team Goals with Strategy**: Tools like OKRs connect daily tasks to strategic objectives, focusing teams on delivering real value.
5. **Simplifying Governance**: Streamline sign-offs or cross-team approvals to remove bottlenecks.

Middle Management as Agile Enablers

Middle managers are the linchpins of Agile transformation, translating leadership's strategic vision into actionable plans. By fostering psychological safety within their teams, aligning daily work with organizational objectives, and championing iterative practices, they ensure that Agile principles permeate all levels of the organization. For example, a financial services firm saw a 15% improvement in time-to-market after training middle managers to facilitate cross-functional retrospectives. This focus on empowering middle managers bridges the gap between strategy and execution, enabling organizations to scale agility effectively.

This transformational change is more effective when employees are invited to participate rather than being compelled. By adopting an invitation-based approach to change, leaders create an environment of trust and mutual respect, fostering higher engagement. This method empowers individuals to take ownership of transformation, ensuring long-lasting and meaningful outcomes. When teams feel invited to contribute rather than obligated, their commitment to the process strengthens, leading to sustainable cultural shifts.

While these practices drive alignment and cultural change, metrics are crucial for evaluating their effectiveness. For a detailed discussion of leadership metrics and measurement methods, see '**Measuring Leadership Effectiveness in Transformation**' (page 106).

Effective leadership practices go beyond process management; they extend to creating behavioural norms that reinforce agility at all levels of the organization.

Personal Reflection

When I was CTO at a financial institution, leaders initially saw Agile as a 'team-level fix'. I spent time coaching each executive, showing them the direct link between Agile principles and strategic gains. Once they understood how their daily behaviour impacted the team's mindset, the cultural shift took hold.

Setting Expectations to Foster Agility

Leadership is conspicuously absent from Agile's core teachings. While the Manifesto emphasizes collaboration and adaptability, it provides little guidance on the role of leaders in fostering these behaviours. Highly Agile organizations thrive not because of rigid adherence to Agile practices but their leaders create environments where behaviours such as experimentation, cross-boundary problem-solving, and proactive decision-making are expected. These behaviours are not optional; they are cultural norms reinforced by clear leadership expectations and accountability structures.

Leadership is the foundation upon which organizational agility is built. In highly Agile organizations, leaders establish clear expectations that go beyond role definitions or job descriptions. They foster a culture where individuals are expected to:

- Solve problems proactively without waiting for explicit directives.
- Navigate beyond their immediate responsibilities when necessary.
- Collaborate openly, speaking to whomever is needed to resolve issues, regardless of hierarchy.
- Test solutions iteratively, even in the absence of complete certainty.

These expectations create a shared understanding of what it means to act with agility. Leaders who model these behaviours amplify their impact, embedding agility into the fabric of their organizations.

The Leadership Commitment Gap: Why Agility Stalls

At a global insurance firm, Agile was announced with fanfare – new frameworks, training, and Agile coaches were deployed. Yet six months later, teams still operated in silos, and leadership continued demanding rigid project roadmaps. The issue? Leaders themselves hadn't changed. They expected Agile to work at the team level while clinging to old management habits. Without leadership commitment, Agile remains a superficial exercise rather than a true transformation.

Setting clear expectations is only the first step – sustaining agility requires continuous leadership reinforcement. Research from *The Evolution of the Agile Organization* report from PA Consulting highlights a stark reality: 60% of leaders acknowledge that embedding and scaling agility is a major struggle.

One of the most common pitfalls is a lack of sustained leadership commitment. Many executives endorse agility in principle, yet their actions fail to reflect this intent, leading to fragmented transformations and inconsistent adoption. While leaders may advocate for agility, their engagement often fades over time, causing organizations to revert to traditional hierarchies and decision-making patterns.

To counteract this, leaders must move beyond surface-level support and actively demonstrate their commitment to agility by:

- **Making unanimous and unwavering commitments** across the executive team to align transformation efforts.
- **Participating in key Agile ceremonies**, such as **Program Increment (PI) planning**, to signal hands-on involvement.
- **Redefining leadership metrics** to prioritize **customer outcomes over traditional KPIs**.
- **Establishing clear non-negotiables** in Agile transformation to prevent **backsliding into old habits**.

Without these elements, agility risks becoming a superficial exercise rather than a fundamental organizational shift. Leaders who fail to internalize these commitments inadvertently reinforce traditional hierarchies, slowing decision-making and stifling innovation. Sustained engagement is the defining factor between superficial Agile adoption and a truly adaptive organization.

Moving Beyond Superficial Practices

Organizations often fall into the trap of performing Agile rituals without embodying Agile values. Daily stand-ups, retrospectives, and sprint planning become routine activities that provide the appearance of agility but fail to drive meaningful outcomes. To combat this, leaders must focus on the principles that underlie these practices: open communication, accountability, and customer-centricity.

By prioritizing outcomes over rituals, leaders ensure that Agile ceremonies remain purposeful. For example, a retrospective should not simply catalogue past successes and failures; it should challenge the team to experiment and evolve, iterating not just on work processes but on how the team collaborates and communicates.

Through these practices, leaders can shift their organizations away from superficial rituals and towards a deeper, outcome-driven culture of agility.

Leaders as Champions of Agility

Leaders can't simply oversee from the sidelines; they have to embody agility themselves. When they remove silos, promote open feedback, and facilitate cross-team connections, they signal that experimentation is welcome. Shifting from a hierarchical mindset to *servant leadership* fosters genuine collaboration.

Dave Snowden describes leaders as catalysts who spark emergent solutions rather than forcing compliance. Key adaptive leader habits include:

- **Transparency**: Share decisions and data widely.
- **Experimentation**: Test ideas in short cycles, celebrating insights from 'failures'.
- **Comfort with Uncertainty**: Show teams how to handle ambiguity productively.

Without these guiding behaviours, no Agile process will truly embed. Yet, cultural and structural realities can still hinder leaders, even with the best intentions.

Challenges in Leadership and Cultural Transformation

While leadership plays a pivotal role in any transformation, it's essential to recognize the challenges that leaders may face in shifting organizational culture:

- **Resistance to Change**: Longstanding mindsets or fear of obsolescence hinder new methods.
- **Misalignment of Goals**: Inconsistent priorities and communication gaps undermine synergy.
- **Skill Gaps**: Missing competencies (such as facilitation or emotional intelligence) hamper effective leadership.
- **Lack of Agile Mindset Understanding**: Without a clear grasp of Agile as a mindset rather than just a process, leaders may struggle to support meaningful transformation.

According to the 2023 State of Agile Report, 41% blame 'lack of leadership participation' for stunted Agile efforts. Often, leaders publicly back agility but fail to model or reinforce it. A solution is leadership retrospectives, where top-level decision-makers examine their own processes and collaboration. One manufacturing company cut decision-cycle times by 25% after identifying leadership communication gaps in such a retrospective.

Reflecting on common leadership critiques offers a pathway to refine leadership approaches and better align them with Agile objectives.

Learning from Leadership Critiques in Agile Transformations

Critics often note a mismatch between theoretical Agile and leaders' real behaviour, like rigid governance or ignoring team feedback. Dave Snowden also warns that over-focusing on frameworks can stifle creativity. Leaders must fluidly adapt structure to context, bridging oversight with autonomy, ensuring cultural alignment, and emphasizing ethical practices.

Turning valid critiques into improvements requires weaving empowerment with appropriate governance and addressing cultural inertia head-on.

Navigating Critiques to Drive Change

These critiques aren't just complaints – they're signals that reveal necessary refinements. Leaders can:

- **Transform Rigid Frameworks** into flexible guidelines.
- **Balance Adaptability and Governance** via tools like OKRs.
- **Align Culture and Values** through open discussion of fears, skill-building, and repeated reinforcement of Agile ethics.

Personal Reflection

I once led a distributed project with team members in three continents. By establishing rotating meeting times and encouraging asynchronous retros, we respected cultural work-hour norms. Seeing each locale's unique approach to problem-solving was eye-opening, and it underscored how culture-driven agility hinges on genuine inclusivity.

Leaders who welcome critiques often find renewed momentum and authenticity in their Agile efforts. A big part of this involves helping teams let go of outdated routines.

Letting Go of the Old to Embrace the New

Letting go can be the toughest part of transformation. People fear losing proven methods and stable roles. Leaders must provide emotional backing, showing how new Agile approaches add meaning rather than threaten livelihoods.

A financial services firm overcame middle-manager pushback via empathy-driven workshops. Managers shared anxieties and then worked together to redefine their roles. This acceptance process eased the transition from old ways to new Agile norms, ensuring deeper commitment.

Sometimes, leadership tries to remove the hierarchy but fails to supply Agile-friendly structures. Servant leadership is pivotal at all levels. Freed from top-heavy controls, teams need help coordinating dependencies and balancing system-wide priorities. Furthermore, real culture change typically follows new behaviours, not the other way around. By reinforcing collaborative, iterative habits, leaders eventually embed them as cultural norms.

Practical Step: Encourage open sessions where staff safely voice discomfort about changes. Acknowledge and adapt – this empathy fosters buy-in that speeds up transformation. However, measuring leadership success is crucial to see whether these shifts truly move the needle.

Measuring Leadership Effectiveness in Transformation

Change thrives with feedback loops. By tracking leadership effectiveness, organizations see how well transformations align with strategic aims.

Key Metrics

1. **Employee Engagement Surveys**: Gauge team morale and empowerment.
2. **360-Degree Feedback**: Gather multiple viewpoints on leadership behaviours.
3. **Agility Metrics**: Watch for time-to-market, pivot speed, or number of validated experiments.
4. **Leadership Dashboards**: Connect leadership actions (like building trust or clarifying goals) to improvements in culture and output.

For instance, a telecom company tracked leadership agility via dashboards showcasing team feedback. Enhancing transparency created a 15% jump in productivity, and data-informed leadership strategies were spotlighted.

Linking leadership actions to organizational outcomes provides real insights for ongoing refinement. The table below illustrates potential metrics:

Leadership Action	Measurable Outcome	Metric
Promoting Psychological Safety	Builds trust, boosts collaboration, and elevates engagement	Employee engagement scores and team collaboration surveys
Encouraging Regular Feedback	Ensures continuous alignment and refinement	Retrospective satisfaction, action completion
Supporting Experimentation	Fuels innovation and adaptability	Innovation rates (e.g. number of new ideas piloted)
Modelling Agile Values	Improves trust and fosters team alignment	Trust index, alignment with strategic OKRs
Aligning Team Goals with Strategy	Links daily work to broader organizational priorities	OKR success rates, productivity improvements

By measuring these aspects, organizations can identify areas for improvement and ensure that leadership is effectively driving transformation. Building on these measurements, leaders can identify specific gaps and refine their approaches, bridging divides that impede Agile progress.

Addressing Leadership Gaps in Agile Transformations

Leadership often meets criticism for failing to bridge Agile ideals with practical realities. Common concerns: rigid use of frameworks, weak governance, or disregard for cultural fit. A structured approach addresses these challenges.

1. **Misuse of Frameworks**
   o **Issue**: Overly rigid frameworks stifle creativity and hamper outcomes.
   o **Solution**: Leaders must shift from strict compliance to facilitating autonomy and context-driven tools.
2. **Over-Adaptation Without Governance**
   o **Issue**: Flexibility can devolve into chaos without guardrails.
   o **Solution**: Adopt adaptive governance like OKRs to keep teams aligned while preserving autonomy.
3. **Cultural Resistance**
   o **Issue**: Teams fear letting go of old processes or losing stable roles.
   o **Solution**: Invest in training, conduct open forums for dialogue, and show how Agile thinking can enrich job experiences, not eliminate them.

Practical Actions

- **Empowering Teams**: Go beyond frameworks by granting autonomy, ensuring psychological safety, and celebrating lessons from failures.
- **Balanced Governance**: Use flexible frameworks like OKRs to maintain alignment without stifling initiative.
- **Championing Culture**: Make cultural alignment an explicit goal, embed Agile values into policies, and cultivate ethical leadership that promotes fairness.

The Path Forward

When leaders tackle these issues head on, critiques become catalysts for rethinking and refining. Adaptive leaders adopt a holistic approach – serving as catalysts, not dictators – so that Agile principles seep into the cultural fabric.

Conclusion

Leadership and culture form the strategic core of real Agile transformation. Leaders who only implement frameworks miss the deeper shift needed. By prioritizing open collaboration, simplifying excessive processes, and actively championing iterative mindsets, leaders build organizations ready to flex in uncertain conditions.

Reflect on your own leadership. Are you fostering a collaborative environment or inadvertently drowning teams in rituals? Think about clarifying roles, encouraging bold experimentation, and connecting daily work to broader goals. With these changes, agility moves from process to practice and becomes a lasting driver of value.

Leaders don't just adopt Agile; they model it. Agile endures in environments where leaders demonstrate adaptability, trust, and a willingness to uproot obsolete norms. Real transformations begin with leadership that fully inhabits agility's values.

Cultural transformation starts at the top. Leaders set the tone for psychological safety, experimentation, and resilience – the foundation of the Culture element in CLEAR. The next chapter expands on empowering teams by building supportive environments that spark high performance. Ultimately, true agility isn't imposed – it grows through cultural ownership and continuous learning.

Call to Action

As an adaptive leader, assess your daily interactions. Are you living empathy, resilience, and openness in front of your teams? Commit to steps like leadership retrospectives, new governance experiments, or advanced coaching. Then, share outcomes with fellow leaders – collectively reinforcing an organization-wide culture of Agile leadership.

Key Takeaways

- **Adaptive Leadership Is Essential**: Leaders must inspire and motivate teams, modelling Agile values to drive cultural change.

- **Leadership Influences Organizational Culture**: Policies, vision, and structures embed Agile principles into the organization's DNA.
- **Emotional Intelligence Matters**: Leaders who practise personal, emotional, and collective intelligence create environments where teams thrive.
- **Middle Management Plays a Crucial Role**: Engaging middle managers helps bridge the gap between strategy and daily operations.
- **Measuring Leadership Effectiveness Is Key**: Using metrics and feedback loops to assess leadership impact ensures sustained transformation.

CLEAR Model® Connection

- **Culture**: Lasting Agile adoption happens when cultural values align with collaboration and trust.
- **Leadership**: Leaders bridge cultural principles with day-to-day tasks, ensuring Agile isn't just talk.
- **Execution**: Intentional follow-through makes Agile principles tangible.

Key Takeaway: Leadership commitment is not just about supporting Agile in words but embedding it into daily operations, decision-making, and strategic priorities. Leaders must actively demonstrate agility in their approach.

Leadership Self-Assessment Quiz

- **Agile Mindset:**
  - o Do you encourage experimentation and learning from failure?
- **Empowerment:**
  - o How often do you delegate decision-making to your team?
- **Communication:**
  - o Are you transparent and open in your communications?
- **Support:**
  - o Do you ensure your team has the resources and autonomy needed to achieve their goals?

Action Plan: Cultivating an Agile Culture

1. **Define Cultural Attributes:**
   - o Identify the desired cultural traits that support Agile.
2. **Gap Analysis:**
   - o Compare the current culture with the desired state.
3. **Leadership Development:**
   - o Implement training programmes to develop Agile leadership skills.
4. **Recognition Systems:**
   - o Reward behaviours that exemplify Agile values.
5. **Monitor Progress:**
   - o Regularly assess cultural shifts and make adjustments as needed.

Chapter Summary

Leadership underpins Agile success by setting strategic direction, modelling collaboration, and forging a culture of continuous learning. Frameworks alone can't drive true agility; leaders who live Agile values day to day inspire a transformation that endures.

6

Team-Centric Agility – Leading from the Middle Out

No one can whistle a symphony. It takes an orchestra to play it.

H.E. Luccock

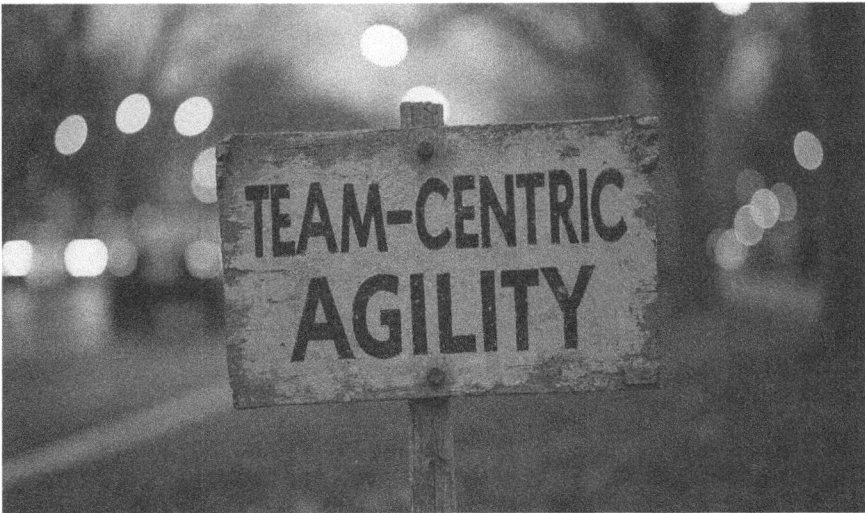

What You'll Gain

- **For Senior Leaders and Executives**: Learn how to foster truly empowered, self-managing teams that deliver strategic value.
- **For Mid-Level Leaders**: Discover practical techniques for nurturing team autonomy, open communication, and continuous improvement.
- **For Students or Early-Career Professionals**: Understand the core principles of building psychologically safe, innovative, and purpose-driven Agile teams.

From Strategy to Execution

Lisa, an engineer at a fintech startup, sat in a tense retrospective. Deadlines were missed, and the project manager's quick fix – 'Just work faster' – only fuelled frustration. The real culprits were shifting priorities and top-down decisions that eroded ownership. While the company called itself 'Agile', the teams felt powerless.

True empowerment arises when teams have genuine ownership over their work and the trust to execute it. When Agile transformations only push tasks downward without granting autonomy, agility remains superficial. The most enduring Agile success stories stem from communities of practice (CoPs) and champion networks that grow organically, creating spaces where teams shape – and own – their agile mindset.

However, many organizations still treat Agile as a top-down initiative, expecting teams to 'be Agile' while leadership remains stuck in traditional ways of working.

The truth? Agile only succeeds when teams are empowered, self-organizing, and adaptable.

But simply calling a group of people a 'team' doesn't make them Agile. To achieve true agility, teams need:

1. **Autonomy** to make decisions and own their work.
2. **Psychological safety** to take risks and innovate.
3. **Cross-functionality** to break silos and deliver real value.
4. **A shared mission** that aligns them with business outcomes.

Why Traditional Teams Struggle with Agility

Most organizations still structure teams based on control rather than empowerment and adaptability.

1. Command-and-Control Structures

- Decisions are made at the top, with teams waiting for approval.
- Leaders dictate how work should be done rather than trusting teams to figure it out.
- Speed is sacrificed for control, leading to slow delivery cycles.

Fix It: Shift to decentralized decision-making – empower teams to own their work.

2. Functional Silos Instead of Cross-Functional Teams

- Traditional teams are structured by function (e.g. marketing, IT, HR) rather than outcomes.
- Silos create bottlenecks – teams have to 'hand off' work between departments.
- Lack of cross-functional collaboration slows delivery.

Fix It: Build cross-functional teams that contain all the skills needed to deliver value independently.

Personal Reflection

Reflecting on my leadership journey, I realized real breakthroughs happened when I stepped back, relinquishing control and letting teams carve their path. In these moments, empowerment wasn't gifted from above; it thrived where leaders built the right environment and trusted teams to self-manage.

Chapter 5 highlighted how leadership shapes culture and strategy. This chapter shifts perspective to the team experience, revealing how leaders' actions influence everyday collaboration, autonomy, and learning. We'll outline how psychological safety, trust, purpose, and continuous growth produce Agile teams that can turn strategic ambitions into tangible outcomes.

A recurring theme is authentic purpose. Agile endures when teams grasp a compelling 'why'. When they believe in the mission, like helping customers navigate financial burdens, frameworks become secondary. Tying Agile efforts to purpose transforms them from rituals into a meaningful movement.

With purpose secured, leaders must also cultivate open communication, risk tolerance, and clarity. This begins with establishing high-performing Agile teams.

Personal Reflection

As a leader in a high-pressure role, I once believed giving teams autonomy meant stepping back entirely. But in one transformation, I saw a self-organizing team struggle – deadlines slipped, collaboration faltered, and frustrations grew. Instead of staying hands-off, I leaned in as a coach, helping them build a structure without micromanagement.

That experience taught me that Adaptive Leadership isn't about stepping back – it's about knowing when to guide and when to empower.

The 5 Pillars of High-Performing Agile Teams

Teams that thrive in an Agile environment must embrace five key principles, as discussed on the following pages:

1. Teams must be self-organizing and autonomous

The Problem

- 'We're called a "self-organizing team" but we have to get manager approval for every decision.'
- 'We're expected to take ownership, but leadership still micromanages us.'
- 'Autonomy is encouraged – until we make a decision that leadership doesn't like.'

The Solution

Teams must be given the authority and accountability to make decisions without constantly seeking approval.

Actionable Steps

- Define decision boundaries. Teams should know what they can decide without escalation.
- Trust, don't control. Give teams the space to innovate.
- Measure teams by outcomes, not adherence to process.

Self-organizing teams move faster and innovate more than controlled ones.

2. Psychological Safety Must Be a Priority

The Problem

- 'We're told to take risks, but leadership only rewards safe bets.'
- 'Our team avoids conflict instead of discussing problems openly.'
- 'Mistakes are blamed on individuals instead of being treated as learning moments.'

The Solution

A culture of psychological safety allows teams to challenge, experiment, and learn.

Actionable Steps

- Encourage constructive debate. All ideas should be open to challenge.
- Reward learning, not just success. Innovation comes from experimentation.
- Leaders should model vulnerability. Admit when you don't know something – normalize learning.

Psychological safety fuels creativity, innovation, and true agility.

3. Cross-Functional Collaboration Is Essential

The Problem

- 'We need marketing's help, but they work in a different sprint cycle.'
- 'IT and business don't collaborate – they operate like separate worlds.'
- 'Dependencies kill our ability to move fast.'

The Solution

Cross-functional teams own end-to-end value delivery, reducing dependencies and improving agility.

Actionable Steps

- Build teams around outcomes, not functions. Every Agile team should contain all the necessary skills to deliver value independently.
- Encourage shared goals. Business and technical teams should be aligned around the same outcomes.
- Remove bottlenecks. Identify and eliminate hand-off dependencies between teams.

Agile teams must be cross-functional to deliver real agility.

4. Agile Teams Must Be Outcome-Driven
The Problem

- 'We measure our success by sprint velocity, not customer impact.'
- 'We're shipping features, but are they solving real problems?'
- 'Agile should help us deliver faster – but faster doesn't mean better.'

The Solution

Agile is not about speed – it's about delivering meaningful results.

Actionable Steps

- Define success based on outcomes, not output. What impact are teams having?
- Use customer feedback to drive priorities. Agile must be linked to user needs.
- Measure agility by results, not rituals. Stop obsessing over velocity – focus on impact.

Agile teams must be driven by real impact, not process adherence.

5. Leadership Must Support and Enable, Not Dictate
The Problem

- 'Leadership talks about agility but still controls every decision.'
- 'We don't feel trusted to experiment or take risks.'
- 'Agile is just a buzzword – leaders still expect rigid planning.'

The Solution

Leaders must shift from controlling to enabling, creating an environment where teams thrive.

Actionable Steps

- Empower, don't dictate. Leaders should guide, not command.
- Remove barriers. Simplify approval processes and eliminate bureaucracy.
- Encourage continuous learning. Foster a growth mindset at all levels.

Adaptive leaders build adaptable teams.

Psychological Safety: Where It Goes Wrong and How to Get It Right

One thing to note here is that psychological safety is often misunderstood, and in some organizations, it is dangerously overused as a slogan rather than a reality. Too often, teams are told they are in a 'safe space' – but when they test that assumption by questioning leadership decisions, pushing back on unrealistic deadlines, or admitting mistakes, the response tells a different story.

The reality is that **psychological safety is not just about eliminating fear – it is about fostering an environment where honest conversations can happen without hidden consequences**. If a leader claims to embrace safety but rewards only those who conform, the concept loses meaning. If employees are encouraged to challenge assumptions but later penalized for questioning authority, psychological safety is an illusion.

Simply saying, 'This is a safe space' does not make it one. A psychologically safe workplace does not mean there are no consequences for actions – it means that transparency, constructive debate, and learning from failure are not met with retaliation. Without this, Agile efforts become performative rather than effective.

True psychological safety means that teams not only feel safe to speak up but also that their concerns lead to genuine engagement rather than performative listening. Leaders who say, 'We value open feedback', must also prove that feedback drives action. Without this, the term becomes nothing more than empty corporate jargon.

To Move from Rhetoric to Reality, Leaders Must:

- Encourage dissenting views and act on concerns rather than just acknowledging them.
- Ensure that psychological safety coexists with accountability, so that openness does not excuse poor performance but enables improvement.
- Recognize that trust and psychological safety are built through actions, not just words.

When psychological safety is real, it accelerates innovation, strengthens collaboration, and builds resilient teams. But when it is just a phrase, it does the opposite – breeding cynicism, fear, and disengagement.

Finding the Sweet Spot of Disagreement

Not all disagreement is harmful. In fact, some tension is essential for innovation. Teams that fall into constant agreement may be too polite to surface useful challenges. On the other hand, teams steeped in hostility will shut down risk-taking altogether.

In adaptive teams, innovation tends to peak when the culture allows for *generative disagreement*, where ideas are questioned with respect, and people feel safe to challenge without it becoming personal.

When teams are stuck in a 'culture of nice', they avoid conflict and hold back feedback to keep harmony, often at the cost of truth. A 'culture of harsh' does the opposite, prioritizing bluntness or dominance over psychological safety. Neither promotes agility.

What leaders must cultivate is a *culture of candour*, where dissent is welcomed, but never weaponized.

Ask yourself: *Is your team too agreeable to move forward, or too abrasive to move together?*

Rethinking Hierarchy – The Networked Organization

Traditional hierarchies slow decision-making and limit innovation. Instead, companies like Haier have adopted micro-enterprise models, where small, self-sufficient teams operate with autonomy. These networked teams are not just Agile in process but in structure, ensuring adaptability at scale.

Adaptive leaders foster cross-functional, self-organizing teams, empowering individuals to own decisions rather than waiting for approvals. Organizations that embrace fluid team structures are better positioned to handle complexity and change.

Conflict and Resistance Management

At a retail tech firm, two senior designers clashed: one championing user experience, the other engineering feasibility. Tension ballooned, slowing progress. Rather than mandate a quick compromise, the Agile coach ran a 'conflict resolution sprint' where both sides mapped their priorities to broader company goals. The result: an integrated solution uniting user needs with technical constraints.

Conflicts don't have to derail progress. Viewed correctly, they spur valuable reforms. The tables below show how to tackle conflict.

Framework for Managing Conflict and Resistance

The table below highlights four essential actions – diagnose, discuss, experiment, and follow up – that help leaders discover the true source of friction, organize balanced conversations, test targeted fixes, and monitor ongoing progress.

Action	Guidance	Example
Diagnose the Root Cause	Use retrospectives or one-on-one conversations to discover underlying reasons for conflict or resistance.	In a retrospective, a team member reveals that unclear goals are causing frustration and leading to missed deadlines.
Facilitate Open Dialogue	Provide a neutral setting where concerns can be discussed without judgment or fear.	A Scrum Master arranges a conflict-resolution workshop where team members role-play challenging situations to boost empathy and understanding.
Pilot Solutions	Experiment with small changes to address the issues identified, then collect feedback on their effectiveness.	A team struggling with missed deadlines agrees to adopt shorter sprints with a tighter scope, resulting in more consistent delivery.
Follow Up and Iterate	Check in periodically to confirm solutions remain effective and make adjustments if needed.	The leader runs quarterly surveys to gauge ongoing team morale and spot new concerns before they escalate.

Toolkit: Conflict Resolution Process

While the framework above shows how to manage conflict step by step, this process outlines the essential questions leaders should ask at each stage. It encourages swift identification of core issues, constructive conversations, and continuous improvement.

Stage	Key Question	Action
Identify	What is the root cause of the conflict?	Use retrospectives to surface concerns.
Facilitate	How can we address this constructively?	Organize a neutral team discussion.
Resolve and Iterate	Is the solution working?	Gather feedback and adjust approaches.

Addressing Resistance During Agile Transformation

A global financial services firm faced significant resistance when transitioning from traditional project management to Scrum. Team members expressed concerns about losing control over their work and felt overwhelmed by the new processes. Using Adaptive Leadership techniques, the organization achieved the following:

- Conducted anonymous surveys to identify specific fears and frustrations.
- Held team workshops to clarify the benefits of Agile while addressing concerns openly.
- Piloted Scrum practices in one department to gather feedback and refine the approach before scaling.

The result: Increased team buy-in and roughly a 30% improvement in project delivery timelines.

By addressing resistance constructively, the organization turned potential setbacks into a catalyst for growth, aligning teams with the Agile vision.

With effective conflict management strategies in place, leaders can turn their attention to clarifying roles and responsibilities, ensuring that every team member understands their contribution to the shared vision and goals.

Clarifying Roles and Responsibilities

At a financial services firm, product managers kept overriding developers' sprint plans, creating chaos. The team felt disempowered, and velocity dropped by around 30%. When leadership clarified roles – defining clear boundaries between prioritization and execution – team morale rebounded, and delivery cycles stabilized. This shows why role clarity isn't bureaucracy – it's a crucial enabler of team empowerment.

Accountability without influence breeds frustration. Agile leaders must ensure that team responsibilities align with genuine decision-making power and clear channels to influence outcomes. If teams are held accountable but lack real authority or support, role clarity alone won't resolve underlying tensions. Leaders must actively provide teams with the tools, autonomy, and resources necessary to meet their responsibilities effectively.

Clear roles and responsibilities are essential for building effective collaboration. When individuals understand exactly what they contribute and how it ties to overarching goals, accountability and teamwork improve. This clarity acts as a foundation for achieving shared objectives.

Engaging the Team in Role Definition: Jointly crafting a RACI matrix – mapping who is Responsible, Accountable, Consulted, and Informed – establishes accountability and reduces confusion.

Maintaining Flexibility: Keep roles adaptable, allowing shifts as projects evolve so that boundaries don't hinder innovation.

At Atlassian, teams employ a RACI matrix to minimize confusion and speed up workflows. This visual alignment clarifies ownership and ensures each role complements, rather than duplicates, others.

With well-defined roles, teams can more easily build trust and collaborate effectively. At that point, they're positioned to develop deep trust, open communication, and an inclusive culture – key drivers of success.

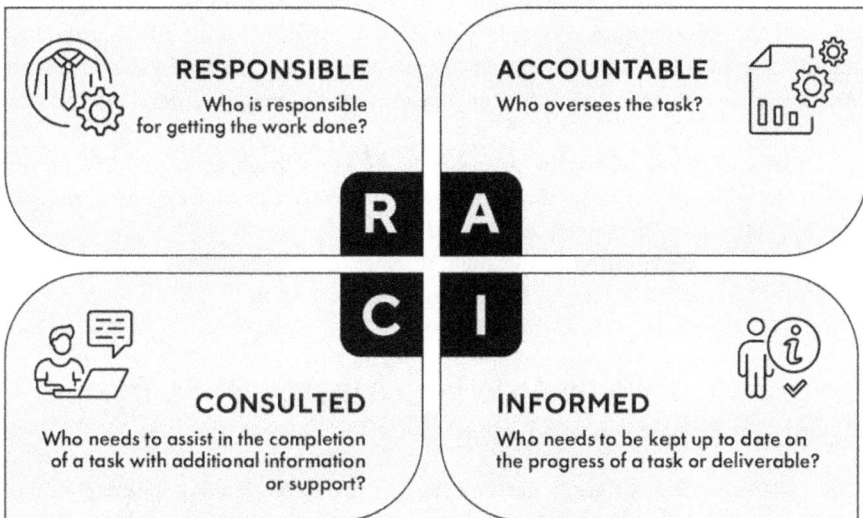

RESPONSIBLE
Who is responsible for getting the work done?

ACCOUNTABLE
Who oversees the task?

R A

C I

CONSULTED
Who needs to assist in the completion of a task with additional information or support?

INFORMED
Who needs to be kept up to date on the progress of a task or deliverable?

RACI matrix (Responsible, Accountable, Consulted, Informed)

However, these roles must not be rigidly fixed. Agile teams thrive when individuals are empowered to take on multiple responsibilities based on their skills and the team's needs. For example, a Scrum Master can effectively contribute as a Delivery Manager or Business Analyst when required. Encouraging such flexibility not only optimizes resources but also builds resilience within teams, particularly in tight-budget scenarios.

While responsibility frameworks like RACI can provide clarity, enforcing them too rigidly can stifle agility. In some organizations, strict adherence to predefined roles has discouraged collaboration and hindered skill development, leading to siloed teams and reduced adaptability. Leaders must foster an environment where overlapping responsibilities are embraced as opportunities for growth and collaboration rather than as constraints.

Middle Management as a Potential Bottleneck

Middle management is pivotal to the success or failure of Agile transformations. When middle managers resist change, remain isolated, or lack clarity about their new roles, agility stalls. Adaptive leadership must proactively equip and support middle management as active agility champions rather than passive bottlenecks. By clarifying expectations, providing autonomy paired with accountability, and involving middle management early in Agile decision-making, organizations create essential conduits rather than blockages to Agile maturity.

Strategic Agility Enablers

Too often, the Project Management Office (PMO) is seen purely as a guardian of process. But in high-agility organizations, PMOs have evolved. They now play a critical role in enabling enterprise-wide adaptability.

Modern PMOs actively support cross-functional collaboration, help teams select the most suitable delivery approach (Agile, predictive, or hybrid), and directly contribute to strategy execution. In these organizations, PMOs also drive talent development, support continuous improvement, and ensure alignment between project delivery and strategic outcomes.

If your PMO is still seen as the 'process police', it's time to reimagine its role. As a core pillar of business agility, a forward-thinking PMO bridges strategy and execution, empowering teams to work with focus, flexibility, and purpose.

Once roles are well-defined, teams find it easier to form the deep trust required for open collaboration and inclusion – key elements we'll explore next.

Building Empowered Agile Teams that Cultivate Trust, Collaboration, and Inclusion

Trust underpins effective Agile. It nurtures cooperation, fosters innovation, and promotes inclusive teamwork. Leaders build trust through consistent transparency and by acknowledging everyone's input. Diversity – across backgrounds and ideas – also energizes creative solutions.

Ways to Encourage Trust and Collaboration

1. **Consistency**: Meeting commitments and delivering on promises.
2. **Shared Decision-Making**: Explaining rationale fosters ownership.
3. **Celebrating Contributions**: Recognizing wins builds positive morale.
4. **Inclusion:** Actively seeking diverse talent and guaranteeing all voices are heard.

Google's Project Aristotle found that psychological safety and trust were the top drivers of high-performing teams. By emphasizing open dialogue and fair participation, Google harnessed collective expertise more effectively.

Psychological safety is the foundation of the Culture element in the CLEAR Model®. Without it, Agile teams will never truly self-organize or innovate.

When trust and inclusivity form the norm, teams engage more fully, tackling challenges together. This synergy intensifies when everyone unites around a common vision.

True agility isn't just about speed and responsiveness; it's about fairness, equity, and access. The most effective Agile teams prioritize *justice, equity, diversity, and inclusion (JEDI)* as core leadership principles. Agile transformations that ignore these aspects risk creating exclusionary structures that ultimately weaken adaptability.

Key aspects of JEDI in agility include

- **Equitable Decision-Making:** Ensuring all voices contribute to strategic choices.
- **Inclusive Structures:** Creating Agile teams that reflect the diversity of the communities they serve.
- **Fair Access to Opportunities:** Breaking down systemic barriers that limit participation.

Companies that embrace these principles create more resilient and innovative teams, ensuring that agility works for everyone, not just a select few.

By embedding these principles into agility, leaders create a culture where adaptability is not just about efficiency but about ensuring fairness, access, and inclusion for all team members.

Aligning Around a Shared Vision and Goals

A unifying mission lifts team motivation. Clear objectives – co-created with the team – link daily tasks to organizational strategy, amplifying a sense of meaning.

- **Collaborative Goal Setting:** Involve the entire team in defining targets.
- **Highlight the Bigger Picture:** Show how tasks support organizational impact.
- **Constant Reminders:** Frequent goal reviews to keep everyone aligned.

At Atlassian, 'alignment sessions' help teams define and refine their objectives, swiftly adjusting to any shifts. This synergy, built on trust, clarifies how each person's work counts.

Teams stay more engaged when a bigger purpose is visible and relevant. Consistent feedback loops also keep them on track and spark continuous evolution.

Encouraging Open Communication and Feedback

Transparent communication cements alignment and adaptiveness. While psychological safety allows honesty, structured mechanisms ensure it isn't overlooked. Through daily check-ins, retros, and open Q&A, teams stay coordinated and handle issues early.

Building on Psychological Safety

- **Feedback Systems:** Anonymous surveys or 360 reviews to unearth hidden concerns.
- **Facilitated Transparency:** Leaders share wins, failures, and challenges widely.
- **Collaboration Tools:** Slack, Teams, or Trello for asynchronous or quick updates.

GitLab, a fully remote company, thrives by mixing asynchronous communication and thorough documentation. With clarity, distance and time zones matter less.

Clear communication lays the groundwork, but action is what earns trust.

Show, Don't Tell – Turning Ideas into Action

Words alone rarely shift behaviour. Teams gain confidence when they see solutions in motion, not just discussed in theory. Leaders who demonstrate ideas through experiments build belief and speed up buy-in.

Practical Demonstration Tactics

- **Pilot First:** Test ideas in small, low-risk settings to show real impact.
- **Prototype Fast:** Quick models make abstract concepts tangible and testable.
- **Feedback on Delivery:** Invite input while the work is still live, not after.

Visible action removes ambiguity and encourages shared ownership. This approach cuts delays, builds trust, and focuses everyone on what matters most – results.

Even with strong intent, if these actions become too rigid or overused, they can start doing more harm than good.

Tip: Demo user stories back to the team; seeing the outcome first-hand feeds pride and energy.

When Agile Creates More Stress Than Value

Agile promotes transparency, accountability, and continuous improvement – but these very principles can backfire when misapplied. Many teams experience ceremony fatigue, where excessive Agile rituals leave little room for focused work. Instead of enabling agility, rigid frameworks can create frustration, disengagement, and burnout.

Some Agile ceremonies, originally designed to enhance collaboration, can become counterproductive when overused.

- **Retrospective Fatigue:** Teams often repeat the same discussions, leading to disengagement.
- **Backlog Refinement Overload:** Hours spent grooming tasks can delay real progress.
- **Stand-ups Losing Impact:** Updates become a routine checkbox rather than a valuable touchpoint.

To prevent Agile from becoming an administrative burden, teams need to rethink the frequency and necessity of rituals. Adjusting the cadence of ceremonies and introducing asynchronous alternatives can reduce fatigue while maintaining alignment.

Cultural differences also influence how teams respond to Agile structures. Some cultures value structured feedback, while others prefer indirect discussions. By adapting Agile to fit the team's work style, organizations can maintain engagement without forcing rigid, one-size-fits-all approaches.

Reframing these struggles opens the door to a better path – one where continuous improvement is shaped by smarter feedback.

Leveraging Feedback Loops for Continuous Improvement

Frequent feedback loops – through retrospectives, daily stand-ups, or peer reviews – fuel small adjustments, building an adaptive culture.

- **Sprint Retros:** After each iteration, teams dissect what went well and what to refine.
- **Peer Critiques:** Constructive reviews drive personal growth and synergy.
- **Data-driven:** Analytics reveal bottlenecks and highlight best practices.

Through these loops, teams spot issues swiftly and learn from them. It's an iterative process that fosters ever-improving workflows. With this foundation, empowerment and self-management become feasible, letting teams make decisions effectively.

For feedback to drive lasting improvement, it must be paired with learning – building skills, not just awareness.

Fostering a Culture of Continuous Learning

A learning culture ensures teams stay fresh and fluid. Encouraging professional growth, knowledge-sharing, and personal development not only bolsters morale but also drives adaptability.

Key Learning Strategies

- **Professional Development:** Workshops, conferences, or certifications aligned with the domain.
- **Knowledge Sharing:** Brown-bag sessions or wikis to spread best practices.
- **Personal Growth:** Tailored learning paths that meet each person's ambitions.

IBM's 'Think40' mandates at least 40 hours of learning per year for each employee. This keeps them at the forefront of innovation, fostering ongoing refinement. When everyone invests in learning, the organization evolves rapidly.

A culture of continuous learning sparks creativity. By mixing these efforts with dedicated space for experimenting, teams can pivot their fresh skills into real innovations.

Encouraging Innovation and Experimentation

A global healthcare firm struggling with lengthy product cycles launched an 'Innovation Lab'. Like Google's 20% rule, employees got reserved time to test ideas. A year later, three new revenue-driving features emerged. *Innovation* thrives when experimentation is safe, not an afterthought.

Leaders Can:

- **Dedicate Time:** 'Innovation sprints' or partial work hours for side projects.
- **Organize Challenges:** Hackathons or idea contests spur creative synergy.
- **Enable Fast Prototyping:** Provide quick, user-centric test platforms.

3M – with its 15% rule – gave birth to Post-it Notes, a prime example of empowered employees exploring personal passions leading to breakthrough products.

Where learning meets experimentation, teams produce an endless pipeline of improvements. Yet conflicts may arise with fresh ideas; effective resolution fosters a stable environment.

Implementing Effective Conflict Resolution Strategies

Conflict is part of healthy collaboration, indicating psychological safety and diverse views. Properly guided, disagreements yield better outcomes.

Conflict Resolution Essentials

- **Encourage Early Dialogue:** Tackle issues swiftly to avoid festering resentment.
- **Focus on Interests Over Positions:** Understand deeper motivations for lasting solutions.
- **Facilitated Mediation:** When friction escalates, a neutral figure can guide respectful discussion.

In fact, teams frequently emerge stronger after constructive conflict, turning tension into momentum. While conflict resolution is vital, so is preserving an overall balance, so teams don't burn out, leading to the question of well-being.

Promoting Work-Life Balance for Agile Teams

Effective agility also respects personal boundaries. Overworked members can't sustain creativity or pivot effectively. Striking the right workload is essential to preserve morale and long-term performance.

Methods to Support Work-Life Integration

1. **Flexible Scheduling:** Align working hours with employees' personal peak times or obligations.
2. **Respect Personal Time:** Avoid constant after-hours messaging.

3. **Wellness Initiatives:** Provide mental health support, gym benefits, or social activities.

Hybrid Work: Some see it as an advantage, boosting accessibility for parents or those with disabilities. Others feel it blurs boundaries, prolonging work hours. Leaders must clarify expectations – remote presence shouldn't mean 24/7 availability. Focus on output, not presence, to maintain fairness and equity.

Buffer, a social media management firm, endorses an unlimited vacation policy. The result: employees balance rest with productivity responsibly, driving both satisfaction and project success.

As remote and hybrid setups gain ground, balancing these dynamics grows crucial. Let's see how best to equip scattered or partly distributed teams for success.

Supporting Remote and Distributed Teams Effectively

Remote or hybrid arrangements require additional adaptation. *Agile* can still thrive, provided teams have well-defined communication, trust, and the correct digital tools.

Key Tactics

- **Tech Stack:** Tools like Zoom, Trello, Slack, or MS Teams for synchronous and asynchronous collaboration.
- **Clear Protocols:** Standard expectations for response times and meeting etiquette.
- **Virtual Team-Building:** Online social events or unstructured chat spaces to sustain personal connections.

Automattic, the WordPress parent company, is fully remote, succeeding through asynchronous communication and documented best practices. Physical distance is no barrier when clarity and trust are top priorities.

Personal Reflection

I recall a cross-functional team whose members barely spoke at first. By hosting casual 'show-and-tell' sessions, we built personal connections. After a few sprints, their morale soared, and they began proactively solving issues, showing me that true team-centric agility hinges on trust and personal ownership.

With the fundamentals laid out, let's pull them together into a consolidated toolkit that leaders and teams can adopt to sustain strong, autonomous Agile teams.

Toolkit for Building Empowered Agile Teams

Empowerment involves combining psychological safety, autonomy, and a culture of accountability. Below are recommended steps:

Establish Clear Goals and Vision

- **Action:** Conduct workshops clarifying objectives and linking them to organizational outcomes.
- **Benefit:** Heightened commitment and alignment.

Promote Autonomy

- **Action:** Let teams choose their paths, so long as they remain aligned to strategic goals.
- **Benefit:** Accelerates decisions and nurtures ownership.

Provide Necessary Resources

- **Action:** Offer the training, tools, and support required for Agile practices.
- **Benefit:** Removes barriers so teams can focus on impact.

Foster Open Communication

- **Action:** Implement routine retrospectives, feedback loops, and Q&A forums.
- **Benefit:** Boosts transparency and early detection of issues.

Encourage Continuous Learning

- **Action:** Sponsor e-learning, workshops, or certifications.
- **Benefit:** Ensures teams stay adaptive, with fresh perspectives fuelling innovation.

Adaptive Leadership in Action: In each of these steps, leaders bring the CLEAR Model® to life. By shaping a purpose-driven culture, modelling open leadership, driving execution, staying flexible, and responding to feedback, they create an empowered, high-performing team environment.

Distributed teams require more than just digital collaboration tools – they need leadership approaches that acknowledge different time zones, work habits, and communication styles. The challenge is not just technical; it's about making distributed work seamless and effective.

Agile in Distributed Teams: The Reality Check

One of the most persistent struggles in modern Agile is its incompatibility with distributed teams when applied rigidly. Traditional Agile ceremonies assume co-located teams, but today's workforce is often spread across multiple time zones. This creates logistical challenges that many organizations fail to address.

Take daily stand-ups, for example. The idea of a quick morning huddle becomes impractical when a development team spans India, Europe, and North America. What was intended to be a 15-minute sync often turns into a 45-minute meeting that forces some members to log in at inconvenient hours, reducing engagement and effectiveness.

A better approach is to embrace asynchronous updates. Some companies have successfully shifted to Slack-based check-ins or written updates instead of real-time calls, allowing team members to share their progress on their own schedules. Others use a hybrid model – maintaining a short weekly live touchpoint while handling most communication asynchronously. These adjustments preserve Agile's core values – collaboration and rapid feedback – without forcing teams into unnecessary fatigue.

With these strategies, teams thrive – innovating, iterating, and delivering consistent value. As we'll see, synergy at the team level serves as the linchpin for organization-wide agility.

Conclusion

Teams empowered with clear goals, trust, and psychological safety form the backbone of any Agile organization. True empowerment stems from a culture that fosters ownership, open dialogue, and constant learning. Leaders are pivotal in setting up these conditions.

Consider whether your teams feel safe proposing bold ideas. Are roles and priorities transparent? Are you facilitating a culture of shared learning and autonomy? By refining collaboration norms, role clarity, and policies, you create the conditions for Agile excellence.

Empowering teams isn't about enforcing top-down frameworks; it's about fostering trust, clarity, and the freedom to experiment. Leaders who invest in psychological safety, conflict resolution, and well-defined roles see their teams flourish.

The next chapter expands the discussion from team-level empowerment to broader organizational impact. Adaptive leadership must scale agility beyond individual teams, creating an integrated culture that sparks innovation across the enterprise.

Call to Action

As an adaptive leader, consider how you can strengthen team ownership and a culture of experimentation. What immediate step could you take to nurture psychological safety or clarify responsibilities? Commit to removing barriers, inviting feedback, and championing knowledge sharing. Share your insights and results with peers – collectively, you'll reinforce the transformation and magnify your impact.

Key Takeaways

- **Psychological Safety as a Cornerstone:** Team members should feel safe taking risks, sharing ideas, and voicing concerns.
- **Empowerment Leads to High Performance:** Autonomous, self-managing teams are more agile and engaged.
- **Continuous Learning Drives Adaptability:** Ongoing development keeps teams competitive and responsive to change.
- **Diversity and Inclusion Enhance Innovation:** A diverse workforce fuels better solutions.
- **Effective Communication Is Essential:** Clear, transparent dialogue underpins alignment and collaboration, which is crucial for remote/hybrid contexts.

CLEAR Model® Connection

- **Culture:** A climate of trust and collaboration underpins effective Agile practices.
- **Leadership:** Leaders empower teams to work autonomously and champion psychological safety.

Key Takeaway: Agile is not just about speed – it's about sustainable, empowered teams. Leaders must create environments where trust, collaboration, and psychological safety drive performance.

Team Empowerment Checklist

- **Team Charter Template:**
  o Define team purpose, roles, and operating principles.
- **Psychological Safety Checklist:**
  o Ensure the environment encourages open communication and risk-taking.
- **Collaboration Tools Assessment:**
  o Evaluate tools that facilitate teamwork. Select the most suitable ones.

Facilitation Guide: Building Self-Organizing Teams

1. **Workshop Planning:**
   o Set objectives and prepare materials.
2. **Ice-Breaker Activities:**
   o Foster trust and familiarity among team members.
3. **Role Definition Exercises:**
   o Clarify responsibilities and expectations.
4. **Goal Setting:**
   o Collaboratively establish team goals and metrics.
5. **Feedback Mechanisms:**
   o Implement regular check-ins and retrospectives.

Chapter Summary

High-performing Agile teams rest on a foundation of psychological safety, purpose, and iterative feedback. This chapter has shown that nurturing autonomy, clarity, and continuous learning underpins genuine agility. Empowered teams – fuelled by supportive leadership and trust – drive lasting impact.

End of Part 3

Empowered teams and a supportive culture are the bedrock of any Agile success story. Part 4 examines the five core elements of business agility, uniting strategy, culture, and delivery to produce results that stand the test of time.

Part 4

The Key Elements for Business Agility

CLEAR Focus: Culture, Leadership, Execution, Adaptability, and Responsiveness

Teams gain strength when they link all five parts of the CLEAR Model® in one shared effort. This section uncovers how Culture, Leadership, Execution, Adaptability, and Responsiveness fit together to shape a flexible and productive approach. Each element works with the others, guiding leaders and teams towards clear goals and steady outcomes, whatever the circumstances.

7

Defining and Leading Business Agility

To improve is to change; to be perfect is to change often.

Winston Churchill

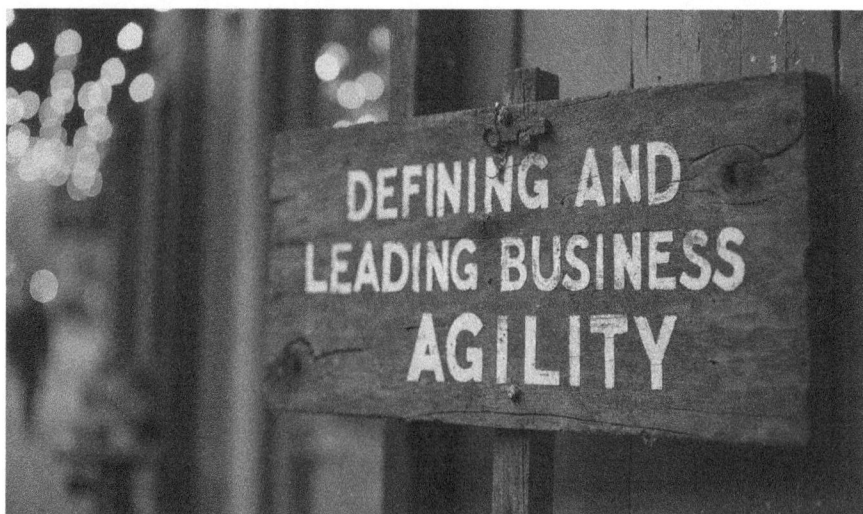

What You'll Gain

- **For Senior Leaders and Executives:** Understand how agility moves beyond IT and into every part of the enterprise, creating adaptability at scale.
- **For Mid-Level Leaders:** Learn to integrate Agile thinking into finance, HR, marketing, and other areas to spark cohesive transformation.
- **For Students or Early-Career Professionals:** Grasp why enterprise-wide agility focuses on more than frameworks, ensuring the entire organization stays flexible and future-ready.

Business Agility: More Than Just Agile Teams

Adaptive leaders must recognize that genuine agility involves the whole organization, not just a few 'Agile islands'. When a CFO at a global retailer complained about slow supply chain responses, even though 'Agile teams' were in place, the reason was clear: agility was siloed. True business agility transforms every function – marketing, HR, finance – into collaborative partners that adapt swiftly to market shifts.

Here's the uncomfortable truth: Agile at the team level doesn't automatically make a company Agile.

- If leadership still operates in annual budget cycles, the business isn't Agile.
- If big strategic decisions take months to approve, the business isn't Agile.
- If innovation is limited to small experiments instead of driving real change, the business isn't Agile.

Personal Reflection

Reflecting on my experience, taking Agile beyond IT sparks broad ripple effects: marketing embraces iterative cycles, HR adopts continuous feedback, and finance shifts toward flexible budgeting. Agility becomes the enterprise's unifying DNA, not just a method in certain corners. Yet many organizations remain anchored by slow-moving governance, budgeting, or compliance routines, ignoring the real reason agility stalls: leadership hasn't anchored the mindset everywhere.

A researcher posed a challenging question to me recently: '*Why are some organizations unable to turn like speedboats? Why do slow-moving enterprises struggle, despite being "Agile"?*'

The answer is simple: Agile frameworks do not guarantee agility. Many large organizations have adopted Agile ways of working, but their fundamental structures – governance, budgeting, approvals – still operate in a traditional, slow-moving fashion. They may call themselves Agile, but in reality, they remain Agile in pockets, not Agile at scale.

True business agility means that every part of the organization is empowered to respond to change. It's not just IT and product teams working in sprints – it's finance enabling dynamic funding, HR fostering adaptive talent strategies, and leadership creating decision-making autonomy. The real challenge isn't Agile adoption; it's breaking the deep-seated habits that keep businesses anchored to slow-moving processes.

This chapter builds on the CLEAR Model® introduced in Chapter 1, illustrating how adaptive leaders apply its principles to drive holistic change across entire enterprises. By expanding agility beyond delivery teams and embedding it into strategy, operations, and leadership culture, organizations can unlock business agility at scale.

Before we see how this adaptation spans departments, let's clarify what 'Business Agility' really means.

What Does Business Agility Really Mean?

> Business agility refers to an organization's capability to adapt swiftly and efficiently to changing market conditions, customer preferences and technological advancements. It encompasses flexibility, adaptability and responsiveness in decision-making, operations and management. Agile organizations foster a culture of continuous learning and improvement, enabling them to navigate uncertainties and disruptions while staying ahead of the competition.
>
> *Giles Lindsay – Clearly Agile: A Leadership Guide to Business Agility*

Business agility isn't just a buzzword – it's about thriving in uncertainty. Agile organizations don't just react to change; they anticipate, adapt, and outperform competitors.

Think of it like a top-tier athlete: they don't just train for one event – they build flexibility, endurance, and resilience. The same applies to businesses. The best don't just survive change; they use it as fuel for innovation.

Business agility involves aligning adaptability, customer focus, and a growth mindset across all layers of the organization, beyond any single department. The aim is to transform the entire enterprise into a receptive, streamlined environment founded on ongoing learning, iterative improvement, and sometimes radical change.

Agile Teams → Deliver work iteratively, adapt to feedback, and improve efficiency.

Business Agility → An entire organization's ability to sense, adapt, and respond to change quickly.

Agile Teams = 'We deliver software faster.'

Business Agility = 'We can pivot our entire strategy based on new market conditions.'

Business Agility Canvas

Leaders and teams need a single page that links goals, ways of working, and proof of value. Use this canvas to build that shared view, then keep it live as work evolves.

How to run it:

- Bring a cross-functional group and cap the session to one page of notes.
- Write short bullets, not essays. Mark the top three bets and the top three constraints.
- Assign an owner for each action and a date to check progress.
- Review monthly so the canvas stays real, not shelfware.

Why it helps:

- Aligns language across business units.
- Exposes bottlenecks early.
- Ties outcomes to flow, not activity.

BUSINESS AGILITY CANVAS

Purpose: A quick way to align strategy, ways of working, and outcomes across the CLEAR pillars

1. Purpose & Outcomes (why now?) • North Star / value thesis • 90-day outcomes (customer + business)	2. Customers & Value Target segments • Current pains / jobs-to-be-done • Proof of value (signals you'll track)	3. Work Design & Flow • Value streams / teams • Cadence & WIP limits • Definition of Done / quality rules
4. Teams & Talent • Skills we have / gaps • Role shifts (from control to coaching) • Learning plan this quarter		5. Tech & Enablers • Platforms, automation, data needed • Tech debt hotspots to tackle
6. Governance & Funding • Decision rights close to the work • Rolling funding model & guardrails	7. Feedback & Learning • User touchpoints (weekly/fortnightly) • Experiment backlog & review rhythm	8. Measures that Matter • Flow: lead time, throughput, ageing WIP • Outcomes: adoption, retention, NPS, ROI
9. Risks & Constraints • Top 3 policy/process constraints • Mitigations and owners	10. 90-Day Bets • Bet, hypothesis, measure, owner, date	

Why Most Businesses Struggle with Agility

Even companies with high-performing Agile teams fail to achieve Business Agility because of these common barriers:

1. **Leadership Still Operates in Traditional Management Models**
   o Teams are Agile, but executives still demand fixed long-term roadmaps.
   o Leaders expect adaptability at the bottom but maintain rigid structures at the top.
   o Risk aversion prevents bold, strategic pivots.

Fix It: Leadership must embrace agility first. If executives don't model adaptability, the organization will never follow.

2. **Decision-Making Is Too Slow**
   o Agile teams move fast, but critical decisions still take weeks or months.
   o Business approvals require multiple layers of sign-off.
   o Competitive opportunities are missed due to bureaucratic delays.

Fix It: Decentralize decision-making – empower teams and leaders at all levels to respond to change quickly.

3. **Annual Budget Cycles Kill Agility**
   o Traditional budgeting assumes certainty in an uncertain world.
   o Agile teams need flexibility, but finance locks in yearly spending plans.
   o Large-scale Agile transformations stall because funding doesn't support iterative growth.

Fix It: Move to rolling, adaptive budgets based on real-time market conditions.

But what does this transformation look like in practice? Executives, investors, and stakeholders often ask for tangible proof that agility delivers real business value. Measurable business outcomes are where this comes into play.

Executives are often asked, 'How does Agile improve the bottom line?' The answer lies in real, quantifiable benefits that go beyond team productivity and directly impact revenue, cost efficiency, and customer satisfaction.

1. Agility's Measurable Business Outcomes

Below are real-world examples of how Agile transformation has translated into tangible business results:

Company	Outcome of Agile Transformation
Financial Services Firm	Reduced time-to-market by 45% for new products
Retail Company	Increased customer satisfaction (NPS) by 20 points
Telecom Provider	Reduced operational costs by 30% through Lean-Agile practices
Healthcare Organization	Cut regulatory approval time by 25% using iterative processes

Agility enables faster adaptation, reduces delays in decision-making, and allows organizations to prioritize value delivery over rigid compliance processes.

Still, one critical but underused tool in this transformation is the Fixed Date, Variable Scope approach. It allows teams to deliver against important deadlines without compromising agility. This model has always aligned with Agile values – prioritizing the most valuable work first and delivering it within a committed timeframe. The problem isn't the approach; it's the avoidance of the hard conversations needed to agree what's flexible and what's not. Too often, delivery becomes a cycle of vague promises and ritualized sprints, while business leaders wait for results that don't come. To restore commercial trust, leaders must treat Agile as a means to improve delivery confidence – not an excuse to avoid it.

2. Connecting Agile to Revenue Growth

Executives must link agility to profitability and shareholder value. A few key ways Agile drives revenue:

- **Customer-Centricity:** Agile organizations iterate based on real-time feedback, leading to higher customer retention.
- **Speed to Market:** Reducing product delivery cycles results in faster monetization of innovations.
- **Operational Efficiency:** Decentralized teams reduce costly bottlenecks in decision-making.

When Agile is implemented beyond IT and into finance, HR, and strategic planning, the entire business benefits. These shifts create a direct competitive advantage, positioning companies to respond swiftly to market opportunities while keeping operations streamlined.

To sustain these advantages, leadership must do more than approve Agile initiatives – they must actively model and scale agility across the organization. This brings us to a critical factor in business agility: the role of Adaptive Leadership.

Tip: Track finance, customer, social, and ecological results together to see whole-of-system value.

Scaling Adaptive Leadership Across Organizational Levels

When Lorraine became COO of a logistics firm, she saw top-level decisions stifling local adaptation. 'We say we're agile, but decisions still funnel upward.' To solve this, she introduced 'decision-making autonomy zones', allowing teams to address problems without waiting for sign-offs. The result?

- Shipment delays plummeted.
- Customer satisfaction soared.

The lesson is clear: Adaptive Leadership doesn't rely on processes alone – it gives teams authority where it matters. But leadership agility alone isn't enough. Agile teams can only thrive if the entire business structure supports agility, from strategy and decision-making to funding and operations. Leadership agility falls under the Leadership element of the CLEAR Model®. Without adaptive leadership, scaling agility becomes impossible.

This is where the Four Critical Areas of Business Agility come in.

The Four Critical Areas of Business Agility

To embed agility beyond teams, organizations must focus on these four critical areas:

1. **Leadership Agility:** Adaptive leadership, not rigid hierarchy.
2. **Strategic Agility:** Fast decision-making, not slow approvals.
3. **Structural Agility:** Flexible operating models, not rigid org charts.
4. **Financial Agility:** Dynamic funding, not fixed budget cycles.

1. Leadership Agility – Agility Starts at the Top
The Problem

Many organizations expect Agile teams to be flexible, but leadership maintains traditional, risk-averse structures.

Common Issues

- Leaders demand five-year plans instead of adaptive strategies.
- Executives still manage with rigid KPIs, not learning-based outcomes.
- Leadership pushes agility downward but doesn't model it themselves.

The Solution

Leaders must model agility first. If executives don't embody adaptability, the organization won't follow.

Actionable Steps

- Replace fixed long-term plans with adaptive strategies.
- Move from command-and-control to empower-and-enable leadership.
- Encourage bold, data-driven decision-making – even in uncertainty.

Agility must start at the top – or it won't happen at all.

2. Strategic Agility – Making Faster, Smarter Decisions

The Problem

Even companies with Agile teams struggle to make decisions quickly.

Common Issues

- Months-long approval processes delay innovation.
- Decisions funnel upward, creating bottlenecks.
- By the time a decision is made, the opportunity is gone.

The Solution

Decentralized decision-making fuels agility.

Actionable Steps

- Empower teams with decision-making autonomy.
- Shorten approval processes – eliminate unnecessary sign-offs.
- Use real-time data to drive business pivots.
- Speed of decision-making = speed of adaptation.

3. Structural Agility – Designing for Change, Not Stability

The Problem

Most organizations are structured for efficiency, not adaptability.

Common Issues

- Rigid hierarchies slow down innovation.
- Siloed departments prevent cross-functional collaboration.
- Teams need approval for every little change.

The Solution

Businesses must be designed for agility, not bureaucracy.

Actionable Steps

- Move toward network-based structures, not rigid hierarchies.
- Encourage cross-functional collaboration between business and tech teams.
- Create 'two-speed organizations' – stable core + fast-moving innovation units.

Agility requires organizations that can flex and adapt.

4. Financial Agility – Funding Based on Learning, Not Fixed Plans

The Problem

Most companies fund Agile teams with rigid, outdated budgeting processes.

Common Issues

- Finance expects detailed forecasts, even in volatile markets.
- Innovation funding requires a full business case before experimentation.
- Agile projects are forced into traditional budget cycles.

The Solution

Agile businesses need flexible, learning-based funding.

Actionable Steps

- Use rolling budgets that adjust based on real-time needs.
- Fund teams based on impact, not fixed plans.
- Eliminate bureaucracy in financial approvals.

If budgets aren't Agile, the business isn't Agile.

Transparency as a Leadership Superpower

In many organizations, decisions are made behind closed doors, creating a lack of trust. Yet companies like Buffer practise radical transparency, openly sharing salaries, financials, and strategy with employees. The impact? Higher trust and more aligned teams.

Adaptive leaders make financial, strategic, and operational decisions visible, ensuring teams understand not just the 'what' but the 'why' behind choices. When employees have access to real data, they engage more deeply in the organization's success.

Bridging Leadership Agility with Execution

Leadership must coordinate strategy and daily execution across all levels – C-suite, mid-level, and team leads. The Four Pillars of Business Agility ensure that leadership agility translates into organizational agility, breaking down barriers between strategy, execution, and funding.

The CLEAR Model® (explored in detail shortly) still acts as a unifying guide, but these Four Pillars provide the foundation for scaling agility at an enterprise level.

Ownership and accountability sit at every leadership level. Many leaders never take accountability for their actions and decisions. When one layer fails, gaps appear elsewhere. Adaptive leadership needs clear structures that spread ownership through all organizational layers. The approach below shows how this responsibility can cascade through the organization.

Approach to Scaling Adaptive Leadership

The table below highlights how leadership responsibilities can be distributed across three key layers. Rather than relying solely on new methods, it shows the importance of empowering people with the right focus, autonomy, and accountability at each level.

Level	Role	Actions	Example
Senior Leadership	Set strategic direction, ensure cross-functional alignment, and model adaptive behaviours.	– Define and communicate the organization-wide vision for business agility. – Create psychological safety at scale by encouraging open dialogue at executive levels.	A CEO hosts quarterly 'Ask Me Anything' sessions to align the executive team and foster transparency.
Middle Management	Translate strategy into action by bridging executive vision and team-level execution.	– Serve as change agents, promoting cross-functional collaboration. – Balance autonomy with accountability through delegation and trust-building.	A department head introduces shared OKRs (Objectives and Key Results) to unite different teams.

Level	Role	Actions	Example
Team Leads	Empower teams to use Agile principles effectively while resolving day-to-day obstacles.	– Encourage team autonomy by delegating decision-making. – Facilitate regular retrospectives to motivate change.	A development lead invites team members to rotate facilitation roles during retrospectives, strengthening ownership and collaboration within the group.

Toolkit: Adaptive Leadership Cascade

While the table above outlines who does what at each level, it's helpful to see a more structured approach for joining these practices together. The following table offers a toolkit – or 'cascade' – ensuring leaders remain aligned from top to bottom and that Adaptive Leadership becomes part of the organization's shared mindset.

Level	Focus	Key Actions	Example
Senior Leadership	Strategy and culture	Communicate vision; foster alignment	Quarterly alignment sessions
Middle Management	Execution and alignment	Balance autonomy and accountability	Shared OKRs for cross-functional goals
Team Leads	Empowerment	Remove blockers; enable team autonomy	Rotating facilitation in retrospectives

By cascading Adaptive Leadership principles in this way, organizations make sure agility isn't seen as a separate initiative but as an everyday, shared approach. Although frameworks and tools can be helpful, they only succeed when the right leadership mindset exists at every level – bridging strategy and execution so everyone remains focused on genuine, sustainable growth.

One of the primary reasons that Agile transformations fail is that leadership sees agility as a set of processes to be 'rolled out' rather than a deeper cultural shift. As we'll see throughout this chapter, leadership alignment is essential – without it, transformations remain superficial. Real agility emerges when leaders actively model the behaviours that empower teams to adapt, experiment, and deliver value incrementally.

Many executives believe that hiring Agile coaches or implementing frameworks like SAFe or Scrum will instantly transform their organizations, but this overlooks the reality that agility is a leadership-driven practice. Effective leaders do not just sponsor Agile initiatives;

they actively participate in creating an environment where teams can adapt, experiment, and deliver value incrementally. Without this shift in leadership behaviour, Agile remains a surface-level transformation rather than an embedded organizational capability.

Personal Reflection

At a growing travel startup I worked with, departmental managers were hesitant to adopt Agile approaches if they had to share resources with marketing or operations. Once we established a shared OKR framework that encouraged cross-department collaboration, productivity soared, and we saw how quickly an aligned approach can amplify business agility.

Emphasizing Accountability with Influence

A recurring pitfall – often dubbed 'responsibility theatre' – occurs when individuals are assigned grand accountabilities but lack genuine influence or resources to fulfil them. Leaders set lofty targets, yet teams remain hamstrung by budget constraints, rigid hierarchies, or approval bottlenecks. This gap leads to frustration and burnout, undermining agility at its core.

Key Principle: If you expect teams or leaders to be accountable, ensure they also have the authority and support to make decisions, experiment, and shape outcomes. Otherwise, 'responsibility theatre' replaces real ownership, stalling true business agility.

Governance as a Maturity Enabler

Adaptive leadership requires governance frameworks designed explicitly to enable, not hinder, agility. Effective governance sets clear guardrails, ensuring alignment, accountability, and rapid decision-making. Mature Agile organizations explicitly integrate agility within governance processes, using structured but flexible guidelines to balance freedom with accountability. This encourages strategic alignment without sacrificing team-level responsiveness.

Defining Business Agility: Diverse Perspectives

Business agility means harnessing change for customer advantage. Digital anthropologist Brian Solis calls it an open, perpetual drive to deliver new value. Agile Manifesto co-author Arie van Bennekum highlights how integrating marketing, legal, and beyond is crucial – Agile can't remain an IT phenomenon.

Why It Matters: By embedding agile mindsets across every function, leaders spark synergy, break silos, and build an organization able to sense and respond to shifting conditions. This approach resonates with the CLEAR Model®, which systematically connects culture, leadership, and execution with adaptability and responsiveness.

While business agility remains a competitive advantage, its impact extends beyond corporate performance. True agility influences how organizations and societies adapt to uncertainty, making agility more than just a business imperative – it's a mindset that applies across industries, governments, and communities.

Agility as a Societal Force

Agility doesn't just improve business outcomes – it strengthens *social resilience*. The ability to rapidly adapt, respond to crises, and empower communities mirrors the same principles found in Agile enterprises. When agility is embedded at a societal level, it ensures that communities, governments, and institutions remain responsive to their people's evolving needs.

Key Drivers of Societal Agility Include:

- **Resilience and Adaptability**: Nations and institutions must be able to pivot based on social, economic, and environmental challenges.
- **Empowered Communities**: Self-organizing networks play a critical role in societal stability, from grassroots initiatives to national policy shifts.
- **Technology as an Enabler**: Digital transformation allows governments and organizations to respond faster to emerging issues.

Agility is no longer just a corporate strategy; it is a way of structuring entire ecosystems to remain responsive, just, and effective in uncertain times.

Shifting from Agile to Agility

Adaptive leaders must see agility as a holistic perspective, not just a process. In marketing, for instance, teams could iterate on campaigns weekly, pivoting quickly based on user feedback, just like in software. This agility arises from fostering psychological safety, iterative thinking, and real-time feedback.

Outcomes matter more than ceremonies. By emphasizing user feedback and continuous reflection, organizations stay on track for real customer value. Similarly, dissolving rigid boundaries fosters a rapid flow of ideas throughout the enterprise, weaving resilience into the corporate DNA.

But principles alone don't build agility – leaders need a way to make them actionable at scale.

Operationalizing Agility with CLEAR

To embed agility at scale – across teams, functions, and even broader ecosystems – leaders need more than tools. They need a cohesive model that connects mindset to method. That's where the CLEAR Model® comes in.

Introduced in Chapter 1, CLEAR provides a structured way to activate agility across the organization. Rather than viewing it as a set of team rituals, CLEAR embeds agility into how the organization thinks, decides, and delivers – turning it into a system, not just a style.

Now, let's see how these principles come to life in real-world scenarios.

CLEAR Model® in Action

A large fintech successfully applied the CLEAR Model® to reinvigorate its ways of working:

- **Culture:** Embraced open feedback, letting frontline staff propose process improvements.
- **Leadership:** Shifted from a directive to a facilitative style, offering employees more autonomy.
- **Execution:** Formed small, cross-functional squads, shortening product launch times by around 40%.
- **Adaptability:** Started weekly retrospectives across the business, allowing quick pivots in response to consumer data.
- **Responsiveness:** Deployed real-time dashboards to drive proactive, evidence-based decisions.

This holistic approach led to greater staff engagement, higher customer satisfaction, and faster innovation cycles. CLEAR goes beyond 'just another Agile method' by tackling culture, leadership, and execution cohesively – so improvements don't fizzle out or stay stuck in pockets of the organization. Doing so helps leaders achieve tangible benefits, like faster innovation cycles, improved employee engagement, and stronger customer satisfaction, without relying on piecemeal improvements.

Enabling Strategy

Leaders often find themselves juggling disjointed improvements – tweaks to culture, scattered leadership initiatives, or new tools – without a unifying strategy. The CLEAR Model® brings these efforts together into a single adaptive system so you can move beyond one-off enhancements toward continuous evolution. By interlinking culture, leadership, execution, adaptability, and responsiveness, you build a foundation for long-term agility, where every decision, every team interaction, and every process shift aligns with sustainable growth and innovation.

A key advantage of the CLEAR Model® is its role in reducing risk at an organizational level. By fostering adaptability and responsiveness, leaders can anticipate potential disruptions before they become critical threats. This approach transforms agility into a proactive risk-management strategy, ensuring that teams can detect, assess, and address risks in real-time. Whether facing regulatory compliance challenges, shifting market conditions, or operational uncertainties, organizations leveraging the CLEAR Model® create a structured yet flexible framework for continuous de-risking.

In the next section, we'll break down each pillar, showing how these elements interlock to create an integrated approach that supports business agility at scale.

Applying the CLEAR Model® for Tangible Benefits

Building on the CLEAR Model® concepts already outlined in Chapter 1, this section focuses on why each pillar matters to you as a leader – and how it drives real-world outcomes. By aligning these principles with practical steps, you can create a more engaged workforce, deliver consistent value, and pivot quickly in response to changing needs. Below is a closer look at each pillar, plus real examples and tips that leaders can adapt to their own teams.

Culture: 'The Nurturer' – Laying the Groundwork for Innovation

Culture in the CLEAR Model® forms the bedrock of an adaptive organization. Contrary to the belief that agility depends primarily on processes, an environment of trust and transparency enables genuine adaptability. When employees feel safe sharing ideas and experimenting, agility flows naturally rather than being imposed. Additionally, a robust cultural foundation fosters collaboration, constructive feedback, and the confidence to pivot quickly in changing conditions.

Leadership Vignette: Building Trust After Redundancies

A Bristol cloud startup had major layoffs, crushing morale. Fortnightly 'Team Pulse' huddles let remaining staff openly share concerns and propose solutions. Within two months, they introduced a new feature that cut client onboarding time by 15%. Culture is the soil where seeds of innovation sprout.

- **Why It Matters for Leaders**: A strong culture of psychological safety and open dialogue boosts employee morale, spurs creative thinking, and reduces friction across departments.
- **Real-World Example**: At Zappos, a culture of customer service and employee empowerment leads to high satisfaction levels. This aligns with Agile principles, especially continuous improvement, and helps Zappos maintain customer loyalty.
- **Practical Tip**: Conduct cultural assessments to gauge trust, openness, and willingness to experiment. Targeted steps – like collaboration training – can unify attitudes, making agility second nature.

Leadership: 'The Conductor' – Guiding Teams with Vision and Empowerment

Leadership in the CLEAR Model® underscores how a unifying vision, transparent communication, and genuine empowerment replace top-down edicts. Agile leaders inspire continuous learning rather than simply delegating tasks. They champion collaboration across teams, openly share both successes and setbacks and encourage constructive dialogue at every level. By consistently modelling these traits, leaders embed adaptability into the organization's core, making agility more than a buzzword.

Leadership Vignette: Transparent Direction in EdTech

A Midlands EdTech had overlapping efforts on tutoring software. The new CTO initiated weekly 'Focus Sessions' for lead developers to align. Code duplication dropped by 20%, enabling deeper product enhancements. A small nudge in leadership approach overcame big misalignments.

- **Why It Matters for Leaders**: By modelling curiosity, honesty about challenges, and a willingness to pivot, you set a tone that encourages bold experimentation and problem-solving.

- **Real-World Example**: Satya Nadella's 'learn-it-all' mindset at Microsoft revamped a previously closed culture into one that thrives on innovation, elevating collaboration, flexibility, and feedback across teams.
- **Action Step**: Create 'open forums' or town halls that foster shared decision-making. Reassure teams that mistakes can be learning moments, ensuring a high-trust environment that's crucial for agility.

Execution: 'The Artisan' – Turning Plans into Results without Losing Flexibility

Execution in the CLEAR Model® focuses on delivering tangible outcomes. Rather than blindly applying frameworks like Scrum or Kanban, Agile teams maintain a continual feedback loop to recalibrate swiftly. This results-driven mindset ensures each sprint or iteration produces real value, all while allowing room to adjust when customer needs shift. By concentrating on progress over strict procedures, teams minimize waste, meet strategic goals, and sustain momentum in competitive markets.

Leadership Vignette: Streamlining the Delivery Pipeline

A London-based fintech missed deadlines. Daily 15-minute check-ins replaced extended sign-offs, uniting devs, QA, and product owners for instant feedback. Release cycles halved from monthly to fortnightly – proof that streamlined routines can accelerate results.

- **Why It Matters for Leaders**: Effective execution prevents wasted time and effort, ensures customer needs are met, and keeps teams nimble in shifting conditions.
- **Real-World Example**: Toyota's Just-In-Time (JIT) production exemplifies Agile execution – manufacturing 'only what's needed when it's needed', eliminating waste and remaining tightly in sync with customer demand.
- **Action Step**: Encourage short, frequent retrospectives that identify immediate roadblocks and adapt workflows right away. This keeps your organization aligned with strategic aims and customer expectations.

Adaptability: 'The Shape-Shifter' – Embracing Rapid Change with Confidence

Adaptability in the CLEAR Model® is about pivoting proactively rather than just reacting when market conditions shift. Leaders who practise scenario planning and encourage innovation ensure teams stay ready for whatever comes next. By anticipating disruptions early, they enable faster decision-making and build organizational resilience. This approach also nurtures cross-functional collaboration, as fresh perspectives often spark inventive solutions to new challenges.

Leadership Vignette: Quick Pivot Rescues a Data Project

At a Glasgow analytics provider, a large client abruptly demanded encryption mid-project. Rather than push back deadlines, the Head of Engineering assigned a cross-functional 'rapid response' group to handle it. Delivery didn't skip a beat, securing a crucial client relationship.

- **Why It Matters for Leaders**: Market disruptions can come from anywhere – competition, technology, or consumer trends. Building adaptability helps your organization remain calm under pressure and seize emerging opportunities.
- **Real-World Example**: Netflix pivoted from DVDs by mail to streaming, illustrating how foresight and a willingness to adopt new technology keep a company ahead of customer demands.
- **Practical Advice**: Try scenario planning regularly – map possible challenges and plan responses. This structured anticipation helps teams move swiftly and intelligently during uncertainty.

Responsiveness: 'The Sprinter' – Swift, Informed Reactions to Market Changes

Responsiveness in the CLEAR Model® goes beyond broad adaptation; it's the ability to detect signals – customer feedback, market changes, internal data – and respond with speed and precision. Streamlined communication channels help crucial insights reach decision-makers instantly, allowing prompt adjustments. In turn, teams can tailor products or services in near real-time, maintaining a decisive edge in rapidly evolving markets.

Leadership Vignette: Real-Time Reactions in Digital Retail

A Cardiff e-commerce upstart saw a surprise traffic spike from social media. The Product Lead promptly assigned extra server capacity and launched a two-day sale on popular items, boosting sales by 25%. Immediate responsiveness captured a fleeting market surge.

- **Why It Matters for Leaders**: By staying attuned to the most current insights, you can outpace slower competitors, capture untapped user needs, and rapidly refine products or services.
- **Real-World Example**: Zara's 'fast fashion' approach uses real-time buying trends to adapt product lines almost weekly, staying perpetually relevant in a tough market.
- **Tip for Responsiveness**: Integrate user polls, analytics dashboards, and quick-turnaround surveys into your daily processes. Equip teams with the authority to act on new data and keep pace with evolving conditions.

Making Sense of It All

Fusing these five pillars builds an adaptable 'system' rather than a collection of tasks. Each pillar strengthens the others: Culture fosters openness for Leadership to unify vision, Execution translates plans into quick wins, Adaptability spots new directions, and Responsiveness acts swiftly. This synergy ensures that agility becomes your organization's default mode of operating.

Continuous calibration is crucial: markets and technologies never stand still, so agility can't be static. The CLEAR Model® helps leaders unify strategy, daily tasks, and collaborative norms, shaping a truly agile enterprise. Next, let's explore practical tools to track progress and refine strategies as you embed CLEAR.

Bringing It All Together: The Power of the 'Agile Quintet'

When you combine the five CLEAR pillars as personified by the Agile Nurturer, Conductor, Artisan, Shape-Shifter, and Sprinter, you create a unified system rather than a set of isolated practices. For instance, the Nurturer (Culture) establishes an environment of trust and creativity, allowing the Conductor (Leadership) to guide teams with a shared vision. The Artisan (Execution) then turns that vision into tangible results through iterative cycles. Meanwhile, the Shape-Shifter (Adaptability) anticipates changes and readies the organization to pivot, and the Sprinter (Responsiveness) delivers rapid, data-driven actions whenever market opportunities arise.

This synergy matters because each character complements the others, creating a fluid balance across the organization. The Nurturer fosters trust and creativity, which in turn allows the Conductor to align teams around a clear vision. The Artisan then transforms that vision into iterative, high-quality outcomes, while the Shape-Shifter and the Sprinter keep the organization ready to pivot and seize opportunities. By fostering an environment where these 'characters' collaborate, leaders expand perspective and maintain a holistic approach to agility.

But it's not always smooth sailing. Conflicts can arise between these different aspects of agility. The Sprinter's need for speed might clash with the Artisan's focus on perfection, while the Shape-Shifter's push for change can test the Nurturer's emphasis on stability. That is where the Conductor steps in, balancing these tensions and guiding everyone toward shared goals. Becoming Agile isn't an overnight process; it demands patience, effort and a willingness to embrace change. You can't upskill people overnight. You may meet resistance or old habits that die hard, and some team members will feel safer sticking with the status quo. Start small, celebrate quick wins, and show, rather than merely tell, the value of a more Agile approach.

Crucially, this approach does not require five separate people to fill each role; rather, it encourages every team member, especially those in leadership, to internalize elements of each character. When people embrace the Nurturer's empathy alongside the Conductor's clarity, the Artisan's diligence, the Shape-Shifter's adaptability, and the Sprinter's swift responsiveness, the organization transforms into a collective engine of agility and resilience.

Consider a new product launch that demands rapid iteration. The Nurturer's supportive environment can fuel bold thinking, the Conductor can align creative ideas with business goals, and the Artisan can execute those ideas in small, refined increments. As the Shape-Shifter spots emerging trends or roadblocks, the Sprinter swiftly implements any pivots, ensuring the organization never misses a market opportunity. Each 'character' amplifies the strengths of the others, creating a culture of continuous improvement where speed, precision, and adaptability coexist.

By animating the five CLEAR pillars through these characters, leaders move beyond a checklist of practices and harness a dynamic interplay of skills and mindsets. This is how businesses evolve beyond surface-level 'Agile transformations' and forge a truly adaptive, future-ready organization.

Continuous Learning: The Unseen Core

At a leading consumer electronics company, leaders realized their biggest risk wasn't competition – it was stagnation. Teams were efficient, but weren't learning from past failures. To address this, the leadership introduced 'failure retrospectives' – structured sessions where teams analysed failed initiatives to extract insights. Over time, innovation cycles accelerated, and costly mistakes decreased. This case illustrates that continuous learning isn't just an Agile principle – it's the key to sustainable business agility.

At the core of CLEAR is Continuous Learning – the practice of consistently evolving skills, strategies, and mindsets. This principle sustains agility by fostering a culture that adapts as industry landscapes change. Embracing this learning mindset not only enables immediate improvements but also contributes to long-term benefits that strengthen organizational agility.

Example of a Learning Culture

A consulting firm implemented learning sessions, encouraging employees to explore new industry trends and share knowledge across teams. This approach not only advanced organizational agility but also spurred innovation across projects.

Actionable Insight

Organizations can enhance learning by investing in AI-driven Learning Management Systems (LMS), which provide personalized learning paths to keep employees engaged with relevant, up-to-date knowledge. This investment ensures that the workforce remains agile and ready to respond to evolving demands.

Long-Term Benefits of Business Agility

The 2024 Business Agility Report shows deeper cultural shifts and operational flexibility typically blossom after multiple years of consistent effort. If your enterprise invests wholeheartedly, it can see:

- Stronger Employee Engagement
- Reduced Operational Costs
- Higher Customer Satisfaction
- Greater Innovative Capacity

Leaders who treat agility as a continuous journey, not a quick fix, set realistic goals. Combining CLEAR with ongoing learning cements these benefits, building an enterprise that remains nimble and stable simultaneously.

Interactive Tools for the CLEAR Model®

Leaders and teams often ask, '*How do we measure our progress and identify where to improve?*' Below are four tools you can use to gauge your organization's alignment with the five pillars, boost adaptability, and plan a step-by-step rollout.

1. CLEAR Diagnostic

This diagnostic helps you measure how closely your organization aligns with each pillar:
Instructions: Rate each statement from 1 (Strongly Disagree) to 5 (Strongly Agree).

Pillar	Description	Score
Culture	Our organisation fosters psychological safety and encourages open feedback.	
	Team members feel included and valued.	
Leadership	Leaders demonstrate emotional intelligence and adapt to changing conditions.	
	Decision-making is transparent and guided by shared values.	
Execution	Teams connect their goals to the organisation's strategy.	
	Metrics focus on outcomes and real value, not just outputs.	
Adaptability	Teams experiment freely and pivot based on feedback.	
	Scenario planning is conducted to prepare for challenges.	
Responsiveness	Feedback loops are built into daily work.	
	Teams use data to make proactive decisions.	

Scoring Guide

- 35–50: High Alignment. Your organization is well-positioned for post-Agile demands.
- 20–34: Moderate Alignment. Concentrate on the lower-scoring pillars to increase agility.
- Below 20: Low Alignment. Address cultural and leadership gaps first to establish a stronger base.

2. Adaptability Checklist

This short list pinpoints steps that strengthen your organization's capacity to flex:

- Do teams test new methods or tools?
- Are lessons from retros kept for future improvements?

- Does leadership encourage flexible thinking when it comes to goals?
- Are resources available for quick pivots?
- Is scenario planning included in strategic discussions?

If you answer 'No' to anything:

- Pick a sponsor to champion change in that area.
- Host brainstorming sessions to resolve identified issues.
- Check progress regularly and adapt strategies as needed.

3. Post-Agile Leadership Diagnostic

A tool to evaluate an individual leader's readiness for the challenges of post-Agile leadership.
Instructions: Answer Yes/No for each question and identify areas for growth.

Diagnostic Questions

- Do I actively seek feedback from my team and stakeholders?
- Am I comfortable making decisions in uncertain or ambiguous situations?
- Have I fostered an environment where team members feel safe taking calculated risks?
- Do I encourage iterative improvements and experimentation?
- Am I focused on outcomes rather than rigid adherence to processes?

Actionable Results

- **5 Yes**: You're well-prepared for post-Agile leadership.
- **3–4 Yes**: Focus on areas where you answered 'No' to strengthen your adaptability.
- **0–2 Yes**: Consider deeper engagement with Adaptive Leadership principles and training.

4. CLEAR Model® Implementation Roadmap

Follow these stages to bring CLEAR to life in your organization:

Step 1: Assess Your Current Culture

- Conduct the CLEAR Diagnostic to identify strengths and gaps.
- Gather input from teams via surveys or focus groups.

Step 2: Identify Leadership Gaps

- Conduct the Post-Agile Leadership Diagnostic to evaluate leadership readiness.
- Create a leadership development plan targeting emotional intelligence and decision-making skills.

Step 3: Set Measurable Execution Goals

- Align team objectives with organizational strategy using OKRs (Objectives and Key Results).
- Focus on delivering outcomes that directly impact customer value.

Step 4: Develop Adaptability with Iterative Improvements

- Introduce scenario planning to anticipate challenges and opportunities.
- Encourage teams to experiment with new methods and review outcomes regularly.
- Use the Adaptability Checklist to spot where teams may need extra support and to monitor overall progress in building flexibility.

Step 5: Build Responsiveness into Feedback Systems

- Implement real-time feedback mechanisms, such as dashboards and customer surveys.
- Conduct regular retrospectives to refine processes and ensure alignment with goals.

Checklist

- Have you assessed your organization's culture and identified gaps?
- Are leadership skills aligned with the demands of post-Agile challenges?
- Do your team goals align with measurable outcomes?
- Are iterative improvements part of your team's workflow?
- Are feedback loops actively influencing decision-making processes?

These interactive tools help you track how CLEAR takes shape in your workplace. They also highlight improvement areas so you can adjust strategies and maintain momentum.

Embracing Business Agility with the CLEAR Model®

Adaptive leaders must push beyond one-off Agile adoptions. The CLEAR Model® fosters a deeper shift, embedding an iterative mindset across all functions. Instead of sporadic improvements, the entire enterprise unifies behind consistent learning, synergy, and Agile leadership.

By weaving Culture, Leadership, Execution, Adaptability, and Responsiveness into daily norms, teams innovate more freely, pivot quickly, and achieve consistent alignment. The result is holistic enterprise agility. Next, we'll see how leadership ensures successful CLEAR implementation across the board.

Having explored how the CLEAR Model® enhances business agility, the next step is understanding how leadership ensures its successful implementation. Adaptive leadership bridges strategy, culture, and execution, enabling organizations to embed agility into their DNA.

Integration of Adaptive Leadership with the CLEAR Model®

Scaling agility across an organization is no small feat. The CLEAR Model® provides a comprehensive framework for embedding agility into every function. As discussed above, leadership buy-in is the linchpin. Leaders must do more than authorize transformations; they must model adaptive behaviours to embed agility across the enterprise.

Mapping Adaptive Leadership to the CLEAR Model®

Pillar	Description	Example
Culture	Adaptive leaders shape a culture of psychological safety, continuous learning, and inclusivity.	A CEO introduces open forums to encourage honest feedback, fostering trust and collaboration.
Leadership	Leaders at all levels model agility through transparent communication, ethical decision-making, and responsiveness to change.	A department head implements regular strategy reviews, ensuring alignment with evolving customer needs.
Execution	Adaptive leadership ensures teams focus on delivering customer value over merely following processes.	A Scrum Master pivots sprint goals mid-cycle to address a critical client need.
Adaptability	Leaders promote flexibility by empowering teams to experiment and learn from failures.	An organization runs 'safe-to-fail' experiments to test new product ideas without fear of repercussions.
Responsiveness	Adaptive leadership reduces decision-making bottlenecks, enabling rapid responses to market shifts.	A financial services firm introduces real-time dashboards to accelerate insights and actions.

Conclusion

Adaptive leaders must champion the scaling of agility beyond IT, unifying entire enterprises in continuous learning, cross-functional synergy, and user-centric innovation. The CLEAR Model® provides a structured approach to embedding these principles at every level.

Consider how your leadership fosters synergy or stifles it. Are you bridging departmental divides? Are your budgeting or governance processes responsive to new data? By embedding Agile principles across all functions, businesses can transition from isolated Agile teams to a cohesive, future-ready organization.

Business agility is not about frameworks – it's a leadership imperative that redefines how organizations plan, execute, and evolve. Those who adapt will unlock continuous value and be prepared for shifting business realities.

The next chapter builds on these ideas, providing concrete tactics for scaling agility across multiple departments and ensuring the organization remains adaptable at all levels.

Call to Action

As an adaptive leader, keep pushing agility outward. Start by auditing where agility stalls – maybe budgeting in finance or rigid compliance in HR. Then, link each domain to Agile values: short feedback loops, empowered decisions, and transparent data. Challenge departmental assumptions and invite cross-team synergy to embed agility fully.

Key Takeaways

- **Agility Goes Beyond IT**: A flexible mindset and iterative methods can strengthen performance across diverse teams.
- **CLEAR Model® Unifies Efforts**: Culture, Leadership, Execution, Adaptability, and Responsiveness create a strong core for Agile action.
- **Ongoing Feedback and Trust Matter**: Frequent check-ins, open communication, and supportive leadership keep teams aligned.
- **Learning Is a Priority**: Regular reflection and willingness to adapt help embed agility into everyday operations.
- **Leaders Drive Sustainable Agility**: By modelling inclusive behaviours and genuine accountability, leadership paves the way for lasting improvement.

CLEAR Model® Connection

- **Culture**: Shared values and open interaction anchor agility across the organization.
- **Leadership**: Leaders drive an adaptive outlook beyond any single department or function.
- **Execution**: Day-to-day operations must align with strategic goals, ensuring cohesive agility.
- **Adaptability**: Remaining flexible allows approaches to shift as circumstances evolve.
- **Responsiveness**: Quick, well-informed reactions keep teams on track to deliver value.

Key Takeaway: Business agility isn't about applying Agile methods everywhere but embedding a mindset of continuous adaptation, execution, and responsiveness at all levels of the organization.

Business Agility Assessment Tool

- **CLEAR Model® Domains to Evaluate:**
  - Culture, Leadership, Execution, Adaptability, Responsiveness.
- **Scoring Criteria:**
  - Rate each domain on a scale from 1 (low agility) to 5 (high agility).
- **Analysis:**
  - Identify areas of strength and opportunities for improvement.

Strategic Roadmap Template for Enhancing Business Agility

1. **Set Clear Objectives:**
   - Define what business agility means for your organization.
2. **Align Initiatives:**
   - Ensure all projects support agility goals.

3. **Invest in Technology:**
   o   Leverage tools that enable flexibility and rapid response.
4. **Develop Talent:**
   o   Train employees in Agile practices and mindsets.
5. **Measure Impact:**
   o   Establish KPIs/OKRs to measure progress towards greater agility.

Chapter Summary

The CLEAR Model® supports adaptability by uniting its core pillars into a cohesive whole. By applying these concepts beyond IT, leaders can extend agility across all departments, fostering synergy, innovation, and a resilient, well-prepared organization for the future. The upcoming chapter explores methods for scaling these changes, ensuring that agility becomes an enduring organizational strength.

8

Scaling Agile Across the Enterprise

'The art of progress is to preserve order amid change and to preserve change amid order'.

Alfred North Whitehead

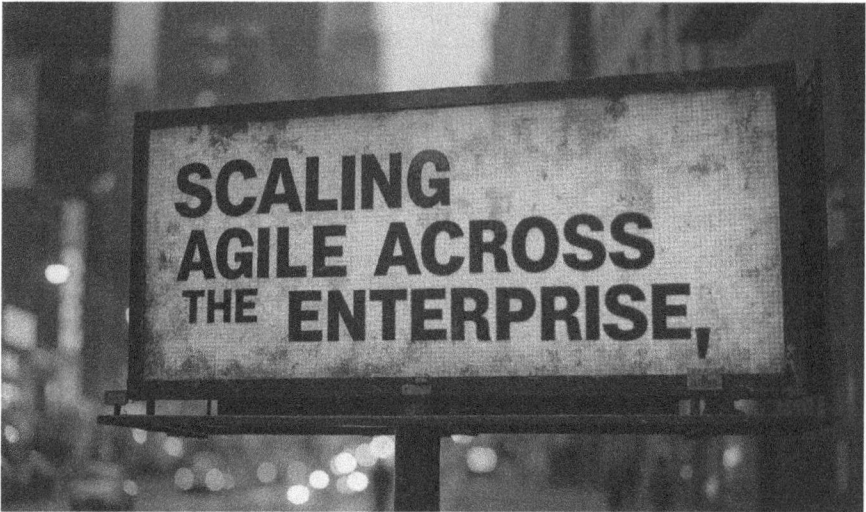

What You'll Gain

- **For Senior Leaders and Executives**: Find out how to merge Agile principles across finance, HR, and other core functions, boosting overall impact.
- **For Mid-Level Leaders**: Learn how to champion cross-team collaboration and keep your department aligned with Agile goals while meeting operational demands.
- **For Students or Early-Career Professionals**: Understand how enterprise agility fosters your growth, from early tasks to advanced responsibilities, so you can thrive in a flexible setting.

Scaling Enterprise Agility: Uniting Every Function for Lasting Impact

In many companies, Agile practices have taken root in isolated departments, yet true transformation requires every part of the business to evolve together. Consider a large retail chain where the IT team embraced Agile methods and delivered impressive results, but marketing, HR, and finance continued with their traditional routines. This separation created bottlenecks that prevented the company from reacting quickly to market changes.

Agile is not merely a set of tools for one team; it is a mindset that must be shared across the entire organization. When functions such as HR adhere to fixed recruitment cycles or finance relies on static annual budgets, the promise of agility remains unfulfilled. Each department needs the freedom to learn, adapt, and coordinate so that decisions reflect real-time insights and collective intelligence.

Personal Reflection

I recall working with a manufacturing firm where only the product development team had adopted Agile practices. When we gradually extended these principles to procurement and logistics, the transformation was striking: communication improved, lead times shortened, and a sense of shared purpose emerged. This experience taught me that sustainable agility happens when every department is part of the conversation and open to change.

Different functions face their own unique challenges. Finance teams, for instance, are bound by strict reporting cycles and risk controls that can seem incompatible with Agile's iterative nature. Yet, by aligning Agile principles with these essential practices, organizations have unlocked efficiencies and made their processes more responsive. Similarly, marketing can shift from annual campaign planning to a dynamic approach that rapidly incorporates customer feedback, yielding better results and stronger market connections.

Another key factor is the need for cultural integration. Bringing together diverse departments means reconciling different priorities and success measures. When teams from varied backgrounds collaborate, a common language and shared objectives become essential. Creating a unified vision that connects each department's metrics to Agile values not only streamlines decision-making but also sparks innovation as teams build on each other's insights.

This chapter explores practical ways to extend Agile thinking across all functions. We will examine how to break down entrenched silos, foster cross-department collaboration, and embed Agile values throughout the organization. Before diving into detailed tactics, it is essential to clarify what scaling enterprise agility truly means and how it can serve as the foundation for a more responsive and innovative future.

Has SAFe Killed Agile?

Few frameworks have sparked as much debate as the Scaled Agile Framework (SAFe). Proponents argue it provides structure for large-scale Agile implementations. Critics claim it has turned Agile into 'corporate theatre', stripping away agility in favour of rigid processes and excessive governance.

SAFe's popularity cannot be denied – many enterprises have adopted it as their default scaling method. But has SAFe actually improved agility, or has it just created a more complex version of the top-down control Agile was designed to avoid?

In many organizations, SAFe reintroduces layers of decision-making, approvals, and governance, diluting Agile's core values. Teams follow SAFe rituals, but autonomy is reduced. Instead of customer-driven agility, they operate within predefined playbooks, leading to what some call 'fake Agile' – where teams go through the motions but remain trapped in old corporate structures.

Post-Agile leaders must challenge this trend. Scaling Agile should not mean adding complexity – it should mean simplifying decision-making, increasing autonomy, and focusing on business outcomes. The more leaders treat SAFe as a rigid rulebook, the less agility they actually get.

Challenge for Leaders: Are you truly scaling agility, or are you scaling processes? Adaptive leaders should question whether SAFe is serving agility or replacing it with compliance-driven bureaucracy.

Multi-Functional Agility for Holistic Growth

Having established agility's broader role, the next step is to ensure its principles flow through every function – marketing, HR, finance, and more. Instead of isolated department-level changes, leaders can align the entire enterprise around customer focus, iterative learning, and empowered teams:

- **Foster Experimentation**: Enable data-driven, iterative cycles so teams can test ideas and learn quickly.
- **Break Down Silos**: Promote cross-department collaboration rather than confining agility to IT alone.
- **Empower Teams**: Delegate authority so teams can adapt in real-time and avoid top-down bottlenecks.
- **Leverage Technology**: Use real-time analytics and decisions to stay responsive and customer-centric.

For instance, Zara transformed its product development by blending continuous feedback with near-immediate production cycles. By reacting swiftly to consumer preferences, Zara slashed design-to-market times to just a few weeks, proving that agility can resonate well beyond software teams.

According to the 2024 Business Agility Report, mature organizations no longer limit Agile to a handful of departments; they reimagine their entire structure around adaptability. Leaders create a single, cohesive system that unites culture, leadership, and execution goals.

Reimagining your entire organizational structure means weaving the core elements of the CLEAR Model® into daily operations. These five components form a cohesive system that helps leaders build sustainable agility across departments. Rather than simply 'doing

Agile', your teams can function as a unified force primed to adapt swiftly and deliver meaningful results – together, they truly 'Act as One'.

Dual Operating Systems and Structural Agility

For agility to extend beyond IT and into enterprise-wide transformation, organizational structures must evolve. John Kotter, a leadership and change management expert, developed the Dual Operating System model, which provides an approach that balances stability with adaptability – combining a traditional hierarchical structure for core operations with a network-based structure that fosters innovation and rapid change.

This aligns with the CLEAR Model® by ensuring that its pillars are embedded in the fabric of both strategic and operational work. That alignment often breaks down in a space many leaders overlook – the space between teams and the next level up. Mike Burrows (2025) calls this 'the space between', where accountability, identity, and support often get muddled. It's not the delivery–strategy gap; it's where cross-team coherence either holds or breaks. The Responsiveness pillar in CLEAR helps leaders strengthen these mid-level layers before misalignment takes root.

The challenge for many leaders is not in introducing Agile teams but in integrating them effectively into the broader business model without disrupting necessary governance and stability.

To Apply Structural Agility in Practice

- Organizations should create an adaptive network of cross-functional teams operating alongside the traditional hierarchy.
- Executive sponsors must support experimentation zones where new initiatives can be tested without bureaucracy.
- Leaders should act as connectors between hierarchical functions and Agile teams, ensuring alignment without micromanagement.

By rethinking structures through an adaptive lens, organizations can create a model where innovation thrives without compromising business continuity.

With leadership driving the implementation of the CLEAR Model®, the next focus is aligning it with key domains of business agility. This alignment ensures the model addresses the unique needs of diverse organizational functions.

Aligning the CLEAR Model® with the Domains of Business Agility

At the Business Agility Conference UK 2024, Evan Leybourn highlighted five domains of enterprise agility: Responsive Customer-Centricity, Engaged Culture, Value-Based Delivery, Flexible Operations, and People-First Leadership.

ENGAGED CULTURE	RESPONSIVE CUSTOMER CENTRICITY	PEOPLE-FIRST LEADERSHIP	FLEXIBLE OPERATIONS	VALUE-BASED DELIVERY
Cultivate a Learning Organization	Fiercely Champion the Customer	Foster Authentic Relationships	Adapt Strategies Seamlessly	Unleash Workflow Creatively
Engage Transparently & Courageously	Sense & Respond Proactively	Empower with Accountability	Fund Work Dynamically	Prioritize.
Embed Psychological Safety	Integrate Diverse Ideas	Realize People's Potential	(Re)organize Structures Fluidly	Deliver Value Sooner
Act as One			Balance Governance & Risk	Seize Emergent Opportunities

Domains of Business Agility – Business Agility Institute

Pairing These with the CLEAR Model® Yields

- **Culture ↔ Engaged Culture**: Fosters trust, safety, and a learning mindset.
- **Leadership ↔ People-First Leadership**: Elevates transparency, accountability, and empowerment.
- **Execution ↔ Value-Based Delivery**: Prioritizes outcomes over tasks.
- **Adaptability ↔ Flexible Operations**: Remains fluid, reconfiguring processes to match new challenges.
- **Responsiveness ↔ Responsive Customer-Centricity**: Ingests feedback, swiftly adjusts decisions in real-time.

Linking these domains with CLEAR ensures that agility saturates every corner of the enterprise. The next sections illustrate how intangible factors – like sustainability, ethics, and professional standards – reinforce business agility's deeper purpose.

The CLEAR Model® complements these domains by offering a structured approach to embedding agility into every layer of the organization.

Customer-Centricity and People-First Leadership

The 2024 Business Agility Report shows that organizations' ability to 'Fiercely Champion the Customer' has risen by 20% in recent years – a clear sign of renewed focus on proactive customer engagement. Leaders who excel in this area not only respond promptly but also integrate diverse ideas into their customer strategies, boosting outcomes. Teams should move beyond reacting and invest in capabilities that enable early sensing and swift, market-aware responses.

The same report indicates that 'People-First Leadership' remains difficult for many organizations despite some progress. Authentic relationships and employee growth strongly shape how leadership is perceived. Empowering teams with autonomy and accountability often takes years, explaining why true people-first leadership is so elusive yet essential for fostering high-performance, engaged teams. Aligning these principles with the CLEAR Model® ensures a cohesive approach that influences every domain of business agility.

Being an Effective Coach

Coaching is central to building genuine business agility. Great coaches guide people to insights they didn't know they had, blending human-centred development, domain expertise, and practical facilitation.

In Agile, coaching isn't merely about frameworks – it's about highlighting the *why* behind them. By concentrating on core principles and mapping a clear learning path, coaches help teams internalize and apply Agile values effectively.

For example, a coach who uses systems thinking plus inherent simplicity helps teams see how their work relates to bigger goals. Templates, checklists, and structured materials can also provide practical collaboration tools. Woven into transformations, coaching ensures teams develop not only new practices but also the critical thinking required to adapt and thrive. This resonates with the CLEAR Model®, underscoring how culture, leadership, and adaptability together drive business agility.

Culture and Engaged Culture

The Culture pillar of the CLEAR Model® centres on cultivating a learning environment, embracing transparency, and nurturing adaptability – all fundamental to business agility. It aligns directly with the *'Engaged Culture'* domain from the Business Agility Institute, which spotlights the importance of fostering a learning organization, practising *courageous transparency*, embedding psychological safety, and acting as one.

Encouraging open communication and removing departmental barriers helps unify diverse groups under a shared goal. The CLEAR Model® offers practical assessment tools that help leaders pinpoint cultural gaps and then design targeted improvements. After establishing a supportive culture, leadership orchestrates conditions where Agile approaches can truly thrive.

Leadership and People-First Leadership

Within CLEAR, Leadership establishes the tone for Agile practices by highlighting vision, empowerment, and adaptability. Leaders demonstrate these values through openness and engagement, encouraging teams to act autonomously and think proactively. This dovetails with the 'People-First Leadership' domain, which promotes trust, accountability, and each individual's full potential.

By practising radical transparency, leaders reinforce agility's transformational power. This authenticity makes employees feel valued and energized, enhancing both culture and strategic alignment.

Execution and Value-Based Delivery

Execution in CLEAR translates Agile thinking into consistent, value-focused initiatives that serve organizational goals. This aligns with Value-Based Delivery – working on high-impact tasks early and staying ready for new opportunities.

Iterative feedback loops keep teams customer-centric, continuously updating priorities as needs shift. The CLEAR Model® interweaves regular refinement and feedback to ensure execution remains aligned with an evolving marketplace.

Adaptability and Flexible Operations

Adaptability within CLEAR underscores how rapidly an organization can pivot in volatile markets. This vision complements Flexible Operations, covering seamless strategy adjustments, fluid team structures, and risk-aware governance.

Practising scenario planning and forward-thinking leadership helps teams restructure swiftly. By making adaptability a core value, organizations maintain momentum despite market turbulence.

Responsiveness and Responsive Customer-Centricity

Responsiveness in CLEAR centres on swift, data-driven decisions shaped by continuous feedback. This concept links directly to Responsive Customer-Centricity, emphasizing deep customer understanding and proactive assimilation of fresh ideas.

Establishing real-time data channels enables immediate feedback and quick product refinements. The CLEAR framework advocates for user-insight mechanisms, like customer feedback loops or analytics dashboards, so leaders can stay steps ahead of the competition.

Validating the CLEAR Model® Principles

The principles embedded in the CLEAR Model® are reinforced by external research findings. The *Evolution of the Agile Organization* report from PA Consulting highlights five critical dimensions that define an Agile organization. These dimensions closely align with the pillars of the CLEAR Model® and further validate the approach:

- **Centre on Your Customer**: Agile organizations prioritize customer needs in decision-making, integrating feedback loops and co-creation processes. This aligns with **Responsiveness**, where rapid customer insight drives adaptability.
- **Speed Up Time-to-Value**: Successful Agile businesses reduce cycle times, iterating quickly to deliver continuous value. This echoes **Execution**, ensuring teams translate agility into measurable outcomes.
- **Build to Evolve**: Agility is not a one-time transformation but an ongoing process requiring structural flexibility and cultural adaptability. This mirrors **Adaptability**, where an organization remains resilient in shifting markets.
- **Design for Simplicity**: Flattening hierarchies and reducing bureaucracy enhances agility and responsiveness. This complements *Culture and Leadership*, reinforcing decentralized decision-making and lean operations.

- **Liberate Your People**: Empowering employees at all levels fosters innovation and rapid problem-solving. This resonates with *People-First Leadership*, which encourages trust, autonomy, and accountability.

By assessing their organizations against both the CLEAR Model® and these research-backed dimensions, leaders can ensure they are embedding agility holistically rather than treating it as a process-driven initiative.

Embedding Sustainability and Ethics in Business Agility

Adaptive leaders must see agility's potential for broader impact, beyond short-term profit. Tying iterative cycles to ethical goals, like green initiatives, can yield significant gains. A global consumer goods firm integrated an environmental lens into retrospectives, slashing packaging waste by roughly 30% over two years.

When combined with Agile approaches, ethical frameworks, or DEI (diversity, equity, and inclusion) goals flourish. Emphasizing 'Agile for good' fosters societal impact while boosting brand reputation. Meanwhile, upholding professional standards ensures Agile's credibility remains solid.

Tip: Pair every profit KPI with one eco-social KPI so decisions stay balanced.

Professionalizing Agile for Long-Term Credibility

As Agile soared in popularity, some corners commercialized it heavily, diluting its essence. To sustain effectiveness, Agile practitioners must maintain ethical standards, robust coaching standards, and peer-reviewed best practices.

Leaders Can Champion Professional Integrity by:

- Encouraging Transparent Certifications: Focus on real mastery, not superficial badges.
- Promoting Peer-Reviewed Principles: Keep Agile knowledge evolving and validated.
- Upholding Coaching Values: Emphasize client-centric solutions over dogmatic frameworks.

When agility is regarded as a serious, ethically grounded discipline, it can expand responsibly into broader 'purposeful' initiatives that benefit society and the planet.

Purposeful Agile – Aligning Agile with Broader Societal and Environmental Goals

Purposeful Agile extends beyond corporate walls, addressing climate issues or social inequities. By hooking iterative processes to philanthropic or green objectives, businesses can innovate solutions that tackle global challenges. For instance, a clothing retailer using Agile cycles to test sustainable materials or a social enterprise refining processes to better serve underprivileged communities.

Examples

- **Patagonia:** Aligning Agile thinking with sustainability, emphasizing repairs and ethical supply chains.
- **Unilever:** Driving agility in product R&D to reduce waste and adopt greener formulas.

Adaptive leaders see agility not just as a revenue multiplier but as a means to do more with their resources, proactively benefiting people and the planet.

Business Agility in Practice

Large, customer-centric enterprises like Tesla quickly iterate on products, bridging R&D with real-world user data. Amazon's relentless focus on customer service and rapid experimentation exemplifies enterprise agility. These methods reflect Jim Highsmith's call to return to agility's core values – simplicity, adaptiveness, and a focus on people.

Reimagining Agile further underscores that these core values – creativity, continuous learning, and human-centred approaches – should unify entire organizations. Companies that internalize these values are more likely to remain resilient and quickly adapt to new opportunities.

Jim Highsmith suggests using Agile as a compass, balancing processes with responsiveness. By focusing on outcomes, not rituals, Tesla and Amazon stay ahead of competitors while placing the customer front and centre.

Agile's drive is not limited to boosting productivity or cutting time-to-market; it extends to building an ethical, sustainable, and innovative ecosystem. Balancing short-term sprints with long-term visions, these companies keep Agile from devolving into rigid 'corporate theatre'.

Addressing Psychological Safety and Burnout

Though Agile offers numerous advantages, it's not without challenges. Studies reveal that heavy workloads contribute to high burnout rates, particularly in software engineering and other tech-centric roles. Ensuring a psychologically safe environment encourages open discussions around workload, enabling teams to adapt processes to avoid burnout.

The pervasive 'do more with less' culture seen in startups is unsustainable and contradicts true Agile principles. Adaptive leadership must shift from survival mode to sustainable growth by balancing resources, capacity, and psychological safety. Leaders should actively monitor workload demands, ensuring teams have adequate support rather than pushing them into perpetual overdrive.

Psychological safety is critical in hybrid teams, yet many employees report feeling disconnected and overlooked compared to their in-office colleagues. This is particularly true for younger professionals, as research suggests employees in their teens and early 20s benefit from at least four days in the office to build relationships and gain informal mentorship.

The cultural divide in hybrid work is also widening. While some leaders view remote work as detrimental to productivity, others see it as an opportunity to tap into underrepresented talent, such as parents, caregivers, and those with disabilities, who might otherwise struggle with rigid office demands. Organizations must acknowledge both perspectives and design hybrid models that prioritize fairness, career progression, and genuine inclusion rather than defaulting to 'one-size-fits-all' mandates.

Return-to-office policies have highlighted clear divisions between senior management and operational staff. Leaders often prefer employees to return physically, believing it improves collaboration. Operational teams, however, frequently prefer remote options due to improvements in flexibility and work-life balance. This tension risks widening cultural divides unless leaders actively manage expectations and clearly communicate the reasons behind policy decisions. Additionally, mental health and employee well-being must be a priority as teams adjust to increased office presence after long periods of working remotely.

Adaptive leaders should integrate mental health considerations into Agile transformations. This includes realistic sprint commitments, balanced workload distributions, and supportive leadership that addresses stress factors early. An organization that invests in well-being fosters both employee satisfaction and long-term agility. Yet deeper structural barriers also affect how far agility can go.

Human Debt – The Balance Between Agility and Employee Well-Being

Agility has revolutionized business responsiveness, but at what cost? The concept of Human Debt refers to the long-term impact of Agile work practices on employee well-being. Just as companies monitor technical debt, they must also track the cumulative stress, fatigue, and burnout caused by Agile intensity.

Key Aspects of Human Debt

- **Pace vs Sustainability**: Agile promotes rapid iteration, but relentless cycles can exhaust teams without built-in recovery.
- **Psychological Safety and Workload Management**: Teams require mechanisms to balance autonomy with structured workload management.
- **Measuring Human Impact**: Just as velocity and throughput are measured, organizations must track well-being metrics and adjust Agile practices accordingly.

Leaders must ensure Agile does not become a productivity trap, where constant iteration leads to exhaustion rather than sustainable progress.

Conclusion

Leaders who look beyond IT and embrace agility across finance, HR, marketing, and other core functions unleash the full potential of adaptive thinking. As seen in this chapter, scaling Agile ways of working requires a willingness to disrupt old silos, sponsor open communication, and guide teams toward continuous learning and user-centred innovation.

Consider where your own organization might be holding back progress. Do budget cycles clash with iterative experimentation? Are compliance rules and decision hierarchies slowing timely action? By embedding Agile values – collaboration, rapid feedback, and empowered autonomy – into every department, businesses can move from pockets of 'Agile' activity to a truly responsive enterprise.

Enterprise agility isn't merely about following a certain framework or running a set of sprints. It's a leadership duty that resets how an organization plans, executes, and matures. Those who align their teams around this mindset will discover repeated gains and stand ready for tomorrow's demands.

As an adaptive leader, integrating the CLEAR Model® equips you to drive transformative change. Embracing its core elements not only strengthens your organization's resilience but also empowers you to make agile, informed decisions amid uncertainty.

The next chapter builds on these ideas, providing concrete tactics for scaling agility across multiple departments and ensuring the organization remains adaptable at all levels.

Call to Action

As an adaptive leader, keep extending agility beyond its usual boundaries. Identify where departmental routines slow progress, whether in marketing campaign approvals or HR's talent strategies. Then, each function is linked to Agile fundamentals: regular feedback loops, delegated decision-making, and open data sharing. Urge your teams to examine old assumptions and promote unified efforts, ensuring that agility becomes a shared mindset rather than a set of scattered initiatives.

Key Takeaways

- **Enterprise-Wide Agility Needs Leadership and Culture**: Departments embrace autonomy when leaders champion it.
- **Scaling Frameworks Must Stay True to Agile Roots**: SAFe or similar methods should enhance collaboration, not stifle it.
- **Cross-Functional Teams Drive Better Results**: Frequent reviews and collaborative squads push outcomes forward.
- **Continuous Learning Underpins Growth**: Regular reflection avoids rigid approaches and keeps efforts aligned.
- **Well-Managed Workloads Protect Enthusiasm**: Fair duties and mutual trust allow staff to maintain energy and avoid burnout.

CLEAR Model® Connection

- **Culture**: Place trust at the centre of group interactions so fresh ideas can emerge.
- **Leadership**: Leaders demonstrate openness and curiosity, showing that agility goes beyond mechanical practices.
- **Execution**: Teams focus on short, iterative achievements that align with bigger goals, adapting as feedback arises.
- **Adaptability**: Encourage small experiments and scenario thinking so teams can pivot when conditions shift.
- **Responsiveness**: Establish quick feedback loops and transparent data to capture emerging opportunities promptly.

Key Takeaway: Scaling Agile requires weaving these five pillars into daily practice, ensuring your entire organization stays nimble and prepared for the next challenge.

Functional Agility Scorecard

- **Metrics to Evaluate:**
  - o Select two or three agility indicators per department (e.g. speed of decisions, openness to experimentation, user focus).
- **Scoring Criteria:**
  - o Rate each department's agility on a 1–5 scale.
- **Action Plan:**
  - o Discuss improvement steps in monthly leadership huddles.
  - o Adjust support or training as needed.

Cross-Team Pilot Approach

- **Pilot Initiative:**
  - o Choose an initiative that involves at least two non-technical departments (e.g. finance and HR).
- **Execution:**
  - o Form a dedicated squad to run short sprints.
  - o Share insights weekly.
- **Learning and Scaling:**
  - o Document what works and what doesn't.
  - o Publicize results to encourage multi-department collaboration.

Chapter Summary

Expanding Agile methods beyond IT builds a culture of trust, empowered leadership, focused delivery, flexible structures, and swift action. This won't be instant, yet with perseverance and the right support, you can create an organization that adapts, learns, and grows through every stage of its journey.

By encouraging cross-functional synergy, balancing people's workloads, and staying close to user feedback, leaders can shape an environment where agility stands firm across all departments, becoming a collective way of working rather than a passing initiative.

9

Operational Agility – Breaking Down Silos for Adaptive Execution

If you want to go fast, go alone. If you want to go far, go together.
African Proverb

What You'll Gain

- **For Senior Leaders and Executives**: Learn how to expand Agile far beyond IT into finance, HR, operations, and more to build a cohesive, responsive organization.
- **For Mid-Level Leaders**: Discover ways to adapt Agile to the unique needs of different departments, aligning each function around shared goals and continuous learning.
- **For Students or Early-Career Professionals**: Understand how iterative thinking, cross-department collaboration, and a unifying mindset can transform traditional business structures into adaptive, future-ready enterprises.

Agility Can't Stop at Teams – It Must Scale Across the Entire Organization

Adaptive leaders must realize that business agility extends well beyond tech teams. Jenny, COO of a healthcare provider, saw her IT squads flourish under Agile, yet finance, HR, and operations lagged behind. The CFO asked, *'Agile's fine for tech, but does it really work everywhere else?'* The answer: Truly transformative agility emerges once iterative, adaptive thinking permeates every function.

Many organizations claim to be Agile, but their structure is anything but.

- HR still operates with slow hiring and rigid job roles.
- Finance still demands detailed annual budgets.
- Operations still follow strict, top-down approval chains.
- Marketing still runs long campaign cycles that don't adapt to customer needs.

Agile teams can't succeed if the broader organization operates in silos.

Operational Agility ensures that every function – HR, Finance, Marketing, and beyond – adapts to change with the same speed, flexibility, and responsiveness as Agile teams.

Governance is often the final barrier. Many teams evolve, but their organizations still govern with policies that belong to another decade. If agility is going to thrive, governance needs to shift from control to enablement. It must support change, not stall it.

At the core of this shift is a blunt reality: productivity is now a make-or-break capability. Execution isn't just about speed or quality – it's about translating strategic priorities into daily progress across every layer of the business. When done well, it becomes a durable edge.

This chapter explores:

- The key barriers preventing Operational Agility.
- How HR, Finance, and other business functions must adapt.
- Practical strategies for breaking down silos and enabling cross-functional agility.

The Role of Agile Coaches in Expanding Business Agility

One of the most overlooked but essential components of organizational Agile transformation is the role of coaches. Many organizations invest in training but lack internal expertise to guide teams through the transition. Agile coaches serve as transformation enablers, helping businesses bridge the gap between theory and real-world application.

Effective Agile Coaches

- Facilitate the application of Agile concepts in business environments beyond IT.
- Help leaders foster a culture of psychological safety and iterative learning.
- Provide structured guidance to prevent Agile from becoming a mechanical process rather than a mindset shift.

Companies that integrate experienced Agile coaches early in their transformation see higher adoption rates and sustained agility across business functions.

Personal Reflection

Over the years, I've personally coached leaders who discovered that even small steps toward agility can produce meaningful change outside traditional tech settings. One Sales department greatly improved its pipeline management by shifting from quarterly reviews to short, focused cycles. In another case, HR adapted sprint retrospectives to enhance staff well-being programmes, leading to faster improvements and a noticeable boost in employee satisfaction. Although each department had its own learning curve, these successes underscored an important truth: Agility thrives wherever teams dare to iterate, collaborate, and experiment.

This chapter delves into how organizations can expand agility beyond IT, weaving iterative thinking into every department. By blending practical steps, real-world anecdotes, and an awareness of cultural subtleties, you'll discover new ways to align people around common goals. The result is a stronger, more adaptive environment where every function, not just software development, contributes to sustainable growth.

Challenges and Strategies for Scaling Business Agility

A global telecom firm successfully introduced Agile in software but struggled to expand it to HR and procurement. Siloed budgeting and a risk-averse culture slowed progress. By overhauling HR policies to support dynamic teams, shifting budgeting to rolling forecasts, and introducing lighter governance, they saw cross-team collaboration improve and product lead times drop.

The Number One Killer of Agility: Functional Silos

One of the biggest obstacles to scaling agility across an organization is the persistence of functional silos. These silos create rigid, disconnected workflows that hinder collaboration, delay decision-making, and slow down responsiveness.

- Traditional functions operate on their own timelines, disrupting cross-team collaboration.
- Teams remain focused on departmental objectives rather than broader organizational goals.
- Critical decisions take too long because different departments do not share priorities or data effectively.

A stark example of this challenge comes from Nokia. The company's slow response to the smartphone revolution was not due to a lack of innovation – its research teams had developed advanced mobile technologies well ahead of competitors. The real issue was internal silos. There was little collaboration between R&D, marketing, and leadership, which meant that breakthrough ideas failed to reach the market in time. Meanwhile, companies like Apple and Google moved quickly by ensuring seamless coordination between product development, marketing, and executive strategy.

Silos create friction. Agile organizations work to remove it.

Key Challenges in Scaling Business Agility

- **Resistance to Change**: Long-standing roles and hierarchies often resist Agile's collaborative style.
- **Cultural Barriers**: Without psychological safety, new ways of working cause confusion or burnout.
- **Leadership Gaps**: Agility demands executive buy-in – leaders must do more than give lip service.
- **Coordination Across Units**: Different departments can find it tough to align in short cycles.
- **Rigid Processes**: Complex structures block quick pivots and iterative feedback.
- **Legal and Regulatory Constraints**: Strict rules can limit Agile flexibility, especially in finance or healthcare.

Strategies to Overcome These Barriers

- **Invest in Training**: Educate employees and leaders on Agile principles and cross-team alignment.
- **Lead by Example**: Leadership must show, not just tell – model adaptive behaviours.
- **Start Small, Scale Up**: Use pilot projects to highlight benefits and build internal advocates.
- **Foster Continuous Improvement**: Encourage safe-to-fail experiments for learning.
- **Break Down Silos**: Create cross-functional squads and unify metrics.
- **Manage Compliance**: Work with legal and regulatory experts to embed agility within constraints.

By deliberately tackling these pain points, leaders can expand agility beyond IT teams and build an enterprise that swiftly responds to market shifts.

Bureaucracy kills agility. Buurtzorg, the Dutch healthcare company, eliminated layers of management, giving nurses full autonomy to make decisions for patient care. The result? Faster responses, higher satisfaction, and more engaged employees.

Adaptive leaders create freedom within a framework, ensuring essential guardrails exist while allowing teams to self-manage. They remove policies that serve no real purpose and replace them with trust-based decision-making.

Integrating Lessons from Agile Criticism

Scaling agility enterprise-wide doesn't ignore valid critiques. Common criticisms can guide how to refine your approach:

- **Balancing Strategy and Iteration**: The CLEAR Model® unites daily sprints with broader strategic aims.
- **Avoiding 'Corporate Theatre'**: Culture changes, not just ceremonies, ensure authenticity.
- **Embracing Ethics and Sustainability**: Factor in inclusive practices, data privacy, and green initiatives.

Practical Steps

- **Balanced Scorecards**: Align Agile efforts with strategic and ethical targets.
- **Agile Workshops**: Reinforce Agile values across all business units.
- **Frequent Feedback Loops**: Adapt quickly while maintaining accountability.

Example: A multinational financial services firm overcame siloed divisions by piloting a single Agile division, cutting time-to-market by 30% and raising staff engagement by 20%. They then scaled successes across other departments, bridging leadership gaps early to sustain momentum.

Improving Task-Based Feedback

When feedback centres on tasks and results rather than personal traits, teams feel safer to experiment and share ideas. This approach helps avoid blame, reduces defensiveness, and directs everyone's attention to outcomes instead of personalities. For instance, if a project slips behind schedule, discuss the tasks or processes that need refining, rather than singling out individuals. Leaders who shift the lens from 'Who messed up?' to 'How can the team refine its work?' create a healthier environment for ongoing learning.

Operationalizing Agile Across the Business

Julian, a transformation lead at a finance firm, found that 'Agile is a tech thing' was the biggest barrier. Instead of forcing frameworks, he tied agility to business objectives. Finance experimented with iterative funding, HR with Agile hiring, and executives explored adaptive decision-making. The outcome? Agility was no longer pigeonholed in IT – it took root in the entire organization.

When scaling beyond IT, avoid drowning in bureaucracy. The goal is to embed Agile thinking. Spotify's squads and tribes exemplify how autonomy meshes with alignment. Where standard frameworks like SAFe or LeSS can become cumbersome, the CLEAR Model® offers a flexible leadership lens to keep agility dynamic.

Context Matters: Finance might adopt rolling forecasts, while HR might prefer itera-tive feedback cycles. Each function customizes Agile to its reality – the synergy of these varied adaptations yields a unified, enterprise-wide mindset.

Scaling Agile Beyond Frameworks: Decomposition and Recombination

Traditional approaches to scaling Agile, such as SAFe or LeSS, often focus on adding hierarchical layers to coordinate multiple teams. While these frameworks bring structure, they also introduce rigidity, reducing an organization's ability to adapt quickly. Instead of viewing scaling as a top-down implementation, an alternative approach – rooted in complexity science and the work of Dave Snowden – emphasizes decomposition and recombination.

Decomposition, a concept from complexity theory, is the process of breaking down large, complex systems – whether they are teams, projects, or workflows – into smaller, autonomous units that can operate independently. This fragmentation allows for flexibility, reducing dependencies and enabling teams to adapt at their own pace. However, breaking things apart is only half of the equation.

Recombination, also drawn from Snowden's work, is the act of dynamically reintegrat-ing these decomposed elements into new configurations based on evolving needs. Rather than enforcing rigid structures, recombination allows teams, processes, and even entire business functions to reform in ways that maximize responsiveness and innovation.

This approach moves beyond the assumption that agility at scale requires a linear replication of small-team Agile practices. Instead, it recognizes that complex systems thrive when individual components can interact dynamically, adjusting to context rather than adhering to predefined frameworks. Snowden's principles highlight that true agility comes not from layering processes but from understanding how to break down complex-ity into manageable parts and reassemble them in ways that allow for emergence and adaptability.

The Problem with Linear Scaling

Many large organizations default to rigid frameworks that attempt to scale Agile by rep-lication rather than adaptation. However, true agility comes from understanding how to deconstruct and reassemble teams and workflows to match evolving business needs. However, complexity theory suggests that effective scaling is not a matter of linear expan-sion but rather fragmentation followed by adaptive recombination.

For example, rather than creating rigid organizational layers, companies can design loosely coupled teams that dynamically form and reform around emerging priorities. Spotify's Squads, Tribes, and Guilds model reflects this principle by enabling small, focused teams to work autonomously while maintaining alignment with organizational objectives.

How Decomposition and Recombination Enable Scaling Agility

1. **Breaking Work into Modular Components**
   - o Instead of treating business agility as a monolithic transformation, organizations should decompose workstreams into smaller, interdependent functions. This enables faster learning cycles and more efficient allocation of resources.
   - o **Example**: Finance teams moving from annual budgeting to rolling forecasts, adjusting plans in response to real-time market data.

2. **Contextual Recombination for Flexibility**
   - o Recombining decomposed elements allows teams and functions to collaborate fluidly rather than being bound to a fixed operating model.
   - o **Example**: HR moving from fixed job roles to skill-based teams, dynamically forming and dissolving based on the needs of the business.

3. **Ecosystem-Wide Agility**
   - o Scaling isn't limited to internal operations. Organizations must decompose value chains, identifying where collaboration with external partners can create more responsive ecosystems.
   - o **Example**: Automotive manufacturers working with software firms to rapidly iterate on in-car digital services instead of locking features into years-long development cycles.

Traditional scaling frameworks often introduce unnecessary complexity and slow adaptation. By focusing on decomposition and recombination, organizations can scale in a way that maintains flexibility while avoiding rigid hierarchies. Breaking down work into smaller, autonomous units allows for emergent design, ensuring that agility remains dynamic rather than static. Leaders should embrace this modular approach to create systems that can evolve as business needs shift.

A key enabler of operational agility is Lean thinking, which refines Agile by eliminating waste, optimizing flow, and focusing on value creation across all business functions.

Lean Thinking and Agile: Eliminating Waste to Maximize Value

While Agile is often associated with software development, its roots share many principles with Lean thinking – a philosophy that originated from Toyota's production system. At its core, Lean focuses on eliminating waste (muda), optimizing flow, and maximizing value delivery – all of which directly complement Agile practices.

Key Lean Principles That Enhance Agile Effectiveness Include

- **Eliminating waste (Muda)**: Identifying activities that do not add customer value and removing them, reducing bottlenecks and inefficiencies.

- **Continuous Improvement (Kaizen)**: A mindset of small, incremental improvements that aligns with Agile's iterative cycles.
- **Pull Systems and Flow**: Delivering work just-in-time based on customer demand, improving efficiency, and reducing delays.
- **Empowered Teams**: Lean advocates decentralized decision-making, much like Agile's emphasis on self-organizing teams.

How Lean Strengthens Agile in Business Operations

In Agile transformations beyond IT, Lean thinking helps organizations focus on outcomes over output. For example, instead of just completing sprints or measuring velocity, teams should optimize value flow across the organization, whether in product development, HR, finance, or customer experience.

The Combination of Lean + Agile Enables Organizations to:

- Reduce delays in decision-making (**Lean Flow**).
- Increase efficiency without sacrificing flexibility (**Agile Responsiveness**).
- Align teams around delivering value rather than completing tasks.

By integrating Lean principles into Agile transformations, organizations can achieve a more holistic, sustainable agility that extends across all business functions.

But this alignment between Lean and Agile only works when Lean is properly understood. In many organizations, that's not the case. Lean is often misused – applied as a shortcut to cut costs rather than as a way to improve value delivery. When that happens, it not only weakens the system but also undermines trust and long-term capability.

When Lean Gets Lost: Misuse and Misunderstanding

There's a growing misconception that Lean is synonymous with cutting costs, reducing headcount, or pushing teams to do more with less. In some companies, Lean is reduced to a blunt instrument – used to eliminate roles under the guise of efficiency while overlooking the human cost and long-term risk to capability.

But that's not Lean.

At its core, Lean is about eliminating *waste*, not people. It's about learning what customers truly value and continuously improving how that value is delivered – with dignity, respect, and shared purpose. When Lean is misunderstood as a cost-cutting exercise, it breaks trust, damages morale, and erodes the very flow it aims to optimize. This distortion turns Lean into 'cut' thinking – focused on short-term optics, not long-term resilience.

This is where agility offers a better lens.

Agility begins with adaptability, not austerity. It doesn't assume we know the answer – it encourages learning through iteration, collaboration, and context-based decision-making. Rather than squeezing more output from fewer hands, agility expands the potential of teams by encouraging experimentation, distributed leadership, and psychological safety.

Lean, when done right, can complement agility by refining flow and clarifying value. But when used as a tool for downsizing rather than improvement, it undermines both performance and trust. Agility puts people at the centre of change. It adapts with them, not around them.

The most successful organizations don't just claim to be Lean – they live it through a culture of reflection, respect, and purposeful improvement. But when Lean is misapplied, agility becomes the safeguard. It reminds leaders to ask better questions – not 'How can we reduce headcount?' but 'How can we improve value while keeping people engaged, skilled, and proud of their work?'

Agility protects what Lean *should* be.

As organizations mature in their internal Agile and Lean practices, a new challenge emerges – extending agility beyond their own walls. True business agility isn't confined to departments or functions; it must flow across the broader network of partners, vendors, and collaborators. That's where ecosystem coaching comes in.

Ecosystem Coaching – Agile Beyond Single Organizations

A multinational automaker found its suppliers slowed Agile cycles. Their fix? Embedding Agile coaches within supplier teams. Over six months, the entire value chain became more responsive, forging stronger alignment and fewer bottlenecks. This underscores that agility doesn't stop at your organizational boundary – it extends to partners, clients, and industries.

Ecosystem Coaching Fosters

- **Industry-Wide Collaboration**: Sharing Agile practices across supply networks.
- **Cross-Company Learning**: Building Agile knowledge collectively.
- **Public Sector Influence**: Some governments adopt Agile for policy-making, broadening agility's reach.

In short, agility is an ecosystem-wide game. By connecting with external stakeholders who share iterative methods, you reduce friction and spark novel solutions.

The next section explores why context is the defining factor in successful Agile scaling and how businesses can adapt accordingly.

Scaling with Context in Mind

Scaling Agile across an enterprise is a complex undertaking, often fraught with challenges when a uniform approach is applied. Context-driven agility ensures that scaling efforts respect the unique needs of each department while maintaining alignment with overarching business objectives.

For example, an HR department focusing on talent acquisition may find value in Kanban's visual workflow, while a product development team thrives using Scrum's iterative cycles. An effective way to ensure agility aligns with business functions is through decomposition and recombination – breaking work into modular units and reforming them dynamically to match shifting priorities. This approach allows agility to complement, rather than disrupt, operational efficiency.

This approach also mitigates resistance to change, as teams feel empowered to adapt methods to their realities. Businesses can scale agility effectively by focusing on outcomes rather than adherence to predefined frameworks, fostering a culture of collaboration and adaptability across the organization.

Applying Decomposition and Recombination to Different Business Functions

While decomposition and recombination provide a powerful model for scaling agility, their application varies depending on the business function. Different areas of an organization require different approaches to maintain agility without introducing unnecessary complexity.

Finance: From Annual Budgeting to Rolling Forecasts

Traditional finance functions often rely on rigid, annual budgeting cycles that struggle to adapt to real-time economic changes. By decomposing financial planning into rolling forecasts, organizations can adjust their budgets dynamically, responding to new insights rather than being constrained by static plans. This enables more informed decision-making and resource allocation that aligns with shifting priorities.

Human Resources: Breaking Down Job Roles into Skill-Based Teams

HR departments typically organize employees into predefined job descriptions with rigid career paths. However, as businesses require greater adaptability, HR can decompose roles into skill-based teams, where individuals are assigned to projects based on evolving business needs rather than fixed job functions. This model allows organizations to optimize talent deployment and foster continuous learning.

Operations: Fragmenting Supply Chains for Greater Resilience

Supply chain agility is essential for responding to disruptions. Organizations can recombine resources dynamically by decomposing supply chains into smaller, independent units, such as regional distribution hubs or vendor-managed inventory models, to address shifting demands. This approach ensures greater responsiveness in volatile market conditions.

Different business functions require tailored approaches to decomposition and recombination. Finance benefits from rolling forecasts, HR thrives with skill-based teams, and operations gain resilience through decentralized supply chains. Rather than applying a uniform scaling model, leaders should contextualize agility, ensuring that each function adopts modularity to enhance its adaptability and efficiency. By doing so, organizations can sustain agility across all departments, driving long-term responsiveness and innovation.

By scaling with context in mind, organizations can ensure that agility complements, rather than clashes with, departmental goals. Decomposing rigid structures and enabling recombination across teams ensures agility flows beyond product teams, extending into finance, HR, operations, and beyond.

To scale effectively and sustainably, the structure itself must support flow. That's where organizational design frameworks like Team Topologies offer a powerful approach.

Designing for Flow with Team Topologies

Structural agility means more than cross-functional teams – it means designing those teams for flow. The *Team Topologies* model offers a fresh way to do that, advocating for stream-aligned teams that own value end-to-end, supported by enabling and platform teams that reduce cognitive load.

Adaptive leaders don't just shuffle boxes on an org chart – they rethink how work flows through the system. They focus on interaction modes, boundaries, and team purposes, not just headcount. By embracing organizational design principles that prioritize flow and fast feedback, they unlock performance and reduce friction.

Consider this: Is your org designed to deliver software, or designed to manage hierarchy? The difference shows in the speed and quality of your outcomes.

As structure evolves to support flow, Agile practices can extend into every business function, not just product or IT.

Applying Agile Principles Across All Business Functions

Case: A European bank embedded Scrum squads in marketing and HR. Marketing's short cycles replaced annual campaigns, while HR used continuous feedback loops for staff development. Collaboration soared, time-to-market shrank, and satisfaction rose.

Agility Can Reshape Non-tech Domains by:

- **Experimentation**: Real-time iteration in marketing, finance, and HR.
- **Collaboration:** Breaking down departmental barriers.
- **Empowered Teams:** Delegating decisions to the closest stakeholders.

The next sections examine specific departmental stories, from HR to legal, illustrating how Agile fosters innovation, synergy, and responsiveness well beyond IT.

Agile in Human Resources

By **Riina Hellström,** Agile HR pioneer, author (*Agile HR – Deliver Value in a Changing World of Work*)

Human-centric design is fundamental in product development. Just as companies develop products for customers, HR creates and maintains 'people products' for employees, leaders, and candidates. These include processes, frameworks, policies, services, and development – all of which benefit from Agile practices.

Traditionally, HR has operated in silos, with specialists designing processes that may lack deep business understanding or real-world user insights. These are then rolled out company-wide in a one-size-fits-all manner.

Modern HR teams have embraced a user-centric mindset, integrating Agile ways of working to increase value, improve speed, enhance employee experience, modernize people products (Tech and UX), and boost efficiency.

With five generations working together, each with different preferences for communication and collaboration, HR must balance scalable, standardized practices with personalized experiences.

Agile Principles in HR

Here's how Agile principles apply to HR, using onboarding as an example:

- **Human centricity**: Understand user needs, validate assumptions, and design intuitive touchpoints with minimal bureaucracy (while respecting legal and privacy constraints).
  Example: *Replace dull compliance materials with engaging, interactive corporate training.*
- **End-to-end journeys**: Take a holistic view of the employee experience to support success from the start.
  Example: *Align HR, IT, Communications, and Facilities for a seamless onboarding process.*
- **Co-creation, testing, and feedback**: Identify root problems, involve employees early, and test before scaling.
  Example: *Develop and test three versions of a 'first-day experience' with new hires before finalizing.*
- **Product thinking and incremental delivery**: Focus on high-impact changes rather than full-scale overhauls.
  Example: *Improve the most critical onboarding gaps instead of redesigning everything at once.*
- **Quarterly prioritization and capacity management**: Break work into smaller releases and adapt based on business priorities.
  Example: *If an urgent M&A integration arises, HR reprioritizes accordingly.*
- **Release thinking**: Sync HR initiatives with business unit planning cycles for smoother adoption.
- **Continuous improvement**: HR teams evolve their performance over time, often with Agile coaching.
  Example: *Thales' Talent Acquisition team improved performance by 72% YoY by adopting Agile HR practices.*

Unlike software teams, HR often doesn't focus on a single product or value stream, which would make Scrum a poor fit. Agile HR isn't about copying IT methods – it requires a modernized HR mindset and an adaptive approach to Agile. Lean-Agile ways of working must align with HR's value streams and operational realities, ideally guided by professionals who understand both Agile and HR.

Why Agile HR Matters in Business Transformation

For a business to succeed in transformation, HR must be involved early and upskilled in Agile. Otherwise, HR can become a blocker, designing performance, reward, and talent products for traditional line management rather than an Agile, team-based organization. HR must assess and update these products to align with Agile business value streams.

If your HR teams need a modern, human-centric mindset and want to create great people products and experiences, explore the Agile HR Community at agilehrcommunity.com.

Agile in Marketing

By **Pam Ashby**, Marketing Agility Strategist and Coach

Customer centricity is central to Agile working, making marketing a key driver of broader business agility. Marketing identifies, anticipates, and meets customer requirements profitably, forging a deeper understanding of customers' needs and building relationships that power the brand. Agile Marketers use agility to focus on genuine customer delight and tangible business outcomes rather than just staying 'busy'. The five values of the Agile Marketing Manifesto illustrate this:

1. **Focusing on Customer Value and Business Outcomes Over Activity and Outputs**
   Marketers must avoid equating 'busy' with 'productive'. Agile keeps the team value-driven and safeguards against burnout.
2. **Delivering Value Early and Often Over Waiting for Perfection**
   Market changes are too fast for big-bang launches. Sharing work early and gathering real feedback fosters loyalty and buy-in.
3. **Learning Through Experiments and Data Over Opinions and Conventions**
   Relying on past wisdom can waste resources. Test, validate, and ensure branding or content resonates with actual customer needs.
4. **Cross-Functional Collaboration Over Silos and Hierarchy**
   Collaboration – between art directors and copywriters, agencies and clients, or sales and helpdesk – opens new possibilities and fuels innovation.
5. **Responding to Change Over Following a Static Plan**
   Agile marketers iterate in short bursts, testing and adapting to serve audiences more effectively than any long-term fixed plan would allow.

Because marketing shapes behaviour and brand perception, it holds pivotal levers for advancing enterprise agility. By aligning value delivery across teams, marketers influence the organization's success in staying customer-focused and responsive.

Real-World Example: NatWest Group

In 2021, NatWest Group marketing aimed to:

- Become more customer-centric
- Increase speed to market
- Reduce hand-offs between teams
- Accelerate strategic initiatives

Challenges

- Changing ways of working for a 220-strong marketing function
- Building new mindsets alongside Agile processes

- Planning iteratively based on evidence and feedback
- Prioritizing effectively across the entire function

Key Learnings

- Mindset outweighs method
- Jargon can obstruct the clarity of purpose
- Agile requires finding the most important tasks, dividing them, testing, refining, and improving
- Transparency and collaboration sharpen goal-setting and prioritization
- Regular interaction, coupled with enjoyment, fosters strong teams

Results

- Clear goals backed by robust prioritization
- Autonomy to deprioritize low-value tasks
- 51% increase in finance applications from one campaign
- Podcast listening exceeding targets by over 240%

For further insights into Agile marketing, consider free Marketing Agility Community events on Meetup.com or join the Agile Marketing Alliance.

Agile in Finance

By **Daniela Forsgård**, Agile CFO

Achieving full business agility requires applying Agile principles to finance operations and business planning.

Traditionally, budgeting has been the backbone of financial planning, yet it remains a rigid, time-consuming process. Companies spend months setting an annual budget, often led by siloed finance teams focused on detail and control. In a complex and evolving business environment, these budgets quickly become outdated, limiting their usefulness in decision-making. Meanwhile, finance teams continue producing heavy variance analyses that add little business value.

Agile financial planning enables continuous adaptation to market conditions while fostering a finance team that is responsive, collaborative, and business-focused.

Agile Budgeting

An Agile budgeting process is iterative, flexible, fast, and decentralized. Instead of an annual plan that quickly loses relevance, Agile budgeting follows a rolling schedule, typically with quarterly planning cycles. In this approach, nine months are reassessed, and three new months are planned each quarter. The rhythm should align with business needs and market dynamics.

Frequent updates improve flexibility and enable just-in-time resource allocation, ensuring funds are directed to the highest-value initiatives. By first defining strategic priorities and then setting financial plans accordingly, organizations ensure resources drive meaningful outcomes.

To keep the process efficient, financial planning inputs must be simplified and supported by automation, streamlining data collection and analysis. A decentralized approach encourages local decision-making, fostering trust, engagement, and accountability. Transparency, combined with a balance of top-down guidance and bottom-up initiatives, accelerates execution while reducing the need for excessive oversight. Making financial planning a regular part of daily operations further strengthens adaptability.

The Agile Finance Team

An Agile finance team is collaborative, responsive to change, and focused on delivering insights that drive business value.

By working across functions, finance teams remain close to the business and better support strategic decision-making. Acting as trusted business partners not only improves business outcomes but also increases motivation and professional growth within the finance team.

A culture of continuous improvement fosters an Agile mindset, helping finance teams embrace change as an opportunity rather than a disruption. Adopting elements of Agile ways of working improves efficiency, shifting the focus from rigid control to value creation. This results in more relevant reporting and analysis, providing better insights for informed decision-making.

The Agile Finance Manifesto (www.theagilefinancemanifesto.org) outlines values and principles that bring finance and Agile closer together.

By embracing Agile budgeting and an adaptive finance team, organizations gain greater flexibility, stronger collaboration, improved efficiency, and better decision-making, positioning themselves ahead of the competition.

Agile in Sales

By **Marina Alex**, Modern Management Expert

Traditional Sales No Longer Work

Sales has changed. Cold calls, aggressive pitches, and manipulation tactics no longer deliver results. Buyers now control the process – researching products, reading reviews, and comparing options before engaging with sales. A decade ago, salespeople had the upper hand. Now, customers often know exactly what they want before a conversation even begins.

Modern buyers don't need a pushy salesperson; they need an advisor – someone who understands their challenges, offers insights, and guides them toward the right decision. Companies that fail to adapt face declining sales, unresponsive prospects, and outreach that feels intrusive rather than helpful.

The Sales and Marketing Divide

A longstanding disconnect between sales and marketing is one of the biggest barriers to success. Marketing focuses on lead generation, while sales are measured by closed deals. The result? A broken funnel. Marketing blames sales for not converting leads. Sales blame marketing for poor-quality prospects. Millions are wasted, and customers experience a disjointed buying journey.

The Solution: Agile in Sales

Agile in Sales eliminates silos by aligning sales, marketing, and post-sales teams around a shared goal – revenue. With common KPIs and cross-functional collaboration, businesses remove inefficiencies and create a seamless experience from first contact to ongoing service.

Instead of leads being tossed between departments like a hot potato, Agile in Sales ensures an integrated, continuous process, maximizing conversions and customer satisfaction.

A Real-World Example: The TV Shopping Success

A TV shopping company in Tennessee faced stagnating sales. Instead of hiring more staff, they formed a cross-functional team, integrating sales, marketing, and content creation to produce TV content that directly drove sales.

The result? $20 million in additional revenue within a year. Same people, same company – a radically different approach. The key was breaking silos and fostering collaboration.

How to Implement Agile in Sales

Businesses can apply Agile in Sales with three simple steps:

- **Joint Planning Sessions**: Sales and marketing align on objectives and strategy at the start of each week.
- **Regular Demonstrations (Demos)**: Weekly reviews showcase what worked and what didn't and refine strategies based on real customer data.
- **Agile Retrospectives**: Teams analyse performance, gather customer feedback, and continuously improve.

The Power of Retrospectives: Why They Drive Sales

Unlike traditional sales reviews, which focus on blame and missed quotas, Agile retrospectives centre on learning and growth. Teams reflect on:

- What strategies delivered the best results?
- Where did customers engage most?
- What feedback did customers provide?
- How can we improve next week?

By systematically refining their approach, companies can *double sales* simply by optimizing efforts based on real customer insights.

The Future of Sales Is Agile

Traditional sales tactics are obsolete. Customers demand value, trust, and expertise. Agile in Sales fosters collaboration, aligns incentives, and continuously improves the sales process.

The future of sales isn't about pushing – it's about advising, adapting, and evolving. Companies that embrace Agile in Sales will thrive in this new era of customer-driven selling.

Agile in Legal

By **Ondřej Dvořák**, co-founder at AgiLawyer, Legal Agility Coach

The legal profession is evolving due to technology, cybersecurity risks, shifting client expectations, remote work, regulatory pressures, and alternative service providers. Traditional management often struggles to keep up.

Agile's Role in Legal Complexity

Legal work ranges from the complicated (where expert analysis solves known unknowns, like regulatory compliance) to the complex (where solutions emerge iteratively, such as adapting to AI-driven tools). The Cynefin Framework highlights the need for adaptable strategies. Agile offers legal teams a dynamic, transparent approach – shifting from rigid planning to responsive, data-driven decision-making.

The Agile Legal Manifesto in Practice

While no formal Agile Legal Manifesto exists, Agile principles – designed for software development – translate well into legal work. Collaboration, adaptability, and client-focused delivery help legal teams stay responsive to change.

People and interactions over processes and tools

Strong relationships and direct communication remain central to legal practice. While automation, legal tech, and case management systems improve efficiency, they should enhance – not replace – human expertise. Agile fosters a culture where legal teams engage closely with clients and colleagues to create human-centred solutions.

Delivering value over exhaustive documentation

Legal work is often document-heavy, but excessive perfectionism can slow progress. Agile prioritizes working drafts and iterative feedback – whether for contracts, opinions, or agreements – keeping clients engaged and refining outputs as needed.

Client collaboration over rigid contracts

Legal engagements require detailed contracts, but Agile encourages open communication and regular check-ins, ensuring teams stay aligned with evolving client needs and strengthening trust.

Responding to change over following a fixed plan

Regulatory shifts, new case law, or emerging risks can quickly make static legal strategies obsolete. Agile legal teams use iterative planning to adapt as new developments arise, maintaining both flexibility and stability.

Real-World Examples of Agile in Legal

Legal teams across sectors have successfully adopted Agile to enhance efficiency, transparency, and client engagement:

- **Holubová advokáti (12 professionals – boutique law firm)**
  Specializing in travel law, personal injury, and succession planning, this firm implemented Agile task-tracking tools to improve transparency, prioritization, and collaboration, leading to faster case handling and balanced workloads.
- **KLB Legal (40 professionals – mid-sized firm)**
  Known for capital markets and class-action lawsuits, KLB Legal adopted Agile and Kanban to break down complex legal processes into manageable tasks, improving resource allocation, transparency, and client satisfaction.
- **JetBrains' In-House Legal Team (30 professionals – software company)**
  As part of a global organization with 2,000+ employees, JetBrains' legal team integrated Agile tools like YouTrack to align legal processes with business goals, improving cross-department coordination and compliance tracking.
- **Linking Help NGO (300 pro bono lawyers – humanitarian legal aid)**
  In response to the Russian-Ukrainian War, this NGO used Agile and Kanban to coordinate legal aid across 30 countries. Their system enabled real-time case tracking, rapid response strategies, and transparent collaboration, ensuring timely support for thousands of refugees.

Agile's Impact on Legal Work

Agile provides legal teams with a flexible, structured, and transparent approach to managing complex legal challenges. By embracing iterative processes, client collaboration, and AI-driven efficiency, legal professionals can navigate regulatory shifts, strengthen client relationships, and drive better legal outcomes.

These examples illustrate how Agile principles can be tailored to fit different business functions, enhancing adaptability, collaboration, and customer focus across the organization. By embracing Agile ways of working, departments beyond IT can drive innovation, improve performance, and respond more effectively to the dynamic demands of today's business environments.

Personal Reflection

When I coached the HR department at a fintech organization, they struggled to fill roles quickly. We applied Agile sprints to the recruiting pipeline – daily check-ins, rapid feedback from hiring managers, and consistent iteration on job specs. Hiring time dropped by 20%, and HR gained new respect as a strategic partner.

Beyond these examples, agility continues to prove its value across various sectors, illustrating its adaptability and relevance beyond traditional domains.

Agile Across Industries: From Regulation to Innovation

Agile ways of working are proving valuable far beyond IT, reshaping industries that rely on regulation, risk management, and customer responsiveness. From banking and retail to healthcare and manufacturing, organizations are using Agile principles to enhance decision-making, improve responsiveness, and drive efficiency.

Agile in Banking: Risk and Responsiveness

Financial institutions operate under strict regulations, making agility seem counterintuitive. Yet, banks that embrace Agile improve responsiveness while maintaining compliance. ING Bank, for example, restructured its operations using Agile frameworks to enhance cross-team collaboration, cutting time-to-market for financial products by 30%. Agile methods help banks balance compliance with customer-driven innovation, ensuring new services reach the market without unnecessary delays.

Agile in Retail: Adapting to Consumer Behaviour

Retailers thrive on shifting consumer trends. Agile ways of working help brands iterate on customer feedback, optimize inventory, and personalize shopping experiences. Zara applies Agile principles in its supply chain, adjusting product lines weekly based on real-time sales data, reducing waste, and responding faster to demand shifts. Digital retailers also use Agile-driven A/B testing to refine customer experiences dynamically, demonstrating how agility strengthens business resilience.

Agile in Healthcare: Improving Patient Flow and Care Coordination

Healthcare providers are applying Agile methods to improve efficiency and patient outcomes. For example, some hospitals use Agile principles to optimize surgery scheduling, reducing delays and increasing the number of successful procedures per day. By applying iterative improvements, hospitals enhance patient flow, cut wait times, and create a more responsive healthcare system that adapts to real-time demands.

Agile in Manufacturing: Driving Innovation and Efficiency

Manufacturers are embracing Agile to streamline supply chains and accelerate product development. Companies like Dyson and Lego apply Agile principles to prototype, test, and refine products faster, ensuring they remain at the forefront of innovation. Agile-driven approaches such as modular manufacturing and continuous feedback loops enable faster adaptation to market shifts while reducing waste and inefficiencies.

Agile in Politics: Policy Development and Crisis Response

While government structures are traditionally slow-moving, some have applied Agile thinking to policy-making, emergency response, and citizen services. The UK Government

Digital Service (GDS) introduced Agile frameworks to improve online service efficiency, reducing development cycles from years to months. During the COVID-19 crisis, Agile methods accelerated policy decisions and vaccine rollouts, proving that iterative approaches enhance public sector responsiveness.

By extending Agile beyond IT, industries once seen as rigid or highly regulated are discovering new ways to stay competitive, improve service delivery, and adapt to uncertainty. Success depends on balancing Agile flexibility with industry constraints, ensuring agility enhances, not disrupts, core operations.

Agile in Mergers and Acquisitions: A Competitive Advantage

Mergers and acquisitions (M&A) are complex, high-stakes initiatives where agility is often the difference between success and failure. Traditionally, M&A relies on rigid integration roadmaps, but Agile principles can create faster, more adaptive integration processes.

How Agile Benefits M&A

- **Faster Due Diligence**: Agile enables cross-functional teams to analyse risk iteratively instead of waiting for exhaustive reports.
- **Flexible Integration Plans**: Traditional M&A plans focus on 100-day integrations, often leading to delays. Agile companies use incremental integration (e.g. onboarding key teams first, followed by iterative rollout).
- **Cultural Agility**: The biggest M&A failures stem from cultural misalignment. Agile promotes team-level decision-making, reducing resistance to change.

By embedding Agile thinking into M&A strategy, companies can accelerate value realization and reduce risk.

The benefits of Agile extend beyond corporate giants and regulated industries. Increasingly, non-profits and charities are also leveraging Agile ways of working to navigate funding challenges, manage stakeholder expectations, and maximize social impact.

Agile in the Third Sector – Adapting Agility for Non-Profits

Non-profits and charities face tight budgets, donor expectations, and the challenge of delivering impact efficiently. While agility is often linked to commercial businesses, many non-profits are applying Agile principles to improve collaboration, prioritize resources, and respond quickly to crises.

Why Agility Matters in the Third Sector

- **Resource Constraints**: Agile helps organizations focus on high-impact work, using iterative approaches to test initiatives before committing full resources.

- **Stakeholder Expectations**: Transparency in Agile methods allows for better reporting to donors and funders.
- **Crisis Response**: Many non-profits operate in high-pressure environments. Agile frameworks enable rapid adaptation to changing needs.

Real-World Agile in Non-Profits

RNLI's Agile Response to Funding Challenges

During the pandemic, the Royal National Lifeboat Institution (RNLI) lost 60% of its fundraising income. Agile methods helped them refocus on digital engagement and cost efficiency, keeping operations running despite financial uncertainty.

CleanWaterKenya's Lean-Agile Approach

Facing a 40% funding cut, CleanWaterKenya used weekly Agile sprints to prioritize initiatives, cut costs, and exceed fundraising targets.

How Non-Profits Can Apply Agile

- **Prioritize Impact**: Start small, focusing on quick wins over large, slow-moving projects.
- **Use Data for Fundraising**: Adjust donor engagement based on real-time insights.
- **Break Down Silos**: Encourage cross-functional collaboration across fundraising, operations, and programmes.
- **Test and Adapt**: Pilot initiatives with low-cost experiments before scaling.
- **Track Progress Transparently**: Use iterative reporting to keep stakeholders informed.

As non-profits and charities embrace agility, they increasingly rely on digital tools to enhance fundraising, streamline operations, and engage with stakeholders. This highlights a broader trend – technology as a critical enabler of agility in both social and corporate sectors.

The Role of Technology in Business Agility

Technology underpins Business Agility by driving faster decision-making, seamless collaboration, and real-time adaptability. The right tools enable organizations to respond swiftly to market shifts, customer expectations, and operational disruptions.

Collaboration and Communication

Agile organizations rely on technology to break down silos and foster cross-functional teamwork. Platforms like Slack, Microsoft Teams, and Zoom enable real-time discussions, allowing remote and hybrid teams to align quickly. Integrated workflow tools, such as Miro and Jira, enhance visibility into projects, keeping teams focused on delivering value without unnecessary bottlenecks.

Data-Driven Decision-Making

Business Agility thrives on informed decision-making, where data analytics and AI-powered insights play a crucial role. Platforms like Google Analytics, Power BI, and Tableau provide real-time market trends, customer behaviour insights, and performance metrics. This allows organizations to pivot strategies rapidly, refine product offerings, and personalize customer experiences. For example, retailers leverage predictive analytics to forecast demand and optimize inventory, reducing waste and improving profitability.

Cloud Computing and Scalability

Scalability is a key pillar of agility, and cloud computing enables businesses to expand or contract their operations without heavy infrastructure investments. Amazon Web Services (AWS), Microsoft Azure, and Google Cloud empower companies to deploy solutions faster, scale resources dynamically, and improve disaster recovery resilience. Agile enterprises use cloud-based platforms to ensure teams can access critical data and applications anytime, anywhere.

Automation and AI in Agile Workflows

Automation streamlines repetitive processes, freeing up teams to focus on high-value work. Robotic Process Automation (RPA) tools like UiPath and Automation Anywhere reduce manual effort in finance, HR, and customer support. AI-driven assistants and chatbots improve response times, enhance customer service, and support 24/7 engagement. Agile businesses use AI-powered sentiment analysis to track brand perception and adapt marketing strategies in real-time.

Cybersecurity and Resilience

As agility increases speed, security must keep pace. Cloud-based security solutions, zero-trust architectures, and real-time threat detection ensure that agility does not come at the cost of vulnerabilities. Companies like CrowdStrike, Palo Alto Networks, and Darktrace use AI to detect and neutralize cyber threats before they disrupt operations, maintaining business continuity in an ever-evolving risk landscape.

Technology as the Engine of Agility

When used effectively, technology does more than support agility – it embeds it into daily operations. From AI-driven insights to cloud-based collaboration, businesses that invest in the right tech stack build resilience, responsiveness, and continuous innovation into their DNA.

Measuring Business Agility

Two retail companies attempted to scale Agile, but their results differed significantly. Company A tracked Agile adoption using only team velocity and backlog completion rates, while Company B measured broader indicators – cross-functional collaboration, employee engagement, and customer satisfaction. After a year, Company A saw limited business impact, while Company B improved customer retention by 15% and reduced time-to-market for new products. This comparison highlights the importance of measuring agility beyond IT metrics – aligning it with business value and strategic outcomes.

Organizations must additionally measure progress to verify whether the transition to Business Agility is working. Defining relevant metrics and assessing performance regularly highlights weaknesses and verifies alignment with strategic aims.

Key Metrics

- **Time to Market**: Measuring how quickly products or services are delivered.
- **Customer Satisfaction Scores**: Assessing how well customer needs are met.
- **Employee Engagement Levels**: Evaluating involvement and commitment.
- **Adaptability Indicators**: Monitoring the ability to respond to changes.
- **Innovation Rate**: Measuring the frequency of new ideas implemented.

Actionable Steps

- **Set Clear Objectives**: Define what Business Agility means for the organization.
- **Implement Regular Reviews**: Schedule assessments to evaluate progress.
- **Utilize Feedback Loops**: Gather input from customers and employees.
- **Use Visual Dashboards**: Implement visual aids to monitor metrics effectively.

These measures guide leaders in refining their approach and focusing on areas yielding the biggest impact.

Armed with these metrics, leaders can pinpoint where to refine their approach, guiding the practical steps needed to implement business agility effectively.

Implementing Business Agility in Practice

Real-world adoption demands structured planning that is mindful of each organization's unique context. Essential actions include:

1. **Developing a Roadmap**: Outline transformation phases with clear milestones.
2. **Engaging Stakeholders**: Include employees, customers, and partners for broader buy-in and insights.
3. **Customizing Agile Practices**: Fit methods to your organizational culture – avoid blindly copying frameworks.
4. **Providing Ongoing Support**: Provide coaching, training, and resources for teams.

5. **Addressing Remote Models**: Adopt specific guidelines and collaboration tools that maintain strong distributed teams.

By methodically planning and executing these steps, organizations embed agility into everyday operations. Such a focus keeps the organization forward-looking and ready for changes and disruptions.

By following these strategies and understanding current trends, organizations can anticipate future shifts and position themselves advantageously for what comes next.

The Future of Business Agility

As global business grows more interconnected and uncertain, Business Agility remains a critical success factor. Trends like digital transformation, remote work, and enhanced customer experiences prove the need for agile, responsive organizations.

Agile is also expanding into sustainability, as indicated by Agile & Digital Solutions expert Scott Seivwright's remarks at the Business Agility Conference UK 2024. Agile's flexibility supports swift environmental compliance, fosters green innovation, and builds robust supply chains. By integrating sustainability into Agile, organizations reduce waste and support eco-friendly products and processes – a synergy that underscores Agile's evolving relevance in broader social and environmental contexts.

For instance, some organizations incorporate Agile cycles into developing renewable energy technologies or applying circular economy principles. Embedding these approaches positions them well to meet rising expectations for responsible corporate behaviour.

Business Agility Can:

- **Enhance Innovation**: Iterative structures and collaboration spark creative breakthroughs.
- **Improve Engagement**: Autonomy and openness keep employees motivated.
- **Strengthen Competitiveness**: Quick responsiveness to market changes outperforms less adaptive competitors.

Since Business Agility remains a continuous journey, organizations that commit to lifelong learning and adaptability will stay best equipped to handle new complexities. Aligning Agile practices with pressing priorities like sustainability extends agility's benefits beyond internal performance to lasting societal and environmental impact.

Conclusion

Business agility extends beyond IT, encompassing iterative cycles, cross-functional collaboration, and data-informed decisions across the enterprise. Adaptive leadership weaves these elements together, ensuring every function – finance, HR, marketing, legal – evolves from siloed processes to an integrated, user-centric approach. The CLEAR Model® ensures alignment between culture, leadership, and execution.

Consider whether your organization operates with genuine agility. Are your finance and HR teams able to pivot, or are they constrained by static plans? Do employees have the freedom to innovate, or are they bogged down by bureaucracy? By breaking down silos and embedding iterative thinking, organizations can unlock efficiency, synergy, and long-term resilience.

Scaling agility across functions is about cultivating an adaptive culture, not just deploying frameworks. Organizations that embed these principles will remain competitive and responsive in an unpredictable business landscape.

The next chapter examines how Agile practices resonate across different cultures and generations, ensuring adaptability becomes a unifying force for all teams.

Call to Action

As an adaptive leader, reflect on which departments or processes remain rigid. Could finance test rolling forecasts or lean budgeting? Could HR run sprints for performance reviews? Are marketing teams leveraging short, iterative cycles? Identify one or two pilot projects outside IT and champion them. Keep measuring, iterating, and sharing success stories to inspire broader organizational transformation.

Key Takeaways

- **Cross-Functional Synergy**: Agility thrives when departments unite around shared goals.
- **Department-Specific Approaches**: Tailor methods to each area's unique needs, from Finance to HR.
- **Leadership Alignment Is Key**: Leaders who champion inter-team collaboration enable real progress.
- **Incremental Changes Build Momentum**: Small pilots spark interest and let you refine your approach.
- **Practical Tools Accelerate Adoption**: Checklists, roadmaps, and clear actions help teams grasp Agile methods more easily.

CLEAR Model® Connection

- **Execution**: Translating Agile principles into real-world action creates measurable outcomes.
- **Responsiveness**: Broadening Agile beyond IT calls for fast adjustments to different departmental needs.

Key Takeaway: Agile is not an IT initiative; it is an operational strategy. Organizations that embed Agile principles across functions will be more resilient and responsive to change.

Cross-Functional Agility Checklist

- **Set a Shared Objective:**
  - o Bring managers from different areas together to identify a common target.
- **Clarify Roles:**
  - o Ensure that each participant knows how they contribute to meeting the objective.
- **Remove Barriers:**
  - o Address current hurdles – process bottlenecks, communication gaps, or missing resources.
- **Pilot a Joint Sprint:**
  - o Run a short collaboration period where teams work toward a shared outcome.
- **Review and Adapt:**
  - o After the pilot, gather feedback, note lessons, and adjust for the next cycle.

Scaling Roadmap for Multi-Department Coordination

1. **Form Cross-Department Squads:**
   - o Create small groups with a mix of expertise, aiming for a balanced perspective.
2. **Agree on Feedback Routines:**
   - o Schedule frequent check-ins so teams can address issues early and share insights.
3. **Gradually Expand the Approach:**
   - o Once initial squads show success, add more teams or expand the scope of collaboration.
4. **Encourage Shared Learning:**
   - o Keep a record of what works, what doesn't, and any improvements for future squads.

Chapter Summary

Agility shouldn't be confined to IT. By deploying iterative thinking in finance, HR, operations, and other domains, leaders generate synergy, resilience, and swift value delivery. This chapter illuminated how to tailor Agile to each function's needs, unify teams, and leverage the CLEAR Model® for cohesive transformation. Next up: how agility evolves further across diverse cultures and generations, forging a truly adaptive organization.

End of Part 4

Those five elements shape a unified approach that ties day-to-day tasks to strategic aims. Next comes a look at how these ideas stay strong when fresh technology and roles appear. In Part 5, we'll look at the evolving Agile organization, examining how to stay flexible and relevant in a world that never stops changing.

Part 5

The Evolving Agile Organization

CLEAR Focus: Adaptability and Responsiveness

The future of Agile depends on continuous adaptability and a responsive approach to new technologies, roles, and workplace dynamics. This section explores how AI, automation, and emerging trends can enhance Agile's relevance in the evolving business world.

10

Agility Across Cultures and Generations – Leading in a Diverse World

Diversity is not about how we differ. Diversity is about embracing one another's uniqueness.

Ola Joseph

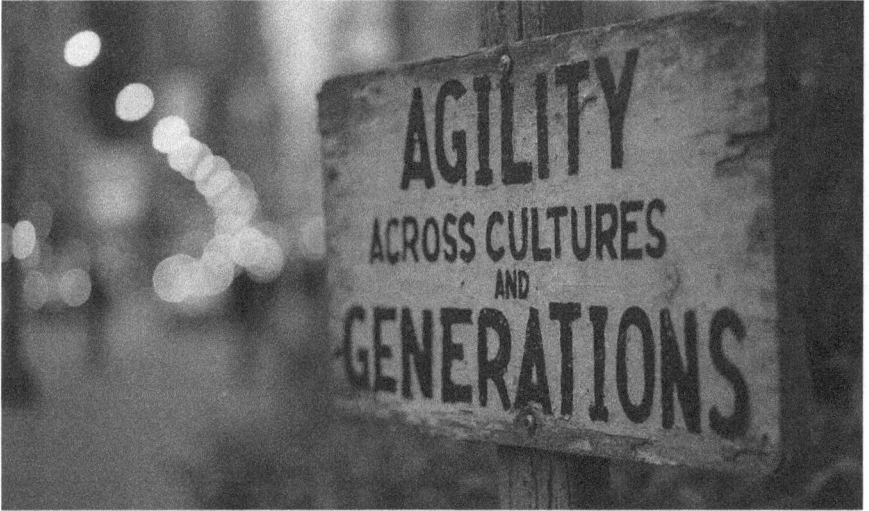

What You'll Gain

- **For Senior Leaders and Executives**: Discover how to customize Agile for different global and generational contexts, harnessing diversity for higher performance.
- **For Mid-Level Leaders**: Learn ways to align multicultural and multigenerational teams, respecting local norms and bridging generation gaps.
- **For Students or Early-Career Professionals**: Understand how Adaptive Leadership guides Agile across cultural nuances and generational preferences, ensuring lasting impact.

Culture-Building Agility

Adaptive leaders must recognize that culture and generational shifts are reshaping workplaces. By 2025, around 30% of the workforce will be Gen Z, mixing with veteran Baby Boomers and bridging multiple communication styles. This collision of attitudes, hierarchies, and traditions can derail agility if not managed carefully.

Generational shifts and global expansion are creating workplaces where expectations collide. This chapter explores how adaptive leaders bridge both generational and cultural gaps to keep agility principles intact.

How do adaptive leaders bridge generational gaps, drive collaboration, and build high-performing teams across cultures? The answer lies in culture-driven agility – the ability to adapt leadership styles to fit diverse teams while keeping agility principles intact.

A global software firm faced tension between Tokyo, Berlin, and New York teams. European squads preferred open debate, while Japanese colleagues valued consensus, and younger staff pushed for rapid iterations. Agile success required adapting practices to each cultural context – balancing self-organization with deeper trust-building and a structured approach. Leaders who honoured local norms while preserving core Agile values saw productivity and engagement soar.

Personal Reflection

Having led teams across continents, I've seen firsthand how cultural nuances can either hinder or enhance Agile adoption. In India, where hierarchical norms run deep, a team thrived once we introduced structured leadership roles while progressively encouraging open dialogue. The team adapted Agile principles without disrupting cultural norms by modelling collaborative decision-making and promoting trust through clear communication. Conversely, in the Netherlands, open dialogue and flat hierarchies expedited decision-making. These experiences underscored a central truth: recognizing and adjusting to cultural dynamics is crucial for Agile success.

Agility Isn't One-Size-Fits-All – It Must Adapt to Culture and Generations

Most Agile frameworks were created in Western, individualistic cultures such as the US and Europe. However, agility means different things in different cultural settings.

A leadership style that works in one country may fail in another.

- In Japan and South Korea, hierarchy is deeply respected – self-organizing teams may struggle without leadership guidance.
- In Germany and Switzerland, process rigour is valued – fast iteration without a clear structure may cause friction.
- In the US and Scandinavia, autonomy is celebrated – top-down leadership can slow teams down.

Similarly, different generations (Boomers, Gen X, Millennials, and Gen Z) have distinct expectations of work, collaboration, and leadership.

To scale agility globally, leaders must understand these cultural and generational differences and adapt accordingly.

Extending earlier discussions that dismissed the misconception that Agile is geographically or industrially confined, this chapter explores how to adapt Agile principles for varied cultural contexts, ensuring true impact in a globalized environment. Before delving into specific adaptations, let's briefly clarify how different cultural realities can shape Agile outcomes.

We'll examine how adaptive leaders can interpret cultural nuances to guide Agile adoption, explore how they tailor practices in emerging markets, and outline strategies for leaders to drive cross-cultural collaboration. By acknowledging and respecting cultural differences, organizations can successfully implement Agile across diverse regions.

Cultural Impact on Agile Adoption

A multinational bank's European and Asian branches faced varied adoption speeds: the European units quickly embraced Agile self-organizing teams, while Asian teams, accustomed to hierarchical management, resisted the shift. Leaders responded by shaping 'cultural agility coaching', merging consensus-building with iterative processes. The outcome? Asia-based teams integrated Agile without sacrificing cultural norms.

Agile succeeds only if it fits the culture. A method championed in one region may falter in a society valuing hierarchy or indirect communication. By acknowledging local values, leaders smooth tension, build trust, and accelerate Agile acceptance.

Historical power imbalances often re-emerge as hidden barriers in Agile adoption. Adaptive leaders must recognize structural inequalities to ensure Agile practices promote genuine autonomy rather than replicating outdated power dynamics. For instance, in hierarchical cultures, leaders need to consciously empower teams through structured, incremental delegation of decision-making power rather than abruptly imposing self-organization.

In my experience leading cross-continental teams, cultural alignment fosters smoother transitions. For instance, in India, where hierarchies run deep, teams responded well to structured roles while gradually adopting open collaboration. Meanwhile, a Dutch environment prized directness and immediate iteration. Each approach thrived because it aligned Agile with local expectations.

Agile's core remains universal: collaboration, iterative cycles, and a user-focused mindset. How leaders apply these principles depends on each cultural context, recognizing unique communication styles, risk tolerances, and group dynamics.

Once we grasp how culture shapes Agile outcomes, it's equally important to note that generational differences also influence how teams communicate, share feedback, and prioritize goals.

Adaptive Leadership for Cross-Cultural and Generational Agility

The heart of Adaptive Leadership is recognizing and working across diverse cultural and generational perspectives, ensuring inclusivity, trust, and alignment.

Agile isn't one-size-fits-all, especially in multicultural and multigenerational teams. Adaptive leaders customize how they lead, communicate, and collaborate by understanding team dynamics and tailoring their approach accordingly. This means going beyond frameworks and cultivating environments where different backgrounds become innovation drivers.

Framework for Culturally Adaptive Leadership

The table below outlines practical steps for leaders to customize their approach when working with culturally diverse teams. Rather than imposing a uniform style, adaptive leaders modify communication, collaboration, and expectations to fit different cultural norms, yielding stronger cohesion and mutual respect.

Action	Guidance	Example
Assess Cultural Norms	Use frameworks such as Hofstede's Dimensions to understand attitudes toward hierarchy, communication styles, and risk tolerance.	A leader working with a high-context culture allocates time for informal relationship-building before moving to formal discussions.
Adapt Communication Styles	Tailor language and delivery. In low-context cultures, be direct and structured; in high-context cultures, nuance and context matter.	In a multinational team, the leader provides explicit instructions for some members and a more conversational tone for others to ensure clarity.
Foster Inclusivity	Promote spaces where every cultural and generational perspective is seen as a strength.	A team lead hosts cultural exchange sessions, allowing members to share traditions, building empathy and mutual respect.
Support Cross-Cultural Collaboration	Encourage clear protocols and the use of appropriate technology to enable global teams.	A global automotive firm held role-playing workshops to explore communication differences between European and East Asian teams, improving trust and reducing misunderstandings.
Enable Tools and Team Building	Use platforms like Slack or Teams for async updates and plan virtual or on-site team-building activities.	Distributed teams hold regular check-ins, summary updates, and cultural recognition sessions to create unity across time zones.

Generational Agility: Bridging Age Gaps

Team dynamics can also shift dramatically across different age groups, each with its own communication style and outlook. Adaptive leaders know how to bring out the best in each generation, as they all have different mindsets about work, hierarchy, and agility:

Generation	Traits	Agility Strategy
Baby Boomers (1946–1964)	Prefer structure, value experience, and hierarchy.	Position Agile as structured continuous improvement; emphasize clear roles and learning over disruption.
Gen X (1965–1980)	Independent, value flexibility and autonomy.	Highlight Agile's adaptability in managing priorities; support self-led leadership.
Millennials (Gen Y) (1981–1996)	Purpose-driven, feedback-focused, and seek growth.	Make Agile meaningful; build in mentorship and regular feedback cycles.
Gen Z (1997–2012)	Digital-first, expect fast feedback and growth.	Use collaborative tech tools and offer accelerated skill-building opportunities.

When leaders adapt feedback methods and career paths to generational needs, they unite all ages under shared Agile goals. For instance, a team might run Slack updates for Gen Z and schedule workshops for Gen X, striking a collaborative balance.

Toolkit: Cross-Cultural Leadership Checklist

While the previous table focuses on cultural nuances, the checklist below spotlights common challenges leaders face in diverse teams – and how to handle them effectively. It serves as a quick reference to ensure smooth communication and collaboration, regardless of cultural or generational differences.

Challenge	Leadership Strategy	Example
High-context culture struggles with direct feedback	Use relationship-building and informal discussions.	Pre-meeting coffee chats to build trust.
Generational friction in team roles	Assign tasks aligned with generational strengths.	Boomers as mentors, Gen Y leading innovation.

Example: Bridging Cultures and Generations

A global software company struggled with collaboration across its multicultural teams. By adopting Adaptive Leadership practices, the organization carried out the following:

- Conducted team workshops to explore cultural differences and align on shared values.
- Introduced reverse mentoring schemes where Gen Z employees trained senior colleagues on emerging technologies.
- Balanced formal and informal communication styles, creating a unified team dynamic.

The result: Improved team cohesion and a 25% increase in the pace of delivery across multicultural teams.

While Adaptive Leadership offers practical strategies for addressing cultural and generational diversity, frameworks like Hofstede's Cultural Dimensions provide deeper insights into the nuances of cultural behaviours and their influence on Agile practices.

Hofstede's Cultural Dimensions and Agile Practices

Dutch social psychologist Geert Hofstede's Cultural Dimensions Theory illustrates how Agile principles interact with diverse cultural characteristics, offering a lens to align practices with team-specific realities. He identified six key dimensions of culture that shape how people work, lead, and collaborate.

Example

- **Power Distance Index (PDI)**: In high PDI cultures, teams may prefer clear hierarchies and structured leadership; low PDI cultures naturally align with self-organizing Agile teams.
- **Uncertainty Avoidance Index (UAI)**: High UAI contexts gain comfort from detailed planning phases, while lower UAI cultures adapt easily to iterative change.
- **Individualism vs Collectivism (IDV)**: Agile thrives in collaborative settings, though more individualist environments may require explicit reinforcement of collective goals.
- **Long-Term Orientation (LTO)**: Cultures with high LTO want to see strategic, long-term value in Agile roadmaps; short-term-oriented ones might prefer quicker wins.
- **Masculinity vs Femininity (MAS)**: High MAS cultures focus on competition and achievement, while low MAS cultures emphasize collaboration and work–life balance.
- **Indulgence vs Restraint (IVR)**: High IVR cultures embrace flexibility and creativity, while low IVR cultures favour discipline and structured processes.

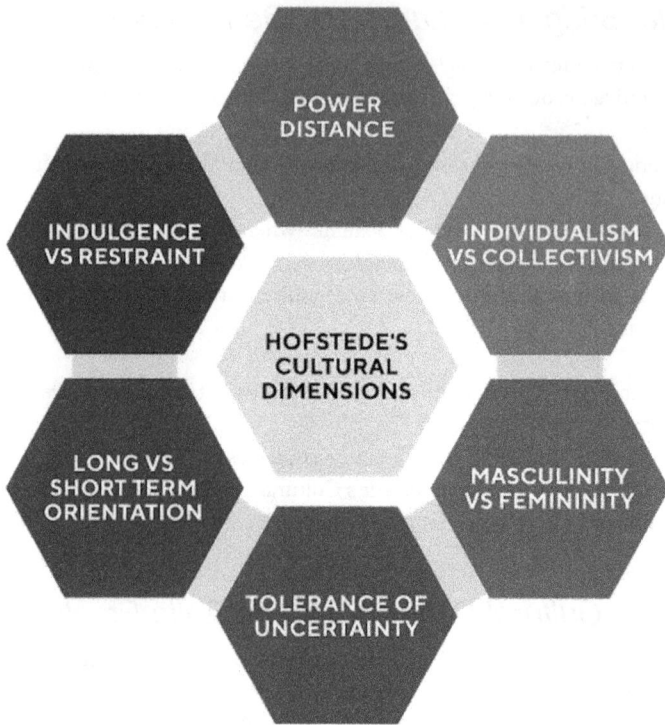

Hofstede's cultural dimensions

Grasping these dimensions allows leaders to pre-empt cultural barriers and tailor Agile strategies effectively.

Among these dimensions, power distance and uncertainty avoidance play a particularly influential role in shaping how Agile practices unfold.

Team Dynamics: Power Distance and Uncertainty Avoidance

Power distance and uncertainty avoidance strongly influence how teams adopt Agile. Low power distance cultures (Denmark) often embrace open dialogue and cooperative decision-making, mirroring Agile's self-organization. In high power distance contexts (Malaysia), leaders must deliberately encourage participation via structured feedback loops, for example, to strengthen collaboration.

When it comes to uncertainty avoidance, high UAI cultures (like Japan) benefit from formal risk assessments in sprint planning, reducing anxiety while building trust in iterative processes. Low UAI cultures (like Sweden) need minimal adjustments for Agile's short cycles. Attentive leaders can help teams flourish across cultural predispositions by applying targeted strategies.

For example: In Japan, which exhibits high uncertainty avoidance, teams often appreciate detailed plans. Adapting Agile by incorporating thorough planning phases can align well with local expectations.

Beyond power structures and comfort with ambiguity, communication style also shapes how Agile teams exchange ideas and feedback.

Communication Styles: High-Context vs Low-Context Cultures

American anthropologist and cross-cultural researcher Edward T. Hall's concept of high- and low-context cultures highlights how emotional intelligence influences communication. Some assume Agile's direct, frequent communication fits every setting, but not all teams function best under directness. High-context cultures rely on unspoken cues and shared context (common in Japan and China), often leaving words unsaid. Low-context cultures (such as the US and Germany) prefer explicit communication, with nothing left to guesswork.

Agile teams in high-context environments should invest time in trust-building to decode subtle signals and fortify alignment. Low-context teams can benefit from explicit instructions and openness. Misunderstandings occur when someone from a direct culture interprets indirect communication as dishonest. Leaders who adjust to these nuances facilitate strong collaboration among multicultural teams.

Leaders must develop cultural intelligence to guide teams through these subtleties gracefully.

Cultural Intelligence

Adaptive leaders excel by growing their cultural intelligence (CQ), allowing them to transform diversity into a valuable advantage. CQ encompasses:

- **Cognitive Awareness**: Understanding norms, communication styles, and values across different cultures.
- **Motivational Engagement**: Showing genuine willingness to learn, adapt, and appreciate diverse viewpoints.
- **Behavioural Adaptability**: Modifying actions to fit cultural contexts.

For example: A US tech firm in Japan prioritized relationship-building during onboarding, fostering trust in its Agile teams. For high uncertainty-avoidance cultures like Japan's, adding structured planning phases built alignment and confidence.

With strong cultural intelligence, leaders can refine Agile practices for diverse cultural settings. Likewise, generational differences also shape collaboration in workplaces, reinforcing the need for a flexible, inclusive approach to leadership. Leaders who recognize both cultural and generational traits can form cohesive teams that capitalize on distinct viewpoints and experiences.

Just as cultural intelligence aids cross-border collaboration, an understanding of generational diversity is equally vital for uniting teams within the same organization. Let's look at how generational traits intersect with Agile adoption.

HIGH CONTEXT		LOW CONTEXT
How things get done depends on relationships with people and attention to group processes	01	Things get done by following procedures and paying attention to the goal.
One's identity is rooted in their groups, i.e., family, work, and culture.	02	One's identity is rooted in oneself and one's accomplishments.
Social structure and authority are centralized; responsibilities are at the top.	03	The social structure is decentralized; responsibility goes further down.
Space is communal; people stand close to each other, share the same space	04	Space is compartmentalized & privately owned; privacy is important, so people are farther apart.

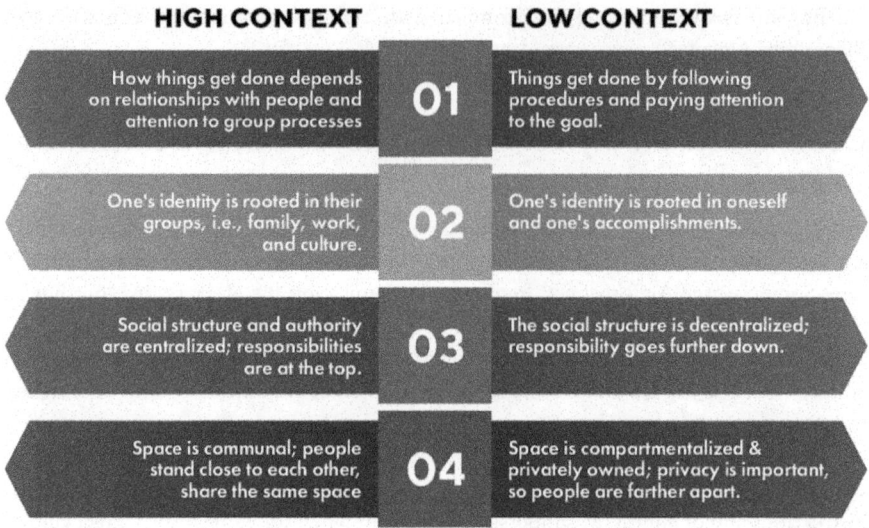

High-Context vs Low-Context Cultures

Generational Dimensions: Adapting Agile Across Age Groups

At a global consulting firm, a project team faced a divide: senior members, accustomed to Waterfall approaches, preferred structured plans, while younger team members advocated for rapid sprints. Tensions surfaced during retrospectives – senior members saw them as redundant, while younger colleagues viewed them as crucial for learning. The breakthrough came when the team introduced hybrid Agile-Waterfall workflows, aligning detailed planning with flexible execution. This case highlights that bridging generational gaps in Agile requires compromise, mutual respect, and tailored implementation.

Each generation contributes different work styles, technology habits, and collaboration preferences to Agile teams. Research by Dr Jean Twenge and Pew Research Center identifies characteristic outlooks and communication styles for Gen X, Millennials (Gen Y), Gen Z, and the upcoming Gen Alpha, each shaping how they engage with Agile approaches:

- **Gen X**: Often values self-reliance, balancing tried-and-true methods with new ideas.
- **Gen Y (Millennials)**: Typically seeks purpose and meaning, thriving in collaborative, growth-oriented environments.
- **Gen Z**: Digitally native, expects immediate responses and open communication, often comfortable experimenting with virtual tools.
- **Gen Alpha**: Likely to embrace future technologies and flexible work arrangements once they enter the workforce.

Adapting to these generational needs may mean refining feedback formats, meeting styles, and tools. Gen X might appreciate a mix of structured discussions and open collaboration; Gen Y frequently wants continuous feedback aligned with a deeper mission; Gen Z thrives on constant interaction through messaging apps; Gen Alpha may demand new digital channels not yet mainstream.

For example: In one project, Gen Z staff excelled with Slack and Trello, while Gen X colleagues preferred scheduled workshops. Combining real-time updates with structured learning bridged the generational gap.

A key trend shaping generational Agile adoption is the growing resistance to traditional promotion structures. Recent workforce data highlights that younger generations, particularly Gen Z, are increasingly rejecting middle management roles in favour of lateral career moves or specialist paths. This shift impacts Agile leadership pipelines, requiring organizations to rethink how they develop future Agile coaches, Scrum Masters, and product leaders.

Additionally, technology influences how each generation engages with Agile frameworks. Gen Z, being digital natives, is comfortable with AI-driven analytics, real-time dashboards, and asynchronous collaboration tools. Meanwhile, Gen X and Boomers often prefer structured meetings and formalized planning cycles. Understanding these differences allows leaders to design Agile workflows that respect diverse work preferences while maintaining team cohesion.

Bridging Generational Gaps in Agile Teams

To overcome these differences and ensure inclusive Agile adoption, organizations can refine Agile implementation through the following strategies:

- **Flexible Career Pathways**: Offer leadership alternatives beyond traditional management, allowing Gen Z employees to grow in influence without rigid hierarchical promotions.
- **Hybrid Agile Models**: Combine structured planning cycles with flexible, real-time collaboration to engage both traditional and tech-driven work styles.
- **Tailored Agile Leadership Development**: Support the next wave of Agile leaders through mentorship and skill-based career progression, reducing reliance on formal promotions.
- **Reverse Mentoring**: Pair younger employees with seasoned professionals for mutual skill-sharing.
- **Tailored Feedback Loops**: Provide frequent feedback for Millennials and Gen Z while aligning it with the structured expectations of Gen X.
- **Hybrid Tools**: Blend interactive platforms with traditional methods to suit varied preferences.
- **Tailored Onboarding**: Customize onboarding programs to address varying comfort levels with technology.
- **Feedback Adaptation**: Deliver feedback in formats aligned with generational preferences, such as structured reviews for Gen X and real-time updates for Gen Z.

Aligning Agile with generational inclinations ensures all team members feel supported and engaged.

This cultural sensitivity doesn't just build internal trust – it also strengthens your position in the talent market. Beyond performance, a healthy culture has become a competitive edge in attracting and keeping top talent. Millennials and Gen Z professionals often select employers based on purpose, inclusion, and growth opportunities – not just compensation.

In one survey, candidates were more likely to accept offers when the onboarding process included storytelling from leaders about how values come to life inside the company. Culture is no longer just an internal concern; it defines your external reputation. Leaders who invest in cultural integrity position their organizations as destinations for top talent.

Meanwhile, communication with senior stakeholders often needs precise, outcome-focused terminology, particularly when discussing the strategic or financial impacts of Agile.

Adapting Language for Senior Leadership

Some senior executives have grown sceptical of Agile terms due to previous frustrations or unmet promises. This has led to so-called 'Agilesplaining', where Agile jargon struggles to resonate with C-level leaders fixated on strategic results. Leaders can sidestep negative associations by avoiding jargon-heavy labels, instead emphasizing neutral, outcome-focused terms like 'adaptive approach' or 'continuous improvement'.

Research by John Kotter shows leadership language affects how teams adopt new methods, while Amy Edmondson, a Harvard Business School professor known for her work on psychological safety, underscores how words foster openness and commitment. Publications from *Harvard Business Review* and McKinsey confirm swapping old, overused Agile labels for value-oriented phrases can ease leader buy-in.

Bridging the Gap for Business Owners

Many senior sponsors wonder whether Agile will bring more income or just lead to extra meetings. Their top concerns are increasing revenue, reducing costs without harming quality, and staying ahead of rivals. When explaining Agile, skip complicated terms and emphasize how it helps cut waste, boost delivery, or lift sales figures.

Owners often want short cycles, fewer errors, and faster feedback. Highlight practical gains, such as less rework and clear performance metrics, rather than vague talk of mindset changes. This approach secures stronger support by showing how Agile can directly improve the bottom line.

Practical Tips

- **Reframe Terminology**: Swap 'Agile transformation' with phrases like 'adaptive growth strategy'.
- **Demonstrate Impact**: Showcase data on shorter delivery cycles, better customer satisfaction, or revenue improvements.

- **Build Trust Through Results**: Use pilot projects to display measurable progress, lowering leadership scepticism.

Adapting language isn't about hiding Agile truths; it connects with senior executives who seek clarity, stability, and tangible results. Learn from the language of the company. A simpler, outcome-centric vocabulary lets them view these methods with fresh optimism, bridging hierarchical and generational divides. Yet keeping a standard, inclusive language for Agile supports better alignment across the organization.

A Unified, Straightforward Language for Agile

A European healthcare company working with offshore teams in Brazil and Vietnam noticed that complex Agile jargon led to misunderstandings. Terms like 'product increment' and 'definition of ready' were misinterpreted, causing misalignment. To resolve this, they replaced technical Agile terms with plain language, ensuring all teams had a shared understanding of objectives. The result? Fewer miscommunications and smoother collaboration. This case reinforces that clarity in Agile language enhances global teamwork.

Even when adapting 'Agile-speak' for executives, another larger challenge persists: the Agile community itself often uses a jumble of frameworks, each loaded with unique terms. Over time, such jargon can mystify teams and leaders.

This fragmented language can spark confusion. One team's 'retro' might mean a formal meeting, and another's an informal chat. Terms like 'user story' might carry varying levels of detail. Miscommunication creeps in when people assume they share definitions but are actually misaligned.

Beyond team-level clarity, the broader conversation around agility in business is also shifting. More organizations are moving away from framework-heavy language toward practical, outcome-driven discussions. Instead of talking about specific Agile methods like 'Scrum' or 'Kanban', leaders are focusing on business agility, adaptability, and responsiveness.

Key Shifts in Agile Language

- **Outcome-Oriented Framing**: Businesses now prioritize agility as a means to improve *resilience, customer focus, and decision-making* rather than simply implementing frameworks.
- **Avoiding Buzzwords**: Terms like 'Agile transformation' can create resistance, while language centred around continuous learning, adaptability, and rapid feedback loops resonates more widely.
- **Cross-Disciplinary Integration**: Agile is now merging with systems thinking, behavioural science, and product management, making language more accessible to different audiences.

Clarity fosters trust and synergy. A *consistent, plain-spoken terminology* prevents friction and ensures everyone, especially leaders, sees Agile as practical, not a buzzword.

Practical Actions

- **Use Outcome-Oriented Terms**: Replace Agile-heavy terminology with business-friendly language like 'value delivery' or 'results-driven iteration'.
- **Check Understanding**: Pause to confirm that different teams interpret keywords the same way.
- **Remain Flexible**: Recognize that language evolves – aim for clarity over rigid definitions.

A simpler shared vocabulary not only streamlines daily activities but also upholds Agile's values of transparency and collaboration.

Tip: Craft a shared glossary at kickoff; consistent terms cut rework and build trust across cultures.

Beyond Agile Labels

Beyond adapting language for leaders, Agile's evolution extends further. As Agile matures, it transcends the need for explicit labels. Mike Cohn (n.d.), an Agile author, trainer, and co-founder of the Scrum Alliance, suggests that once organizations fully absorb agility, they needn't call it 'Agile'. Instead, adaptability, collaboration, and customer focus become part of the organization's everyday routines.

One client replaced words like 'sprint' with 'iteration' to calm sceptical senior leaders. Branding practices as 'value-focused' rather than 'Agile' overcame biases and illustrated that delivering outcomes, not following a label, is what truly counts.

Historically, project management also progressed from fixating on Gantt charts to focusing on results. Similarly, agility becomes standard practice when baked into culture, overshadowing frameworks or rituals. Leaders must model adaptive behaviours and cultivate an environment where agility evolves organically; focusing on measurable outcomes resonates with C-level executives.

This evolution eliminates the superficial 'Agile theatre' of checklists and ceremonies, emphasizing authentic adaptability. Indeed, leaders must ensure any new approach suits their unique organization, balancing networks and hierarchies rather than blindly adopting trendy methods. Enter Dave Snowden's perspective on how to create 'sustainable agility' without falling for the next big hype cycle.

Yet transcending labels alone isn't enough – leaders must reconcile the interplay between networks and hierarchies to ensure agility endures.

Balancing Networks and Hierarchies for Lasting Agility

Dave Snowden warns about '*old wine in new skins*' – cycling through new frameworks without addressing deeper structures. Real agility merges flexible, network-based innovation with hierarchical stability. Amazon, for example, integrates strong leadership with competence-based networks.

Key

- **Use Each Structure Where It Fits**: Networks for speed and creativity, hierarchies for safety or regulated tasks.
- **Focus on Results Over Hype**: Avoid illusions that brand-new frameworks alone solve cultural or structural barriers.
- **Contextual Approach**: Evaluate each situation to find the right mix of network autonomy and hierarchical governance.

Leaders who adopt 'both-and' thinking craft sustainable agility rather than chasing the latest methodology.

Pitfalls of Chasing the Next Big Thing

Companies frequently jump on new frameworks, hoping to solve deep-rooted problems. Instead, they often yield superficial transformations, driven more by marketing hype than by genuine solutions.

Leaders can avoid these cycles by focusing on context-based strategies – evaluating what's truly needed rather than blindly adopting the newest frameworks. Introducing network concepts in a company reliant on rigid hierarchies can create chaos if readiness isn't addressed.

Context-Driven Agility

According to Snowden, choose 'the right method for the right context'. Understand your organization's culture, size, and regulatory environment to decide how to combine networks and hierarchies effectively.

1. **Hierarchies**: Provide clarity, accountability, and consistency – valuable in regulated or large-scale environments.
2. **Networks**: Promote innovation, collaboration, and rapid decision-making – perfect for dynamic customer-facing settings.

Adaptive leaders switch between these modes, building resilience by embedding Agile thinking in a context that balances structure with flexibility.

Breaking the Cycle of Superficial Change

To defeat the 'old wine in new skins' syndrome, leaders must develop a culture of critical thinking and adaptability:

1. **Focus on Outcomes Over Frameworks**: Don't rigidly apply a methodology; aim for genuine results.

2. **Empower Teams with Contextual Tools**: Let teams adapt methods to their unique challenges while keeping broader goals in sight.
3. **Promote Continuous Learning**: Encourage regular experimentation and feedback to fuel iterative improvements.

By grounding transformations in relevance and results, organizations cultivate enduring agility, escaping hype-driven bandwagons.

In global organizations, avoiding superficial transformation becomes even more complex. Let's explore how leaders can unify multicultural teams so that authentic agility takes root across cultural boundaries.

Strategies for Multicultural Teams

Leaders with cultural intelligence can create welcoming environments that appreciate and effectively coordinate across cultural differences. The following practices can ensure diverse teams excel:

1. **Flexible Communication Styles**: Incorporate visuals or multilingual resources, maintain clarity, and facilitate inclusive dialogues.
2. **Time Zone Management**: Rotate meeting times, encourage asynchronous updates, and respect regional schedules.
3. **Cultural Sensitivity Training**: Offer workshops on cultural awareness and potential conflicts.
4. **Team-Building Activities**: Either virtual or in-person, such events cultivate trust and shared understanding.

For example: A global IT company that used both virtual collaboration tools and cultural awareness sessions aligned Agile teams spanning Asia, Europe, and the Americas. They saw fewer miscommunications, boosted alignment, and enhanced project outcomes.

When leaders integrate cultural intelligence with practical strategies, they create inclusive, high-performing Agile teams that flourish in multicultural environments.

As an adaptive leader, how are you developing your cultural intelligence to lead effectively in diverse settings? What steps can you take to enhance your team's cultural awareness and adaptability?

Examining how multinational corporations implement Agile globally provides valuable insights into best practices and potential pitfalls.

Case Study 1: IBM: Integrating Agile Across Global Teams

What Happened: IBM, spanning 170+ countries, faced varied cultural norms. Rather than forcing a single method, they established a core Agile vision, allowing each region to adapt frameworks to local traditions.

Why It Matters: They empowered teams to tweak sprint lengths or roles, ensuring cultural comfort. Executive commitment and training enabled synergy while respecting diversity.

Adaptive Leadership Lesson: Leaders served as facilitators – an inclusive approach that balanced global standards with local needs, improving collaboration and faster alignment on strategic goals.

Adaptive Leadership in Action

- **Culture (C)**: Allowed local adaptation without losing shared Agile vision.
- **Leadership (L)**: Executives visibly championed regional autonomy.
- **Execution (E)**: Each region tested Agile cycles but maintained consistent reporting.
- **Adaptability (A)**: Promptly refined processes based on local feedback.
- **Responsiveness (R)**: Reactions to local challenges remained swift, ensuring global synergy.

Case Study 2: Spotify: Squads, Tribes, and Global Collaboration

What Happened: Spotify's flexible model (Squads, Tribes, Guilds) emphasizes autonomy plus alignment. Deploying it globally, they varied planning details or retrospective styles by region, respecting local communication norms.

Why It Matters: Some teams used structured sprint planning in high uncertainty avoidance cultures; others used open dialogues for low power distance societies. This adaptability balanced innovation with local acceptance.

Adaptive Leadership Lesson: Letting each region tailor Agile while preserving guiding principles (autonomy, transparency, user focus) fosters consistency and avoids 'one-size-fits-all' friction.

Adaptive Leadership in Action

- **Culture (C)**: Emphasized local relationship norms while upholding the Squad/Tribe structure.
- **Leadership (L)**: Encouraged each region's leaders to tweak details.
- **Execution (E)**: Maintained iterative cycles but adapted communication forms.
- **Adaptability (A)**: Freed teams to pivot processes as needed.
- **Responsiveness (R)**: Real-time adjustments to user data or cultural feedback.

Both companies highlight that cultural adaptation in Agile is not about forcing a specific culture but about encouraging positive behaviours that emerge organically. Leaders should facilitate rather than dictate, creating resilient teams that reflect agility's essence. Let's see how these principles also appear in emerging markets, with unique cultural and economic conditions that demand thoughtful Agile adoption.

Agile Practices in Different Markets

Emerging Markets

Emerging markets aren't automatically incompatible with Agile. On the contrary, their rapid growth and technological leaps can welcome Agile's adaptability. However, it's vital to tweak Agile approaches to address local values, traditions, and resource constraints.

Asia: Balancing Hierarchy and Collaboration

India

India's IT industry has embraced Agile practices extensively, becoming a global hub for software development. However, traditional hierarchical structures and deep respect for authority can pose challenges. Team members may be hesitant to voice dissenting opinions or challenge decisions made by superiors, which can inhibit the open communication Agile requires.

To address this, organizations in India are encouraging leadership to model transformative behaviours, fostering an environment that drives both cultural and operational change. Training programmes focusing on soft skills, open communication, and team-building exercises help bridge the gap between hierarchical norms and Agile's emphasis on equality within teams. By gradually introducing Agile practices and allowing time for cultural acclimation, Indian companies are successfully integrating Agile ways of working while respecting cultural values.

- **Power Distance Index**: High
- **Individualism vs Collectivism**: Collectivist
- **Uncertainty Avoidance Index**: Medium–High
- **Long-Term Orientation**: Medium–High
- **High-Context Culture**

Strategies for Adaptation

- **Leadership Training**: Developing leaders who encourage open communication.
- **Cultural Sensitivity Programmes**: Helping teams understand the value of voicing opinions.
- **Gradual Implementation**: Introducing Agile practices in phases.

China

In China, collectivist values and high power distance influence team dynamics significantly. Team cohesion and group harmony are highly valued, and there is a strong emphasis on maintaining face and avoiding conflict. Agile adoption in China focuses on leveraging these collectivist tendencies to enhance collaboration. Teams work closely together, and the sense of collective responsibility aligns well with Agile's emphasis on teamwork.

However, the hierarchical nature of Chinese organizations can conflict with Agile's self-organizing principles. Leaders in China often act as facilitators who guide teams while respecting the existing hierarchy. By balancing traditional leadership roles with Agile facilitation, organizations can navigate cultural expectations and still reap the benefits of Agile practices.

- **Power Distance Index**: High
- **Individualism vs Collectivism**: Collectivist
- **Uncertainty Avoidance Index**: Low
- **Long-Term Orientation**: High
- **High-Context Culture**

Strategies for Adaptation

- **Leveraging Collectivism**: Emphasizing team goals over individual achievements.
- **Balancing Hierarchy and Autonomy**: Leaders act as facilitators while respecting hierarchy.
- **Building Trust**: Investing time in relationship-building.

Africa: Driving Innovation Through Agile
South Africa

South African tech firms are increasingly adopting Agile ways of working to spur innovation and competitiveness. The country's diverse cultural landscape presents both challenges and opportunities. Teams often comprise individuals from various ethnic backgrounds, each bringing different perspectives and communication styles.

To harness this diversity, South African companies emphasize inclusive practices that value each team member's contributions. Team-building activities and cultural awareness training help foster trust and understanding among team members. By creating an environment where diversity is celebrated, Agile teams in South Africa can leverage a wide range of ideas and experiences to drive innovation.

- **Power Distance Index**: High
- **Individualism vs Collectivism**: Mixed (tending towards Collectivist)
- **Uncertainty Avoidance Index**: Medium
- **Long-Term Orientation**: Medium
- **Low-Context Culture**

Strategies for Adaptation

- **Embracing Diversity**: Leveraging multicultural teams for innovation.
- **Inclusive Practices**: Promoting equality and open dialogue.
- **Community Engagement**: Aligning projects with local needs.

Kenya and Nigeria

In rapidly growing tech hubs like Nairobi and Lagos, there is a young, dynamic workforce eager to embrace new methodologies. Agile practices are appealing because they offer a flexible and responsive approach to product development, which is essential in fast-paced markets.

Organizations in these regions leverage Agile to accelerate development cycles and respond quickly to customer needs. Challenges such as limited resources and infrastructure are addressed by adopting lean Agile practices that maximize efficiency. By tailoring Agile ways of working to suit local contexts, tech firms in Kenya and Nigeria are positioning themselves competitively on the global stage.

Kenya

- **Power Distance Index**: High
- **Individualism vs Collectivism**: Collectivist
- **Uncertainty Avoidance Index**: Medium–High
- **Long-Term Orientation**: Low–Medium
- **High-Context Culture**

Nigeria

- **Power Distance Index**: High
- **Individualism vs Collectivism**: Collectivist
- **Uncertainty Avoidance Index**: Medium–High
- **Long-Term Orientation**: Low–Medium
- **High-Context Culture**

Strategies for Adaptation

- **Leverage Mobile Technology**: Utilize mobile platforms to overcome infrastructure challenges.
- **Adopt Lean Practices**: Focus on delivering Minimum Viable Products (MVPs) to validate ideas quickly.
- **Community Engagement**: Participate in local tech communities to share knowledge and resources.

Latin America: Integrating Flexibility with Tradition

Brazil

Brazilian organizations often navigate between formal hierarchical structures and a flexible approach to work. There is a strong emphasis on personal relationships and communication, which can both aid and hinder Agile adoption. While the collaborative nature of Brazilian culture aligns with Agile principles, hierarchical decision-making can conflict with team autonomy.

To overcome this, companies in Brazil are combining Agile practices with existing processes, creating a hybrid approach that respects cultural norms while introducing new ways of working. Engaging stakeholders early and ensuring alignment of expectations help smooth the transition. By focusing on the benefits of Agile, such as improved efficiency and customer satisfaction, organizations can gain buy-in from all levels.

- **Power Distance Index**: High
- **Individualism vs Collectivism**: Collectivist
- **Uncertainty Avoidance Index**: High
- **Long-Term Orientation**: Medium
- **High-Context Culture**

Strategies for Adaptation

- **Hybrid Approaches**: Combining Agile with existing processes.
- **Stakeholder Engagement**: Ensuring alignment across levels.
- **Cultural Integration**: Respecting traditions while introducing new practices.

Mexico

In Mexico, strong family and community ties influence workplace dynamics. Team members value close relationships and often prefer face-to-face interactions. This collectivist culture can enhance teamwork but may also lead to challenges in giving and receiving constructive feedback.

Strategies for Agile adoption in Mexico include building on collectivist values to strengthen team cohesion. Establishing clear communication channels and setting expectations around feedback help mitigate potential misunderstandings. Emphasizing the shared goals of the team and the organization fosters a sense of unity and purpose, aligning well with Agile ways of working.

- **Power Distance Index**: High
- **Individualism vs Collectivism**: Collectivist
- **Uncertainty Avoidance Index**: High
- **Long-Term Orientation**: Medium
- **High-Context Culture**

Strategies for Adaptation

- **Strengthen Team Cohesion**: Organize team-building activities to leverage close relationships.
- **Balance Hierarchy with Empowerment**: Respect traditional structures while encouraging team autonomy.
- **Enhance Communication Practices**: Provide training to navigate indirect communication styles.

To understand these adaptations in a broader context, it's instructive to compare how established economies approach Agile, revealing both similarities and contrasts.

Comparisons with Established Economies

Established economies – like the UK, US, Japan, or Germany – often feature enduring organizational traditions that shape how Agile is received. Understanding local tendencies (whether direct or indirect communication, hierarchy, or freedom) is crucial. For instance:

United Kingdom

In the UK, a relatively low power distance and high individualism encourage open dialogue and personal accountability. Teams may prefer direct communication and balanced decision-making. Adaptive practices can blend well with a culture that values both independence and cooperation as long as leaders emphasize clear goals and practical benefits.

- **Power Distance Index**: Low
- **Individualism vs Collectivism**: Individualist
- **Uncertainty Avoidance Index**: Low
- **Long-Term Orientation**: Medium
- **Low-Context Culture**

Strategies for Adaptation

- **Clear Communication**: Use straightforward language and clear objectives.
- **Inclusive Decision-Making**: Involve team members in shaping solutions.
- **Emphasize Practical Value**: Show tangible benefits of adaptive methods.

United States

The USA's cultural traits often feature low power distance and high individualism, coupled with an openness to change and innovation. Adaptive practices align well with a direct communication style and a results-oriented mindset. Leaders should highlight goals, outcomes, and opportunities for personal growth.

- **Power Distance Index**: Low
- **Individualism vs Collectivism**: Individualist
- **Uncertainty Avoidance Index**: Low
- **Long-Term Orientation**: Low
- **Low-Context Culture**

Strategies for Adaptation

- **Results Focus**: Emphasize measurable outcomes and improvements.
- **Frequent Feedback**: Offer regular updates to maintain engagement.
- **Empowerment**: Encourage personal initiative and experimentation.

Japan

Japan's cultural framework includes medium–high power distance, collectivist values, and very high uncertainty avoidance. Teams often favour thorough planning and value group harmony. Adaptive methods succeed when leaders incorporate structured planning phases, build trust over time, and respect indirect communication cues.

- **Power Distance Index**: Medium–High
- **Individualism vs Collectivism**: Collectivist
- **Uncertainty Avoidance Index**: High
- **Long-Term Orientation**: High
- **High-Context Culture**

Strategies for Adaptation

- **Structured Planning**: Add detailed preparation to align with preferences.
- **Relationship-Building**: Invest in trust before expecting open debate.
- **Subtle Communication**: Recognize non-verbal cues and indirect feedback.

Germany

Germany's low power distance and individualist traits combine with a preference for planning and structure. A relatively high uncertainty avoidance encourages thorough preparation. Adaptive practices work well when framed as systematic, well-organized approaches that deliver quality and efficiency.

- **Power Distance Index**: Low
- **Individualism vs Collectivism**: Individualist
- **Uncertainty Avoidance Index**: High
- **Long-Term Orientation**: High
- **Low-Context Culture**

Strategies for Adaptation

- **Thorough Preparation**: Provide clear frameworks and defined processes.
- **Quality Emphasis**: Highlight how adaptive methods improve outcomes.
- **Logical Communication**: Keep discussions direct, reasoned, and fact-based.

Adjusting adaptive methods in different cultural contexts – whether in emerging markets or established economies – means blending global principles with local realities. Leaders who recognize variations in power distance, individualism, uncertainty avoidance, long-term orientation, and communication style set the stage for truly effective teamwork. This approach fosters innovation, growth, and sustainable progress in diverse settings. Building on these insights, let's examine how to facilitate effective collaboration among cross-cultural teams, ensuring that Agile thrives across boundaries.

Breaking Myths: One Size Fits All?

Many mistakenly believe Agile practices apply globally without modifications. In truth, culture influences how Agile fosters new behaviours and trust. Leaders who adapt Agile values to local norms – while preserving core Agile principles – see better, more authentic results.

Transformation in Agile means adapting while upholding fundamental values. Recognizing local nuances prevents unnecessary friction and sustains true improvements in collaboration, speed, and innovation. With this viewpoint, we can explore common global adoption challenges and strategies for scaling Agile effectively.

Challenges and Strategies in Global Agile Adoption

Scaling globally demands nuance. Different ethics around timekeeping, communication, or hierarchical respect can hamper synergy if leaders assume a single approach. Combine strong leadership, local adaptability, and continuous learning to succeed.

Key Challenges

- **Differing Work Ethics**: Varying attitudes to time, deadlines, or directness.
- **Organizational Hierarchies**: Self-organizing teams clash with top-down mindsets.
- **Resistance**: Concern about heavier workloads or scepticism about new methods.
- **Language Barriers**: High vs low-context styles hamper consistent communication.
- **Leadership Gaps**: Without leadership modelling Agile behaviours, transformations languish.

Strategies to Overcome

- **Leadership Commitment**: Leaders must actively exhibit transparency and adaptability.
- **Contextual Training**: Tailor Agile education for local norms.
- **Pilot Projects**: Show quick wins and replicate.
- **Safe-to-Fail Experiments**: Reinforce continuous learning.
- **Silo-Busting**: Cross-functional squads unify multiple regions or departments.
- **Localized Adjustments**: Tweak sprint lengths or roles to match cultural comfort.

Example: A financial services provider overcame departmental silos by running an Agile pilot in one division – success triggered expansion across the enterprise.

Tracking progress within global Agile teams involves collecting team satisfaction data, delivery metrics, and cultural integration markers and refining the approach as needed.

Measuring Success in Global Agile Teams

Evaluating the efficacy of Agile across diverse cultures demands careful tracking. Important metrics include:

- **Team Satisfaction Surveys**: Continuous feedback on collaboration and communication.
- **Delivery Metrics**: Monitoring timelines, quality, and stakeholder happiness.
- **Cultural Integration**: Gauging how effectively teams navigate cultural differences.

Regularly examining these metrics pinpoints improvement areas, guiding context-aware adaptations to keep Agile successful within unique local realities.

Conclusion

Adaptive leaders must tailor Agile to cultural and generational dynamics, forging synergy from diversity. This chapter explored how variations in power distance, communication style, and generational outlook influence the adoption of iterative, collaborative workflows. By aligning Agile's core principles – transparency, fast feedback, and continuous learning – with local norms, leaders can drive meaningful transformation.

Consider whether your Agile approach is adaptable to different cultural and generational contexts. Are you applying Agile in a way that respects varying communication styles and decision-making structures? Success comes from bridging these differences rather than imposing a one-size-fits-all approach.

Agility flourishes when it respects diverse perspectives while maintaining its core values. By fostering inclusivity and recognizing unique cultural strengths, organizations can build a truly resilient and innovative workforce.

The next chapter explores how to measure Agile maturity, ensuring that these cross-cultural and generational adjustments lead to sustainable improvements rather than temporary fixes.

Call to Action

As an adaptive leader, review your team's cultural and generational mix. Are communication styles or hierarchical norms hindering Agile? Could pilot tests or simpler language unify your diverse workforce? Pick at least one immediate step – like cultural training, adjusting ceremonies for high-context members, or bridging generational friction – and see how it elevates collaboration.

Key Takeaways

- **Cultural Awareness Is Essential**: Recognizing cultural nuances amplifies Agile adoption.
- **Adaptation Boosts Effectiveness**: Adapting Agile to local realities ensures success.

- **Inclusive Communication Is Vital**: Address linguistic and cultural styles for cohesive teamwork.
- **Leadership Is Crucial**: Leaders must champion and exemplify Agile's adaptive behaviours.
- **Diversity Fuels Innovation**: Different backgrounds and viewpoints sharpen creativity and outcomes.

CLEAR Model® Connection

- **Culture**: A supportive mindset determines whether Agile thrives or stalls.
- **Adaptability**: Teams and leaders must evolve practices over time for lasting success.

Key Takeaway: Agile transformations fail when culture is misaligned with Agile principles. Leaders must actively shape a culture of trust, innovation, and continuous learning.

Cross-Cultural Collaboration Checklist

- **Cultural Awareness Training:**
  - o Schedule sessions to educate teams about cultural differences.
- **Communication Protocols:**
  - o Establish guidelines that consider language barriers and time zones.
- **Team-Building Activities:**
  - o Organize events that foster mutual understanding and trust.

Global Agile Implementation Guide

1. **Cultural Assessment:**
   - o Research cultural dimensions relevant to your teams.
2. **Adaptation Strategies:**
   - o Modify Agile practices to respect cultural norms.
3. **Inclusive Leadership:**
   - o Encourage leaders to model culturally sensitive behaviours.
4. **Feedback Loops:**
   - o Implement mechanisms for continuous improvement across cultures.

Chapter Summary

Agility must adapt to different cultural norms and generational expectations. This chapter detailed how local traditions, power dynamics, and generational outlooks shape Agile's success and how leaders can unify these differences into a high-performing, innovative force.

11

Outcome-Based Agility – The Metrics That Actually Matter

What gets measured gets managed.

Peter Drucker

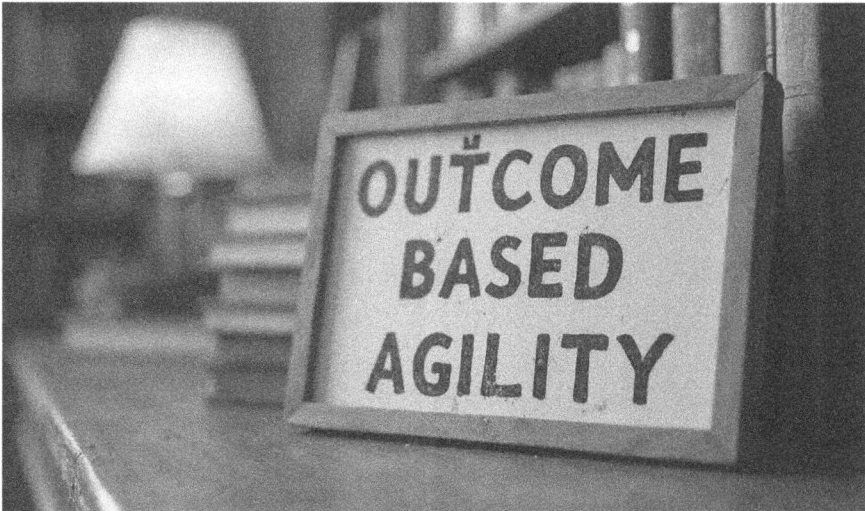

What You'll Gain

- **For Senior Leaders and Executives**: Learn how to measure Agile maturity so you can confirm that your transformation delivers genuine business value and strategic alignment.
- **For Mid-Level Leaders**: Discover specific maturity models, tools, and metrics to track both team performance and leadership effectiveness, ensuring continuous improvement.
- **For Students or Early-Career Professionals**: Understand why measuring progress, not just activity, is essential for moving beyond basic Agile adoption toward a culture of outcomes.

Recognizing the Need to Measure

Amy, a transformation lead at a global financial services firm, sat in a tense strategy meeting. Senior executives were wrestling with a tough question: *Is our Agile transformation actually driving business success?* The CEO leaned forward. *'Our teams are running sprints, but are we truly Agile?'*

Many leaders share this dilemma. They adopt frameworks, track sprint velocities, and run retros, yet real outcomes remain fuzzy. Measuring Agile isn't about process adherence; it centres on delivering real business value – people do what they are measured on. Adaptive leaders must check if agility produces meaningful gains, such as faster time-to-market, improved customer satisfaction, or stronger strategic alignment.

Personal Reflection

Throughout my years guiding Agile transformations, I've seen measurement act as both a mirror (revealing gaps and blind spots) and a map (highlighting the path to deeper agility). For instance, a financial institution discovered that although it aced sprints, it failed to measure customer impact. By shifting focus from output to outcomes, morale soared, and Agile became a strategic differentiator.

Take a financial institution I worked with. Their Agile adoption looked solid on paper – teams delivered features on time, and sprint metrics were strong. But their assessment revealed a glaring issue: they weren't measuring customer impact. Their output-focused approach left them disconnected from real value. By shifting their focus to outcomes – like reducing time-to-market and improving customer satisfaction – their teams regained purpose, morale soared, and Agile finally delivered strategic impact.

This chapter debunks the myth that Agile success is about process adoption. Instead, it introduces a new measurement framework focused on business results, customer outcomes, and adaptability.

Agile Isn't About Moving Fast – It's About Delivering Real Value

Most organizations today measure Agile the wrong way.

They focus on output, not outcomes.

- Teams are rewarded for increasing velocity, but does faster delivery mean better results?
- Organizations track how many user stories are completed, but do customers care?
- Managers report on sprint burndown charts, but is the business actually improving?

Example: The 'Faster, Not Better' Trap at a Global Bank

A major bank implemented Agile and saw sprint velocity increase by 40%. Leadership celebrated. Then, customer satisfaction scores dropped. Why?

- Teams optimized for speed, not customer impact.
- They delivered features but not the right features.
- They followed Agile rituals but failed to deliver real business value.

Agility is meaningless if it doesn't drive real results.

This chapter explores:

- The biggest mistakes companies make when measuring Agile.
- How to shift from vanity metrics to outcome-driven agility.
- A practical framework for measuring Agile success the right way.

The Three Biggest Mistakes in Agile Measurement

1. Measuring Velocity Instead of Value

The most common Agile metric – velocity – measures the number of story points or user stories completed per sprint. But an obsession with velocity leads to rushed work. Teams cut corners to hit targets, and not every feature is equally valuable.

Faster development does not always mean better business results. Comparing velocity across teams is also meaningless because each team estimates differently.

What to Do Instead:

- Focus on customer outcomes, not internal team speed.
- Use velocity only for team forecasting, not performance measurement.
- Reward teams for delivering impact, not just completing work.

Agile is not about speed; it is about delivering meaningful results.

2. Tracking Agile Maturity Instead of Business Impact

Many companies use Agile maturity models to assess progress, but this often leads to a focus on process adoption rather than business outcomes.

- Asking, 'How Agile are we?' becomes more important than 'How much value are we delivering?'
- Companies measure how well teams follow Agile practices instead of focusing on business results.
- Agile transformations stall because they focus on adopting frameworks, not driving impact.

What to Do Instead:

- Track business agility, not Agile maturity.
- Stop obsessing over frameworks and focus on adaptability and results.
- Measure agility by how fast the organization responds to change.

Agility is about adaptability, not process perfection.

3. Using Vanity Metrics Instead of Meaningful Key Performance Indicators

Organizations often track what is easy to measure rather than what actually drives value.
Examples of vanity metrics that do not provide meaningful insights:

- Number of Agile ceremonies completed
- Number of story points delivered
- Number of retrospectives held

Examples of meaningful metrics that reflect real business impact:

- Customer Satisfaction and Net Promoter Score
- Time-to-value for new product features
- Revenue impact of Agile initiatives
- Employee engagement and retention in Agile teams

What to Do Instead:

- Tie Agile success to key business outcomes.
- Track both qualitative customer feedback and quantitative financial impact.
- Use Agile metrics as a tool for learning, not just reporting.

If an Agile metric does not connect to business impact, it is not worth tracking.
Warning: If the dashboard needs a legend, prune the metric list; clarity beats volume every time.

Beyond Story Points – Rethinking Agile Metrics

Story points were meant to measure effort, not value. Yet many teams treat them as currency, optimizing for velocity instead of impact. Even Ron Jeffries, one of the creators of XP, has spoken out against their misuse.

Adaptive leaders shift the spotlight from estimates to evidence. They prioritize metrics like lead time, customer satisfaction, and feature adoption over abstract effort scores. Tools like Evidence-Based Management (EBM) offer a more grounded approach, tying agility to outcomes that matter: predictability, time to market, and delivered value.

Agile isn't a numbers game – it's a value game. The right metrics guide decisions, spark learning, and reveal what's working. The wrong ones just look good in a slide deck.

Tip – Make progress obvious: a visible Kanban wall or live dashboard keeps everyone aligned on real outcomes.

A Framework for Measuring Agile Success

To measure agility effectively, organizations must track three key areas:

1. **Business Outcomes**: Does agility drive better results?
2. **Customer Impact**: Are we solving real user problems?
3. **Organizational Adaptability**: Are we responding faster to change?

1. Business Outcomes – Measuring the Return on Investment of Agility
Key Metrics

- The revenue impact of Agile initiatives
- Reduction in time-to-market
- Cost savings from Agile transformation

Agility should improve business performance, not just team efficiency.

2. Customer Impact – Are We Delivering What Matters?
Key Metrics

- Customer satisfaction (CSAT)
- Net Promoter Score (NPS)
- Feature adoption and user engagement

Agility is only valuable if it improves customer experience.

3. Organizational Adaptability – How Fast Can We Respond to Change?
Key Metrics

- Time-to-decision for strategic pivots
- Speed of responding to market changes
- Frequency of product iterations

Agility is about adaptability, not just delivery speed.

Metrics for Adaptive Leadership Effectiveness

When Paul became CIO at a fintech startup, he noticed a troubling pattern. While Agile ceremonies were in full swing, decision-making remained largely top-down, and teams lacked true empowerment. The company was doing Agile but not being Agile. To shift leadership behaviour, Paul introduced agility-focused leadership metrics.

Over the next few months, leaders were evaluated not on how many Agile meetings they attended but on how quickly they responded to market changes, empowered teams, and fostered cross-functional collaboration. The results were striking – product innovation accelerated, decision-making improved, and employee engagement soared.

Leadership agility is the cornerstone of true business adaptability. Agility is not just about team-level execution; it is a leadership capability that ensures an organization can respond rapidly to change, improve customer outcomes, and create a culture of continuous learning.

But adaptability isn't just visible in outcomes – it starts with mindset. Specifically, how leaders behave when faced with uncertainty.

Gauging Leadership Adaptability

Metrics alone don't reveal whether leaders are adaptable. You need context. Behaviour. And the ability to reflect.

One way to uncover adaptability is through self-assessment. Not abstract traits but grounded actions. Ask:

- When did I last pivot based on unexpected data?
- Do I lead with flexibility when a plan falls apart?
- Where am I most adaptable – tools, people, or process?
- What does my team need from me in moments of uncertainty – and do I deliver?

These questions shift the mindset from an abstract concept to a measurable leadership capability. The goal isn't to label leaders as adaptable or not, but to give them a mirror. Insight becomes action. And that's where agility starts.

Key Leadership KPIs for Business Agility

To measure leadership agility, organizations should focus on metrics that assess decision speed, adaptability, and impact rather than compliance with Agile rituals.

Metric	Description	How to Measure	Example
Psychological Safety Score	Measures the extent to which team members feel safe to express ideas, take risks, and provide feedback without fear of repercussions.	Use team surveys with questions like, 'I feel comfortable speaking up about potential issues'.	A team with high psychological safety reports a 20% increase in innovation-driven ideas during retrospectives.
Responsiveness to Market Shifts	Evaluates the speed and effectiveness of leadership decisions in response to changing customer or market needs.	Track the time from identifying a market change to implementing a strategic adjustment.	A leader reduces the time to pivot product strategy from six weeks to three through streamlined decision-making processes.
Team Autonomy Index	Assesses the degree of decision-making power teams have within Agile frameworks.	Conduct team interviews to evaluate their perception of autonomy in daily work and long-term goals.	Autonomous teams report a 30% improvement in sprint velocity when empowered to prioritize tasks.
Cross-Team Collaboration Index	Captures the frequency and quality of interactions between cross-functional teams.	Use collaboration tools to monitor cross-team project engagement and conduct post-project reviews.	A leader implements bi-weekly cross-team check-ins, leading to a 15% reduction in project delays.

However, effective metrics should always reflect the organization's priorities and values. Role-based or practice-based KPIs, while well-intentioned, often drive the wrong behaviours. For instance, mandating that every team must have a Scrum Master can lead to rebranding existing roles without meaningful change. True agility is better measured through outcomes such as customer impact, business value delivered, and the ability to quickly adapt to changing needs rather than just frequency of releases or time-to-market improvements. These metrics directly link Agile practices to business value, encouraging teams to focus on delivering impactful results rather than adhering to superficial compliance.

Action Plan for Leaders

- **Measure what matters**: Track leadership agility metrics instead of just Agile compliance.
- **Increase leadership transparency**: Share decision-making effectiveness scores with teams.
- **Improve cross-team collaboration**: Conduct regular alignment meetings between product, engineering, and business leaders.
- **Encourage autonomy**: Reduce unnecessary approvals and empower teams to make decisions.

By tracking leadership agility instead of process adherence, organizations foster resilient, high-performing teams that can rapidly respond to market demands.

The Financial Link Between Agility and Performance

A global pharmaceutical company invested heavily in Agile training and frameworks. One year in, executives were frustrated – they saw no meaningful business impact. Teams were sprinting, story points were being tracked, but product cycles weren't accelerating, and revenue wasn't growing.

Everything changed when they started tying Agile investments to financial performance metrics.

Cultural metrics should be treated with the same seriousness as financial ones. Many organizations track cost, delivery, and risk – but fail to measure trust, inclusion, or team morale. Tools like psychological safety scores, employee Net Promoter Scores (eNPS), and culture pulse surveys help leaders quantify how work feels, not just how it performs.

A global bank recently introduced a psychological safety index into its quarterly review process. It triggered targeted interventions when scores dropped, improving team retention and cross-functional collaboration. Measuring culture is not a soft practice. It's a leadership imperative that links directly to agility and long-term value.

By measuring speed-to-market, customer feedback loops, and cost efficiencies, the company cut product development cycles by 25% and increased revenue from new drug releases. The lesson? Agile isn't about ceremonies; it's about business impact.

Agility as a Measurable Financial Lever

Research by PA Consulting confirms that top financial performers also exhibit strong Agile characteristics. The most successful organizations aren't those that have implemented Agile perfectly – they're the ones that use agility to drive revenue growth, reduce operational costs, and enhance customer retention.

Key Business Metrics for Agility

Rather than focusing on Agile maturity, organizations should track how agility directly impacts business results:

- **Customer Impact Metrics**: Measure agility's effect on customer satisfaction and retention.
- **Speed-to-Market Benchmarks**: Track how quickly teams can turn ideas into revenue-generating products.
- **Cultural Agility Indicators**: Assess how well agility is embedded in leadership decision-making.
- **Financial Correlation Tracking**: Monitor whether agility translates into cost savings and increased revenue.

Real-World Example: Agility Driving Business Outcomes

- A 150-year-old manufacturing company reduced lead times by 30%, improving its competitive position.
- A Boston hospital cut patient wait times by 25%, increasing both efficiency and patient satisfaction.
- A fintech company improved customer retention by focusing on rapid customer feedback integration rather than backlog completion.

Are You Measuring Agility or Business Impact?

Many organizations mistake Agile transformation for Agile success. They invest in training, Agile coaches, and frameworks – yet fail to see real improvements. Why? Because they measure success by process adherence instead of business impact.

Instead of Asking, 'How Agile are we?' Leaders Should Ask:

- Are we delivering value faster?
- Are we improving customer experience?
- Are we reducing lead times?
- Are teams empowered to make decisions?

Agile should never be a box-ticking exercise. The most critical measure of success is not how well an organization follows Agile practices – it's how effectively agility translates into real business value.

Maturity Models

Dispelling Myths Around Maturity Models

Myth 1: Agile Maturity = Agile Success

Many organizations assume that climbing an Agile maturity model means they are getting better at Agile. However, maturity models often focus on process adoption, not real agility.

Reality: The most Agile organizations aren't those that score highest on maturity models but those that can pivot quickly in response to market shifts.

Myth 2: More Agile Practices = More Business Value

Companies often believe that the more Agile frameworks, tools, and rituals they implement, the better they will perform.

Reality: Many companies overcomplicate Agile adoption by forcing rigid frameworks, which can stifle innovation instead of enabling it.

Myth 3: Agility Can Be Measured by Checklists

A common mistake is using checklists and maturity assessments to measure progress without tying them to real business impact.

Reality: Agile success should be measured by:

- **How fast an organization can respond to change.**
- **How effectively teams align with customer needs.**
- **Whether agility improves financial performance.**

How to Use Maturity Models Without Losing Agility

Maturity models aren't useless – but they must be used as tools, not targets.

- **DO**: Use them to identify *areas for improvement*.
- **DO**: Adapt them to *fit your industry and business needs*.
- **DON'T**: Treat them as a *scorecard for success*.

Example: A highly regulated bank adapted Agile maturity models to focus on compliance and customer trust rather than just Agile adoption rates.

Key Takeaway

Agility is not about reaching an 'ideal' maturity level. It's about how fast your organization can adapt and deliver value.

Popular Maturity Models

Several maturity models have been developed to assist organizations in assessing their Agile maturity. These models provide structured frameworks for evaluation and improvement. Let's begin with one of the most established frameworks, CMMI, and understand how it adapts to Agile contexts.

1. CMMI (Capability Maturity Model Integration) – Process Standardization with Flexibility

Initially designed for software development, CMMI has five levels of increasing process maturity:

1.   **Initial**: Ad hoc, reactive processes.
2.   **Managed**: Basic processes established.
3.   **Defined**: Organization-wide standards.
4.   **Quantitatively Managed**: Data-driven improvements.
5.   **Optimizing**: Continuous innovation and adaptability.

Where It Helps

- Highly regulated industries (e.g. banking, healthcare) benefit from structured Agile governance.
- Encourages data-driven decision-making, aligning agility with strategic goals.

Where It Fails

- It can create bureaucracy if used rigidly.
- Doesn't measure agility's business impact.

How to Use It Effectively: Instead of focusing on checklist completion, link CMMI assessments to business agility metrics like customer impact, time-to-market, and revenue growth.

2. SAFe Maturity Model – Scaling Agility in Large Enterprises

SAFe (Scaled Agile Framework) provides a structured approach to scaling Agile.

Competency Areas in SAFe Maturity Models

1.   **Lean-Agile Leadership**: Measures how well leaders enable agility rather than command teams.
2.   **Technical Agility**: Assesses automation, DevOps, and engineering practices that improve adaptability.

3. **Business Agility**: Focuses on an organization's ability to respond to market disruptions.

Where It Helps

- Large, complex organizations needing structured Agile adoption.
- Aligns teams across multiple business units.

Where It Fails

- Overemphasis on process compliance rather than business agility.
- Bureaucratic layering can slow down agility.

How to Use It Effectively

- Use SAFe as a guide, not a rulebook.
- Measure agility by how quickly teams respond to change, not by how many SAFe ceremonies they follow.

3. Agile Fluency Model – Team-Centric Business Agility

Developed by James Shore and Diana Larsen, this model focuses on team-level fluency rather than rigid maturity scores.

Fluency Levels

1. **Focusing**: Teams deliver basic business value.
2. **Delivering**: Agile becomes predictable and consistent.
3. **Optimizing**: Agile improves business strategy.
4. **Strengthening**: Agile drives enterprise-wide change.

Where It Helps

- Ideal for mid-sized tech companies or organizations scaling Agile organically.
- Encourages business-driven agility rather than framework adherence.

Where It Fails

- Lacks structured measurement methods, making it harder to track ROI from Agile adoption.

How to Use It Effectively

- Define success in terms of customer outcomes and business agility rather than Agile fluency scores.

4. Custom Models – Tailoring Agile Maturity to Business Needs

For industries like healthcare, fintech, and manufacturing, custom models work best because they align agility with specific business challenges.

Benefits of Custom Maturity Models

1. **Contextual Relevance**: Addresses unique industry challenges (e.g. compliance, security).
2. **Flexibility**: Adapts to changing priorities and customer needs.
3. **Strategic Alignment**: Ensures agility supports financial and operational goals.

How to Use Custom Models Effectively

- Design models that measure business value creation, adaptability, and leadership agility rather than just Agile practices.
- Use business agility metrics (e.g. customer retention, innovation cycles) as key indicators of success.

Key Takeaway

Maturity models should not dictate agility; they should help measure how agility improves business performance.

Visual Aids and Comparisons

Including tools like radar charts or maturity matrices helps stakeholders understand results more effectively. For instance, a radar chart comparing collaboration, adaptability, and delivery metrics highlights areas requiring attention.

Model	Focus areas	Best fit
CMMI	Process standardization	Regulated industries (e.g. finance)
SAFe Maturity Model	Scaling Agile practices	Large enterprises
Agile Fluency Model	Team-level capabilities	Mid-sized tech companies
Custom Models	Tailored to the organization	Unique or niche industries

These tools provide clarity, enabling organizations to effectively align assessments with improvement strategies.

Once you've chosen or developed a suitable maturity model, the next step involves practical assessment methods, starting with self-assessment tools.

Agile Maturity Self-Assessment Tools

Many organizations use self-assessment tools to measure Agile maturity. The problem? Most tools focus on practice adoption rather than real impact.

Instead of Measuring 'How Agile are we?', Organizations Should Ask:

- **Are we responding to customer needs faster?**
- **Are we delivering measurable business outcomes?**
- **Are we improving cross-functional collaboration?**

Recommended Self-Assessment Approaches

- **Agile Business Impact Score**: Measures how agility improves revenue, customer satisfaction, and market responsiveness.
- **Leadership Agility Index**: Assesses leadership's ability to adapt, delegate, and drive innovation.
- **Cross-Team Collaboration Heatmap**: Tracks the effectiveness of Agile collaboration across departments.

How to Use Self-Assessments Effectively

1. Tie results to business agility metrics, not just Agile process adherence.
2. Use assessments to inform leadership decisions about where to improve adaptability.
3. Benchmark against competitors and industry best practices rather than just internal Agile scores.

Key Takeaway

Assessments should measure agility's business impact, not just framework adoption.

Scoring and Visualizing Maturity

Leadership teams often struggle to determine where agility is working and where bottlenecks exist. By using data-driven visualization, organizations can pinpoint how agility contributes to business success and where improvements are needed.

Recommended Visualization Techniques

1. Business agility heatmaps

- Identify which departments adapt quickly versus those still working in silos.
- Highlight where Agile adoption enhances customer outcomes.
- Detect bottlenecks in decision-making that slow down responsiveness.

2. Customer Impact Scorecards

- Track how agility improves customer retention, satisfaction, and Net Promoter Score (NPS).
- Show which Agile initiatives deliver the most business value.

3. Speed-to-market dashboards

- Illustrate how Agile adoption affects time-to-market and revenue growth.
- Compare pre- and post-Agile launch metrics to assess the impact of agility.

How to Use Agility Visualization Effectively

- Ensure data links to business performance indicators, not just Agile metrics.
- Share insights across leadership teams, not just with Agile coaches.
- Use visual tools to drive strategic decisions on where to refine agility.

Key Takeaway

Agility should not be assessed by the presence of Agile frameworks alone but by its measurable contribution to business outcomes.

Leaders sometimes need a straightforward way to gauge organizational agility. The following material introduces the CLEAR Business Agility Radar (CLEAR-BAR), which highlights strengths, concerns, and priorities at a glance.

CLEAR Business Agility Radar (CLEAR-BAR)

Purpose

The CLEAR-BAR helps adaptive leaders quickly pinpoint strengths, concerns, and priority actions within their organization, all aligned to the CLEAR Model® dimensions.

CLEAR Dimensions and Sub-dimensions

CLEAR Dimension	Sub-dimensions for Assessment
Culture	Psychological Safety, Agile Mindset, Collaboration, Shared Value
Leadership	Adaptive Decision-Making, Empowerment, Transparency, Leadership Modelling
Execution	Value Delivery, Quality of Outcomes, Iterative Cycles, Customer Focus
Adaptability	Flexibility to Change, Learning from Failure, Responsiveness to Feedback
Responsiveness	Decision Speed, Customer Interaction Frequency, Alignment with Needs

Symbols for Assessment Levels

Use distinct symbols to indicate performance in each sub-dimension:

- ✓ ✓ (**Double Check**) = Strong performance, minimal worries.
- ✓ (**Single Check**) = Good performance, minor improvements needed.
- ! (**Exclamation**) = Moderate concerns; action required soon.
- ✗ (**Cross**) = Major concerns; immediate attention needed.

Example CLEAR-BAR Table

CLEAR Dimension	Sub-dimensions	Effectiveness	Practicality	Adoption
Culture	Psychological Safety	✓	!	✗
	Collaboration	✓ ✓	✓	✓
Leadership	Empowerment	✗	!	!
	Adaptive Decision-Making	✓	✓	✓ ✓
Execution	Iterative Cycles	✓ ✓	✓	✓
	Customer Focus	!	✗	✓
Adaptability	Learning from Failure	✗	!	!

CLEAR Dimension	Sub-dimensions	Effectiveness	Practicality	Adoption
	Responsiveness to Feedback	!	✓	✓ ✓
Responsiveness	Decision Speed	✓	✗	!
	Alignment with Needs	✓ ✓	✓	✓

Introducing the CLEAR Business Agility Radar (CLEAR-BAR)

Adaptive leaders benefit from rapid insights on organizational health across multiple agility dimensions. The CLEAR-BAR offers a concise visual assessment, highlighting strengths and urgent improvement areas.

Symbols let leadership see exactly where action is needed and where the organization is performing well. This method steers strategic focus to the highest-impact areas, boosting adaptive leadership principles and encouraging meaningful outcomes.

Why CLEAR-BAR Matters for Adaptive Leadership

- Provides a prompt, intuitive assessment that sparks immediate action.
- Avoids confusion that can arise from colour-based charts in black-and-white print.
- Encourages practical application, offering a direct view of agility status so leaders can shift from analysis to leadership action.

This symbol-driven format fits effectively into a printed book and aligns with the CLEAR Model®. It gives a practical tool for leaders who want to reinforce enterprise agility without delay.

Leaders who apply tools like CLEAR-BAR can combine visual diagnostics with deeper qualitative insights, gaining a thorough view of their teams' agility. The next section explores measuring the return on agility transformations, helping leaders justify these efforts at an organizational level.

Demonstrating the ROI of Agile

Many Agile transformations struggle to gain executive support because they do not demonstrate a clear financial impact. For agility to be valued, leadership must see its contribution to revenue growth, cost efficiency, and market adaptability.

How to Measure Agile ROI

- **Customer Retention Rate**: Does agility help improve customer loyalty?
- **Product Development Speed**: Has Agile reduced time-to-market for new products or features?
- **Revenue Impact**: Are Agile-driven products generating higher profits?
- **Cost Efficiency**: Are Agile teams delivering more value while reducing waste?

Example

A digital payments company linked its Agile adoption to a 20% increase in customer retention and a 35% acceleration in product release cycles, leading to higher revenue.

Key Takeaway

The effectiveness of Agile should be measured in business terms – customer value, revenue growth, and operational efficiency – rather than the number of Agile ceremonies completed.

Incorporating Criticism into Assessments

Agile assessments are valuable only if they reflect the real challenges of agility. Many organizations fall into the trap of treating Agile maturity as a checklist rather than a means of achieving meaningful business outcomes. To ensure assessments drive improvement, leaders must evaluate not just Agile adoption but also the broader organizational culture and leadership behaviours that influence agility.

Avoiding the Common Pitfalls of Agile Assessments

1. **Ritualism vs Real Agility**
   o Agile is not about performing stand-ups, retrospectives, or sprints – it is about how well teams respond to change and deliver value.
   o Assessments should evaluate leadership alignment, empowerment, and adaptability rather than just checking whether Agile ceremonies are in place.
   o **Example**: A company that held daily stand-ups but still relied on top-down decision-making realized that true agility required shifting leadership behaviours, not just adding meetings.
2. **Overemphasis on Frameworks**
   o Many assessments measure how closely teams follow Scrum, SAFe, or other frameworks rather than evaluating whether agility drives business results.
   o Teams should be assessed on how effectively they adapt Agile frameworks to their unique context, rather than on rigid process adherence.
   o **Example**: A global bank measured Agile success based on SAFe implementation, but product delivery cycles remained slow. By shifting focus to customer outcomes rather than framework compliance, they identified blockers in governance and decision-making that were slowing agility.
3. **Ethical Blind Spots in Agile Assessments**
   o Agility should not come at the expense of inclusivity, fairness, or ethical considerations.
   o Assessments should include metrics for diversity, psychological safety, and ethical decision-making.
   o Data protection, privacy, and responsible AI usage should also be evaluated as part of Agile governance.

o **Example**: A tech firm discovered that while Agile improved speed-to-market, it also introduced ethical concerns around algorithmic bias in AI products. Integrating ethical reviews into Agile assessments improved both compliance and customer trust.

Key Takeaway

Agile assessments should not focus solely on whether teams follow processes – they should evaluate whether agility is delivering business value, cultural transformation, and ethical decision-making. Leaders must ensure that agility remains flexible, inclusive, and results-driven rather than a bureaucratic exercise.

Using Maturity Assessments to Plan Improvements

Maturity assessments are only valuable if they lead to meaningful improvements. The goal is not to achieve a high maturity score but to ensure Agile practices drive business success.

Steps to Turn Assessment Insights into Action

1. **Identify Strengths and Gaps**
   o Reinforce high-performing areas where Agile is already delivering impact.
   o Pinpoint recurring weaknesses, such as poor stakeholder collaboration or slow decision-making.
2. **Align Improvements with Business Objectives**
   o Agile should enhance strategic goals like customer satisfaction, faster innovation, and cost efficiency.
   o Ensure assessment insights translate into business-driven action plans.
3. **Set Specific Goals for Improvement**
   o Define measurable objectives, such as reducing time-to-market by 15% or improving customer retention.
   o Establish key performance indicators (KPIs) that track both process efficiency and business impact.
4. **Develop an Actionable Roadmap**
   o Assign responsibilities to leaders, teams, and Agile coaches.
   o Identify required training, coaching, or tools to support improvements.
   o Set clear milestones to measure progress.
5. **Monitor and Adjust**
   o Schedule regular check-ins to track whether Agile maturity improvements are leading to better business outcomes.
   o Be willing to pivot if strategies are not producing expected results.

Key Takeaway

The true purpose of Agile maturity assessments is to create a roadmap for continuous business improvement, not just to measure compliance with Agile practices.

Linking Results to Improvements

For Agile transformation efforts to succeed, measurement must be tied directly to business outcomes. Data collected from maturity assessments should inform decision-making and help close performance gaps.

How to Link Maturity Insights to Business Impact

1. **Use Strengths to Address Weaknesses**
   o   If certain teams excel at customer collaboration, leverage their best practices across the organization.
   o   If one department struggles with responsiveness, use high-performing teams as internal mentors.
2. **Prioritize Business Outcomes Over Process Compliance**
   o   Instead of tracking Agile framework adherence, measure whether agility improves speed, customer satisfaction, and product quality.
   o   Shift focus from Agile ceremony participation to metrics like lead time reduction and customer value creation.
3. **Ensure Leadership Accountability**
   o   Senior leaders should actively support agility initiatives rather than delegating responsibility to Agile coaches alone.
   o   Cross-functional alignment should be a leadership priority, ensuring Agile efforts are not isolated within specific teams.
4. **Create Feedback Loops**
   o   Regularly collect input from teams and customers to assess the real-world impact of Agile changes.
   o   Adjust improvement strategies based on tangible business feedback, not just internal Agile assessments.

Key Takeaway

Measuring Agile maturity is not the end goal – using those insights to drive continuous business improvement is what matters most.

Opportunity Flow as a Leadership Mindset

Agile organizations must do more than initiate change – they must manage the full life cycle of opportunities, from discovery to retirement. Jim Highsmith's concept of Opportunity Flow highlights how leaders can balance innovation with operational efficiency.

The Five Phases of Opportunity Flow

1. **Discovery**: Identifying emerging opportunities based on market trends and customer needs.
2. **Startup**: Testing ideas through small-scale investment before full commitment.

3. **Scale**: Expanding successful initiatives with executive sponsorship and resource allocation.
4. **Mature**: Extracting maximum value while preparing for future shifts.
5. **Decline**: Retiring outdated projects to free up capacity for new initiatives.

Why This Matters for Agile Leaders

- Many organizations struggle with agility because they hold onto outdated projects for too long, leading to resource drain.
- Leaders must actively assess whether existing Agile initiatives continue to deliver business value.
- Regularly reviewing Opportunity Flow ensures that agility is applied where it has the most impact.

Key Takeaway

True agility is not just about starting new projects quickly – it's about managing the entire life cycle effectively to sustain long-term adaptability.

Continuous Discovery in Outcome-Driven Teams

High-performing teams don't just optimize delivery – they optimize discovery. Continuous product discovery means testing assumptions early, often, and cheaply – long before a feature hits production.

Adaptive leaders create space for this by backing practices like hypothesis-driven development, weekly customer conversations, and outcome mapping. These aren't new rituals; they're guardrails to ensure teams are solving the right problems before scaling the wrong ones.

Feedback isn't a stage – it's a loop. Whether through user interviews, prototype testing, or behavioural analytics, keeping the voice of the customer close allows teams to course-correct faster. Agile isn't just about shipping more – it's about learning faster. And learning starts with listening.

Breaking Down Silos

One of the biggest barriers to business agility is organizational fragmentation. Teams that work in isolation create misaligned goals, duplicated efforts, and slower decision-making.

Strategies to Improve Cross-Functional Agility

1. **Align Teams Around Shared Business Outcomes**
   o Ensure departments work toward common goals rather than separate, disconnected priorities.
   o Use cross-functional planning sessions to foster collaboration.

2. **Encourage Open Communication**
   - o Implement regular cross-team reviews to discuss dependencies and challenges.
   - o Use visual management tools to keep teams aligned on key objectives.
3. **Reduce Bottlenecks in Decision-Making**
   - o Empower teams with the autonomy to make decisions within their scope.
   - o Ensure leadership enables faster approvals rather than acting as a bottleneck.
4. **Use Data to Improve Collaboration**
   - o Measure how well teams work together, not just their individual Agile performance.
   - o Track cross-team dependencies to identify where silos still exist.

Key Takeaway

Agility requires more than just efficient teams – it demands seamless collaboration across the organization to deliver real business impact.

Personal Reflection

During one of my transformations, the teams initially measured success by 'how many user stories we delivered'. Leadership was unimpressed. Once I got them to pivot to tracking customer retention and time-to-value, we finally got board-level support. Outcome-based agility demands metrics that resonate beyond sprint velocity.

To illustrate all these principles in action, let's consider real-world examples of organizations that leveraged their maturity assessments to achieve tangible outcomes.

Case Study 1: ING Bank's Agile Transformation

Background: ING Bank embarked on a broad Agile journey to better address customer needs and inspire innovation.

Assessment and Findings

- The maturity model uncovered siloed teams, slow decisions, and weak customer focus.
- Varied Agile adoption across departments.

Actions

- **Organizational Restructuring**: Adopting a 'Spotify model' with squads and tribes.
- **Leadership Engagement**: Senior leaders championed an Agile mindset.
- **Coaching and Training**: Heavy investments in building Agile skills.
- **Cultural Shifts**: Emphasized experimentation and continuous learning.

Results

- Faster product rollouts and higher employee engagement.
- Greater resilience in adapting to market shifts.

Lessons

- Integrate structure, culture, and leadership.
- Ongoing leadership support and trust-building sustain success.

Case Study 2: Ericsson's Agile Journey

Background: Ericsson, a telecom giant, aimed to enhance efficiency and drive innovation via Agile for software teams.

Assessment and Findings

- Initial variance in Agile practices hindered consistency.
- Leadership's partial embrace slowed progress.

Actions

- **Custom Framework**: Tailored to Ericsson's context.
- **Training and Coaching**: Building broad-based Agile competence.
- **Community of Practice**: Encouraged knowledge sharing, addressing common hurdles.
- **Regular Assessments**: Ensured data-informed continuous refinements.

Results

- Unified Agile methods across teams.
- Faster cycles, increased product quality, and improved cross-team collaboration.

Lessons

- Tailor Agile practices to local realities.
- Frequent assessment + responsive improvements = consistent progress.
- A robust learning culture cements positive change.

Improving Agile maturity requires more than measuring practices or outputs – it demands a nuanced approach that considers the organization's context. By aligning improvements with contextual realities, leaders can drive meaningful and sustainable progress.

Context as a Driver for Maturity Improvements

Agile maturity is not a one-size-fits-all journey. Organizations in different industries and markets require different agility strategies.

Adapting Agility to Organizational Context

1. **Highly Regulated Industries**
   o Compliance requirements may necessitate a hybrid Agile approach.
   o Agile frameworks should incorporate regulatory checkpoints without slowing down innovation.
2. **Technology-Driven Companies**
   o Faster iteration cycles and product-market fit validation are key priorities.
   o Agility should focus on rapid prototyping, experimentation, and data-driven decision-making.
3. **Customer-Centric Businesses**
   o Agile must prioritize customer experience improvements over internal efficiency gains.
   o Agile teams should work closely with customers to validate assumptions.
4. **Scaling Enterprises**
   o The focus should be on aligning agility across departments rather than optimizing isolated teams.
   o Leadership involvement is critical to preventing agility from becoming fragmented.

Key Takeaway

Agile maturity models must be tailored to an organization's unique challenges and market conditions, ensuring that agility drives relevant business outcomes.

Overcoming Common Challenges

Many Agile transformations fail due to predictable obstacles. Addressing these challenges early ensures long-term success.

Common Pitfalls and How to Address Them

1. **Resistance to Change**
   o Communicate benefits, involve teams from the start, and invest in training to dispel misunderstandings.
   o **Example**: Cisco overcame staff anxiety by organizing workshops to illustrate Agile's benefits, earning trust and buy-in.
2. **Lack of Executive Support**
   o Align Agile with core objectives to present pilot successes.

  o **Example**: Nokia pivoted after realizing leadership involvement was crucial – leaders took Agile training themselves, reigniting momentum.

3. **Inadequate Training and Coaching**
  o Provide real-world education, hire expert coaches, and promote continuous learning.
  o **Example**: ING Bank overcame confusion by building an Agile 'academy' and employing skilled coaches across teams.

4. **Misalignment Between Teams**
  o Cross-functional squads, open communication, 'Scrum of Scrums'.
  o **Example**: Barclays used an enterprise Agile framework with regular multi-team syncs, bridging gaps and boosting knowledge sharing.

5. **Measuring Success Incorrectly**
  o Shift from output metrics to outcome-based indicators.
  o **Example**: Spotify emphasized user satisfaction over feature counts, fine-tuning their approach to maximize customer benefit.

6. **Over-fixation on Tools/Frameworks**
  o Focus on outcomes, letting teams adapt frameworks as needed.
  o **Example**: Atlassian allowed squads to choose their own boards and schedules so long as they supported alignment and strategic goals.

7. **Remote or Hybrid Collaboration**
  o Encourage asynchronous updates, define 'core hours', and integrate social connections.
  o **Example**: GitLab's all-remote model documents everything, ensuring every collaborator, anywhere, can easily align with Agile ceremonies.

8. **Lack of Psychological Safety**
  o Leaders model vulnerability and run 'blameless retros'.
  o **Example**: Google's Project Aristotle showed psychological safety fosters the best team outcomes, fuelling open creativity.

9. **Weak Product Ownership or Vision**
  o Dedicate a product owner with the authority to prioritize and shape the roadmap.
  o **Example**: Netflix invests in strong product owners who unify real-time data insights with a user-centric strategic vision.

10. **Compliance and Regulatory Constraints**
  o Incorporate compliance early in sprints and embed legal/regulatory experts within squads.
  o **Example**: A digital health firm put a compliance officer in its Scrum team, avoiding last-minute compliance fixes that hamper iteration.

Key Takeaway

Agile transformations succeed when they proactively address the cultural and operational barriers that often derail change efforts.

Learning from Past Mistakes

Many failed Agile transformations result from a narrow focus on frameworks rather than outcomes. Reflecting on past missteps can help organizations build more resilient Agile strategies.

Key Lessons from Failed Agile Transformations

- **Overemphasis on Process Over Impact**: Agile success is not about perfect adherence to Scrum or SAFe; it's about delivering better business results.
- **Superficial Adoption Without Cultural Change**: Without leadership buy-in and mindset shifts, Agile remains a surface-level practice rather than a true transformation.
- **Failure to Iterate and Improve**: Agile itself must be applied iteratively; transformation efforts should adapt based on feedback and results.

Key Takeaway

Agile is not a destination but a continuous learning process. Success comes from refining and adapting Agile approaches based on real-world experience.

Conclusion

Measuring agility is not about tracking adherence to Agile frameworks – it is about ensuring agility drives tangible business impact. This chapter has outlined how leaders can shift from measuring process compliance to assessing business outcomes, customer value, and organizational adaptability. The key to sustained agility is continuous assessment and refinement, ensuring that Agile practices remain relevant and responsive to change.

Maturity assessments help organizations move beyond vanity metrics like velocity and Agile ceremonies, instead focusing on real business drivers such as customer retention, faster time-to-market, and innovation capability. By measuring what truly matters, leaders can ensure that agility delivers long-term value rather than becoming a box-ticking exercise.

Agility should not be a static achievement but an ongoing journey. Businesses that embed regular feedback loops and data-driven decision-making into their agility measurement approach will remain resilient in the face of change. Leaders must champion a culture where agility adapts as fast as market conditions evolve, ensuring it remains a core driver of success.

The key takeaway is clear: Adaptive Leaders don't just track output; they champion outcome-based metrics. Agility isn't about measuring activity – it's about measuring impact. The next chapter examines how Agile roles are evolving in response to organizational needs, ensuring teams and leaders can scale agility successfully.

Call to Action

As an adaptive leader, assess whether your current metrics capture the true value of agility. Are you still measuring Agile by story points and sprint velocity or by real business outcomes like customer satisfaction, innovation speed, and strategic impact? Shift your focus – start a maturity assessment, identify improvement areas, and refine your approach. Build a habit of continuous evaluation to ensure agility remains dynamic, relevant, and a driver of lasting business success.

Key Takeaways

- **Measuring Business Agility**: Focuses on delivering customer and market impact rather than just adhering to Agile processes.
- **Using Agile Assessment Models**: Whether established or tailored, models should align with business objectives and industry context.
- **Applying Data-Driven Insights**: Surveys, scorecards, and business impact metrics provide meaningful measurement.
- **Interpreting Results for Growth**: Identify agility bottlenecks, prioritize business outcomes, and drive cross-functional collaboration.
- **Sustaining Agility as a Competitive Advantage**: Use assessments not as compliance tools but as enablers of continuous innovation and market responsiveness.

CLEAR Model® Connection

- **Execution**: Business agility is only valuable when it translates into tangible, strategic results.
- **Responsiveness**: Organizations must measure how quickly they adapt to change, not just how well they follow Agile frameworks.

Key Takeaway: Measuring Agile success requires shifting from activity-based metrics to business-driven, outcome-focused agility. Leaders must ensure Agile initiatives deliver measurable impact.

Business Agility Assessment Framework

1. **Maturity Levels:**
   o Ad Hoc, Managed, Defined, Outcome-Driven, Adaptable.
2. **Key Assessment Areas:**
   o Decision-making speed, cross-functional collaboration, customer-centricity, leadership adaptability, and innovation cycles.
3. **Scoring System:**
   o Evaluate based on adaptability, market responsiveness, and customer impact.

Self-Assessment Questionnaire

- How frequently does your organization pivot based on customer feedback?
- Are Agile metrics tied to business KPIs or internal team output?
- How quickly can leadership implement strategic shifts based on market signals?

Improvement Plan Framework

1. **Identify Business Agility Gaps:**
   o   Use assessment results to highlight areas requiring change.
2. **Set Strategic Objectives:**
   o   Define clear, outcome-focused agility goals.
3. **Develop Targeted Initiatives:**
   o   Implement specific actions that enhance adaptability, speed, and customer value.
4. **Allocate Leadership Accountability:**
   o   Ensure leadership owns agility improvements, not just Agile teams.
5. **Track and Refine Progress:**
   o   Review agility metrics regularly and adapt as needed.

Chapter Summary

Outcome-driven agility requires continuous measurement and refinement. This chapter outlined how leadership metrics, business-focused agility models, and customer impact assessments replace outdated process adherence. By tracking real indicators – like decision-making speed and customer value – organizations move from doing Agile to becoming truly adaptive, ensuring agility remains a strategic advantage.

12

The Evolution of Agile Roles – What's Next for Agile Jobs?

The illiterate of the 21st century will not be those who cannot read and write, but those who cannot learn, unlearn, and relearn.

Alvin Toffler

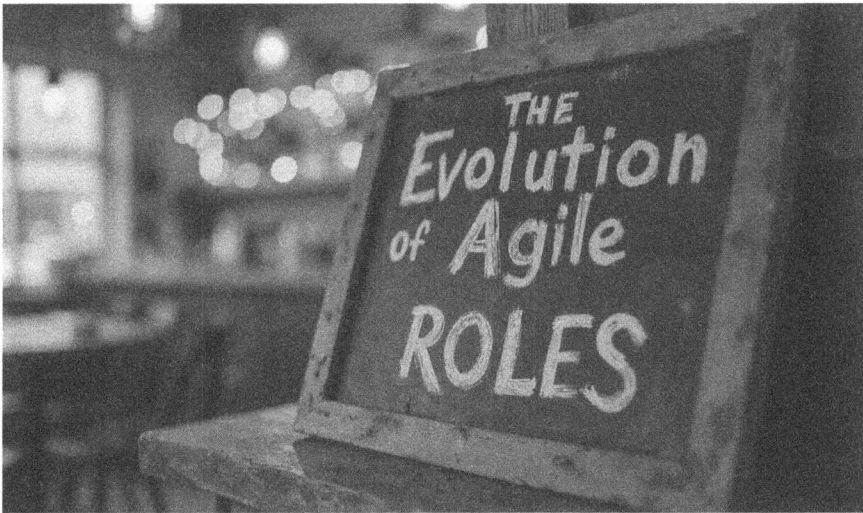

What You'll Gain

- **For Senior Leaders and Executives**: Understand how Agile roles evolve alongside emerging technology, strategic shifts, and new collaboration styles – and why these roles are still vital.
- **For Mid-Level Leaders**: See how traditional Agile functions like Scrum Master and Product Owner expand beyond frameworks to shape culture, strategy, and business impact.
- **For Students or Early-Career Professionals**: Discover skills that future-proof Agile careers, focusing on leadership, tech-savviness, and cross-functional collaboration.

The Evolution of Agile Roles

Samantha, an established Agile Coach, felt uneasy scanning a new industry report on AI's effect on Agile. Headlines claimed that automation was taking over backlog management and even replacing some coaching. She thought: *'Are Agile roles just going to vanish?'*

The truth is more nuanced. Agile roles aren't dying – they're changing shape. With AI handling routine tasks, Agile professionals must evolve beyond process facilitation and become strategic enablers of innovation and adaptability.

Case in point: Capital One recently restructured teams, eliminating many Scrum Master and Agile Coach positions. This ignited panic across the Agile community. However, upon closer look, those responsibilities were folded into leadership roles or integrated within cross-functional teams, raising the bar for Agile practitioners to align more closely with strategy, commercial outcomes, and cultural transformation.

Personal Reflection

In my early years, I saw Agile roles as fixed – overseeing sprints, planning backlogs, etc. Then, I met a Product Owner bridging sales and engineering to deliver game-changing results. It dawned on me: Agile roles shift and expand, shaping how teams collaborate and deliver.

This chapter, building on earlier explorations of supportive environment – focuses on how these roles are mutating, challenging the myth that they might fade away. We'll also reveal essential skills to stay relevant and push beyond mere frameworks.

When Agile first emerged, organizations introduced new roles such as Scrum Masters, Product Owners, and Agile Coaches to support implementation and guide transformation.

But as Agile matures, these roles are shifting – or disappearing entirely.

The Agile job market is changing:

- Companies no longer need Agile cheerleaders – they need adaptable leaders.
- Agile frameworks are becoming less important than Agile thinking.
- AI and automation are replacing repetitive Agile tasks.

Agile Jobs Are Evolving, Not Disappearing

When Max joined his company as a traditional Scrum Master, his primary responsibilities were organizing daily stand-ups and ensuring sprint backlogs were well-maintained. Five years later, automation had streamlined these tasks, and Max found himself in a new role – Agile Strategy Lead. Instead of tracking user stories, he now facilitated executive-level Agile adoption, focusing on business agility rather than just team processes. This shift highlights the broader transition from operational Agile roles to strategic enablers of transformation.

This also reflects a larger industry shift: Agile professionals must adapt, aligning more closely with business outcomes, leadership, and technology-driven agility.

Agile professionals often describe their career journeys as akin to continuous learning in fields like medicine or education. Rather than mastering a static skill set, they cultivate ever-expanding expertise and experience. Like a general practitioner in healthcare, Agile practitioners adapt their abilities to meet evolving organizational needs, focusing on maintaining a flexible approach rather than pursuing an endpoint of mastery.

Roles That Are Shifting

- **Scrum Master**: As teams become self-managing, the need for facilitators is diminishing.
- **Agile Coach**: Many organizations are embedding agility into leadership, reducing reliance on external coaches.
- **SAFe Consultants**: Large-scale frameworks are losing traction as organizations favour simplicity.

Roles That Are Thriving and Emerging

- **Adaptive Leaders**: Agile professionals who integrate strategy, execution, and change leadership.
- **AI-Augmented Product Owners**: Leaders who leverage AI for better decision-making.
- **Flow Managers**: Experts in value stream optimization, moving beyond rigid Agile frameworks.

As Agile continues to serve as a catalyst for organizational transformation, those fulfilling these roles are likewise evolving. Forward-thinking leaders recognize that Agile practitioners are vital in driving cultural shifts and embedding continuous improvement in the company. As discussed previously, Agile itself remains highly relevant; its associated roles – Scrum Master, Agile Coach, and Product Owner – are likewise shifting rather than disappearing altogether. Now, they often transcend frameworks and rituals, becoming drivers of cultural change and adaptability while also focusing on the commercial outcomes Agile was always intended to enable.

Personal Reflection

I've personally seen Scrum Masters progress from scheduling stand-ups to spearheading transformative efforts. In one instance, a Scrum Master led a cross-departmental initiative that eliminated long-standing inefficiencies, cutting operational costs by more than 15%. Such scenarios remind us that Agile roles extend far beyond frameworks; they enable enduring change.

Key Observations

- **Scrum Masters** become change agents, aligning leadership and encouraging continuous improvement.
- **Agile Coaches** evolve into leadership mentors, integrating Agile mindsets at all levels of an organization.
- **Product Owners** expand into cross-functional strategists, partnering with marketing, sales, and support to ensure product visions match market opportunities.

Another vital factor supporting the evolution of these Agile roles is how teams can move skills where they are needed most. This leads us to the idea of talent fluidity.

Talent Fluidity as a Value Amplifier

Adaptive leadership increasingly depends on talent fluidity – the ability to shift skills across projects and teams. Organizations that proactively build talent fluidity amplify their agility by quickly aligning skills with strategic priorities. Leaders must foster cultures encouraging continuous learning, flexible role definitions, and internal mobility. Doing so enables quicker responses to new opportunities, boosts creativity, and sustains high-value delivery through continuous talent reallocation.

Yet, Agile professionals are not the only ones shaping how work gets done. A growing movement is empowering business users to develop their own digital solutions – without needing technical expertise. The Citizen Developer Movement is redefining the boundaries between business and technology, accelerating innovation while raising new challenges for Agile teams.

The Citizen Developer Movement and Agile Roles

The emergence of low-code and no-code platforms is democratizing software development. Business users, often without formal coding experience, can now build applications, automate workflows, and improve operational efficiency without waiting for IT. Platforms like Microsoft Power Apps, Mendix, and OutSystems allow employees to create their own solutions, reducing the backlog for software teams.

From a business agility perspective, this shift aligns with Agile principles:

- **Faster Iteration**: Business teams can rapidly test and deploy solutions.
- **Decentralized Decision-Making**: Employees closest to a problem can develop solutions without bottlenecks.
- **Cross-Functional Collaboration**: Agile Coaches and Scrum Masters can facilitate citizen-led innovation, integrating it into Agile workflows.

Impact on Agile Roles

This movement potentially reshapes Agile roles in several ways:

1. **Scrum Masters as Enablers**
   Instead of focusing solely on ceremonies, Scrum Masters can support citizen development initiatives, ensuring that Agile principles – like iterative improvement and user feedback – are embedded in these efforts.
2. **Product Owners as Business Innovators**
   Product Owners can now co-create solutions with business stakeholders, leveraging citizen developers to prototype and refine applications before full-scale development.
3. **Agile Coaches as Governance Guides**
   With business users building applications, governance becomes critical. Agile Coaches can ensure that citizen development aligns with security, compliance, and long-term agility goals.

Challenges and Considerations

While the benefits are significant, there are risks:

- **Shadow IT**: Unregulated development can lead to security and compliance issues.
- **Scalability**: Not all citizen-developed apps are built for long-term growth.
- **Skill Gaps**: Non-technical users may lack the experience to design robust, maintainable solutions.

To Address These, Agile Leaders Should

- Establish **governance frameworks** that support citizen development without stifling innovation.
- Provide **training** on Agile practices, iterative feedback, and Lean principles.
- Encourage **Scrum Masters and Agile Coaches** to support, rather than control, citizen-led innovation.

As citizen developers take on a more active role in building digital solutions, Agile professionals must adapt. Just as AI is transforming Agile workflows, low-code/no-code development is pushing Agile beyond software teams and into business-led innovation. This shift underscores the need for Agile roles to evolve from facilitators to enablers of enterprise-wide agility.

Agile Roles: Adapting to Avoid Obsolescence

As organizations reach higher maturity, they often reduce strictly defined Agile positions like 'Scrum Master' or 'Agile Coach'. Instead, they blend Agile competencies into everyday leadership or cross-functional squads. This fosters strategic agility rather than limiting it to a single framework.

Adaptive leaders see the big picture: Skilled Agile professionals are crucial for cultural shifts, bridging silos, and championing continuous improvement. By expanding their strategic and technological perspective, these individuals become transformation enablers, not just Agile framework experts.

A Note on Integrity in Evolving Roles

As Agile roles evolve, it's important to avoid performative rebranding. Moving into areas like product strategy or business consulting requires more than new titles – it demands real experience, accountability, and outcomes delivered. The shift from Scrum Master or Agile Coach to roles with broader influence must be earned through exposure to commercial pressures, team leadership, and tangible results. Without this foundation, role evolution risks becoming hollow. The future of Agile depends on substance over spin.

Moving from Framework-Focused to Adaptive Function

A major telecom discovered that simply scaling Scrum company-wide wasn't enough. They re-labelled Product Owners as 'Value Delivery Leads', emphasizing ROI and user satisfaction. Agile Coaches pivoted to broader 'business agility' across finance, HR, and operations. This approach replaced a rigid process emphasis with Agile roles that align with the company's deeper strategic aims.

In many cases, roles are taking on responsibilities akin to doctors in a healthcare system: mixing broad knowledge with specialized insights where needed. An Agile Coach might remain hands-on with one team while also guiding cross-departmental transformations. That synergy ensures both practical relevance and strategic sway.

Results

- Teams can unify short-term wins with long-range adaptability.
- Cross-functional alignment fosters real-time collaboration.
- Agile roles integrate more deeply with the business side.

Personal Reflection

I recall working with a longtime Project Manager who feared becoming obsolete under Agile. We reframed her role into a facilitator of collaboration, coaching teams on backlogs and identifying cross-team dependencies. She embraced it fully, proving that Agile roles aren't replaced; they adapt to the new reality.

New and Evolving Roles

As Agile expands beyond IT, new roles are emerging across industries. In healthcare, 'Agile Care Coordinators' use iterative methods to enhance patient journeys. In finance, 'Agile Investment Analysts' apply lean experimentation to portfolio strategies. Meanwhile, manufacturing firms now employ 'Agile Supply Chain Managers' to streamline operations using iterative planning. These roles illustrate how Agile thinking is adapting to industry-specific challenges.

As Agile roles expand, new ones emerge. Agile Transformation Leaders or Agile Ways of Working Leaders coordinate entire organizations toward Agile's transformative potential. Working with various teams, they embed Agile culture at the core of strategic decisions, championing continuous improvement and change. Meanwhile, Enterprise Agile Coaches operate at higher levels, scaling Agile practices and mindsets beyond single teams. By collaborating with senior leadership, they ensure alignment with broader strategic objectives.

Definitions

- **Agile Transformation Leaders (or Ways of Working Leaders)**: Guide companies through adopting and scaling Agile by embedding principles into the culture, influencing strategic choices, and driving organizational change.
- **Enterprise Agile Coaches**: Focus on scaling Agile mindsets, leadership behaviours, and practices across the organization. They bridge the gap between top executives and delivery teams, ensuring strategic alignment while fostering a culture of collaboration, adaptability, and continuous learning.

With these roles defined, we can explore practical examples of organizations that have successfully integrated them into their Agile ecosystems.

Real-World Examples

Capital One: As part of a broader move toward operational efficiency, Capital One integrated Agile principles into leadership and long-term planning. Enterprise Agile Coaches worked hand in hand with department heads, speeding up product delivery and aligning corporate goals more effectively.

Tesla: Famous for blending Agile practices into hardware and manufacturing, Tesla's Product Owners collaborate across R&D and engineering to create disruptive, market-leading products. This illustrates how Agile roles can extend beyond software, yielding real-world innovation and outcomes.

These examples demonstrate that as Agile roles evolve, individuals must be prepared for continuous learning and skill refinement, spanning strategic, cultural, and technical spheres.

Embracing Lifelong Learning and Overcoming Challenges

Practitioners must commit to perpetual skill expansion – embracing new methods, tools, and insights. Resistance to change is common, so Agile professionals should use tactics like quick wins, alliance-building, and transparent communication to demonstrate the value of Agile and gain support.

Mirroring the ongoing training of medical professionals, Agile's approach to learning must never be static. Practitioners continually refine their capabilities to guide teams that can thrive despite uncertainties and complexities.

Future-Proofing Your Agile Career

To stay relevant in the evolving Agile job market, professionals must:

Shift from Process Expert to Adaptive Leader

- Agile framework knowledge alone won't future-proof a career.
- Leadership, decision-making, and strategic thinking will.

What to Focus On

- **Change Leadership**: Leading Agile transformations, not just coaching teams.
- **Enterprise Agility**: Scaling agility beyond IT into business strategy.
- **Outcome-Based Leadership**: Measuring success by business impact, not Agile rituals.

Embrace AI and Data-Driven Agility

- AI isn't a threat – it's an opportunity.
- Agile professionals must learn how to leverage AI, not fear it.

What to Focus On

- **AI-Augmented Decision-Making**: Using AI to enhance backlog prioritization.
- **Data-Driven Agility**: Measuring agility based on real business outcomes.
- **Intelligent Automation**: Eliminating repetitive Agile tasks through AI tools.

Master Value-Driven Agility, Not Just Frameworks

- Framework knowledge alone won't keep Agile professionals relevant.
- Delivering measurable value will.

What to Focus On

- **Customer-Centric Agility**: Aligning Agile work with real customer impact.
- **Business Agility Metrics**: Measuring agility by value, not process compliance.
- **Product-Led Agility**: Using Agile to drive business growth, not just team efficiency.

Agile professionals who evolve from process managers to value-driven leaders will shape the future of agility.

Developing New Skills for Evolving Roles

With Agile roles expanding, professionals must sharpen an array of abilities:

- **Leadership and Strategy**: Align Agile with organizational objectives, bridging daily iteration and market realities.
- **Cross-Functional Collaboration**: Unite diverse departments, connecting technology, operations, finance, or marketing.
- **Emotional Intelligence and Communication**: Master relationship-building, conflict resolution, and dialogue that fosters psychological safety.
- **Tech Proficiency**: Harness AI, machine learning, and analytics for predictive risk management and real-time iteration.
- **Continuous Learning**: Adapt to new frameworks, tools, and leadership approaches.
- **Commercial Acumen**: Understand how efficiency, user satisfaction, or innovation affects financial performance.

Personal Reflection

One Scrum Master I knew used data analysis to identify hidden workflow bottlenecks, increasing project ROI by 18%. This cross-cutting skill set exemplifies the critical intersection of technology, finance, and leadership that future Agile roles demand.

Comparisons with healthcare spotlight how both generalist and specialist expertise can strengthen an Agile team. For instance, the NHS uses a flow system to triage patients according to urgency, illustrating the value of adaptability. Likewise, Agile roles demand a mix of broad-based agility and, when necessary, focused specialization.

Moreover, a rising number of Agile-focused workshops and courses can sometimes lead to overcommercialization. George Bernard Shaw's quip – *'Those who can, do; those who can't, teach'* – remains a cautionary note. History's greatest minds combined profound expertise with practical application, unlike instructors who sometimes lack a solid track record. Adaptive leaders must ensure learning remains grounded in experience, not merely dogma. Reflecting on this, ask yourself:

> As an adaptive leader, are you providing opportunities for your Agile practitioners to develop these new skills? How can you support their growth to meet the evolving demands of the future of work?

While developing new skills is essential, practitioners may face various challenges as they transition into these evolving roles. Recognizing and addressing these challenges is crucial for successful adaptation. However, as professionals strive to enhance their skill sets, they may encounter practical obstacles and need strategies to overcome them.

Challenges Faced by Agile Practitioners in Evolving Roles

Agile professionals stepping into broader-impact roles may encounter:

1. **Cultural Pushback**: Teams or managers reluctant to expand beyond familiar tasks.
2. **Steep Skill Curve**: Shifting to strategic or technical scopes that require new learning.
3. **Role Ambiguity**: Unclear responsibilities when bridging multiple departments.
4. **Increased Complexity**: More stakeholders mean more potential friction.
5. **Need for Balanced Authority**: Practitioners may lack direct managerial power, relying on influence, persuasion, and trust.

Resilience and adaptability remain critical, helping Agile professionals stay the course amid ever-evolving circumstances. Agile is inherently open-ended, demanding continual innovation, learning, and a 'beginner's mind', all of which can boost agility in volatile environments. Acknowledging these challenges guides us to solutions for ensuring roles evolve effectively within a broader organizational change context.

Developing and Supporting New Competencies

Organizations play a central role in advancing Agile careers:

1. **Provide Training and Development**: Invest in programmes that equip Agile professionals with the skills they need.
2. **Communicate the Vision**: Clearly express why evolving Agile roles matter and how they tie to strategic aims.
3. **Encourage Collaboration**: Organize cross-functional efforts to expand awareness of the broader business.
4. **Offer Mentorship and Coaching**: Pair seasoned Agile professionals with those transitioning into expanded roles.
5. **Recognize and Reward Adaptability**: Celebrate individual and team efforts to adapt, reinforcing a growth mindset.

Adhering to these principles ensures organizations can guide Agile practitioners through times of change.

Building on these organizational strategies, let's outline practical steps that Agile practitioners can take to develop the skills needed for their evolving roles.

Practical Steps for Skill Development

For Agile professionals aiming to upskill:

1. **Pursue Advanced Training**: Enrol in leadership, strategic management, or emerging tech courses.
2. **Engage in Cross-Functional Initiatives**: Find opportunities to collaborate across departments and gain holistic insights.
3. **Develop Soft Skills**: Join workshops or coaching sessions on communication, conflict resolution, and emotional intelligence.
4. **Stay Current Technologically**: Attend industry events or read relevant journals to keep pace with AI, Machine Learning (ML), and emerging technologies.
5. **Build Commercial Understanding**: Cultivate knowledge of the business's financial drivers – revenue, savings, efficiency gains – to clarify your team's overall impact.

By combining self-driven growth with supportive leadership, Agile practitioners can adapt successfully, benefitting both themselves and their organizations.

Adaptive leadership can empower these evolving roles by promoting continuous learning, encouraging cross-functional skill acquisition, and ensuring roles adapt as organizational needs evolve. Yet, beyond leadership support, fostering integration across functions and disciplines further solidifies the position of Agile roles in the future of work.

A vital strategy to support the evolution of Agile roles is recognizing and encouraging the integrative nature of Agile work, requiring a holistic approach that brings together various fields and perspectives, moving beyond specialization. Organizations can foster this integration by promoting collaboration across teams and disciplines, reducing the 'silo effect' that hinders comprehensive, Agile solutions. To accomplish this, leaders must adopt specific practices that nurture these evolving roles, guiding Agile professionals toward broader organizational impact.

Leadership Practices for Evolving Agile Roles

Agile leadership is about deep motivation, not top-down dictates. Achieving organizational change relies on inspiring teams to adapt willingly, not forcibly. Just as personal change (e.g. quitting smoking) often depends on intrinsic reasons, effective Agile leadership fosters autonomy, clarity, and genuine commitment.

1. **Build Trust and Psychological Safety**
   o Encourage safe-to-fail experimentation and open dialogue.
   o Promote emotional intelligence training so teams handle interpersonal friction constructively.

2. **Empower Teams and Individuals**
   o Grant real autonomy matched with accountability for outcomes.
   o Invest in continuous learning to expand skill sets and keep roles dynamic.
3. **Drive Collaboration and Alignment**
   o Break departmental silos with cross-functional initiatives.
   o Routinely synchronize objectives so each function sees the overarching vision.
4. **Foster Innovation and Experimentation**
   o Allow small, low-risk pilots to test new ideas.
   o Embrace a culture of iteration – fail fast, learn quickly, refine for next time.
5. **Align with Organizational Strategy**
   o Link Agile roles to top-level goals, ensuring that daily work advances the mission.
   o Offer mentorship for Agile practitioners stepping into more strategic realms.

By adopting these practices, leaders can facilitate the effective evolution of Agile roles, ensuring these practitioners are equipped to drive the next stage of Agile transformation within their organizations. As these leadership practices take hold, Agile professionals must also adapt to external changes, particularly the influence of emerging technologies.

Leadership in Agile is not about exerting control but about fostering understanding. Teams perform best when they have clarity about their work and its purpose. This requires leaders to focus on equipping teams with the knowledge and tools they need to make informed decisions. By prioritizing understanding over authority, leaders empower their teams to navigate challenges with confidence and autonomy.

Technological Advancements Shaping Agile Roles

Technological shifts – from AI to automation – are redefining Agile roles, not replacing them. Agile practitioners must embrace these shifts, leveraging technology to enhance decision-making, workflow optimization, and business impact.

- **AI and ML Applications**: Practitioners should learn how AI can perform predictive analytics, helping anticipate project risks and suggesting backlog prioritization based on historical data.
- **Leveraging Automation**: Mastering relevant tools allows teams to reduce manual effort and focus on strategic work. AI-powered assistants can now automate backlog management, generate user stories, and highlight process bottlenecks – but leadership and strategic thinking remain human responsibilities.
- **Data-Driven Agility**: By analysing real-time data, Agile professionals can identify trends in user behaviour and adjust priorities dynamically, ensuring Agile work remains outcome-focused rather than process-driven.

As automation expands, new Agile roles are emerging to maximize the benefits of AI:

- **AI-Augmented Product Owners**: These professionals leverage AI insights to enhance product strategy, ensuring prioritization is data-driven rather than intuition-based.

- **Flow Managers**: Rather than focusing on Agile ceremonies, Flow Managers optimize value streams across entire organizations, improving efficiency beyond traditional Agile frameworks.

The Shift: From Process Management to Decision Enablement

AI is no longer just an efficiency tool – it is reshaping the role of Agile professionals.

- AI can **automate backlog management**, reducing the manual effort of prioritization.
- AI can **generate user stories** based on historical data, customer feedback, and predictive models.
- AI can **identify performance patterns** across Agile teams, highlighting productivity bottlenecks.

However, while AI enhances efficiency, it cannot replace leadership, strategic thinking, and human intuition. Agile professionals must shift from process facilitators to decision enablers – leveraging AI-driven insights while making the critical calls that machines cannot.

The Future of Agile Jobs Lies in Skills AI Can't Automate

- **Critical Thinking and Decision-Making**: AI can suggest priorities, but leaders must weigh trade-offs and navigate uncertainty.
- **Complex Problem-Solving**: AI can analyse patterns, but humans must interpret context and balance competing business needs.
- **Emotional Intelligence and Team Leadership**: AI doesn't inspire, mentor, or build trust – people do. Agile professionals must strengthen their ability to coach, influence, and align teams.

Far from displacing human expertise, AI magnifies it by handling routine processes so teams can channel energy into creativity, leadership, and strategic agility. The future belongs to Agile professionals who leverage AI to enhance agility, not those who resist it.

The Role of Human Expertise in an AI-Driven Agile World

A multinational retail company implemented AI-driven sprint planning to automate backlog prioritization. While efficiency improved, teams struggled with prioritizing nuanced, high-impact decisions. Agile Coaches stepped in, using AI insights as a starting point while guiding strategic trade-offs based on customer feedback and business objectives. This example highlights that AI can enhance Agile execution, but human expertise remains crucial in driving meaningful agility.

While AI can streamline various Agile processes, it falls short of human aptitude for creativity, empathy, and refined judgment. Concepts like 'Extreme Agile' propose automating large segments of workflow, raising questions about the future of coding and other roles. Yet many experts, including Tobias Mayer, argue that programming is an art, requiring skill, empathy, and an understanding of context that AI cannot replicate. As a result, AI is best viewed as a companion tool that complements, rather than replaces, human strengths.

The Impact of AI on Job Security in Agile Roles

Although AI can automate repetitive tasks – like building dashboards or predicting sprint backlogs – Agile roles themselves remain secure because they centre on problem-solving, empathy, strategic thinking, and cultural influence. Far from rendering Scrum Masters or Agile Coaches obsolete, AI augments their reach by handling mundane duties and freeing them to focus on higher-value work: coaching teams, driving alignment, and guiding complex decisions that demand human insight. In fact, as AI capabilities increase, Agile practitioners who harness AI for predictive analytics or automated reporting will find themselves in even greater demand. These professionals can interpret AI outputs, maintain psychological safety, and facilitate crucial trade-offs that no algorithm can fully manage.

Looking Forward

Instead of fearing job displacement, Agile professionals can view AI as a strategic ally. By staying informed on AI tools, developing data fluency, and refining leadership soft skills, they become indispensable. As the Agile community has always adapted to new methods and technologies, it can readily incorporate AI to accelerate innovation while keeping the human touch that fosters real trust and collaboration. In this sense, AI complements the Agile mindset, reinforcing rather than replacing the continuous improvement principles that drive organizational success.

That said, a few practical habits help ensure AI supports the team without compromising clarity, trust, or delivery quality. These are not rules to enforce, but principles to guide how Agile teams integrate AI responsibly into everyday work.

1. Know What Not to Share

Not all content should go into an AI tool. Teams can agree on what is fine to include, what needs editing, and what stays out completely. Customer details, strategic discussions, and sensitive internal documents should be handled with care. This avoids unintentional exposure.

2. Keep the Human in Charge

Agile is built on human values – judgment, empathy, and collaboration. AI can assist, but it should not replace the thinking, listening, and leadership that comes from people. Roles like Scrum Master or Product Owner must remain grounded in human insight.

3. Check Before Trusting the Output

AI-generated suggestions should be reviewed by the team before being put into use. Whether it's a backlog item, a test scenario, or a delivery forecast, human validation ensures accuracy and avoids costly mistakes.

4. Make It Clear When AI Helped

If AI played a part in what the team produced, especially anything public or customer-facing, this should be noted. Keeping a simple record of where and how AI contributed protects clarity and avoids confusion about authorship.

These habits don't require ceremonies or checklists. Just a little discipline and shared understanding help teams use AI confidently while protecting the integrity of their work.

Beyond AI, another major force shaping modern Agile roles is the shift toward remote and hybrid work, demanding new ways to preserve human collaboration across distances.

Thriving in Remote and Hybrid Environments

Modern Agile teams often operate remotely or in hybrid modes, challenging leaders to reevaluate ceremonies and team dynamics. Establishing trust, ensuring robust communication, and maintaining a sense of shared purpose become paramount.

In many cases, asynchronous collaboration tools – like virtual boards and video briefings – supplement or replace live interactions. Success depends on emphasizing results over mere activity and offering the flexibility teams need to operate at their best.

A prime example is an Agile Coach who used Miro for virtual retrospectives, enabling distributed teams to share lessons and perspectives effectively. Engagement soared, affirming that with the right approach, remote teams can thrive.

While hybrid models offer flexibility and can enhance productivity, business leaders remain divided on their long-term viability. Some, like former retail executives, argue that home working is part of the UK's productivity decline, with workers becoming less engaged and efficient. In contrast, a study by Stanford University and the Shenzhen Finance Institute found that hybrid working arrangements, where employees spend three days in the office and two at home, are just as productive as full-time office attendance. The research involved more than 1,600 graduate workers at the Chinese travel agency Trip.com and found that people who worked from home two days per week were just as likely to be promoted as those who were fully office-based. Hybrid workers were also much less likely to quit their jobs, especially women, non-managers, and people with long commutes.

The hybrid model also raises tensions between employers and employees, with some companies requiring staff back full-time while others embrace hybrid work as a way to boost motivation and workforce participation. The data suggests a growing gap in experiences, particularly between junior and senior staff – the latter tending to come in more often, which may impact mentorship and career growth. Leaders must ensure that hybrid work does not inadvertently disadvantage remote employees, particularly in visibility, networking, and development opportunities.

Adapting to Remote and Hybrid Work Environments

Building on trust, communication, and adaptability, Agile ways of working can be successfully adapted to remote settings by:

- **Virtual Facilitation Skills**: Use interactive approaches to keep virtual meetings lively and productive.
- **Remote Collaboration Tools**: Gain proficiency with platforms like Zoom, Microsoft Teams, and Miro to maintain team momentum.
- **Time Zone Management**: Implement flexible core hours, asynchronous communication, and rotating meeting schedules to accommodate global teams.
- **Fostering Psychological Safety**: Encourage inclusivity in retrospectives and decision-making, ensuring all voices are heard.

For instance, an IT services firm that moved to flexible working hours and asynchronous stand-ups managed to boost engagement and cut meeting fatigue by over 30%. Leaders and practitioners can study success stories from thought leaders to refine their remote Agile practices.

The Future of Agile Roles

At the Business Agility Conference UK 2024, various speakers explored the future of Agile roles. Evan Leybourn stressed that Agile experts must bridge strategy and execution to enable true business agility. Philippe Guenet, another well-known voice in Agile, highlighted how these roles shape cultures of constant innovation and adaptability by guiding teams through major transformations. These perspectives reinforce the idea that Agile roles are central to orchestrating organizational change rather than being overshadowed by it.

Demand for Agile experts remains robust, yet it's evolving. Companies want those who understand Agile enough to customize it, help navigate modern challenges, and embed Agile culture across different functions. With emerging areas like AI and sustainability, Agile practitioners can apply iterative methods to accelerate and refine innovation. This ongoing evolution requires professionals to expand their skills in leadership, strategy, and cross-functional engagement. By embracing these roles, Agile experts stay at the forefront of guiding transformative change.

Shifting Focus to Organizational Agility

A growing number of Agile professionals are shifting their attention beyond IT, championing agility across broader functional areas. This ensures an organization-wide capacity to respond to market pressures and remain competitive. For example, in the UK social care sector, applying Agile concepts cut wait times from eight weeks to two, demonstrating the sizable impact of organizational-level agility over piecemeal improvements.

Additionally, as societal focus on ethics and sustainability increases, Agile practitioners can integrate these values into product development, balancing responsiveness with a sense of responsibility. This holistic outlook underscores the long-term relevance of Agile roles in shaping cultural and operational pivots.

Conclusion

Agile roles now extend far beyond daily stand-ups and backlog refinements. Today, they serve as strategic enablers, bridging silos, shaping culture, and driving measurable business value. As automation reduces routine tasks, Agile professionals must evolve – expanding their leadership capabilities, deepening their commercial awareness, and continuously learning.

Consider whether your organization is enabling this shift. Are Agile roles constrained by process adherence, or are they evolving into strategic leadership positions? By empowering Agile practitioners to act as enablers rather than just facilitators, organizations can cultivate a culture of innovation and adaptability.

True agility demands roles that go beyond ceremony and actively contribute to business outcomes. This requires leaders to redefine Agile responsibilities to align with modern business challenges.

The next chapter explores how emerging technologies like AI and machine learning are reshaping Agile, requiring leaders to integrate these advancements thoughtfully and effectively.

Call to Action

As an adaptive leader, reflect on whether your Agile teams spend more time in ceremonies than in delivering meaningful outcomes. Encourage them to experiment with advanced tools (AI, low-code) and strategic thinking. Initiate skill-building programmes for roles like Agile Strategy Lead or Enterprise Agile Coach. Celebrate cross-functional initiatives. This fosters an Agile workforce that grows alongside your business objectives.

Key Takeaways

- **Agile Roles Are Expanding**: They go beyond managing frameworks to shaping culture, strategy, and measurable outcomes.
- **New Skills Are Essential**: Leadership, emotional intelligence, commercial acumen, and tech-savvy form the backbone of evolving Agile positions.
- **Organizations Must Support Transition**: Training, mentorship, and cultural backing equip practitioners to adapt effectively.
- **Technology Shapes Roles**: AI, machine learning, and automation are shifting focus from routine tasks to high-value innovation.
- **Organizational Agility Trumps IT-Only Focus**: Embedding Agile throughout all departments boosts competitiveness and responsiveness.

CLEAR Model® Connection

- **Leadership**: Leaders guide role evolution, fostering growth and team flexibility.
- **Adaptability**: Responsibilities must shift to suit changing structures and hybrid work.

Key Takeaway: Agile isn't about rigid role definitions; it's about flexibility. Leaders should enable teams to define roles based on skills, outcomes, and value delivery rather than predefined job titles.

Role Evolution Matrix

- **Traditional Roles vs Emerging Roles:**
  - o Align existing roles with future-required skills and competencies.
- **Skill Development Plan:**
  - o Identify training needs for roles including Agile Coach, Scrum Master, and Product Owner.

Career Pathways Template

1. **Define New Roles:**
   - o Clearly describe responsibilities and expectations.
2. **Competency Framework:**
   - o Outline the skills and knowledge required.
3. **Development Opportunities:**
   - o Provide access to training, mentoring, and on-the-job learning.
4. **Progression Paths:**
   - o Show how roles can evolve over time within the organization.

Chapter Summary

Agile roles have evolved far beyond basic frameworks. This chapter demonstrated how they adapt to emerging tech, cross-functional needs, and strategic opportunities. In an AI-driven, hybrid world, Agile roles endure by shifting emphasis, becoming catalysts for organizational agility, bridging cultural divides, and championing user-centric outcomes.

13
Tech-Enabled Agility

The future belongs to those who prepare for it today.

Malcolm X

What You'll Gain

- **For Senior Leaders and Executives**: Insight into strategically integrating emerging technologies with Agile practices to strengthen responsiveness and innovation.
- **For Mid-Level Leaders**: Practical steps to smoothly combine Agile workflows with new technologies, balancing technical advancement and ethical responsibilities.
- **For Students or Early-Career Professionals**: Awareness of the emerging skills required for careers at the intersection of Agile and cutting-edge technologies.

Agile Meets Emerging Technologies

AI adoption has surged by over 120% year-on-year, yet 65% of leaders admit they feel unprepared to lead AI-driven teams. This creates a paradox: technology is advancing rapidly, but leadership capabilities aren't keeping pace. How can organizations embrace the power of emerging technologies while preserving Agile's human-centred principles?

David, the CTO of a global logistics firm, faced this challenge. During a high-stakes meeting, he vented his frustration: *'We claim to be Agile, but our technology decisions are stuck in the past'.*

The room fell silent. Many companies adopt Agile processes but fail to upgrade their technology accordingly. This gap limits their ability to stay competitive.

Technologies like AI, machine learning, blockchain, quantum computing, and IoT aren't just transforming industries – they're reshaping agility itself. The belief that Agile can't keep up with technology is outdated. The most forward-thinking organizations are not just adapting Agile to work alongside technology but fusing the two. This creates something I have coined as **Agile Next**, where AI-driven insights, automation, and decentralized technologies enhance agility rather than replace it.

The question is no longer whether Agile can adapt to emerging technologies, but how quickly organizations can adopt Agile Next to maintain a competitive edge.

Innovation also needs to leave its silo. It thrives when it's embedded into everyday roles, not confined to a department. Leaders must build teams where testing ideas, suggesting improvements, and using tech creatively are part of everyone's day job.

This chapter explores how these innovations, when thoughtfully woven into Agile processes, boost adaptability and drive strategic transformation. By understanding how emerging technologies reinforce core Agile principles, we can uncover the potential benefits for organizations that use both in tandem.

How Emerging Tech Enhances Agile

Personal Reflection

Early in one transformation project, I watched AI predictive analytics revolutionize sprint planning. By analysing past sprint performance, identifying bottlenecks, and forecasting workload distribution, the system provided data-driven recommendations that improved resource allocation. Initially sceptical, the team came to rely on these insights to balance capacity, optimize sprint commitments, and proactively address risks, dramatically shortening delivery timelines within a few months. Experiences like these show the immense possibilities of blending Agile and emerging technologies.

Organizations integrating Agile with these innovations stay competitive and on the cutting edge. Although Agile's emphasis on flexibility and collaboration remains invaluable, integrating these technologies also introduces unique challenges. Realizing their full impact demands thoughtful navigation of technical complexities, skill gaps, and inevitable resistance to change. Leaders must foster continuous learning and collaboration to address these barriers effectively.

To lay the groundwork, let's examine how Agile and emerging technologies intersect, showcasing opportunities for increased adaptability and strategic alignment.

The Intersection of Agile and Emerging Technologies

A financial services firm once quarantined AI under 'Research and Development', stalling its broader adoption. When AI specialists joined Agile squads, fraud detection time dropped by 40%. This move exemplifies how advanced technologies thrive under collaborative, iterative conditions.

Why Agile and Tech Fit So Well

- **AI and ML**: Provide data-driven insights for predictive decision-making.
- **Blockchain**: Secures tamper-proof records, aligning with Agile's call for transparency.
- **IoT**: Streams real-time data into backlogs, enabling swift user-centric pivots.
- **Quantum Computing**: Potentially solves complex problems in minutes, accelerating Agile cycles.

Yet deploying these powerful tools in an Agile context demands Adaptive Leadership. Leaders must clarify vision, train teams, and embed ethical considerations. That's where the CLEAR Model® fosters synergy, integrating its core pillars into tech adoption.

Emerging Technologies and Adaptive Leadership

Emerging technologies promise efficiency and innovation, but demand Adaptive Leadership to navigate complexity. Leaders must align technology adoption clearly with organizational goals to avoid misalignment or inefficiencies.

Leadership Strategies for Technology Integration

The first table below highlights core actions that adaptive leaders can take to align emerging technologies with organizational goals. These strategies ensure teams remain skilled, motivated, and ethically guided when implementing new tools or systems.

Action	Implementation Guidance	Example
Assess Team Readiness	Evaluate whether your teams have the skills and mindset to adopt new technologies. Offer training and upskilling where needed.	A leader sets up machine learning workshops to boost team skills, enabling them to better leverage AI-driven tools.
Foster Collaboration Between Humans and Technology	Ensure technology complements human creativity and decision-making rather than replacing it.	A logistics firm tracks real-time inventory through IoT but depends on employee insights to interpret irregularities and plan strategic responses.

Action	Implementation Guidance	Example
Establish Ethical and Sustainable Practices	Create clear guidelines for responsible technology use, upholding organizational values and long-term sustainability.	A company mandates data privacy reviews for every AI-based customer interaction, building trust while staying compliant with regulations.

Toolkit: Checklist for Adaptive Technology Leadership

While the previous table focuses on high-level leadership strategies, the checklist below offers a practical, step-by-step approach to guide technology adoption. Leaders can use these steps as a quick reference to maintain clarity, spot skill gaps, and uphold ethical standards throughout the integration process.

Step	Action	Example
Assess Readiness	Survey team skills and knowledge gaps.	Use skill assessments to identify gaps in AI capabilities.
Create Collaboration	Design workflows blending tech and human creativity.	Establish cross-functional AI project teams.
Establish Ethical Standards	Define clear guidelines for the ethical use of tech.	Incorporate sustainability goals into retrospectives.

By applying both the strategies and the checklist, adaptive leaders ensure that new technologies enhance, rather than complicate, Agile practices. They also safeguard the organization's ethical and sustainable priorities.

For example, IoT Integration in Logistics

A global logistics firm replaced manual inventory checks with IoT sensors, gaining instant updates on stock levels. Adaptive leadership made this a success by:

- **Upskilling** teams to take advantage of IoT data.
- **Forming** cross-functional squads to address supply chain issues.
- **Establishing** responsible guidelines for data privacy.

Outcome: Efficiency rose by 15%, and supply chain agility improved dramatically.

As organizations refine their approach to integrating technology within Agile, some are pushing the boundaries even further. This leads to exploring more radical approaches, such as Extreme Agile, which leverages AI to reshape workflows and accelerate decision-making.

To understand this emerging approach, let's examine its potential and its limitations.

Extreme Agile: Potential and Limitations

Earlier chapters (1 and 3) introduced the idea of Extreme Agile, which integrates AI deeply into Agile workflows to dramatically enhance productivity and decisions. While the possibilities are vast, so are the constraints. This moment in technology often evokes comparisons to early aviation – machines can automate and accelerate tasks, but they lack the intangible 'soul' necessary for true craftsmanship. Although AI can generate code or automate tasks, its success hinges on preserving Agile's essential human elements: empathy, creativity, and insight.

But as AI expands, there is also a risk that human connection begins to erode. When interactions become mediated by bots and decisions are made by algorithms, the subtle cues of trust, inclusion, and empathy may fade. Adaptive leaders must ensure their culture does not become sterile. Human-centric rituals such as mentorship, storytelling, and conflict resolution must not be sidelined in favour of automated convenience. These are not inefficiencies; they are the very glue that binds Agile teams together.

Leaders must strike a balance between harnessing AI-driven outputs and preserving skilled professionals who can supervise and refine them. With that context, let's explore how AI and machine learning can bolster Agile decision-making.

AI Won't Replace Agile – It Will Transform It

The future of agility isn't just about faster sprints or better retrospectives.

It's about leveraging AI, automation, and data-driven decision-making to:

- **Enhance adaptability**: AI can process vast amounts of data to help teams pivot faster.
- **Eliminate repetitive work**: Automation can free up Agile teams to focus on innovation.
- **Improve decision-making**: AI-driven insights can help leaders make better, faster choices.

Example: Tesla's AI-Driven Agility

Tesla updates its vehicles over-the-air in real-time based on AI-driven feedback, enabling continuous improvement without waiting for long development cycles.

Agility in the AI era isn't about working harder – it's about working smarter.

1. How AI Will Enhance Agile Decision-Making

Traditional Agile decision-making relies heavily on intuition and past experience. AI changes that by providing real-time, data-driven insights.

- **Old Way** → Teams prioritize work based on intuition.
- **AI-Enhanced Way** → AI analyses customer behaviour, suggesting what features will drive the most value.

AI won't replace leaders, but it will make them more informed and effective.

How to Integrate AI into Agile Decision-Making:

- Use AI to analyse backlog priorities based on customer behaviour.
- Leverage AI-driven risk analysis to improve Agile forecasting.
- Automate sprint planning suggestions based on historical data.

2. How Automation Will Eliminate Agile Busywork

Most Agile teams waste time on administrative tasks that AI can automate.

- **Old Way** → Scrum Masters manually track sprint progress.
- **AI-Enhanced Way** → AI automatically updates sprint metrics, predicting roadblocks before they occur.

Automation lets Agile teams focus on high-value work, not admin tasks.

How to Integrate Automation into Agile Workflows

- Use AI-powered tools for backlog grooming and sprint tracking.
- Automate status reporting instead of manual updates.
- Deploy AI-driven workflow optimizations to improve team efficiency.

3. How Predictive Analytics Will Make Agility More Proactive

Most Agile organizations react to change – AI helps them anticipate it.

- **Old Way** → Teams adjust plans after problems arise.
- **AI-Enhanced Way** → AI predicts bottlenecks before they happen.

Predictive analytics makes agility proactive, not reactive.

How to Integrate Predictive AI into Agility

- Use AI forecasting tools to anticipate delivery risks.
- Leverage customer trend analysis to predict future market shifts.
- Deploy AI-driven insights to optimize team performance and workflow efficiency.

4. How Leaders Can Integrate AI into Agile Workflows Today

While AI provides significant benefits, leaders must carefully guide its adoption to enhance, not replace, Agile principles.

Key Leadership Strategies

- **Start Small and Iterate**: AI adoption should follow Agile principles itself. Begin with small-scale AI pilots and refine them based on feedback.
- **Align AI with Business Objectives**: AI tools should support agility by improving value delivery, not just efficiency.
- **Train Teams in AI Literacy**: Agile professionals should understand AI's capabilities and limitations to use it effectively.
- **Balance AI Insights with Human Judgment**: AI can provide recommendations, but leaders must make the final call.
- **Embed AI Governance**: Ethical and security risks must be proactively managed through clear guidelines.

Generative AI in Agile

Leaders are now experimenting with AI-driven prototypes to accelerate user testing, refine backlogs, or even aid developers in drafting initial code snippets. While speed improves, human oversight remains essential to uphold creativity, code quality, and ethical considerations.

For Example:

- AI can analyse patterns in throughput and capacity to project the likelihood of meeting sprint objectives, allowing teams to adjust plans mid-sprint.
- Tools like Microsoft's Azure Machine Learning crunch historical data to predict success rates of upcoming sprints.
- Beyond forecasting, AI-driven tools also handle repetitive administrative tasks, further streamlining Agile workflows.

AI's role in Agile is rapidly expanding. Yet, reports do not indicate that budgets for Agile or Business Agility initiatives are being systematically diverted to AI. While AI investment is increasing, particularly in response to workforce efficiency and automation trends, this does not equate to a funding shift away from Agile. Instead, Agile remains a critical enabler for AI adoption, ensuring organizations remain adaptable and responsive to technological shifts rather than viewing them as competing priorities.

The convergence of AI and Agile is redefining Agile's future. According to Forrester's *The State Of Agile Development, 2025: It's Still Relevant, With Benefits And Challenges*, AI-driven Agile frameworks are streamlining decision-making, automating backlog prioritization, and improving sprint efficiency. These integrations allow organizations to move beyond traditional Agile approaches, leveraging real-time data for continuous learning and adaptability. As AI adoption accelerates, leaders must ensure these advancements align with Agile's core human-centric values, using AI to augment, not replace, collaborative decision-making and team autonomy.

Beyond simple predictive analytics, AI-driven project management tools further streamline Agile workflows, reducing administrative overhead and improving prioritization.

AI-Driven Project Management Tools

Project management tools are increasingly integrating AI and ML to upgrade Agile practices. Atlassian's Jira, a mainstay in Agile project management, now includes AI features that streamline issue prioritization and balance workloads. AI can auto-assign tasks based on individual skill sets and availability, optimizing resource utilization.

Trello's Butler is another AI-powered automation tool that helps teams automate routine tasks, like moving cards or sending deadline alerts. Through a user-friendly interface, Butler eliminates the need for manual updates or programming expertise. While these capabilities automate routine processes, AI's influence on Agile stretches far beyond such tasks, raising the question of which specific use cases merit deeper exploration.

The future of AI in Agile is not just about automation but about how these tools can enhance collaboration, decision-making, and continuous improvement. Leaders who take an informed approach – leveraging AI to reinforce Agile's principles rather than override them – will set their organizations up for sustained success.

Valid Use Cases for AI in Agile Software Development

AI can significantly boost Agile software development by reducing manual tasks and strengthening decisions. Scott Ambler notes several focused AI applications that Agile teams can adopt:

- **Analysing Existing Implementations**: Tools like SonarQube analyse legacy code for improvements.
- **Brainstorming Requirements**: AI solutions like ChatGPT or Gemini contribute ideas during requirement definition.
- **Generating Documentation and Code**: Mintlify and Brave CodeLLM create well-structured code and documentation.
- **Automating Test Creation**: Platforms like TestRigor simplify acceptance test generation.
- **Suggesting Quality Improvements**: Products like Applitools Visual AI spot UI inconsistencies, while Veracode detects runtime security issues.

By employing these solutions, Agile teams reduce manual toil, increase accuracy, and make informed choices at each development phase. Nevertheless, human expertise remains essential for validating AI outputs and ensuring they align with both business goals and ethical standards.

As Agile teams embrace these use cases, they must remain vigilant about the ethical implications of AI integration, ensuring that innovation is guided by fairness, transparency, and respect for privacy.

Ethical Considerations in AI Adoption

AI offers powerful advantages but also presents ethical complexities, such as potential bias, transparency, and data privacy issues. Teams must implement responsible AI practices, including:

1. **Bias Mitigation**: Continuously audit algorithms for embedded biases, particularly in areas like hiring or customer service.
2. **Transparency**: Ensure AI-driven decision processes can be explained to stakeholders to build trust.
3. **Data Governance**: Comply with regulations such as GDPR and maintain privacy and security standards.

Agile teams should collaborate with legal and compliance units to establish guidelines that match their organization's core values. By integrating ethical checks into sprints, teams can foster trust without stifling innovation.

For example: In one company, an AI algorithm inadvertently favoured a certain demographic during recruitment. After auditing and retraining it with more diverse data, the team rectified the bias and reinforced its commitment to equality.

Before integrating emerging technologies, leaders need a structured approach. The Decision Path for Integrating Emerging Technologies provides one such framework, ensuring both operational and ethical considerations remain paramount.

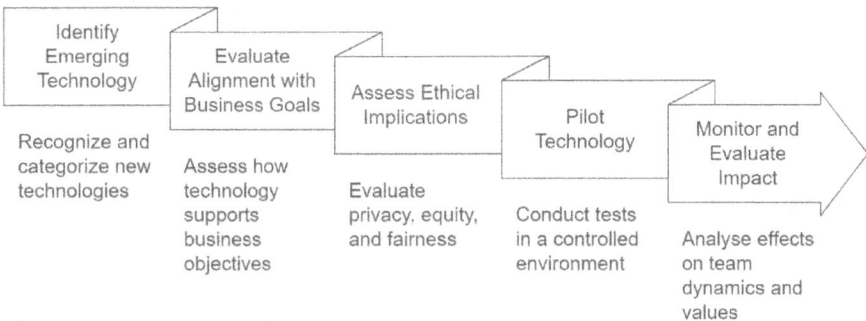

Identify Emerging Technology	Evaluate Alignment with Business Goals	Assess Ethical Implications	Pilot Technology	Monitor and Evaluate Impact
Recognize and categorize new technologies	Assess how technology supports business objectives	Evaluate privacy, equity, and fairness	Conduct tests in a controlled environment	Analyse effects on team dynamics and values

Decision Path for Integrating Emerging Technologies

By following this decision path, leaders must ensure that emerging technologies are carefully evaluated and integrated into their Agile processes, addressing both their operational needs and ethical considerations. This careful approach will help mitigate risks while amplifying the benefits of these transformative tools.

The Future of Agile in an AI-Driven World

AI isn't the enemy of agility – it's an amplifier.

What Will Change?

- AI will replace repetitive Agile tasks.
- AI will enhance decision-making with data-driven insights.
- AI will enable predictive agility, helping teams adapt before change happens.

What Won't Change?

- Agile will still require human leadership, creativity, and problem-solving.
- Teams will still need collaboration and emotional intelligence.
- Agility will still be about adaptability, not just speed.

As an adaptive leader, have you considered the ethical implications of integrating AI into your Agile practices? How can you promote responsible AI use within your teams?

Having established principles for responsible AI use, let's turn our attention to another transformative technology – blockchain – and its potential to enhance transparency and security in Agile workflows.

Blockchain Technologies and Agile

A global supply chain firm leveraged blockchain to enhance Agile product development. Traditionally, tracking product provenance required multiple handoffs, causing bottlenecks. By integrating blockchain into their Agile teams, real-time updates were shared transparently across the network, reducing data reconciliation efforts by 60%. This case highlights how blockchain isn't just about security – it can streamline Agile workflows, making data verifiable and reducing inefficiencies.

Applying Blockchain for Transparency and Security

Blockchain secures Agile environments by recording immutable transaction histories. Agile teams can track sprint backlogs and code changes via blockchain, guaranteeing all modifications are auditable and tamper-proof. Smart contracts can even automate processes like milestone-based payments. IBM's blockchain platform stands out as a tool enabling safe collaboration among distributed teams, demonstrating how decentralized technologies align with Agile's emphasis on accountability and efficiency.

With blockchain's immutable ledgers, Agile teams gain a robust method for confirming that all participants have the same, trustworthy information. This transparency counteracts any perception that Agile may lack rigorous oversight or accountability.

Smart Contracts in Agile Workflows

Smart contracts are self-executing agreements stored on a blockchain. In Agile contexts, they can automate deliverables approval, supplier agreements, or payment releases tied to specific milestones. For instance, once code has passed automated tests and been merged into the main branch, a smart contract can automatically release a payment to a freelancer. This minimizes administrative burdens and guarantees that obligations are met without middlemen.

Real-World Use Cases

Some organizations are already tapping into blockchain-based solutions:

- **Walmart**: Uses blockchain to increase supply chain transparency. This real-time traceability helps rapidly address issues like food contamination, boosting safety and consumer trust.
- **IBM**: Develops blockchain platforms for multi-party collaboration. IBM fosters secure, transparent Agile workflows across organizational boundaries by allowing teams to construct and manage blockchain networks.

As we progress from blockchain to other game-changing technologies like IoT and 5G, we'll see how they further reshape Agile projects, particularly through instantaneous data collection and faster collaboration.

Integrating IoT and 5G Technologies

To understand how these technologies make Agile more data-driven and responsive, we begin by examining the impact of IoT on Agile projects.

Leveraging IoT in Agile Projects

The **Internet of Things (IoT)** links devices that generate real-time data, offering Agile teams valuable insights for decision-making and product development. By relaying live usage metrics, IoT enables rapid adjustments, focusing teams on concrete user needs.

Applications of IoT in Agile

- **Real-Time User Feedback**: Quickly adapt features based on live data about user behaviour by tracking interaction patterns, heatmaps, and in-app feedback loops.
- **Performance Monitoring**: Pinpoint issues early using device performance metrics, guiding sprint priorities through automated alerts, trend analysis, and anomaly detection.
- **Predictive Maintenance**: Analyse sensor data to schedule maintenance or avert failures ahead of time by leveraging machine learning models that detect irregularities before breakdowns occur.

Real-World Example: General Electric (GE)

General Electric's Predix platform collects data from industrial equipment – jet engines, turbines, locomotives – to anticipate failures and optimize performance. By leveraging IoT and machine learning, GE has transformed predictive maintenance, saving millions in operational costs and improving reliability. For Agile teams, this data helps:

- **Spot Patterns and Anomalies**: IoT reveals issues not visible via traditional monitoring, enabling proactive problem-solving.
- **Strengthen Decision-Making**: Real-time insights boost sprint planning accuracy by prioritizing fixes based on actual system performance.
- **Improve Customer Value**: Preemptive solutions reduce downtime, increasing efficiency and enhancing customer trust in GE's services.

This robust feedback loop between IoT devices and Agile iterations can radically improve outcomes. Meanwhile, 5G technology ensures that these data streams and interactions remain swift and reliable, regardless of where team members are located.

Harnessing 5G for Enhanced Collaboration

5G revolutionizes connectivity with high bandwidth and minimal latency, enabling real-time collaboration even among globally dispersed Agile teams. For example, Ericsson leverages 5G to promote quick problem-solving across its global workforce, integrating augmented reality (AR) tools for design and review sessions. This technology makes remote Agile meetings nearly as seamless as in-person interactions.

Real-World Example: Ericsson

As both a 5G developer and end-user, Ericsson integrates 5G to enhance efficiency across its global operations. By embedding high-speed, low-latency connectivity into its workflows, the company accelerates innovation and improves real-time decision-making at scale.

- **Global Team Collaboration**: Minimal latency improves real-time interactions, enabling seamless coordination across distributed Agile teams.
- **AR/VR Tools**: Augmented and virtual reality speed up design reviews and troubleshooting, allowing engineers to diagnose and resolve issues remotely with greater accuracy.
- **Faster Iterations**: High-speed networks streamline testing and deployment, aligning well with iterative Agile cycles by reducing delays in feedback loops.

With connectivity challenges addressed, we can now look toward the horizon of computational power – quantum computing – and explore how it may revolutionize data analysis for Agile teams.

Quantum Computing's Promise

Financial institutions exploring quantum computing for risk modelling found that Agile approaches required adaptation. Since quantum solutions don't yet integrate into day-to-day development, teams experimented with 'Quantum Sprint Prototyping' – short cycles focused on refining algorithms using classical computing while preparing for future quantum implementation. While still evolving, this approach ensures Agile teams are ready when quantum computing becomes mainstream.

The Potential of Quantum Computing

Quantum computing brings a dramatic leap in computational power, allowing Agile teams to rapidly tackle massive datasets. Tasks like risk modelling or scenario planning, which might traditionally take weeks, could be condensed into minutes. Through cloud-based quantum services (e.g. IBM's Quantum Experience), Agile practitioners can tap into emerging quantum capabilities without investing in expensive on-premise hardware. Prepared teams that explore these possibilities can seize competitive advantages while managing inherent risks.

Unlike conventional computers relying on binary bits (0 or 1), quantum computers use qubits (quantum bits that exist in a superposition of both 0 and 1 simultaneously). This enables them to solve extremely complex problems more quickly.

Practical Applications for Agile Teams

- **Risk Modelling**: Quantum computing accelerates large-scale risk analysis, letting teams revise sprint priorities in near real-time.
- **Scenario Planning**: Agile teams can simulate various market or product scenarios in minutes, refining their strategies in retrospectives.
- **Example**: IBM's Quantum Experience helps organizations trial quantum algorithms for workflow optimization.

Quantum computing has significant potential to overhaul how Agile teams handle big data. Organizations must begin preparing to use this technology responsibly, starting with foundational knowledge and expert collaboration.

Agile practitioners can take proactive steps by exploring real-world applications, integrating quantum literacy into learning programs, and fostering partnerships with experts to stay ahead of this technological shift.

Preparing Agile Teams for Quantum Advancements

To anticipate quantum's future impact, Agile teams can:

1. **Develop Foundational Knowledge**: Learn the basics of quantum mechanics and likely use cases.

2. **Stay Informed**: Follow quantum computing breakthroughs to see when and how they might become relevant.
3. **Collaborate with Experts**: Partner with research institutions or quantum-computing firms to remain on the cutting edge.

Before fully adopting quantum capabilities, readiness must be evaluated, and related challenges must be planned.

Challenges and Readiness Assessment

Despite quantum computing's promise, its integration poses obstacles:

- **Limited Access**: Quantum computers are expensive, and cloud-based options from IBM or Google might have restrictions.
- **Specialized Skills**: Quantum algorithms demand expertise in quantum mechanics, requiring new training investments.
- **Security Risks**: Quantum machines may soon undermine existing encryption, forcing organizations to rethink data protection strategies before vulnerabilities emerge.

Agile teams should conduct readiness assessments to measure their abilities, identify gaps, and create plans for bridging them. This theme of assessing and preparing for new technology echoes broader challenges organizations face when weaving emerging tech into Agile workflows.

Challenges in Adopting Emerging Tech

Leaders must ensure that technology elevates Agile's core people-centric ethos rather than overshadowing it. Balancing potential gains against ethical and logistical complications requires a thoughtful approach.

Balancing Opportunities with Risks

Emerging technologies can drive powerful efficiency gains, but come with risks:

- **Technological Debt**: Over-reliance on early-stage technology can become costly if future updates or migrations are complex.
- **Organizational Misalignment**: Adopting AI or other isolated tools can create conflicting objectives. A retailer, for instance, found that siloed predictive analytics systems led to contradictory KPIs across departments.

Technical Complexity and Skill Gaps

Integrating advanced technologies requires specialized technical expertise and a shift in mindset. AI projects call for proficiency in data science; blockchain solutions demand cryptography know-how. To fill these gaps, organizations should:

- **Invest in Training**: Offer workshops, online courses, or certifications.
- **Hire Specialists**: Bring in AI or blockchain experts to mentor existing staff.
- **Collaborate Externally**: Partner with specialized vendors or consultants.

Managing Change and Resistance

Emerging technologies can disrupt routines, triggering pushback from team members who are comfortable with established processes. Agile leaders must manage this transition carefully:

- **Transparent Communication**: Explain how new tools serve broader strategic goals.
- **Involvement**: Include teams in decision-making so they can voice ideas or concerns.
- **Support**: Provide the resources and training needed to ease the transition.

Balancing Innovation with Risk Management

New technologies can introduce security, compliance, or reliability risks. For example, AI tools might inadvertently expose sensitive data, and blockchain solutions could conflict with local regulations. Leaders can mitigate risks by:

- **Risk Assessments**: Identify and plan for potential pitfalls.
- **Compliance Checks**: Align solutions with relevant laws, like GDPR.
- **Continuous Monitoring**: Regularly inspect systems to catch and resolve issues early.

By addressing these complexities, leaders ensure that technology remains a catalyst for greater agility rather than a stumbling block.

Leveraging Technology for Agility

Agile remains integral as AI, automation, and digital platforms expand. Despite concerns, these tools can address longstanding criticisms about slow or rigid Agile processes. Automation relieves repetitive tasks, letting teams focus on creative problem-solving.

True agility emerges when advanced tools merge seamlessly with a collaborative, people-first mindset. Are your leaders guiding teams to adopt new tech while staying anchored to user focus and iterative improvement?

Technology as an Enabler for Agile

- **Augmenting Instead of Replacing**: AI-driven retros can highlight improvement areas, but human empathy remains crucial.
- **Ethical Agility**: Blockchain fosters accountability, while IoT feeds reliable data for retrospective discussions.
- **Preventing Ritual Fatigue**: Automated tasks free time for genuine collaboration.

Implementing these responsibly helps agile teams scale faster, bridging the gap between critics' concerns and actual benefits.

Leaders must also unify the entire organization to handle friction or inertia. Ultimately, it's about aligning advanced tech with Agile values for consistent user value. AI can't fix deeper organizational problems – leadership must shape a culture that embraces both technology and agility.

Safeguarding Agility Through DevSecOps

Adaptive organizations don't trade speed for stability – they embed both into their delivery model. That's why high-performing teams now treat security and operational resilience as part of the development process, not as gates to clear at the end.

This 'shift-left' approach integrates testing, compliance, and security checks early in the workflow, ensuring that agility doesn't come at the cost of safety. Whether it's automated code scanning or real-time monitoring, adaptive leaders build secure pipelines as a foundation, not a luxury.

DevSecOps isn't a buzzword – it's a mindset. It reinforces agility by reducing late-stage surprises and supporting continuous delivery at scale. Leaders who champion this approach enable their teams to move fast and stay protected, creating resilience from day one.

Challenges with AI Development in Agile Frameworks

Research reveals that embedding AI development within typical Agile frameworks can pose difficulties, as AI's iterative demands may differ from conventional software development. Leaders must decide if Agile is the best fit or whether another approach (like Lean experimentation or a hybrid model) might better suit AI's unique needs.

Augmenting Agile Practices with AI: Lessons and Limitations

AI can automate repetitive chores, enhance code quality, and spur iterative development. Leaders can deploy AI tools that add clear value, such as spotting security breaches or analysing substantial datasets. Human oversight remains indispensable to counteract AI's 'hallucinations' or inaccuracies and to ensure outputs align with organizational objectives.

These diverse AI tools can augment Agile workflows in ways that go beyond textual outputs, helping teams make data-driven decisions across various domains.

Intellectual Property and Originality

Leaders should exercise caution with AI-generated outputs to ensure originality and ownership. For instance, using AI to refine a function might be acceptable, but relying on AI to architect an entire system or produce a crucial asset introduces ambiguity over IP rights and ethical concerns. Clarity on the role of AI in these processes is critical.

Start Small and Iterate

AI is best used incrementally:

- Generate or refine small code functions, not entire classes.
- Draft short documentation segments, not full manuals.

Such measured steps minimize risks, allowing teams to pilot tools and refine workflows. AI thus remains an enhancer, not a liability.

By applying these best practices, leaders can seamlessly integrate AI into Agile. The aim is not to replace human judgment but to augment it, forming a collaborative bond that unlocks extraordinary outcomes. As AI takes root, leadership itself must evolve to address both the promise and challenges of an AI-driven workplace.

Leadership in AI-Driven Workplaces

Mark, a CIO at a manufacturer, introduced AI for backlog management. The biggest hurdle was developer anxiety that AI might replace them. Mark reframed AI as 'assistance, not replacement', ensuring teams used AI insights for context while retaining final judgment. They trimmed sprint planning time by 35% and kept morale strong.

Adaptive leadership means blending human creativity with AI data, ensuring automation complements, rather than supplants, collaboration. Real agility grows as teams trust the AI for tasks but guard creativity, empathy, and final accountability.

Key Leadership Approach

1. **Frame AI as supportive**: Reassure teams that they retain crucial creative control.
2. **Champion a Learning Culture**: Encourage employees to tinker with AI, share experiences, and normalize mistakes as part of growth.
3. **Set Ethical Boundaries**: Define acceptable AI usage early, preserving data privacy and fairness.

Personal Reflection

At a data analytics firm I worked with, teams were overwhelmed by new machine-learning pipelines. We created a 'tech buddy' system, pairing experts with novices. Within weeks, novices felt more confident experimenting with the toolchain, and the AI solutions soared in quality, reminding me that Adaptive Leadership addresses both the tool and the team.

Bridging Emerging Technologies with Agile Leadership

Adaptive leaders stand at the forefront, ensuring advanced tech amplifies synergy instead of overshadowing it. AI, for example, can supercharge decisions if leaders cultivate trust and guard the human dimension of agility.

Applying This in Practice

1. **Clarify Purpose**: Articulate how each emerging tech aligns with strategic aims (like shorter lead times or higher user satisfaction).
2. **Maintain Human Oversight**: Let AI or blockchain handle certain tasks while preserving cross-functional reviews and final calls.
3. **Embed Ethics and Transparency**: Whether in AI, IoT, or quantum computing, define usage policies consistent with Agile's open, people-centric ethos.
4. **Upskill Continuously**: Provide ongoing training or communities of practice. Teams flourish when they're free to experiment safely.

Short Real-World Example

A financial firm saw AI backlog prioritization accelerate backlog grooming. Yet they insisted each recommendation be cross-checked for compliance with sector regulations. This hybrid approach reaped gains in speed without sacrificing accountability.

Leaders Must Keep Asking:

- Do new tools serve the end-user or overshadow them?
- Are we building trust by explaining how AI or blockchain decisions are reached?
- What training ensures the entire team remains comfortable and capable?

Key Leadership Questions

- Have I defined clear outcomes for each new technology?
- How do we ensure collaborative decisions are informed, rather than replaced, by AI tools?

- What can we do to make sure that teams have the skills and ethical guidelines needed to handle advanced tech?

By tackling these questions, leaders create an environment where emerging technologies genuinely enhance Agile practices. Rather than letting AI or blockchain impose rigid rules, leadership steers them to amplify collaboration, responsiveness, and continuous learning, safeguarding the human heart of agility.

Future Implications for Agile Ways of Working

The rise of emerging technologies compels Agile ways of working to evolve. Agile frameworks must remain flexible enough to incorporate new tools without losing sight of their guiding principles. This could mean adapting roles, ceremonies, or collaboration methods to accommodate advanced data analytics and automation. Ultimately, a culture of continuous learning is pivotal to sustaining this level of innovation.

Continuous Learning and Adaptability

Teams should commit to learning new skills, staying open-minded about emerging tech, and actively sharing knowledge. This may involve:

- **Lifelong Learning Mindset**: Encouraging personal development through formal courses or in-house mentoring.
- **Knowledge Sharing**: Setting up 'communities of practice' or internal forums for collaborative learning.
- **Experimentation**: Launching pilot projects or innovation labs to explore novel solutions.

Such openness fosters an organization that remains agile regardless of what technology emerges next.

Strategic Planning for Technological Integration

Leaders need strategic roadmaps to align technology with Agile objectives:

Integration Framework for Emerging Technologies

1. **Assess Readiness**: Evaluate team capabilities and organizational culture.
2. **Pilot Projects**: Experiment with small-scale or low-risk trials.
3. **Track KPIs**: Monitor ROI, throughput, and other metrics during pilots.
4. **Scale and Refine**: Roll out successful pilots and update them based on feedback.

When implemented thoughtfully, these steps ensure that new technologies reinforce Agile principles and contribute to sustainable growth.

Conclusion

Emerging technologies such as AI, blockchain, IoT, and 5G can amplify Agile's impact by speeding decisions, automating routine tasks, and deepening live data analysis. Integrated well, they streamline workflows and lift organizational agility. As agentic workforces arrive, with teams operating under greater autonomy alongside AI support, governance must keep pace. We are the last generation to manage only humans. The goal is no longer to watch over static structures but to enable networks of people and systems that learn, decide, and adapt for themselves. Humans have intent; AI doesn't.

Technology should not overshadow Agile's human-centric foundations. Cultural change is more important than technological change. Digital where possible, human where necessary. Agile thrives on trust, collaboration, and iterative learning. Leaders must ensure each technological adoption supports, rather than replaces, these core principles.

Technology doesn't eliminate the need for Agile; it reinforces its importance. By integrating advanced tools into Agile cycles, organizations can remain flexible and responsive while preserving the values that drive success.

The next chapter reinforces the idea that Agile is not a static concept – it is a mindset that must continuously evolve in response to new opportunities and challenges.

Call to Action

As an adaptive leader, align emerging tech with Agile's core. Are you investing in training to close skill gaps and reduce ethical hazards? Are your pilot projects demonstrating genuine user value or just chasing hype? Commit to a synergy of advanced technologies with Agile's collaboration and responsiveness, embedding them in ways that sustain long-term growth.

Key Takeaways

- **Emerging Technologies Enhance Agile**: AI, blockchain, IoT, and quantum computing can amplify agility when integrated thoughtfully.
- **Ethical Considerations Matter**: Address bias, transparency, and data privacy in AI adoption.
- **Framework Adaptation Is Essential**: Agile must evolve to incorporate new technologies while preserving its core values.
- **Continuous Learning Is Key**: Teams should embrace a culture of lifelong learning to stay competitive.
- **Strategic Planning Leads to Success**: Clear objectives, resource allocation, and risk management ensure successful integration.

CLEAR Model® Connection

- **Execution**: Organizations must align technology adoption with core Agile principles.
- **Responsiveness**: Quick iteration helps teams refine how they use AI and emerging tools.

Key Takeaway: Technology should enhance agility, not replace the human-centric principles that make Agile effective. Leaders must balance innovation with adaptability and execution.

Technology Integration Checklist

- **Identify Relevant Technologies:**
  - o AI, Blockchain, Quantum Computing, etc.
- **Assess Readiness:**
  - o Do you have the necessary skills and infrastructure?
- **Pilot Projects:**
  - o Start small to test integration approaches.
- **Ethical Considerations:**
  - o Evaluate potential ethical implications.

Strategic Planning Template for Technology Integration

1. **Set Objectives:**
   - o Specify measurable goals for integrating new technologies.
2. **Resource Allocation:**
   - o Determine budget, personnel, and tools needed.
3. **Risk Management:**
   - o Identify potential risks and mitigation strategies.
4. **Implementation Timeline:**
   - o Create a phased plan with milestones.
5. **Evaluation Metrics:**
   - o Establish KPIs to measure success.

Chapter Summary

Tech-enabled agility merges AI, blockchain, IoT, quantum computing, and more with core Agile values – boosting efficiency without compromising collaboration. Adaptive leaders drive synergy by weaving advanced tools into iterative workflows and safeguarding ethical considerations. Properly integrated, these innovations accelerate outcomes, sustaining Agile's relevance in a fast-evolving future.

End of Part 5

We've seen how Agile must adapt to fresh trends, expanding roles, and shifting cultural needs. But the true key to Agile's future lies in continuous learning and a willingness to reinvent. In Part 6, we'll explore how to keep building upon these foundations, ensuring that Agile remains a catalyst for long-term success – and that your teams are ready for whatever comes next.

Part 6

Continuous Learning and the Future of Agile

CLEAR Focus: Adaptability and Culture

Agility is not a destination – it's an evolving journey. Adaptability ensures resilience, while culture sustains an organization's ability to learn and grow. This section explores how a mindset of continuous learning secures long-term agility and innovation.

14

The Future of Work – How Adaptive Organizations Will Thrive in Uncertainty

The only way to make sense out of change is to plunge into it, move with it, and join the dance.

Alan Watts

What You'll Gain

- **For Senior Leaders and Executives**: Learn why true agility demands a continuous-learning mindset, not a 'one-and-done' project, and how Adaptive Leadership cements agility for the long run.
- **For Mid-Level Leaders**: Discover how to maintain an Agile culture beyond initial wins by reinforcing ongoing improvement, psychological safety, and inclusive collaboration.
- **For Students or Early-Career Professionals**: Understand how continuous learning and a growth mindset sustain agility in fast-evolving workplaces, preparing you to adapt to ever-changing roles.

Sustaining Agility: A Mindset, Not a Milestone

As 'Agile transformation lead' for a multinational firm, Alex thought their journey was complete. Teams were working iteratively, retrospectives were held, and Agile frameworks were in place – yet something felt off. *'Why do we still struggle with adaptability?'* the CEO asked in a leadership meeting. This question is common: many organizations assume that adopting Agile means arriving at a fixed state of agility. But true agility is never 'done' – it's an ongoing process of evolution and refinement.

Agile is often viewed as a project with a clear end. Its power comes from seeing it as a perpetual journey shaped by shifting organizational needs and market forces. This perspective fuels sustained adaptability and drives lasting transformation.

Personal Reflection

Early in my career, I worked with organizations initially pursuing Agile as a 'box-ticking' exercise. Over time, they discovered its deeper transformative impact by embracing it as a mindset. For instance, a retail company I supported saw customer satisfaction soar once they shifted from simply holding Agile ceremonies to truly embedding Agile values in their culture.

In this chapter, we'll reflect on the attitudes, principles, and philosophies underlying Agile. We'll stress the significance of continuous learning, cultural transformation, and the core attributes that keep organizations truly agile over the long term.

Reflecting on the Agile Philosophy

This perspective aligns with Adrian Dooley (founder of the Praxis framework), who argued in an Association for Project Management (APM) blog post titled 'Agile is dead! Long live agility!' that Agile's enduring value lies in advancing broader organizational agility. Rather than just a standalone process, it serves as a foundational philosophy.

Today, Agile principles have become pillars of effective management. They help leaders spark innovation, enhance adaptability, and align teams with ever-shifting priorities.

Organizational agility isn't just a suite of practices – it's a mindset shaped by resilience, adaptability, and continuous improvement. Consider Spotify's evolution from a music-streaming platform into a podcasting powerhouse – a clear example of how agility energizes reinvention and sustained growth. Adaptive leaders can nurture this mindset by encouraging iterative learning and experimentation and by building a culture centred on the customer.

> ## Personal Reflection
>
> At one pharmaceutical company, I encountered rigid processes that made initial Agile adoption difficult. By focusing on cultural transformation – empowering teams to test ideas and iterate – they unlocked levels of innovation they'd never seen. The change didn't just alter processes; it revolutionized work.

As organizations rethink what capabilities matter most, another shift is taking place in how we define and develop leadership strength.

Power Skills: The Missing Middle in Agility

While much attention goes to hard (technical) and soft (interpersonal) skills, leaders now need a third type: power skills, which blend the two and enable strategic transformation. Power skills focus on decision-making in uncertainty, aligning stakeholders, leading change, and shaping the future. These are not just useful, they are essential for leadership that can adapt and thrive.

The CLEAR Model® directly supports power skill development across its five pillars:

- **Culture**: builds trust and psychological safety.
- **Leadership**: brings vision, integrity, and clarity.
- **Execution**: supports decisive, outcome-driven action.
- **Adaptability**: enables learning and resilience under pressure.
- **Responsiveness**: ensures fast, informed action based on feedback.

Power skills sit at the intersection of human connection, strategic insight, and adaptive execution. They help leaders go beyond managing tasks to shape direction, inspire people, and lead with intent. The adaptive leader does not just respond to change, they shape it with purpose and presence.

Leaders play a crucial role in shaping psychological safety, fostering continuous learning, and enabling adaptability. By normalizing vulnerability – for instance, openly discussing mistakes – and consistently modelling constructive feedback, leaders build trust. This trust, in turn, supports frank dialogue, fosters experimentation, and fuels ongoing improvement.

The Project Management Institute (PMI) notes that genuine agility requires challenging the status quo and letting teams shape their working methods. Such an open, flexible stance ensures agility remains a powerful catalyst for navigating customer demands and fast-evolving technologies.

Ultimately, agility is an ongoing transformation, not a one-off initiative. Embracing an outlook that sees change as a constant lets organizations stay nimble, agile, and attentive to both new opportunities and unexpected disruptions. Building on these foundational beliefs, let's examine the characteristics that make Agile genuinely adaptable and resilient.

The Essence of Agility

When Georgina, a newly appointed CIO at a major European retailer, reviewed their Agile transformation progress, she noticed a troubling trend. Teams had adopted Agile ceremonies but resisted change when faced with external pressures. Instead of enforcing more structure, Georgina focused on reinforcing Agile values – coaching teams to embrace adaptability and experimentation. Over time, teams shifted from rigid adherence to Agile rituals to a genuine culture of continuous learning. This case illustrates that agility is not about following set processes – it's about fostering a mindset of curiosity, adaptability, and growth.

Far from being inflexible, Agile can evolve endlessly if integrated into the overarching culture, decision-making, and customer focus. Its essence lies in adaptability, collaboration, and a laser focus on delivering real value.

As an adaptive leader, ask: Does your organization treat Agile as a philosophy, or is it trapped by outdated habits? The ability to continuously adapt is what separates thriving companies from those struggling to keep up. Leaders who embrace a growth mindset encourage teams to learn from every experience – even failures – fostering innovation and resilience. By modelling this mindset, they teach teams to see setbacks as stepping stones for improvement.

Prioritizing people and interactions sits at the core of Agile, emphasizing the power of relationships and open dialogue in handling complexity. Equally central is focusing on Customer Value, ensuring customers' needs guide decisions in a dynamic marketplace.

In the next section, we'll explore how organizations can evolve beyond outdated structures and embrace true adaptability.

Traditional Organizations Are Struggling to Keep Up

Work is changing faster than most organizations can handle. Markets are unpredictable. Employees expect more flexibility. AI is redefining how work gets done. Yet, many companies still operate as if stability is the norm.

Example: Blockbuster vs Netflix

Blockbuster failed because it couldn't adapt to changing consumer behaviours. Netflix, on the other hand, reinvented itself multiple times – from DVD rentals to streaming to AI-powered recommendations.

The companies that will survive aren't the biggest or strongest – they're the most adaptable.

What Is an Adaptive Organization?

An Adaptive Organization is designed to thrive in uncertainty:

Traditional Organizations	Adaptive Organizations
Rigid structures and hierarchies	Flexible, decentralized teams
Fixed job roles	Fluid, skill-based roles
Long planning cycles	Continuous iteration
Office-based work	Hybrid and remote-first mindset
Annual performance reviews	Continuous feedback and learning

The 3 Biggest Shifts Defining the Future of Work

1. Remote and Hybrid Work – Flexibility is the New Norm

The Problem

Many organizations struggle to balance flexibility with productivity.

- Leaders want employees back in the office.
- Employees want autonomy and remote work.
- Hybrid work models are still messy.

The Solution

The future of work is hybrid, but it must be designed intentionally.

What to Do Instead

- Focus on outcomes, not hours in the office.
- Redesign physical office spaces for collaboration, not routine work.
- Use asynchronous communication to avoid remote burnout.

Organizations must stop debating remote work and start optimizing for it.

2. Decentralized Decision-Making – Speed Over Hierarchy

The Problem

Many organizations still rely on top-down decision-making, slowing them down.

- Teams wait for leadership approval instead of acting fast.
- Bureaucracy kills innovation.
- Decisions take weeks when they should take hours.

The Solution

Empower teams to make decisions closer to the action.

What to Do Instead

- Use decision-making frameworks (e.g. RAPID, RACI) to clarify who decides what.
- Push authority to frontline teams.
- Measure decision speed as a core business metric.

Agility at scale requires decentralizing control.

3. Continuous Learning – The Future Belongs to the Fastest Learners

The Problem

Many organizations treat learning as a one-time event instead of an ongoing process.

- Employees are expected to 'figure things out' on their own.
- Training is outdated and irrelevant.
- Learning isn't linked to real-world business impact.

The Solution

The best organizations treat learning as a core business function.

What to Do Instead

- Encourage micro-learning and on-the-job experimentation.
- Create a culture where failure = learning.
- Use AI-driven learning platforms to personalize skill development.

Organizations that don't invest in learning will fall behind.

How Leaders Can Future-Proof Their Organizations

To thrive in the future of work, leaders must:

- Design work for flexibility, not control.
- Distribute decision-making to increase agility.
- Embed continuous learning as a cultural norm.

1. Shift from Managing Work to Managing Outcomes

- **Old Way** → Leaders measure employee success by hours worked.
- **New Way** → Leaders measure success by impact, not presence.

What to Focus On

- Adopt an outcome-based leadership model.
- Move from task supervision to goal alignment.
- Trust teams to work in the way that suits them best.

2. Encourage Cross-Functional Collaboration

- **Old Way** → Teams operate in silos.
- **New Way** → Teams form around business outcomes, not functions.

What to Focus On

- Create cross-functional teams aligned to customer needs.
- Reduce bureaucratic approvals – let teams own their work.
- Use digital collaboration tools to connect teams in real-time.

3. Make Learning and Adaptability a Competitive Advantage

- **Old Way** → Employees are trained once, then expected to keep up.
- **New Way** → Learning is continuous, adaptive, and AI-driven.

What to Focus On

- Encourage daily learning through micro-learning platforms.
- Reward experimentation, not just execution.
- Treat adaptability as a leadership skill.

But adaptability isn't just a trait – it's a repeatable process. The most adaptive organizations build rhythm into how they learn, experiment, and evolve. That rhythm doesn't need to be complex.

The Adaptive Learning Loop

Leaders often speak about learning, but real capability isn't built from disconnected training. It's developed through deliberate cycles of action and reflection.

One helpful tool is the Adaptive Learning Loop:

- **Sense**: Spot early signals, weak trends, and shifts in your context.
- **Act**: Run short experiments. Try a new format, change a routine, or test a bold idea at a small scale.
- **Adapt**: Take time to reflect. What worked? What didn't? What needs adjusting?

This loop builds more than knowledge. It sharpens timing, judgment, and situational awareness – qualities essential to leadership in uncertainty.

Rather than chase trends or wait for clarity, adaptive leaders create learning momentum. The next right step doesn't need to be perfect. It just needs to move you forward.

One way to build learning momentum is through just-in-time reskilling – targeted development delivered at the moment it's needed. Whether it's learning how to use a new AI tool or responding to a fresh compliance requirement, adaptive organizations don't wait for annual programmes. They equip teams in real-time, helping people respond with confidence, not hesitation.

However, adopting these principles often requires revisiting the organization's culture, something we'll explore next.

Overcoming Cultural Barriers

Because Agile transformation depends on cultural change, it's critical to recognize that even deeply rooted behaviours can shift with deliberate, consistent effort. Cultural transformation is essential for enduring agility.

Hierarchical structures and rigid mindsets may reject Agile's flexible, collaborative ideals, so leaders must plan actively to unite these two worlds. By promoting open communication, flattening hierarchies, and encouraging cross-functional collaboration, organizations can start to align norms with Agile's adaptive values.

Revising reward systems so they reinforce collaboration and innovation also nudges the culture toward greater agility. Rewarding teamwork and creativity – instead of just individual outcomes – spotlights the traits that align with an Agile mindset.

Frequent, transparent communication keeps teams engaged, fosters trust, and ensures that Agile principles reach every corner of the organization. Without addressing cultural inertia, Agile risks becoming superficial. By embedding Agile in culture, leaders make sure it endures.

One vital part of dismantling these cultural barriers is leveraging the rich perspectives offered by diverse teams.

Embracing Diversity and Inclusion

A lasting Agile journey depends on diversity and inclusion, both within teams and across the entire organization. Diverse viewpoints spark better problem-solving and innovation, strengthening Agile. Leaders must:

1. **Value Varied Perspectives**: Intentionally include different voices to spot opportunities and mitigate blind spots.
2. **Create Inclusive Spaces**: Make sure everyone feels respected and valued, cultivating a sense of belonging.
3. **Address Unconscious Bias**: Offer training and implement policies that level the playing field for all participants.

Google's 'Project Aristotle' revealed that diverse teams and psychological safety are key contributors to higher performance and innovation, showing that diversity and inclusion are central to unlocking Agile's potential.

> As an adaptive leader, ask yourself: Are you building an inclusive culture that welcomes different perspectives? How might you bring diverse voices into your teams to energize innovation?

Alongside fostering diversity and inclusion, creating a psychologically safe environment is essential for teams to thrive. Psychological safety enables open dialogue and risk-taking, which are critical for sustaining agility. To fully benefit from this diversity, teams must feel safe to share their ideas and take risks, underscoring the importance of psychological safety.

Hybrid Work and Creativity in Agile Teams

Adopting Agile within hybrid work setups sparks new questions about how creativity unfolds. While flexible and remote setups can enhance productivity, certain forms of creativity may flourish more with face-to-face exchanges.

In-person ideation sessions often prompt interactions with both introverts and extroverts, while virtual decision-making can promote frank discussions when freed from hierarchical cues. Hence, a blended approach – combining physical gatherings for ideation with virtual collaboration for execution – can energize Agile teams.

For example: Pair programming used to hinge on two developers sharing the same workstation, but tools like Visual Studio Live Share now enable real-time collaboration from anywhere. These kinds of hybrid solutions carry forward Agile's iterative approach despite geographic distance.

While hybrid work arrangements enhance autonomy and efficiency, creativity and collaboration often require deliberate effort. Some companies report that remote ideation lacks spontaneity, limiting innovation and serendipitous conversations. Leaders in industries like music and finance suggest that in-person collaboration builds stronger relationships, a key factor in long-term business success.

However, employee surveys also highlight that hybrid work is valued as much as an 8% pay rise, suggesting its impact on motivation and engagement cannot be ignored. The challenge for Agile teams is ensuring hybrid structures do not diminish creative energy – crafting intentional touchpoints for collaboration, ensuring hybrid meetings are as engaging as in-person discussions, and maintaining a shared sense of purpose across locations.

Agile's focus on continuous learning means organizations will evolve their methods and find novel ways to remain agile in changing workplaces. Beyond remote versus in-person setups, rapid technological disruption also demands that Agile practices adapt.

The Role of Psychological Safety in Sustaining Agility

Psychological safety unlocks potential, empowering teams to innovate, take risks, and grow together.

- **Encouraging Open Dialogue** means teams must feel safe to express ideas, concerns, and mistakes without fear of negative consequences. This openness leads to better problem-solving and innovation.
- **Fostering Trust** among team members enhances collaboration and enables more effective decision-making. Trust builds a foundation for teams to work cohesively and support one another.
- **Supporting Risk-Taking** allows teams to experiment and take calculated risks, leading to continuous improvement. Embracing experimentation fosters a culture of learning and adaptability.

Leaders play a vital role in creating psychologically safe environments by modelling respectful behaviour and responding constructively to feedback. By demonstrating vulnerability and openness, leaders set the tone for the rest of the team. Fostering such an environment depends on understanding how psychological safety itself evolves – and the stages teams naturally progress through on their journey toward true agility.

The Four Stages of Psychological Safety (Clark's Framework)

Psychological safety doesn't happen all at once – it builds progressively. Timothy R. Clark's model outlines four stages that shape how teams grow:

1. **Inclusion Safety**: Team members feel accepted and valued for who they are.
2. **Learner Safety**: They feel secure enough to ask questions, experiment, and learn without fear of embarrassment.
3. **Contributor Safety**: They feel trusted to share ideas and take ownership of outcomes.
4. **Challenger Safety**: They feel confident challenging the status quo and raising difficult issues, even with leadership.

Without Challenger Safety, teams often hesitate to call out inefficient practices or suggest bold changes. True business agility relies on reaching this final stage. Adaptive leaders must recognize where their teams stand and create the right conditions for trust, learning, contribution, and respectful challenge to thrive.

The Role of Leadership in Sustaining Agility

As Agile roles evolve, adaptive leaders must transition from traditional control to becoming catalysts for ongoing transformation. By backing experimentation and incorporating emerging technologies, they let their organizations respond nimbly to new challenges while staying anchored in core Agile principles. This leadership ensures that agility remains a long-term pursuit, rooted in continuous learning and baked into the organizational culture.

Effective Leadership Practices Include:

1. **Empowering Teams**
   Encourage autonomy so individuals take full ownership of their work, make informed decisions, and feel motivated to drive innovation.
2. **Championing Change**
   Lead by example by demonstrating Agile values in daily actions, fostering a culture where teams confidently embrace new ways of working.
3. **Providing Support**
   Equip teams with the right tools, training, and mentorship to navigate challenges, overcome setbacks, and sustain Agile momentum.
4. **Using Retrospectives**
   Reflect on leadership decisions by asking, 'Have I enabled team autonomy and adaptability?' or 'What feedback did I act on to boost collaboration?' Acting on these insights strengthens Agile alignment.
5. **Modelling Adaptability and Collaboration**
   Stay flexible, adjust decisions based on evolving needs, and pivot strategies when necessary. Engage in Agile ceremonies like stand-ups to reinforce commitment. Foster cross-team collaboration by breaking silos and removing organizational barriers.

By modelling these behaviours, leaders establish trust and set a precedent for the entire organization to embrace Agile as a mindset, not just a process.

In one major telecom transformation, a senior leader transferred decision-making power to team leads. This reduced bottlenecks, sped up product releases, and increased the sense of ownership team members felt.

Leaders can also embrace Agile themselves, adjusting plans based on team input. They may invest in their own Agile education to better grasp the principles and practices their teams are adopting. After all, successful transformations revolve around people. Leadership must nurture a culture where every employee feels valued and becomes an active driver of change.

Yet leadership alone isn't enough – sustaining agility also means committing to continuous learning and growth. We'll see how fostering such a culture helps organizations thrive.

Fostering a Learning Culture

A leading software firm discovered that while teams worked in Agile sprints, innovation was stagnating. Engineers were so focused on meeting sprint commitments that they weren't exploring new ideas. Leadership introduced 'Agile Exploration Days', where teams dedicated one sprint per quarter to experimenting with new technologies. This resulted in breakthrough innovations, proving that a strong learning culture is essential to sustaining agility.

A learning culture is fundamental to sustained agility. Consider how Microsoft's 'growth mindset' initiatives foster creative thinking and experimentation. Supporting cross-functional workshops or using AI-driven learning platforms equips teams for whatever the future may hold. Leaders should celebrate ongoing learning, weaving it into the organization's DNA.

Listening and Knowledge Sharing encourage individuals to exchange ideas and experiences, spurring fresh solutions and boosting team capabilities. Regular seminars, peer coaching, or digital collaboration tools can power this knowledge flow.

Supporting Personal Development by offering individuals training, mentoring, and clear career paths boosts engagement and helps cultivate essential new skills.

Adapting to Change is easier for teams that view change as an opportunity instead of a threat. It also makes them more resilient when industry trends, technologies, or consumer demands shift quickly.

True adaptability demands curiosity and a commitment to learning beyond Agile frameworks. Leaders should explore disciplines such as Lean principles, operational research, and systems thinking to broaden their understanding of agility. These complementary perspectives help leaders move beyond frameworks, creating organizations capable of responding to complexity with creativity and resilience.

Personal Reflection

Midway through an Agile rollout at a financial services firm, we discovered that entire teams lacked basic coding standards. Rather than blame them, we added mini-tutorials and pair programming to each sprint. I saw how quickly people can learn when leadership encourages mistakes as a path to growth.

Leaders can bolster a learning culture by investing in professional development, spotlighting achievements, and encouraging the open exchange of ideas. Lifelong learning is a cornerstone of Agile thinking. However, traditional education and corporate learning structures often fall short of embracing Agile principles.

Applying Agile to Learning and Development

Agile's Role in Education

A university in the UK applied Agile principles to redesign its curriculum, allowing real-time adaptation based on student feedback. Instead of fixed yearly syllabi, they introduced iterative course adjustments, ensuring content remained relevant. This Agile-inspired approach boosted student engagement and learning outcomes, proving that agility can enhance education as much as business.

Agile ways of working are not just transforming workplaces – they are reshaping how individuals learn, adapt, and develop skills. The rigid, syllabus-driven approach to education is giving way to iterative, student-led learning.

How Agile Is Changing Education

- **Iterative Learning Models**: Universities and corporate training programmes are embracing Agile sprints, where content is adjusted in real-time based on student feedback.
- **Self-Directed Learning**: Just as Agile empowers teams, education is shifting toward personalized learning pathways.
- **Cross-Disciplinary Collaboration**: Agile principles are now applied in research, professional training, and executive education.

Companies like Google and IBM use Agile in corporate learning, ensuring employees continuously refine their skills through iteration and feedback loops rather than rigid coursework.

As the role of agility continues to expand across industries and disciplines, its future will be shaped by how effectively organizations embed agility into their DNA, not just as a framework but as a guiding philosophy.

Capability Gap and Affordable Education

A persistent barrier to Agile's widespread success is the 'capability gap': the difference between what Agile can achieve and what is actually being done. Often, the challenge isn't the need for new methods but the difficulty of sharing existing knowledge at scale.

High training costs and the scarcity of incremental learning opportunities widen this gap. Traditional Agile courses, which can be both expensive and content-heavy, risk overwhelming participants with too much information, leading to poor retention. Instead, organizations need affordable, long-term learning models that blend on-the-job practice with live coaching and reinforcement.

Leaders can close the capability gap by prioritizing affordability, seamless integration, and real-world application of learning, ensuring team members can steadily build expertise while contributing to the Agile journey.

Building Resilience Through Continuous Improvement

A fintech startup experienced a major product failure when a highly anticipated feature didn't resonate with customers. Instead of abandoning Agile, leadership leaned into retrospectives, identifying gaps in their customer research. By iterating based on user feedback, they reworked the product and successfully relaunched it within months. This case reinforces that Agile isn't just about speed – it's about resilience and the ability to course-correct effectively.

Continuous improvement drives the resilience needed in modern workplaces. Organizations that internalize this approach grow stronger, more adaptable, and better equipped to handle evolving realities.

Several Strategies Help Build Resilience:

1. **Regular Reflection**: Practices like retrospectives help teams recognize wins, pinpoint challenges, and craft meaningful improvements.
2. **Adaptive Planning**: Rolling wave planning and Agile backlogs let organizations incorporate fresh insights and reprioritize in a short time.
3. **Customer-Centric Focus**: Putting the customer's needs first ensures relevance and cements enduring trust and loyalty.

Growth Mindset vs Resilience and Antifragility

While a growth mindset highlights improvement via effort, resilience focuses on enduring difficulty and adapting. Dave Snowden's notion of 'antifragility' goes a step further, describing how some people or teams can emerge stronger amid chaos. Writer Nassim Nicholas Taleb first used the word 'antifragility' to show how some systems gain from stress rather than merely withstand it. Leaders who nurture antifragility often find their teams respond more robustly to changes and uncertainties.

To maintain that resilience, organizations must break down silos and nurture partnerships inside and outside their borders. Leaders benefit from understanding how thought patterns and assumptions shape organizational behaviour – an idea captured in the 'Mind Map of Human Experience'.

Mind Map of Human Experience

Agile transcends frameworks and processes. It requires leaders to shape the mindsets and mental models throughout the organization. A 'Mind Map of Human Experience' underscores how thinking styles, cognitive frameworks, and metacognition drive behaviour and decisions.

Adaptive Leaders Can:

- **Foster Metacognition** by encouraging teams to reflect on their thought processes and assumptions, challenging unproductive habits, and adopting a more Agile outlook.
- **Enhance Sense-Making** by linking day-to-day tasks with the organization's bigger picture, helping employees find a deeper purpose in their work.
- **Build Dynamic Adaptability** by setting up iterative feedback loops – mirroring how our brains rewire based on new information – so teams evolve continuously in complexity-rich environments.

For instance, if a team clings to believing that 'failure is never acceptable', they'll likely struggle with true experimentation, no matter how well they adhere to Agile ceremonies. Leaders must deliberately shift such beliefs, aligning them with Agile values like collaboration, adaptability, and resilience.

Yet reshaping mindsets alone isn't enough if individuals lack the practical skills or resources. Let's examine how a 'capability gap' can stall Agile adoption and how affordable, incremental education can bridge this divide.

Collaboration Beyond Silos and Boundaries

Agile thrives when teams collaborate across traditionally rigid structures. This includes several layers:

- **Cross-Functional Teams**: By unifying diverse skill sets, organizations address intricate challenges more holistically.
- **External Partnerships**: Bringing in customers, suppliers, or even competitors in certain contexts can foster shared insights and innovative breakthroughs.
- **Global Collaboration**: Adopting remote and international teams boosts creativity and broadens the talent pool.

Real Agile transformations don't happen in isolated pockets – they require teamwork across all levels, stakeholder engagement, and shared ownership of both opportunities and problems. Widespread collaboration strengthens agility and sets the stage for creative solutions.

As dispersed and hybrid work models gain momentum, we'll also examine how they might influence creativity and collaboration.

Today, collaboration often spans both physical and virtual environments. Let's explore how hybrid work arrangements influence creativity within Agile teams – and what it takes to keep them thriving.

Maintaining Agility Amid Technological Disruption

AI, machine learning, and automation are advancing, so agility is vital. Agile must evolve with new technology while keeping its people-first ethic. Gartner predicts that by 2025 over 75% of organizations will run at least one AI-driven process each day. We will become the second most intelligent species on the planet within five years. Are you ready to lead this digital revolution?

Key Strategies

1. **Thoughtful Technology Integration**
   Evaluate how emerging tools can expand customer value and drive transformative change. For instance, offloading routine tasks to AI can free up capacity for human creativity.
2. **Upskill and Cross-Train**
   Motivate team members to gain competencies in emerging technologies, ensuring they can steer how these innovations augment Agile practices.
3. **Leverage Data-Driven Decision-Making**
   Use analytics to anticipate trends and respond swiftly. Keeping data central helps teams pivot effectively in volatile market conditions.

The rapid rise of automation is predicted to replace 45% of routine jobs by 2030. Is your team prepared to pivot and thrive in a redefined working environment?

Agile practitioners can maintain a competitive edge without compromising on values by following these strategies. At the same time, any adoption of technology must also be balanced with sustainability and ethical concerns.

Embracing Sustainability and Ethical Practices

Agile teams increasingly intersect with sustainability and ethics, reflecting broader business priorities:

- **Sustainable Development Practices**: Integrate environmental objectives, whether by minimizing waste or using greener materials.
- **Ethical Decision-Making**: Establish and follow ethical guidelines, reinforcing transparency and accountability.
- **Social Responsibility**: Contribute positively to society through donations, community engagement, or fair supply chains.

A consumer goods firm, for example, integrated eco-friendly design into its Agile product backlog, emphasizing green packaging and minimal waste. The outcome: a stronger bond with eco-conscious consumers. This broader perspective ensures Agile delivers not just market value but societal value, too.

Checking the effectiveness of these initiatives goes beyond raw metrics; it also involves qualitative markers of success.

While Agile practices can integrate sustainability and ethics at a process level, leadership is essential for embedding these principles into the organizational mindset. Adaptive leadership provides the foundation for driving sustainable and ethical decision-making across teams.

Prioritizing Sustainability and Ethics Through Agile Leadership

Agile transformations often focus on speed, collaboration, and responsiveness, but their true potential lies in fostering long-term, sustainable growth. A 2023 Deloitte study found that 64% of global executives rank environmental, social, and governance (ESG) goals among their top three priorities. How is your organization embedding sustainability into its strategic vision?

Adaptive leadership is crucial for embedding sustainability and ethical decision-making into Agile practices, ensuring that organizations not only thrive today but remain resilient and responsible for the future.

The Role of Adaptive Leadership

Adaptive leaders bridge the gap between short-term Agile goals and long-term organizational values. They ensure that decisions made within Agile frameworks align with ethical principles and sustainability goals.

Strategies for Embedding Sustainability and Ethics

Modern organizations recognize that thriving in the long run means caring for both people and the planet. Agile leaders are crucial in weaving ethical and sustainable actions into everyday work. Below, you'll find two resources: the first outlines key steps for leaders to drive positive environmental and social outcomes, while the second offers a quick-reference checklist to keep teams focused on these goals.

Framework: Ethical and Sustainable Actions

Leaders can integrate green initiatives and ethical standards into Agile activities, as shown in the table below, complete with real-world examples.

Action	Guidance	Example
Incorporate Sustainability into Agile Planning	Ensure that sprints, roadmaps, and project goals account for environmental and social impacts.	A manufacturing firm integrates carbon footprint reduction targets into its sprint planning sessions.
Foster Ethical Decision-Making	Equip teams with frameworks to evaluate ethical implications, particularly in AI, data privacy, or supply chain practices.	A leader introduces a decision-making checklist to assess how AI-powered customer solutions affect data privacy.
Create KPIs for Sustainability and Ethics	Track metrics that demonstrate the organization's commitment to eco-friendly, ethical behaviours.	A company measures diversity in Agile teams and monitors energy use during product development to gauge progress on sustainability goals.
Lead by Example	Model ethical behaviours and sustainability practices to emphasize their importance across the organization.	A leader advocates for hybrid work models to cut travel-related emissions, aligning daily practices with the organization's sustainability aims.

Toolkit: Sustainability and Ethics Checklist for Agile Leaders

While the above actions help embed ethical values and eco-friendly thinking, the following checklist offers specific areas to track. Leaders can refer to it regularly, ensuring every team effort supports the broader goals of corporate social responsibility.

Focus Area	Leadership Action	Example
Environmental Impact	Integrate green initiatives into planning.	Carbon-neutral sprint goals.
Ethical AI	Develop frameworks for data governance.	Ensure AI tools respect user privacy.
Team Diversity	Foster inclusive hiring practices.	Diverse teams to reflect global markets.

For Example: Sustainability in Agile Product Development

A global retailer committed to reducing its environmental impact while maintaining Agile delivery timelines. Using Adaptive Leadership, the company:

- Reworked its supply chain to prioritize sustainable materials.
- Introduced sustainability KPIs into Agile sprints, ensuring teams considered environmental impact at every stage.
- Trained Agile teams to identify and eliminate waste during product design.

The Result: A 30% reduction in packaging waste and a significant increase in customer satisfaction due to environmentally friendly practices.

As leaders champion sustainability and ethics, they must also consider how success is evaluated. The next section explores advanced metrics that go beyond traditional outputs, focusing on long-term impact and meaningful progress.

Looking Beyond Output Metrics

Quantitative measures matter, but Agile success also depends on subtler factors that highlight its broader impact:

- **Employee Satisfaction**: Engaged, motivated teams reflect a healthy Agile culture. Pulse surveys or open forums can reveal how people feel.
- **Customer Feedback**: Contented, loyal customers signal that Agile is genuinely creating value.
- **Cultural Alignment**: Observing how deeply Agile principles are embedded – for example, open communication or adaptability – shows whether agility is truly sustainable.

By embracing these qualitative indicators, organizations get a more complete sense of whether Agile is thriving and how to fine-tune it further. In parallel, formal maturity assessments can help guide these improvements.

Assessing where an organization stands in its Agile evolution helps them continuously improve. Models like the Agile Maturity Model (AMM) or Scaled Agile Framework (SAFe) provide structures for analysing processes, culture, leadership, and outcomes.

Consistent re-evaluation spots strengths, gaps, and the next steps, as discussed in Chapter 10. With a clear sense of maturity, organizations are better equipped to evolve Agile in line with modern changes and challenges.

The Future of Agile: Continual Evolution

The future of Agile is deeply intertwined with the evolution of work itself. As new technologies and methodologies emerge, Agile will adapt, integrating these advancements to ensure it remains an effective force in shaping how work is done, fostering innovation, and maintaining a people-centric focus.

Anticipated Developments

1. Integration with Emerging Technologies

   - AI and Data Analytics can handle repetitive tasks and inform decisions.
   - **Future-Proofing Approach**: Create clear AI ethics boards to address bias or privacy, building trust and responsibility in AI's use.

2. Expansion Beyond IT

   - Agile is crossing into healthcare, education, finance, and other realms, creating broader improvements.
   - **Future-Proofing Approach**: Offer cross-sector training and encourage pilot programmes that adapt Agile for non-technical contexts.

3. Emphasis on Sustainability and Ethics

   - Companies are increasingly adopting social responsibility as a core mission.
   - **Future-Proofing Approach**: Integrate eco-friendly metrics and moral considerations into user stories, ensuring they become tangible priorities.

4. Enhanced Remote and Hybrid Adaptation

   - Optimizing Agile ceremonies for remote or hybrid environments remains crucial.
   - **Future-Proofing Approach**: Invest in digital collaboration tools while planning occasional on-site gatherings for deeper alignment.

5. Cultural Agility

   - Continuous focus on inclusivity, diversity, and psychological safety.
   - **Future-Proofing Approach**: Provide unconscious bias training and inclusive policies to ensure that dynamic teams thrive.

Key Actions for Future-Proofing Agile Practices

- Routinely scan emerging social and technological trends.
- Nurture a learning culture that stays current with fresh methods and challenges.
- Establish ethical guardrails for new technologies to stay consistent with Agile's people-first ethos.
- Expand Agile frameworks to include environmental and moral criteria, making them integral rather than afterthoughts.

Fostering Continuous Learning and Innovation

Sustaining agility means championing consistent experimentation, introspection, and refinement. Leaders who encourage inquisitiveness and push teams to question assumptions build a workplace where innovation takes root. Agile ultimately requires more than timely deliveries – its real hallmark is constant learning.

Conclusion

Agility endures when it is embraced as an ongoing mindset rather than a one-time transformation. This chapter highlighted the importance of continuous learning, open collaboration, and iterative thinking in building resilient organizations. Leaders who create environments where adaptability, experimentation, and long-term thinking thrive will sustain Agile's impact well beyond the initial implementation.

Sustaining agility requires an ongoing commitment to reflection and refinement. Agile must be embedded in organizational values, ensuring teams can navigate change with confidence and creativity. The most successful Agile transformations are those that evolve rather than remain static.

Agile's greatest strength is its ability to adapt. Organizations that remain flexible and responsive, rather than clinging to rigid interpretations of Agile, will be best positioned to lead in an unpredictable business environment.

The next chapter explores how Agile can be reimagined to remain relevant in the years ahead, ensuring its principles continue to drive innovation and business success.

Call to Action

As an adaptive leader, set up micro-learning initiatives and run pilot projects that test new ideas in short cycles. Are your retrospectives unearthing meaningful lessons – or just repeating stale patterns? Challenge your team to integrate fresh insights every sprint, turning small improvements into lasting cultural shifts.

Key Takeaways

- **Agile Is a Mindset**: Viewing Agile as a journey boosts resilience and adaptability.
- **Cultural Transformation Is Essential**: Real, sustainable agility demands addressing deep-rooted norms.

- **Leadership Drives Agility**: Leaders must model and uphold Agile's core values.
- **Continuous Learning Builds Resilience**: A learning culture fuels innovation and growth.
- **Collaboration Extends Beyond Boundaries**: Partnering across functions and with external stakeholders enriches Agile practices.

CLEAR Model® Connection

- **Adaptability**: Ongoing adjustments align teams with evolving priorities.
- **Responsiveness**: Timely feedback cycles let leaders address obstacles before they grow.

Key Takeaway: A learning organization is a resilient organization. Leaders must encourage curiosity, feedback loops, and knowledge-sharing to maintain long-term agility.

Continuous Improvement Toolkit

- **Kaizen Board Template:**
  o Visualize ongoing improvement initiatives.
- **Retrospective Techniques:**
  o Introduce varied methods like Start/Stop/Continue or 4Ls (Liked, Learned, Lacked, Longed For).
- **Feedback Collection Tools:**
  o Use surveys and feedback apps to gather insights.

Culture of Learning Guide

1. **Promote Psychological Safety:**
   o Encourage open dialogue without fear of judgment.
2. **Recognition Programmes:**
   o Acknowledge contributions to improvement efforts.
3. **Learning Opportunities:**
   o Provide access to training and development resources.
4. **Set Improvement Goals:**
   o Align individual and team objectives with continuous learning.

Chapter Summary

Agility thrives when an organization continuously learns, experiments, and adjusts. This chapter demonstrated that Agile is never 'done' – it is an ever-evolving cycle of reflection, adaptation, and growth. By nurturing a culture of open dialogue, inclusivity, ethical responsibility, and curiosity, leaders keep agility strong over time.

Embrace continuous learning agility, and your teams will remain resilient, competitive, and ready to face tomorrow's uncertainties.

15

Reimagining Agile – The Path Forward

The best way to predict the future is to create it.

Peter Drucker

What You'll Gain

- **For Senior Leaders and Executives**: Discover how to simplify and reinvigorate Agile, ensuring it aligns with strategic goals and remains adaptive amid today's disruptions.
- **For Mid-Level Leaders**: Learn to prune unnecessary complexity, embrace fresh ideas, and connect Agile practices directly to tangible outcomes.
- **For Students or Early-Career Professionals**: Understand the next phase of Agile evolution – moving beyond frameworks and ceremonies to build a creative, collaborative culture.

Reimagining Agile for a New Era

Paul, a seasoned Agile coach, sensed the tension in a strategic meeting. *'Teams are sticking to Agile ceremonies'*, the CTO admitted, *'but we've lost our adaptive spirit'*. Many organizations reach this point – Agile practices are in place, yet the essence of flexibility wanes.

Agile cannot remain static. It must evolve – not just in methods but also in mindset, leadership, and alignment with emerging trends.

Personal Reflection

I've witnessed transformative results when teams stop treating Agile as a to-do list and nurture it as a fluid, innovative culture. One tech startup, for example, slashed its release cycle by almost 50% simply by removing outdated ceremonies and redirecting that energy into deeper collaboration. When we remove needless complexity, Agile returns to its core impact.

Why Reimagine Agile?

- **Agile Is Not Frozen in Time**: It's a living approach that must keep pace with changing markets, new technologies, and diverse workforces.
- **Avoiding Stagnation**: Leaders risk 'Agile fatigue' if they cling to rigid frameworks. Reimagining keeps the spirit of adaptability alive.
- **CLEAR Model® Link**: *Adaptability* and *Responsiveness* define how Agile thrives long-term. Reimagining ensures these pillars remain strong.

In this chapter, we'll explore the 'Reimagining Agile' movement, which cuts through outdated rituals and reaffirms the original Agile values for modern contexts. We'll see how adaptive leaders, working alongside global thought leaders, guide this ongoing refresh, integrating inclusivity, prioritizing simplicity, and ensuring Agile endures as a powerful method for continuous innovation.

Yet, despite Agile's origins as a flexible and iterative approach, many organizations have unknowingly turned it into a rigid system. Teams go through the motions, but the adaptability that once made Agile powerful is fading. If Agile becomes just another bureaucratic framework, it risks losing its impact altogether. The key to sustaining agility is recognizing that Agile must evolve – not as a fixed process, but as a living, breathing philosophy that continuously adapts. The next section explores why this evolution is essential and how organizations can break free from the constraints of outdated Agile practices.

Agile Was Never Meant to Be Static – It Must Evolve

Agility isn't a framework – it's a mindset. Yet, many organizations have turned Agile into a rigid system full of:

- Ceremony over substance.
- Framework dogma instead of adaptability.
- Process compliance instead of real business impact.

Example: The Agile Plateau at a Global Tech Firm

A global tech company implemented Agile at scale. At first, it worked. However, over time, teams started focusing more on Agile rituals than on delivering value. Sprint velocity increased, but customer satisfaction dropped. The problem?

- Agile became about 'doing Agile' instead of 'being Agile'.

The solution? Leadership cut unnecessary ceremonies, refocused on customer value, and empowered teams to adapt processes as needed.

Result: 35% faster delivery and renewed team engagement.

Agility must be continuously reimagined – if it becomes rigid, it dies.

Redefining Agile's Core Principles for the Future

Agile was never meant to be rigid. The original Agile Manifesto (2001) was about flexibility, iteration, and continuous learning. But over time, Agile has drifted into:

- Process over principles.
- Framework worship instead of business adaptability.
- Metrics that don't measure real success.

Key Shifts for Reimagining Agile

Old Agile Thinking	Reimagined Agile Thinking
Follow the framework	Adapt the framework
Measure velocity	Measure business impact
Rigid sprint cycles	Flexible, outcome-driven iterations
Command-and-control Agile transformations	Agile co-creation with teams
Scrum, SAFe, and LeSS debates	Context-driven agility

Example: The 'Ritual Reset' at a Fortune 500 Company

A large financial services firm stopped focusing on Agile maturity models and instead asked: 'Are we delivering value?'

- They removed stand-ups that had become unproductive.
- They cut meetings that didn't serve a purpose.
- They gave teams full autonomy over how they worked.

Agility means adapting Agile itself, not just following frameworks.

Practical Strategies for Reimagining Agile

1. Encourage Cross-Departmental Collaboration

- Break silos by aligning teams on shared goals.
- **Example**: A global retailer introduced cross-functional Agile squads to improve customer experience, reducing friction between IT, marketing, and operations.

2. Host 'Reimagining' Retrospectives

- Regularly question whether Agile processes still serve their purpose.
- **Example**: A SaaS company eliminated 10 unnecessary meetings per week by identifying wasteful Agile rituals.

3. Use Meaningful Metrics

- Shift from velocity tracking to measuring customer impact.
- **Example**: A healthcare startup tracked patient satisfaction instead of sprint velocity, leading to more impactful Agile development.

4. Model Adaptability as a Leader

- Be visible in Agile stand-ups, adjust plans based on feedback, and stay hands-on.
- **Example**: A tech CEO joins team stand-ups weekly to stay connected to Agile execution.

5. Empower Teams to Shape Their Own Agile Ways of Working

- Trust teams to refine their own Agile processes.
- **Example**: Spotify's Agile teams co-create their own ways of working, leading to more engaged employees.

What Will You Do to Reimagine Agile?

- Challenge every Agile ceremony: Does it still add value?
- Encourage diverse perspectives in Agile transformations.
- Prioritize results over rituals.

Agile is not a destination – it's a movement that thrives on reinvention.

Redefining Agile's Core Principles

A major organization's Agile was stuck in ceremony overkill. Processes stayed, but adaptability vanished. By restoring Agile's original spirit – empowering teams, focusing on actual value, and letting go of rigid steps – they revived creativity. Time-to-market improved by 35%, proving that focusing on core values is essential to re-energize Agile.

As we just read, Agile was never meant to be static. Scrum, XP, and DSDM paved the way for iterative and flexible development long before the Agile Manifesto (2001). Over time, Agile has grown to emphasize collaboration, a customer-first mindset, and continuous learning. As new challenges arise, Agile's basic values must keep evolving.

Agile as a Living Mindset

- **Maturing Beyond Software**: Agile is widely applied to marketing, HR, finance, and other domains.
- **Adaptive Leadership Is Critical**: Leaders who champion evolution ensure Agile's core values don't get lost in frameworks.
- **Future-Focused**: Whether dealing with advanced analytics or global crises, a reimagined Agile stands ready to adapt.

The future belongs to those who dare to refine how they implement Agile. This chapter illustrates how some in the Agile community champion these adaptive transformations, ensuring we keep returning to Agile's guiding spirit.

The 'Reimagining Agile' Movement

The Reimagining Agile movement isn't about replacing Agile – it's about keeping it relevant. Thought leaders across industries are driving this shift, ensuring Agile remains adaptable, simple, and focused on delivering real value.

Sophie, an Agile coach, sensed that her organization had grown complacent, fixated on big frameworks and certificates instead of results. She created Lean-Agile 'labs' to let teams try fresh ideas tailored to their context. The shift from rigid enforcement to co-creation revived excitement and boosted output. This anecdote shows that genuine agility emerges when it's continuously redefined, not prescribed.

Led by figures such as Jim Highsmith (Agile Manifesto co-author), 'Reimagining Agile' reclaims Agile's central purpose – simplicity, adaptability, and continuous improvement. It's not a new manifesto but a renewed commitment to Agile's original power:

- **Stripping Excess**: Removing unhelpful bureaucracy and focusing on the outcomes that truly matter.
- **Reaffirming Core Values**: Emphasizing responsiveness, learning, and deep collaboration.
- **Keeping It Human**: Agile's essence is people-first, not ceremony-first.

Jim Highsmith and others stress that Agile must remain fluid – the Manifesto's 'values over processes' highlight priorities rather than dismissing structure entirely. Adaptive leaders align their teams around these flexible values, ensuring Agile doesn't ossify.

Adaptive Leadership for a Reimagined Agile

- **Simple Over Complex**: Challenge whether each ritual is necessary.
- **Focus on Outcomes**: Move from process metrics (velocity) to genuine impacts (customer delight, learning).
- **Enable Innovation**: Provide autonomy, encourage safe-to-fail experiments, and cut trivial rules.

Highsmith's view underscores that Agile's mission is to deliver meaningful value in a chaotic world. Leaders who embrace these refined Agile ideals reclaim the unstoppable spirit that sparked Agile's origin.

Seasonal Change and the Rebirth of Agile

Agility experts Neil Walker, Nick Perry, and Tobias Mayer compare Agile's progress to the changing seasons, suggesting that a period of decline – or 'winter' – can fertilize the ground for rejuvenation. This perspective frames perceived stagnation or criticism not as a failure but as the beginning of fresh growth. By remembering principles from Neil Walker, such as DEAD: Dynamic, Evolving, Adaptable, and Disruptive, organizations can foster continuous renewal and relevance.

For leaders, this means interpreting moments of crisis or lull as catalysts for reinvention. Indeed, turning disruption into an opportunity for new life is at the core of reimagining Agile. Achieving that renewal hinges on leadership dedicated to guiding and focusing these shifts.

Adaptive Leadership in Reimagining Agile

When Freddie became CIO of a fast-growing fintech company, Agile was already in place, but teams resisted change. Instead of enforcing new frameworks, he encouraged 'Agile Evolution Sessions', where teams openly discussed frustrations and designed their own improvements. This participatory approach turned Agile from an imposed system into a shared mission, demonstrating that Adaptive Leadership fosters ownership and long-term success.

Vision alone isn't enough to reinvent Agile – leaders must create tangible conditions where a reimagined Agile can thrive. The following strategies illustrate how adaptive leaders can nurture dynamic, evolving Agile practices:

Practice	Description
Encourage Cross-Departmental Collaboration	Run workshops where marketing, finance, and engineering teams align on shared goals, sparking broader creative thinking.
Host 'Reimagining' Retrospectives	Dedicate retrospectives to examining whether current Agile practices serve their intended purpose or need recalibration.
Use Meaningful Metrics	Monitor aspects like team morale, innovation, or customer-centric outcomes rather than velocity or story points.
Model Adaptability	Leaders participate in stand-ups, adjust plans in response to feedback, and work alongside teams to maintain continuous improvement.

Practice	Description
Empower Teams	Provide training and autonomy while insisting on accountability, letting teams co-create or refine their own processes.
Cultivate Psychological Safety	Prioritize transparency, celebrate lessons from failures, and protect experimentation from stigma.

By employing these practices, leaders lay the groundwork for experimentation, learning, and inclusive participation – the core ingredients of true Agile evolution.

Personal Reflection

As CTO of a global software company, I introduced bi-monthly 'Agile Reinvention Sessions' to gather input on refining Agile approaches across the business. Using a dashboard that tracked delivery times and customer satisfaction, leadership iteratively tweaked processes, boosting team morale by about 20% in the first three months and elevating product quality in measurable ways.

Adaptive leadership is key to rethinking Agile. By driving collaboration, setting relevant metrics, and authentically living Agile's ideals, leaders ensure that Agile continues to be relevant in modern contexts. Just as important, though, is returning to the timeless Agile values behind each iteration of its expansion.

Emphasizing Core Values and Principles

Two competing automotive firms attempted Agile transformations. The first company focused on enforcing SAFe, requiring teams to follow every structure without adaptation. The second company prioritized Agile's core principles – empowering teams to adapt outcomes-based processes. A year later, the second firm saw a 35% improvement in speed-to-market, while the first reported 'Agile fatigue'. The lesson? Agile succeeds when values drive the transformation, not just process adherence.

Agile's evolution depends on leaders who keep it simple, adaptable, and focused on producing real value. Their task is to continually balance fresh thinking with practicality so that Agile retains its accessibility and impact.

The Reimagining Agile initiative also highlights so-called 'exemplars' – case studies of organizations where Agile has taken root and flourished. These real-world accounts demolish the belief that Agile works only in tech, proving its adaptability across countless industries. They prove that teams can adopt Agile principles to create rewarding workplaces marked by collaboration, creativity, and consistency, regardless of their sector.

This movement doesn't advocate rewriting the Agile Manifesto but instead encourages an evolving platform that suits the future of work, where agility is increasingly decentralized and self-organizing. This adaptability is vital in a world shaped by complexity and rapid changes.

By endorsing inclusivity, curiosity, and collaboration, this wave of reimagining grows beyond software, demonstrating Agile's effectiveness in various sectors. If you're an adaptive leader, consider how reconnecting with Agile's central ideals might rejuvenate your team's performance. Which steps could you take to streamline processes and realign on what truly counts?

Personal Reflection

After years of relying on standard sprints, my DevOps group proposed a rolling release model for continuous integration. It broke from my old assumptions – but once we reimagined our backlog and freed teams from strict two-week cycles, we unlocked faster experimentation and realized Agile is about finding what truly suits your context.

As organizations critically evaluate and reshape their Agile practice, a key insight emerges: success hinges on using methodologies that suit each unique context. This realization paves the way for a 'context-driven' model of agility.

Embracing Context-Driven Agility

Agile's expanding scope reveals the necessity of tailoring solutions to each organization's unique requirements. Leaders who embrace **context-driven agility** find themselves better prepared to tackle intricate and unpredictable environments.

This outlook champions careful analysis of each organization's culture, goals, and challenges, applying only those tools and methods that genuinely provide value. Many agilists, myself included, emphasize 'the right method in the right context', insisting that agility is an ongoing skill to develop, not a product to purchase.

In adopting context-driven agility, companies surpass the boundaries of any one framework, building ecosystems that adapt as business conditions shift. It's a fundamental shift from seeing agility as a set of tools to understanding it as a characteristic intrinsic to organizational health.

Strategies for Context-Driven Agility

1. **Assess Needs**
   o Before selecting a framework or approach, look at team structure, objectives, and pain points.
2. **Pilot Custom Approaches**
   o Begin with smaller test projects, tailoring practices to each team or department's specific goals.
3. **Iterate based on feedback**
   o Regular retrospectives, data analysis, and ongoing dialogue help refine methods to match changing requirements.

Several leading figures championing the Reimagining Agile movement continue to guide and enrich these transformations.

Key Contributors to Reimagining Agile

Among those shaping this initiative with Jim Highsmith are Jon Kern, Heidi Musser, and Sanjiv Augustine, who together formed the Reimagining Agile launch group. Jon Kern, another signatory of the original Agile Manifesto, applies his extensive background in a product-owner capacity at Adaptavist to ensure the concept remains both grounded and forward-looking. Heidi Musser, former CIO of a Fortune 50 company and past board chair of the Agile Alliance, brings deep enterprise and governance experience to the effort. Sanjiv Augustine, author of *Agile Project Management* and *Value Management Office*, contributes a strategic perspective on scaling Agile for modern business needs.

Pioneers like these bring decades of experience to bear, refining Agile so it remains effective and flexible in a rapidly evolving world. Through renewed and refreshed Agile principles, the movement aims to preserve Agile and update it for emerging challenges, keeping Agile core values alive in an age of digital disruption, global competition, and shifting workforce dynamics.

To learn more about the 'Reimagining Agile' movement, visit reimaginingagile.com.

By featuring this effort, we challenge the idea that Agile is outdated. Instead, it evolves. Agile remains future-focused and dynamic, requiring continuous engagement and a willingness to adapt. Beyond the individual leaders guiding this work, reimagined Agile also welcomes a broader range of perspectives and voices.

As these pioneers shape the future of Agile, they also highlight a crucial element for modern workplaces: diversity and inclusion. Let's see how bringing diverse perspectives into Agile can amplify its impact.

Integrating Diversity into Reimagined Agile Practices

A global NGO applied Agile to humanitarian projects across diverse cultural regions. They quickly discovered that standardized Agile frameworks didn't work universally. By integrating local cultural feedback into sprint planning and team structures, they developed an Agile model tailored to regional needs, enhancing responsiveness and impact. This case highlights that reimagining Agile must include diverse perspectives to remain truly adaptable.

Diverse teams continually spark fresh ideas, revealing new solutions to complex business issues. Disproving the notion that uniformity fosters superior outcomes, many global Agile projects benefit directly from cultural and demographic variety. For instance, in one international initiative, local insights informed product design, boosting sales in underserved markets.

Diversity is a critical enabler of agility, enriching both creativity and responsiveness. As Agile frameworks evolve, making space for these differences becomes crucial in driving robust, people-focused outcomes.

Strategies to Integrate Diversity

1. **Foster Inclusive Team Dynamics**
   o Create psychologically safe spaces for people of various backgrounds and experiences.
2. **Promote Diverse Leadership**
   o Leadership teams should mirror the diversity of their workforce, offering a range of perspectives in decision-making.
3. **Adapt Frameworks for Inclusivity**
   o Update Agile ceremonies (like stand-ups or retrospectives) to honour and value different cultures and communication styles.

Practical Ideas

- Rotate who leads daily stand-ups so everyone's voice is heard.
- Provide cross-cultural training to help people understand one another's norms.
- Use anonymous suggestion forms to spark bold ideas and encourage frank feedback.

With a deeper grasp of diversity's role in reimagining Agile, organizations can move on to tangible steps for embedding and sustaining these new Agile approaches.

Reimagining Agile: Practical Steps

To effectively take part in the Reimagining Agile movement, organizations can implement the following strategies:

Practice	Description	Example
Assess Current Practices	Investigate existing Agile processes to identify inefficiencies and refocus on fundamental values.	A global firm sped up time-to-market by streamlining complicated approval workflows.
Refocus on Core Values	Weed out processes that do little more than create bureaucracy, improving overall adaptability.	During retrospectives, explore whether each process or ceremony adds real value.
Integrate Diversity into Agile	Promote inclusive team interactions and make space for varied viewpoints.	Adjust retrospective formats to account for cultural differences, letting everyone contribute comfortably.

Practice	Description	Example
Encourage Experimentation	Build a safety net for trying new ideas and learn from mistakes.	Spotify's flexible 'work from anywhere' culture strikes a balance between structure and freedom.
Invest in Training and Development	Provide teams with the resources they need to understand reimagined Agile values and mindsets.	A technology firm employed dedicated Agile coaches to foster a culture of continuous learning.
Engage with the Agile Community	Join groups and discussions – online or in-person – to keep up with new trends and best practices.	One product team joined an Agile forum to glean insights, eventually adopting advanced backlog-refinement methods.

When executed effectively, these steps let organizations resonate with the Reimagining Agile movement, paving the way for deep transformation. As we look back on these practical actions, we see how this reimagining revitalizes Agile's relevance and secures its place in the future of work.

Reimagining Agile transforms agility from a project-management tool into a broader engine of adaptability, customer focus, and resilience. Adaptive leaders must promote these methods by guiding assessments, encouraging experimentation, and nurturing their teams' ongoing development. By doing so, they create a culture primed for Agile's next chapter.

The most successful Agile transformations are not led from the top, but from within. Corporate Rebels' movement began as an online blog and grew into a global community of people redefining work.

Leaders must move beyond mandating agility and instead foster environments where agility spreads organically. By identifying and supporting change-makers within teams, organizations shift from forcing transformation to enabling it.

Reflecting on Agile's Future

Reimagining Agile is more than just refining frameworks – it's about fostering continuous learning and meaningful change. As an Agile practitioner, take a moment to reflect on the role you play in shaping Agile's evolution.

- What is your hope for Agile in the coming year that is different from previous years?
- How do you want to improve Agile this year?
- What will you contribute to the Agile community to make it a better place?

These questions challenge us to move beyond passive adoption and actively engage in Agile's future. By embracing this mindset, leaders ensure Agile remains a dynamic force that continuously adapts to the needs of modern organizations.

Conclusion

Reimagining Agile means shifting from rigid methodologies to fluid, outcome-driven approaches. This chapter explored how simplicity, flexibility, and people-centred thinking enable Agile to evolve. Leaders who cultivate cultures of collaboration and adaptability ensure Agile remains a powerful tool for transformation.

Agile's future depends on applying its core values in new ways, replacing excessive formality with meaningful progress. When organizations focus on purpose-driven agility, they unlock new opportunities for innovation, resilience, and sustainable success.

Agile is not a destination but a movement that thrives on reinvention. Leaders who embrace its fluid nature will drive progress rather than be constrained by outdated processes.

The next chapter outlines how organizations can develop a strategic roadmap for Agile's future, ensuring leadership, adaptability, and continuous learning remain at the forefront.

Call to Action

As an adaptive leader, challenge every Agile ceremony or process: Does it still deliver value? If not, retire it or adapt it. Encourage wider participation, bring in underrepresented viewpoints, and keep your eye on meaningful results rather than rigid metrics. Reimagine Agile as a dynamic, people-centric system – your team's creativity will soar.

Key Takeaways

- **Agile Is Evolving**: The Reimagining Agile movement shows how Agile adapts to present-day challenges.
- **Core Values Remain Central**: Simplicity, flexibility, and people-first approaches ensure Agile's continuing relevance.
- **Diversity Enhances Agility**: Welcoming varied perspectives enriches innovation and problem-solving.
- **Practical Engagement Is Essential**: Organizations must continually evaluate and refine their Agile practices.
- **Leadership Drives Transformation**: Leaders' actions and behaviours cultivate settings where reimagined Agile can flourish.

CLEAR Model® Connection

- **Adaptability**: Agile remains relevant by evolving alongside new demands.
- **Responsiveness**: Swift reactions to shifts uphold Agile's value in changing conditions.

Key Takeaway: The Agile community must simplify, humanize, and rethink Agile to keep it relevant. Leaders who embrace flexibility and a people-first mindset will drive the next evolution of Agile.

Innovation Workshop Template

- **Objective Setting:**
  - o Define goals for reimagining Agile in your context.
- **Ideation Sessions:**
  - o Use brainstorming techniques to generate ideas.
- **Prototype Development:**
  - o Create small-scale models or pilots of new approaches.
- **Feedback Loops:**
  - o Collect input from stakeholders to refine innovations.

Agile Simplification Checklist

- **Eliminate Redundancies:**
  - o Identify and remove unnecessary processes.
- **Enhance Focus on People:**
  - o Prioritize team well-being and customer relationships.
- **Accessibility Improvements:**
  - o Ensure that all team members understand and use Agile practices.

Chapter Summary

By stripping away unhelpful procedures and celebrating inclusivity, leaders can reignite Agile's transformative power. This chapter revealed how new perspectives and simpler processes yield stronger results. The Reimagining Agile movement encourages us to expand our horizons, maintaining Agile's fundamental values while adjusting to emerging challenges.

Embrace a forward-thinking Agile that fosters creativity and continuous growth. Your teams will deliver greater impact and resilience, staying ready for future disruptions.

16

A Strategic Roadmap for Agile's Future

Vision without action is merely a dream. Action without vision just passes the time. Vision with action can change the world.

Joel A. Barker

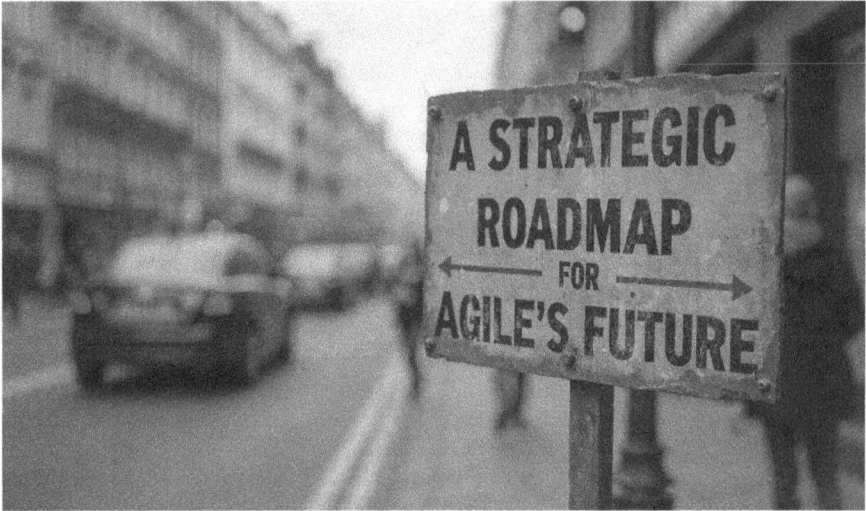

What You'll Gain

- **For Senior Leaders and Executives**: A roadmap to evolve your Agile approach at the strategic level – integrating governance, ethics, and long-term growth.
- **For Mid-Level Leaders**: Practical guidance for connecting day-to-day Agile practices with overarching business strategy, ensuring alignment with wider organizational goals.
- **For Students or Early-Career Professionals**: A clear view of how Agile extends beyond frameworks, influencing culture, ethics, and long-term leadership priorities.

Strategizing for Agile's Future

Sarah, a Chief Transformation Officer at a global bank, scanned the latest Agile adoption report and frowned. *'We've been doing this for five years – but are we actually evolving?'* The issue wasn't Agile itself. It was stagnation, the slow drift into complacency that creeps in when adaptation stops. This chapter explores how leaders can ensure Agile continues to drive meaningful business impact, evolving in step with emerging challenges and opportunities.

Personal Reflection

I've witnessed how agility can determine whether a company thrives or fails. In one case, a client deeply embraced Agile, not only on the production floor but also in strategic decisions, dramatically reducing waste while nearly doubling their speed to market.

Building on the reimagined Agile principles introduced earlier, the following pages provide a strategic roadmap that treats Agile as a dynamic, evolutionary approach to leadership and transformation. It shows leaders how to guide their organizations toward continuous innovation. Adaptive leaders can use this roadmap to shape transformation strategies and steer their organizations confidently into the future.

This strategic roadmap details how leaders can balance operational and strategic agility, tapping into emerging trends to future-proof their organizations. Each pillar in this plan highlights a core leadership trait: resilience, innovation, and fostering a culture of continuous learning.

Leaders can fuel resilience and creativity through scenario planning, helping teams anticipate disruption and adjust before trends overtake them. Leaders who maintain a culture of ongoing learning and technology adoption can position their organizations at the forefront of Agile transformation.

We explore tangible steps to nurture perpetual learning, weave in new technologies, enhance innovation, and reinforce organizational agility – ultimately equipping your organization for sustained success. To achieve these goals, let's first examine the cultural, operational, and strategic dimensions that form the basis of Agile transformation.

Agility's Future: Evolution, Not Stagnation

Agile is not a one-time transformation – it must evolve continuously.

- Markets are shifting faster than ever.
- Technology is transforming how work gets done.
- Employees demand autonomy, flexibility, and purpose.

Yet, many organizations still treat Agile as a checklist, not a mindset.

Example: The Agile Plateau at a Global Bank

Sarah, a Chief Transformation Officer, reviewed her company's Agile adoption report. The data looked good – teams completed more sprints, ceremonies were followed, and frameworks were in place. Yet business results had stagnated.

The issue? Agile had become a routine, not a driver of innovation. Organizations that fail to evolve Agile risk making it just another bureaucracy. The best companies, however, ensure that Agile:

- Drives real business value.
- Adapts to new challenges and technologies.
- Remains flexible and outcome-focused.

This chapter provides a strategic roadmap for the future of Agile – one that keeps it dynamic, relevant, and impactful.

First 100 Days Plan

New or current leaders need early wins and steady habits. This plan sets clear steps, builds trust, and shows progress without noise.

Before you start:

- Pick two pilot teams and record three baselines: lead time, ageing work, and one outcome metric.
- Agree simple guardrails with finance and risk.
- Publish a one-page intent that states why this matters now.

How to use it:

- Follow the four phases as written and avoid adding extras.
- Share a small public dashboard so progress stays visible.
- Hold a short review at day 30, 60, and 100 to lock in learning.

What good looks like by day 100:

- Lead time down, ageing work lower, and two outcome signals up.
- Fewer rules and quicker decisions near the work.
- A repeatable playbook others can adopt.

Purpose: Give new or transitioning leaders a structured start.

Day 1–30: Listen and Learn

- Hold 1:1s with direct reports, skip-levels, and key customers.
- Map current state with Business Agility Canvas (see Chapter 7).
- Identify top five cultural enablers and blockers.
- Run an 'agility health' pulse survey.

Day 31–60: Align and Frame

- Share first findings with leadership team.
- Co-create 12-month CLEAR goals.
- Launch one quick-win project to signal change.
- Set up monthly leadership moves review.

Day 61–90: Act and Embed

- Roll out a cross-team business agility community of practice.
- Adjust governance to shorten decision cycles.
- Launch first 'experimentation cycle' (3–4 small tests with learning reviews).
- Publish Business Agility Canvas results and next quarter's moves.

Day 91–100: Reflect and Commit

- Review progress against Business Agility Canvas and CLEAR measures.
- Share wins, learning, and next-quarter plan with whole organization.

Pillars of Transformation

When Anthony became CEO of a European logistics company, Agile adoption had stalled. Teams followed rituals, but strategic decision-making remained slow. Anthony introduced a Transformation Compass – a model that connected Agile maturity with key business drivers like market expansion, customer experience, and operational efficiency. Within two years, revenue growth accelerated by about 15%, proving that Agile thrives when connected to larger transformation goals.

Success like this often starts not with a full restructure but with removing the constraints that block progress. As Mike Burrows notes, small but critical rules – like rigid approvals or outdated KPIs – can quietly shape behaviour more than any org chart. Before launching a transformation, surface one constraint and ask: What would become possible if this wasn't in the way? The best change often begins by creating permission.

Agile's Strategic Roadmap Is Supported by Three Core Pillars

1. **Cultural Transformation**: Embed a mindset of learning, collaboration, and adaptability.
2. **Operational Transformation**: Streamline workflows for agility, efficiency, and continuous delivery.
3. **Strategic Transformation**: Align Agile principles with long-term vision, innovation, and governance.

By aligning culture, operations, and strategy, organizations can position Agile at the heart of sustained growth. This journey calls for genuine leadership commitment, adaptability, and a willingness to keep evolving. Let's explore these three transformation pillars in detail.

Pillar 1: Cultural Transformation – The Foundation of Sustainable Agility

Agile thrives when it's woven into the company's DNA, not treated as a process to follow.

The Problem

Many organizations:

- Adopt Agile practices but not the Agile mindset.
- Still operate in silos, limiting cross-functional collaboration.
- Fail to create a culture of continuous learning.

The Solution

Leaders must embed agility as a cultural norm.

What to Do Instead

- Encourage experimentation and psychological safety.
- Promote cross-functional collaboration beyond Agile teams.
- Shift from fixed job roles to skill-based, adaptive teams.

Agility is cultural first and procedural second.

Pillar 2: Operational Transformation – Making Agility Real

Operational agility ensures that Agile is not just an IT initiative but a company-wide way of working.

The Problem

- Agile is often confined to software teams, leaving the rest of the business unchanged.
- Many Agile transformations focus on process over value delivery.
- Decision-making remains slow due to outdated governance.

The Solution

Organizations must integrate Agile thinking into finance, HR, operations, and beyond.

What to Do Instead

- Move to adaptive funding models instead of annual budgets.
- Decentralize decision-making to enable faster pivots.
- Use AI and analytics to optimize Agile execution.

Agility is about removing friction, not adding process.

Pillar 3: Strategic Transformation – Aligning Agile with Long-Term Success

Agility is not just about speed – it must connect to a long-term strategic vision.

The Problem

- Many Agile transformations fail because they lack alignment with business strategy.
- Executives still demand fixed long-term plans, conflicting with Agile principles.
- Agile maturity models focus on process adherence rather than business outcomes.

The Solution

Agility must be embedded into strategic decision-making.

What to Do Instead

- Use OKRs to align Agile execution with strategic goals.
- Balance short-term agility with long-term vision.
- Integrate ethical decision-making into Agile governance.

The best Agile organizations don't just iterate – they strategically evolve.

Ethical Decision-Making Framework for Agile Teams

As Agile interweaves with advanced technology, ethical integrity becomes pivotal. Below is a structured approach to ensure decisions respect both Agile's values and broader organizational ethics:

1. **Identify the Ethical Dilemma**
   Define the core issue (e.g. data privacy, fairness, transparency).
2. **Assess Impact on Stakeholders**
   Consider employees, customers, and community – how are they affected?
3. **Align with Organizational Values**
   Cross-check each option with your company's principles and Agile tenets.
4. **Consult Stakeholders**
   Seek diverse viewpoints, including customers and cross-functional teams.

5. **Test Decision Transparency**
    Ask: 'Would we be comfortable defending this publicly?'
6. **Implement and Monitor**
    Decide, track outcomes, and refine as circumstances shift.

Practical Insight: Integrate such checks into sprint reviews or governance sessions. For instance, if adding facial recognition, weigh up both user convenience and privacy implications.

Adaptive Leadership Tip: Make ethics a daily practice, not just a compliance exercise. Model openness, invite questions on fairness or data use, and embed these discussions in retrospectives.

Extending Ethical Thinking Across All Steps

Ethical insights should guide choices across the entire roadmap, not just during formal decisions. When leaders choose new tools, set metrics, or plan sprints, they can invite teams to pause and consider fairness, social impact, and transparency. This approach builds a work culture that values ethics as part of everyday actions rather than a separate process.

A financial services firm used this process before introducing facial recognition for client authentication. By consulting stakeholders, assessing privacy risks, and upholding transparency, the company complied with GDPR while retaining customer trust. They also addressed biases in their algorithms and used input from various teams, boosting confidence in their final product.

- **Example Application**: When considering a new tracking tool, an Agile team examined its effect on employee privacy and ensured its guidelines matched organizational values of openness and respect.
- **Action Step**: What measures will your team take to confirm that every decision adheres to both your values and your overarching vision?

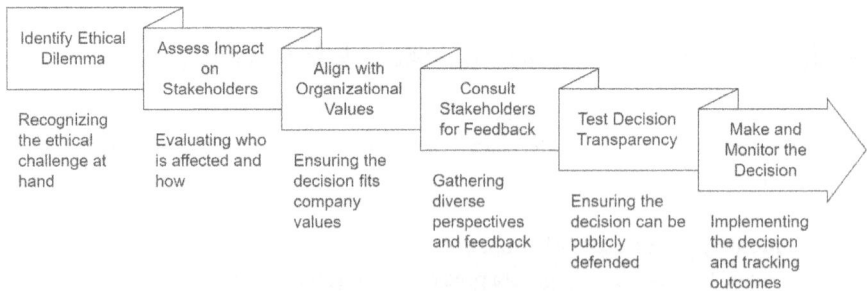

Ethical decision-making framework

Using a structured method like this ensures that new technologies are integrated responsibly, aligning with the organization's goals and ethical code.

While an ethical foundation supports Agile's integrity, achieving true agility also requires aligning short-term actions with long-term strategies to create lasting impact.

Balancing Operational and Strategic Agility

Many firms excel at operational agility – quick iterations, short release cycles – but lack strategic agility, the capacity to shift direction for long-term goals. Leaders must ensure daily improvements align with higher aspirations.

- **OKRs**: Use Objectives and Key Results to bridge short-term iteration with big-picture aims.
- **Governance**: Provide direction without stifling adaptability; measure progress via outcome-based metrics (customer retention, feature adoption).
- **Cross-Level Awareness**: Encourage middle managers to act as coaches who translate strategy into actionable tasks, driving alignment up and down the organization.

Short Example: A logistics firm added 'carbon reduction' to sprint priorities, weaving operational changes (optimized routes) with a strategic sustainability push. This synergy boosted both efficiency and brand reputation.

Charting Agile's Path Forward: Lessons from the Debate

As the conversation around Agile's effectiveness continues, organizations aiming for all-encompassing agility should address these vital areas:

1. **Restoring Authenticity**
   Simplify frameworks to emphasize learning and collaboration over ceremony.
2. **Embedding Ethics and Sustainability**
   Treat environmental, social, and governance considerations as essential, not optional.
3. **Moving Beyond Frameworks**
   'Post-Agile' thinking sees frameworks as flexible tools woven into culture and leadership.

Leaders can broaden the CLEAR Model® to incorporate ethical guidelines and foster collaboration across departments. Rather than seeing critiques as obstacles, treat them as cues to seek improvement and reaffirm authenticity.

Personal Reflection

In one strategic workshop with senior executives, I used a simple one-page roadmap showing quarterly agility goals tied to revenue and market expansion. Their initial scepticism vanished once they saw how an Agile roadmap made big visions more achievable. It underscored that strategic alignment can't be an afterthought – it must be front and centre.

Critics of Agile may pivot to new angles, questioning if Agile can handle emerging technologies or ethical demands around data usage. We should prepare for those critiques by reinforcing our commitment to learning and adapting as demands change.

Overcoming the 'Agile but…' Syndrome

A financial services company faced a common problem – teams were 'Agile' but struggled with decision-making bottlenecks. Leaders realized the issue wasn't the framework but an outdated governance model. By integrating Agile governance – removing excessive approvals and empowering cross-functional decision-making – they reduced project cycle times by 30%. This case highlights that overcoming 'Agile but…' challenges requires addressing underlying structural barriers, not just refining Agile processes.

While some leaders recognize the value of agility, many transformations stall due to compromise and dilution. Research from *The Evolution of the Agile Organization* report from PA Consulting highlights a recurring challenge: the tendency for organizations to claim agility while still clinging to outdated structures. This results in the common 'Agile but…' syndrome:

- 'We're Agile, but we still require multiple layers of approval'.
- 'We're Agile, but we can't decentralize decision-making'.
- 'We're Agile, but teams aren't truly empowered'.

This resistance to full transformation often leads to stagnation and disillusionment, where Agile becomes a superficial branding exercise rather than a real shift in ways of working. To overcome this, leaders must enforce clear non-negotiables in Agile adoption:

- **Commit to Agility at All Levels**: Ensure alignment between leadership, middle management, and teams.
- **Restructure Performance Incentives**: Reward behaviours that drive agility rather than legacy performance indicators.
- **Maintain Consistency in Agile Governance**: Avoid reverting to command-and-control mechanisms under pressure.

These commitments distinguish genuinely Agile organizations from those merely going through the motions. By addressing these challenges head-on, organizations can move from superficial Agile adoption to sustained Business Agility – one that is resilient, responsive, and embedded in everyday decision-making.

The Critics' Next Move: What's Next After 'Agile Is Dead'?

As discussions around the 'death of Agile' wane, critics will likely shift focus. Agile's flexibility – evident in its ability to keep evolving – positions it to respond to new demands, opportunities, and hurdles. Future criticisms might highlight how Agile addresses technological trends, such as AI or data privacy. Debates may arise regarding whether Agile methods can keep up with AI-driven environments or if they need rethinking to accommodate machine learning.

It's clear that 'scale does not kill Agile – corporate theatre kills Agile'. As companies put significant money into Agile transformations (from half a million dollars to $5 million or more), they must redefine success. Instead of clinging to costly frameworks emphasizing superficial compliance over creativity, they should simplify, invest in people, and involve leadership at the core to make Agile truly effective.

We'll also see more scrutiny of how Agile applies to hybrid and remote work environments. As workplaces go digital, sceptics will question whether Agile can hold diverse teams together or if major adjustments are again necessary. Agile's ability to respond to these new critiques hinges on continuous learning and adaptation, ensuring it stays in tune with emerging realities.

Embracing Continuous Learning and Adaptation

Agile thrives on a culture of ongoing development – without it, progress stalls. Leaders who unite strategic vision with day-to-day adaptability foster genuine transformation.

Enter the Strategic Roadmap

Below are 13 tactics across 6 major sections, each linking back to Adaptive Leadership and emphasizing the core components of the CLEAR Model®.

Section 1: Investing in People and Technology

1. Upskilling and Reskilling

Developing your workforce goes beyond technical aptitude. Agile mindsets, flexibility, and strong interpersonal skills stand on par with coding or analytics. Ongoing learning builds resilient teams ready for tomorrow's obstacles. By investing in skills across varied roles, leaders give people the confidence to tackle new demands.

Strategies

- **Upskilling and Reskilling**: Run dedicated courses on AI, ML, data analytics, or cybersecurity through platforms such as Coursera or LinkedIn Learning. Add hands-on labs and industry-backed certifications. Provide seasoned experts to mentor less experienced colleagues. Regularly review skills that are needed to fit emerging goals.
- **Cultivating Agile Mindsets**: Weave Agile values into onboarding and ongoing coaching. Emphasize collaboration, adaptability, and user focus. Invite staff to join Agile ceremonies (e.g. retrospectives, sprint planning). Celebrate actions that reflect Agile ideals and train leaders to model these behaviours.

Example

AT&T channelled over £1 billion into skill-building for advanced technologies and Agile practices. Collaborations with universities gave employees access to degrees and certifications, raising morale and ensuring AT&T's competitiveness. In 2023 alone, AT&T invested $132 million in training, delivering an average of 35 training hours per employee across its 167,000-strong workforce, positioning them strongly against industry peers.

CLEAR Model® Connection

- **Culture**: Encourages a learning environment where evolving skills and mindsets are celebrated.
- **Leadership**: Leaders demonstrate commitment by funding training, coaching, and mentorship.
- **Execution**: Skilled, knowledgeable teams drive more effective daily operations.
- **Adaptability**: Flexible skill sets allow quick pivots to new tools or market demands.
- **Responsiveness**: Trained teams can react promptly to user needs and industry shifts.

2. Advanced Tool Adoption

Introducing tools like AI, IoT, or workflow automation strengthens responsiveness, contradicting the idea that Agile and advanced digital solutions cannot mix. Well-integrated technology enables sharper decisions and quick adjustments to shifting external factors. Leaders must oversee these additions so they enhance delivery while reinforcing agility.

Strategies

- **Using AI and ML**: Introduce AI-enabled project tools (e.g. Jira Align, Asana) for live dashboards and predictive insights. Automate tasks such as sprint planning to lighten admin loads. Set ethical guidelines for AI that are in line with organizational principles.
- **Adopting DevOps**: Implement CI/CD with Jenkins, GitLab, or CircleCI. Integrate development and operations through shared retrospectives. Use monitoring systems (Prometheus, Grafana) for quick fixes and seamless releases.
- **Embracing IoT**: Deploy IoT platforms (AWS IoT Core, Azure IoT Hub) to gather live performance data. Use dashboards to spot trends or predict maintenance needs, refining Agile priorities. Feed IoT insights into sprint reviews to boost product quality and user satisfaction.

Example

Siemens blended IoT and AI into its Agile methods, enabling predictive upkeep in production and smoother product-development cycles. Data from connected devices triggered timely actions, cutting downtime and saving costs.

CLEAR Model® Connection

- **Culture**: Normalizes continual experimentation with cutting-edge tools.
- **Leadership**: Champions adopt technology that aligns with Agile principles and set ethical guidelines.
- **Execution**: Automated processes and real-time insights speed up daily tasks.

- **Adaptability**: Real-time data fosters quick pivots when unexpected issues arise.
- **Responsiveness**: Live dashboards and AI-driven insights enable rapid course corrections.

3. Analytics-Driven Insight

Data analytics underpins Agile decision-making. Live feedback on performance, user sentiment, or changes within the industry helps teams make quick, informed decisions. By embedding continuous data loops, teams base strategic and operational choices on real outcomes. A data-friendly culture is a key facet of Agile growth, letting teams refine processes and improve results.

Strategies

- **Live Decision Support**: Harness solutions like Tableau or Microsoft Power BI for dashboards on user trends and performance. Adjust backlogs and resource allocation to match fresh insights.
- **Continuous Improvement via Metrics**: Track ageing work, defect rates, or cycle durations during retrospectives to spot and fix inefficiencies. Tools such as Jira or Azure DevOps help identify patterns and set action points.
- **User-Centric Adjustments**: Tie analytics from Salesforce or HubSpot to Agile routines. Fold these insights into sprint reviews, ensuring product decisions align with genuine user needs.

Example

Netflix draws heavily on analytics in its Agile framework. By studying user habits and preferences, it refines content recommendations and invests in the shows people want. This approach allows a speedy response to viewer shifts and fuels constant platform improvements.

Ongoing Learning Cycles

Schedule short follow-up sessions a few weeks after any training. Encourage teams to test new skills on real tasks, then gather feedback to decide the next phase of learning. That way, development becomes continuous rather than a one-off event.

CLEAR Model® Connection

- **Culture**: Builds a data-driven mindset that values evidence-based decisions.
- **Leadership**: Embeds analytics into planning and emphasizes transparency of data use.
- **Execution**: Informed by real-time insights, daily tasks and sprints align more closely with user demands.
- **Adaptability**: Data reveals changing trends quickly, prompting iterative adjustments.
- **Responsiveness**: Rapid updates to the backlog or user stories allow near-immediate pivots based on analytics.

Section 2: Enhancing Governance and Organizational Agility

4. Flexible Governance

Adaptive governance blends accountability with responsiveness, allowing prompt pivots without losing direction. Some believe governance dampens agility, but flexible structures can enable frequent adjustments. Leaders measure outcomes (value, alignment, user feedback) over simple output (work hours). Analytics sharpen these data-led choices, promoting openness and clear oversight while allowing quick changes.

Strategies

- **Flexible Governance Frameworks**: Form guidelines that balance control with freedom, such as dynamic approvals. Use digital tools (Miro, Lucidchart) to visualize processes. Update policies through regular review sessions.
- **Outcome-Based Metrics**: Switch from traditional output metrics (hours logged) to user-driven KPIs (satisfaction, feature adoption). Use Power BI or Tableau for live analytics, linking team goals to overall strategic aims.
- **Data-Focused Decisions**: Bring in Google Analytics or Looker for actionable insights. Integrate predictive models to highlight risks and openings. Make data easy to read so teams can act on it swiftly.

Example

A financial services group replaced time-based measurements with indicators like client satisfaction and feature uptake. This drove loyalty up by nearly 30% and improved morale.

Bridging Strategy and Execution

Middle managers shape how strategy comes to life day by day. Encouraging them to be coaches and connectors helps Agile values permeate each level. Leading sprint reviews, guiding junior staff, or advocating fresh ideas ensures top-down aims align with team actions.

CLEAR Model® Connection

- **Culture**: Embeds a trust-based, outcome-oriented ethos.
- **Leadership**: Balances oversight and autonomy, removing bureaucratic hurdles.
- **Execution**: Teams focus on valuable deliverables over administrative tasks.
- **Adaptability**: Governance can flex as market or user needs shift.
- **Responsiveness**: Rapid decision-making speeds up feedback loops.

5. Strengthening Organizational Agility

To embed agility at the organizational level, leaders must push beyond small project teams. Align leadership, strategy, and operations around adaptability. Encourage cross-functional squads and rework rigid leadership setups so that agility flows throughout the hierarchy. This includes giving teams the authority to act and extending Agile thinking well beyond project boundaries. Scaling Agile fosters creativity, speeds up reactions, and nurtures a setting where collaboration cracks tough problems.

Strategies

- **Enterprise Agility**: Unite broad strategic goals with Agile practices through frameworks like OKRs. Promote iterative planning and consistent feedback. Use digital collaboration tools for distributed teams.
- **Adaptive Leadership**: Adopt flatter structures that empower local decisions. Form cross-functional leadership groups to maintain cohesion. Communicate openly with platforms like Slack or Teams. Reassess roles regularly to keep agility intact.
- **Cross-Functional Teams**: Blend skills from finance, marketing, design, etc., for richer solutions. Use brainstorming platforms (Miro) and task trackers (Jira). Hold shared stand-ups across departments for knowledge exchange.

Example

Spotify's 'Squads', 'Tribes', 'Chapters', and 'Guilds' let teams collaborate and act independently. By spreading decision-making, Spotify remains current in a shifting industry.

CLEAR Model® Connection

- **Culture**: Encourages cross-team openness and interdepartmental synergy.
- **Leadership**: Ensures that Agile mindsets and autonomy cascade throughout all levels.
- **Execution**: Larger organizational goals stay connected to day-to-day sprints.
- **Adaptability**: Flattened hierarchies pivot faster, free from layered command chains.
- **Responsiveness**: Regular feedback and flexible structures allow quick realignment with strategic aims.

6. Constant Experimentation

Innovation thrives where testing is welcomed. One organization ran an 'Innovation Sprint' for two weeks, generating three product features that boosted user retention by nearly 20% in six months. Agile draws strength from a culture that sees both successes and setbacks as learning opportunities. Tactics such as innovation labs or incubators allow iterative exploration. Leaders who champion this approach create a balance between creativity and rigour, amplifying Agile's key principles. Partnerships and crowdsourcing also keep the business responsive to broader shifts.

Strategies

- **Psychological Safety**: Give teams the confidence to propose ideas, fail, and learn. While psychological safety should ideally remove the need for anonymity, initially offering anonymous feedback tools can help build trust until team members feel comfortable speaking openly. Leaders should model openness themselves to encourage transparency.

- **Innovation Labs and Incubators**: Allocate dedicated spaces and resources for experimenting with new tech or models. Invite specialists for guidance. Publicize wins from the lab to motivate others.
- **Open Innovation**: Partner with startups, academia, or external communities to generate fresh ideas. Run hackathons or open challenges. Contribute to GitHub or OpenAI forums with proper guidelines for trust and IP rights.

Example

Google's '20% Time' approach encourages staff to devote part of their schedule to passion projects, resulting in products like Gmail and Google News. Supporting this style of experimentation helps Google stay ahead in tech.

CLEAR Model® Connection

- **Culture**: Normalizes trial and error, rewarding learning over fault-finding.
- **Leadership**: Signals trust by offering labs, incubators, and open time to create.
- **Execution**: Regular mini-experiments refine outputs quickly.
- **Adaptability**: Teams quickly shift from failed prototypes to improved solutions.
- **Responsiveness**: Innovations can move from idea to deployment with minimal friction.

Section 3: Embracing Sustainability and Future Challenges

7. Prioritizing Sustainability and Social Responsibility

Sustainability and ethical practice are vital in an era of evolving customer and societal expectations. This might mean eco-friendly product design, careful supply chain oversight, or responsible AI use. Agile's flexibility assists organizations in meeting user demands for ethical conduct. Leaders who set clear sustainability targets help their teams build a business that benefits both society and finances.

Strategies

- **Sustainable Operations**: Factor carbon impact into product design and supply chains. Use life-cycle analytics to spot areas for reduced waste. Collaborate with suppliers who share eco-minded values.
- **Ethical AI and Data**: Draft AI rules that align with data protection policies. Employ tools to detect bias in algorithms. Create transparent dashboards for AI outputs. Train staff on ethical concerns to ensure principled innovation.
- **Community Engagement**: Work with local communities on shared challenges (e.g. education or infrastructure). Host open meetings to gather feedback, sponsor local projects, and share progress to promote further engagement.

Example

Patagonia integrates sustainability into everything it does. The company's iterative methods – inspired by Agile – consistently refine materials and production, gaining customer loyalty and preserving brand identity.

CLEAR Model® Connection

- **Culture**: Internalizes ethical and eco-conscious values, shaping daily decisions.
- **Leadership**: Sets tangible sustainability goals and enforces them across projects.
- **Execution**: Teams incorporate environmental or ethical considerations into backlogs.
- **Adaptability**: Quick adjustments to meet new regulations or community insights.
- **Responsiveness**: Real-time feedback on carbon footprint or supply chain conditions triggers prompt corrective actions.

8. Anticipating and Managing Future Challenges

Scenario planning and resilience strategies help teams prepare for unknowns. Agile squads can run small tests around possible disruptions, adjusting methods as new data emerges. Building such readiness ensures a swift pivot when those difficulties surface. Merging foresight with agility keeps projects on track even under sudden external shifts.

Strategies

- **Scenario Planning with Agile**: Use iterative approaches to imagine possible futures. Include different stakeholders, revisit scenarios often, and adjust assumptions in short cycles.
- **Regulatory Compliance**: Thread compliance tasks into Agile flows so they match legal and industry rules. Automate basic reporting wherever possible. Offer continual training on new regulations.
- **Cybersecurity Preparedness**: Incorporate threat modelling and vulnerability checks into each backlog. Tools like Splunk or CrowdStrike help detect and counter problems. Encourage secure coding and data safety through training and drills.

Example

A multinational pharma group simulated changes in drug approval requirements. By adding compliance milestones to its Agile methods, it preserved launch speed without violating rules.

CLEAR Model® Connection

- **Culture**: Encourages forward-looking, solution-oriented collaboration.
- **Leadership**: Builds resilience by funding scenario planning and compliance readiness.
- **Execution**: Sprints embed tasks for regulatory or security checks, ensuring timely compliance.
- **Adaptability**: Scenario-based sprints refine processes when markets or rules shift.
- **Responsiveness**: Quick course changes avoid delays or non-compliance setbacks.

Section 4: Adapting to New Work Models and Customer Focus

9. Embracing Remote and Hybrid Work Models

With remote and hybrid options growing, Agile teams must update their practices to keep everyone engaged. Possible obstacles include scattered schedules, online fatigue, and ensuring remote workers have an equal voice. Some solutions include shared core hours for live discussions, using video messages for async updates, and rotating meeting facilitators. Empathy, work-life balance, and steady communication help teams stay productive and inclusive, even when spread across locations.

Strategies

- **Digital Collaboration Tools**: Use tools like Slack, Trello, or Zoom for group updates and structured workflows. Monitor usage to avoid overlaps or confusion.
- **Flexible Work Guidelines**: Provide flexible schedules or remote-hybrid structures. Gather employee input to keep practices fair. Offer mental health support and home-office stipends where possible.
- **Virtual Team Building**: Organize online workshops, games, or mini-events to build rapport. Tools like Miro or Gather recreate 'in-person' bonding. Celebrate milestones to lift morale.

Example

GitLab thrives entirely remotely, with over 1,300 staff across 65 nations. Detailed documentation, async communication, and online social activities illustrate that Agile can succeed in distributed setups.

CLEAR Model® Connection

- **Culture**: Fosters inclusive, flexible norms that welcome remote participants.
- **Leadership**: Establishes guidelines ensuring remote workers aren't marginalized.
- **Execution**: Day-to-day sprints adapt to time zones and asynchronous channels.
- **Adaptability**: Teams flex between synchronous and asynchronous collaboration.
- **Responsiveness**: Real-time updates across channels let teams pivot quickly, irrespective of location.

10. Reinforcing Customer-Centric Approaches

Customer demands evolve regularly, making the Agile cycle of frequent adaptation ideal for businesses aiming to stay user-focused. Ongoing feedback loops help teams deliver exactly what customers need. Analytics personalizes products, enabling swift shifts tied to fresh insights. This approach keeps loyalty high and drives growth, as each release adds clear value.

Strategies

- **Customer Feedback Loops**: Gather input rapidly – surveys, usability tests, or in-app prompts. Tools like Qualtrics or Zendesk can spotlight patterns. Reflect on these findings in each sprint.
- **Personalization and Customization**: Harness AI analytics (Tableau, Power BI) to tailor services based on user preferences. Trial changes through A/B tests. Adjust user journeys based on reliable data.
- **Continuous Value Delivery**: Use short-release cycles and incremental improvements, such as new service offerings or streamlined processes. Invite direct customer feedback through surveys, interviews, or focus groups so each update addresses a genuine need, even in non-technical sectors.

Example

Amazon's recommendation engine adjusts content to each user's browsing habits. Ongoing improvements drive satisfaction and repeat business.

CLEAR Model® Connection

- **Culture**: Elevates user value above internal convenience.
- **Leadership**: Ensures feedback loops are well-funded and endorsed at the top.
- **Execution**: Short cycles keep features aligned with actual user behaviour.
- **Adaptability**: Teams pivot quickly upon new feedback or data changes.
- **Responsiveness**: Immediate user insights inform near-instant backlog reprioritization.

Section 5: Collaboration and Diversity

11. Collaborating Across Ecosystems

Silos slow innovation. Partnerships, co-development, and knowledge exchange speed it up. Leaders who foster open collaboration – internally and externally – boost agility and expand shared resources. Forming strategic alliances or contributing to shared projects can also unlock new sectors and expertise.

Strategies

- **Strategic Partnerships**: Collaborate with like-minded partners through real-time channels (Slack Connect, Teams). Formal agreements clarify roles and mutual benefits.
- **Industry Consortia**: Join groups that set standards and share best practices. Transfer collective findings back into your internal efforts.
- **Open Source Contributions**: Engage in GitHub projects aligned with your organization's mission. Gain new ideas while adding your own improvements.

Example

In motoring, brands such as Toyota and Tesla formed alliances to co-create electric car technology more efficiently.

CLEAR Model® Connection

- **Culture**: Breaks down walls, championing shared knowledge and open innovation.
- **Leadership**: Establishes trust-based partnerships, removing interdepartmental or external friction.
- **Execution**: Cross-organization collaboration speeds solution delivery.
- **Adaptability**: Partners can pivot collectively when markets shift.
- **Responsiveness**: Input from multiple sources fosters rapid, holistic improvements.

12. Enhancing Diversity and Inclusion in Agile Practices

A varied workforce sparks creativity and sharpens adaptability. Differences in background and viewpoint often fuel fresh solutions, improving products and processes. Leaders should recruit diversely and ensure tasks and decisions are fairly shared. Providing cultural understanding workshops helps employees collaborate harmoniously across all backgrounds. Encouraging broad participation in governance and planning strengthens innovation and helps solutions resonate with a global audience.

Strategies

- **Inclusive Hiring**: Adopt bias filters in recruitment systems like Greenhouse or Workday. Partner with specialist diversity networks to broaden talent pools. Track hiring metrics to maintain fairness.
- **Cultural Competence Training**: Offer courses on communication and conflict management. Use real-world cases and gather feedback on programme success.
- **Equitable Participation**: Ensure each voice is heard in retrospectives and planning. Rotate facilitators so no single person dominates. Track meeting data to catch any exclusion patterns.

Example

IBM is well known for policies that bring in and keep talent from many backgrounds, boosting problem-solving capacity and making their offerings more wide-ranging.

CLEAR Model® Connection

- **Culture**: Inclusive values encourage open communication and fresh perspectives.
- **Leadership**: Sets the tone by actively recruiting diverse talent and championing equity.
- **Execution**: A broad mix of backgrounds yields innovative, well-rounded solutions.
- **Adaptability**: Different viewpoints foster readiness for multiple market scenarios.
- **Responsiveness**: Inclusive teams respond better to diverse customer needs.

Section 6: Measuring Success

13. Measuring and Demonstrating Agile Success

Clarity on the right KPIs is crucial for guiding Agile improvement. Tracking metrics around the time taken to deliver value, user experience, product quality, or collaboration indicates whether Agile practices align with broader objectives. Frequent reviews help teams steer around issues. Transparent reporting through dashboards or briefings creates unity, motivates teams, and defines what 'success' means for everyone.

Keep It Clear and Visible

Aim for straightforward, shared metrics that teams can interpret at a glance. Overly complex data may hide progress or slow decisions. Public dashboards help everyone see improvements as they happen, strengthening engagement.

Strategies

- **Define Clear KPIs**: Use OKRs or balanced scorecards to link measures (release intervals, user satisfaction, staff engagement) with strategic aims.
- **Review and Adjust Regularly**: Refresh metrics if organizational goals shift. Arrange quarterly data reviews through tools like Power BI or Tableau.
- **Transparent Reporting**: Share real-time dashboards or host regular briefings on key indicators. Offer plain summaries of wins and challenges.
- **Celebrate Progress**: Highlight achievements in retrospectives or with recognition platforms. Reinforce positivity and steady forward momentum.

Example

A software developer ran a live KPI panel for throughput, defect rates, and client ratings. Everyone saw the same figures, which fostered trust, sharpened accountability, and spurred data-driven decisions.

CLEAR Model® Connection

- **Culture**: Builds openness and mutual understanding through visible metrics.
- **Leadership**: Prioritizes relevant KPIs aligned to strategic goals.
- **Execution**: Teams refine day-to-day tasks based on real-time performance data.
- **Adaptability**: Ongoing reviews drive iterative improvement, pivoting as needed.
- **Responsiveness**: Immediate insight into shortfalls or successes triggers swift action.

By combining these techniques – investing in people, embracing technology, refining governance, scaling agility across the organization, experimenting, nurturing sustainability, anticipating the future, adapting work models, focusing on customers, forging partnerships, championing diversity, and measuring success – leaders can create a high-performing Agile culture that remains resilient and innovative.

Lastly, each tactic explicitly aligns with Adaptive Leadership's CLEAR Model®, showing how Culture, Leadership, Execution, Adaptability, and Responsiveness underpin the roadmap for Agile's strategic future.

Adaptive Leader's Toolkit

We've explored many strategies to ensure Agile remains dynamic and future-focused. Below is a short, action-based toolkit you can use immediately to turn big ideas into daily leadership habits. Think of it as your go-to checklist whenever you need to energize teams, solve workflow issues, or nurture a more adaptive culture. But sometimes it's not just about using a better tool – it's about questioning the toolbox itself. If your governance, decision-making, or funding models still reflect outdated assumptions, no new method will fix the core issue. The Adaptive Leader doesn't just add more; they know when to redesign from the ground up.

1. **Pinpoint a Pressing Need**
    Select one project, team, or process that seems bogged down. Aim for something small enough that you can see improvements quickly.
2. **Create a Shared Goal**
    Involve key people in setting a single, clear objective. Co-ownership strengthens everyone's stake in the outcome.
3. **Experiment in Short Bursts**
    Trial fresh ideas for a limited time – perhaps two weeks – and track each day's observations. Keep documentation light so you can adapt fast.
4. **Review and Adjust Fast**
    Schedule quick check-ins to capture lessons. If something isn't working, tweak it rather than pushing through a failing plan.
5. **Celebrate Early Wins**
    Share tangible successes (even small ones) with the wider organization. Early proof of value builds momentum and trust.

These simple steps help leaders transform good intentions into immediate action. Use them alongside the strategic roadmap to maintain progress, spark innovation, and showcase the essence of adaptive leadership.

Next, we'll see how a global energy firm applied many of these ideas to reshape its governance model.

Case Study: Equinor's Governance Transformation Through Beyond Budgeting

How a Multinational Energy Company Enhanced Ethical Governance

Background
Equinor, a global energy firm, found its rigid budgeting processes limited agility and conflicted with its transparency goals. Seeking a solution, Equinor adopted the Beyond Budgeting approach, which leverages Agile principles, decentralization, and ethical oversight.

Actions Taken

- **Eliminated Annual Budgets**: Replaced yearly budget cycles with flexible resource-allocation models, allowing rapid market responses without compromising ethical standards.
- **Implemented Transparency Measures**: Clarified guidelines so all fiscal decisions upheld the company's values and stakeholder expectations.
- **Empowered Teams**: Devolved decision-making to smaller teams, maintaining oversight with frequent reviews and adaptive governance.
- **Adopted Ethical Metrics**: Favoured customer value and environmental impact indicators over short-term financials, anchoring the company's longer-term ethical and sustainable practices.

Outcomes

- **Better Adaptability**: By reallocating resources in real-time, operational efficiency climbed by 30%.
- **Stronger Trust**: Transparent governance reaffirmed stakeholder confidence, bolstering organizational credibility.
- **Sustainable Decision-Making**: Environmental considerations became integral to strategy, reinforcing a resilient, future-ready posture.

Lessons Learned

- **Balance Flexibility with Oversight**: Decentralization fuels agility, yet clear ethical frameworks preserve accountability.
- **Ethics as a Cornerstone of Agility**: By embedding transparency and sustainability into governance, Equinor fortified its agility and resilience.
- **Leadership Support Is Essential**: Leadership buy-in to Agile values and ethical reforms underpinned the company's success.

Equinor's journey underscores the potential of aligning governance with Agile principles to achieve transparency, adaptability, and long-term success. As organizations prepare to embrace Agile's future, these lessons offer valuable insights into the transformative power of Agile practices when applied with purpose and ethical consideration.

Preparing for Agile's Future

Companies that integrate daily execution with overarching strategies will remain competitive over time. As new technologies and Agile frameworks emerge, the Agile mindset provides the flexibility needed to tackle fresh challenges. Leaders who blend a future-focused approach with people-centric thinking ensure that agility drives positive transformation.

Future developments like quantum computing may change data analytics even further, while ethical mandates (around privacy or sustainability) will mould the Agile landscape. Leaders who include these elements keep Agile current and spur teams toward meaningful innovation.

Example: A major manufacturing conglomerate adopted predictive AI maintenance, saving costs and preventing downtime. Their key was using an inclusive Agile governance system that explained the rationale behind each change to every team member.

Looking Ahead: Future Trends

Ongoing trends – like AI, IoT, or remote work – will keep reshaping how organizations employ agility. The leaders who excel will be those who combine hands-on flexibility with long-range objectives, scaling Agile without adding needless layers. Agility evolves with the environment, employees, and customers it serves.

By championing continuous learning, aligning teams to strategic aims, and embedding resilience, companies can outpace the unexpected. Ask yourself: Are you ready to guide your teams toward an Agile-focused tomorrow?

Conclusion

Agile's journey doesn't end with process adoption – it continues through leaders and teams who integrate it into the core identity of their organization. By aligning vision, culture, and execution, businesses can harness Agile's full potential to drive innovation and long-term success.

Sustaining agility requires more than adherence to frameworks; it demands a commitment to continuous improvement and strategic thinking. Those who cultivate an Agile mindset will remain ahead in an evolving business world.

Agile's legacy is one of learning and adaptation. Use this framework not as an endpoint but as a springboard for future growth, ensuring agility remains a competitive advantage.

Final reflections challenge leaders to ask: Is your Agile strategy evolving alongside new challenges, or is it stagnating under rigid structures? The future belongs to those who treat agility as a living, breathing strategy.

Call to Action

As an adaptive leader, envision how Agile principles could redefine your organization's future. *Are you prepared to lead the way in rethinking its principles and practices? What steps will you take today to foster a culture of learning, innovation, and adaptability?* Commit to making Agile a catalyst for meaningful, sustainable transformation.

Key Takeaways

- **Continuous Learning Fuels Agile's Future:** Prioritizing skill development and a learning culture fuels Agile's long-term expansion.
- **Technology Integration Enhances Agility**: AI, ML, and analytics can amplify flexibility and speed when used thoughtfully.

- **Flexible Governance Supports Growth**: Adaptive governance frameworks marry accountability with the freedom to pivot.
- **Organizational Agility Extends Beyond Teams**: Embedding Agile beyond single projects fosters an environment ready to respond to emerging issues.
- **Leadership Drives Future Success**: Leaders must champion both the strategic and human sides of Agile, ensuring continued relevance.

Agile's future isn't about fixed rules but about nurturing a philosophy that supports transformation and discovery. Leaders should merge operational excellence with a strategic vision, ethical governance, and an emphasis on learning.

By synchronizing vision, culture, and strategy, organizations unleash Agile's capacity for resilience and advancement. The journey endures – Agile will keep evolving and be shaped by leaders who embrace innovation and adaptability.

CLEAR Model® Connection

- **Culture**: Ethical, people-first values anchor a healthy Agile environment.
- **Leadership**: Leaders champion upskilling, flexible governance, and a unified strategic vision.
- **Execution**: Seamlessly integrate new technologies, measure outcomes, and keep iterating.
- **Adaptability**: Embrace 'post-Agile' thinking; pivot quickly amid changing demands.
- **Responsiveness**: Constantly align short-term actions with long-term goals for genuine agility.

Key Takeaway: Agile thrives when it's ingrained in both daily operations and strategic direction. Leaders must maintain a learning mindset and guide ethical, responsive practices across the organization.

Strategic Roadmap Template

1. **Vision Articulation:**
   o Define the long-term vision for Agile in your organization.
2. **Current State Analysis:**
   o Assess where you are now in terms of Agile maturity.
3. **Goal Setting:**
   o Establish short-term and long-term objectives.
4. **Initiative Planning:**
   o Outline key projects and actions needed to reach goals.
5. **Resource Planning:**
   o Identify required resources and assign responsibilities.
6. **Monitoring and Review:**
   o Set up mechanisms to track progress and adjust as necessary.

Implementation Guide

- **Communication Plan:**
  - o Develop strategies for keeping all stakeholders informed and engaged.
- **Change Management Strategies:**
  - o Prepare for resistance and plan interventions.
- **Success Metrics:**
  - o Define what success looks like and how it will be measured.

Chapter Summary

This final chapter laid out a strategic roadmap for embedding Agile deeply across an organization through investment in people and technology, flexible governance, sustainability, new work models, improved collaboration, and robust measurement. By aligning these elements under Adaptive Leadership, you create an ecosystem where Agile remains an evolving powerhouse.

End of Part 6

With this final part, you've seen how continuous learning, evolving mindsets, and forward-thinking leadership keep Agile relevant for years to come. As you wrap up your journey through this book, remember: true agility is never static – it grows with each new insight, driving you and your organization toward a future of lasting innovation and resilience.

Conclusion

Agile's Ongoing Evolution

The 'Agile is dead' debate is rooted in myths and frustrations, often sparked by misapplications rather than flaws in Agile itself. Far from signalling the end, these critiques have driven Agile's ongoing evolution. It's no longer just a set of practices; it's becoming a way of thinking embedded across organizations.

Misused frameworks have renewed focus on core principles. As role commodification fades, experience and mindset take precedence over certification. Agile is shedding rigid labels, integrating more deeply into how organizations work and grow.

Leadership's Role in Agile's Transformation

Adaptive leaders are central to this shift. They move beyond enforcing Agile practices to living its values – modelling adaptability, encouraging open dialogue, and enabling continuous learning. By setting direction and giving teams autonomy, they help Agile flourish.

The most effective leaders lead by example, foster feedback, and support bold thinking. They champion experimentation and resilience, making learning, not certainty, the marker of progress.

Agile as a Strategic Philosophy

Agile is no longer confined to software or delivery. It's a broader philosophy that shapes culture, decisions, and strategic direction. Those wondering whether Agile is dead are asking the wrong question – it's not dead, it's different. More embedded. More strategic. More resilient.

Cultivating a Growth-Driven Mindset

This evolution demands a mindset that values responsiveness, innovation, and ongoing value delivery. Leaders must foster open collaboration and support risk-taking without fear of failure. By creating psychological safety, promoting inclusion, and aligning with ethical and sustainability goals, they unlock the full power of agility.

Adaptability is at the heart of resilience. Teams that embrace uncertainty – and leaders who help them do so – turn disruption into opportunity. Every shift becomes a moment to refine, iterate, and improve.

The Future Lies in Adaptability

Agility is about letting go of rigid methods to meet real-world challenges. Its future depends on how well leaders nurture growth, enable experimentation, and prioritize learning.

Agile's values are more vital than ever. When fully embraced, they fuel innovation and long-term success. But the responsibility now lies with you.

Are you ready to lead in a way that keeps Agile principles alive where they matter most?

An Invitation to Shape the Future

The path forward isn't reserved for tech teams or project leads – it's for every leader ready to rewire their organization for agility. Embed Agile deeply, support learning, and lead with purpose. If you do, you won't just transform your workplace – you'll help shape a more adaptive global business culture.

Your next step matters. The potential is in your hands.

Leading Forward: Your Role in Agile's Evolution

Agile is more than a method. It's a mindset – one that helps people solve, learn, and grow together. Every challenge is an opportunity to build better. That begins with how you lead.

The CLEAR Model® has guided this journey, helping you embed agility into the DNA of your organization:

- **Culture** creates space for collaboration and innovation.
- **Leadership** models trust, purpose, and empowerment.
- **Execution** turns vision into action and results.
- **Adaptability** keeps you responsive to real conditions.
- **Responsiveness** enables confident decisions at pace.

Together, these aren't just traits – they're the core of modern agility.

The book has given you the principles, but the impact depends on what you do next. Protect space for experimentation. Support your teams' learning. Lead with clarity through uncertainty. That's adaptive leadership.

Agile will keep evolving.

The question is, will your leadership evolve with it?

Agile is not dead – but the way you lead it will determine its future.

Final Reflection

Years ago, I worked with a manufacturing client that treated Agile as a checklist – stand-ups, sprint reviews, and user stories. But real change only came when they stopped 'doing Agile' and started thinking differently. Leaders shifted from rigidity to adaptability. Teams transformed. Results soared.

That experience confirmed what I've seen time and again: Agile doesn't fail. It adapts – if leaders do. Without that shift, it's just another process. With it, Agile becomes a catalyst for resilience, innovation, and purpose-driven growth.

So the question is simple: **Will you lead the next phase of Agile's evolution?**

Agile was never dead – it was waiting for the right leaders to carry it forward. The future of work belongs to those who learn, adapt, and lead with agility.

One Final Question

So, will you be an Adaptive Leader – or will you let the world move forward without you?

Epilogue – Phoenix Rises Again

The towering headquarters of Phoenix Corp. stood as a beacon of resilience. Once a company teetering on the brink of irrelevance, it had emerged as an industry leader after its first transformation journey, inspired by Sarah and her relentless belief in business agility. But even giants that rise from the ashes must stay vigilant – because in the ever-changing business landscape, complacency is the real competitor.

Five years had passed since Phoenix Corp.'s last transformation. It had achieved what few others had – a sustained streak of innovation and growth. Yet, cracks were beginning to show. Markets were shifting faster than ever, technology was evolving at lightning speed, and new competitors were disrupting industries with unprecedented agility. While Phoenix Corp. had remained steady, it was no longer leading. Teams were falling back into silos, decision-making had slowed, and the company's agility had started to wane.

At the centre of it all was Sarah, now the Chief Transformation Officer of Phoenix Corp. Her first transformation had been guided by the principles of agility outlined in the book *Clearly Agile*. Now, as she sat in a boardroom overlooking the city, she knew it was time for the next chapter. On the table before her lay another book – her well-worn copy of *The Adaptive Leader*, a constant reminder of the journey ahead.

This time, the challenge wasn't just to pivot processes or adapt to disruption – it was to challenge the very myths that were holding Phoenix Corp. back.

Breaking the Myths

The boardroom was silent as Sarah stood, holding up the book. 'We've been here before', she began. 'Phoenix rose once because we embraced change and agility as a mindset. But we've grown complacent. Agility isn't something you achieve – it's something you live. And to move forward, we must break the myths that are chaining us to outdated ways of working'.

She flipped to a page and read aloud: 'Agility is not about doing more, faster – it's about doing the right things at the right time, with clarity and purpose.'

Her words struck a chord. The board members, many of whom had been part of the first transformation, nodded in recognition. They had spent years chasing efficiency, layering new processes over old ones. The result? Complexity disguised as progress.

Leadership must adapt to the terrain instead of imposing an unwavering path. Instead of dragging teams behind predetermined goals, effective leadership involves mapping and adapting to the context, allowing the natural emergence of purpose and progress.

Sarah laid out her vision. It wasn't just about surviving disruption – it was about leading in a post-Agile world. 'We must embed clarity into our leadership, simplify how we work, and align every decision with our core purpose. That's what this book has taught me, and that's the transformation we need now.'

The Journey into the Post-Agile World

The transformation began with leadership. Phoenix's leaders underwent a series of workshops designed to challenge their assumptions and help them embrace clarity and simplicity. Inspired by the leadership lessons in *The Adaptive Leader*, they redefined their roles – not as decision-makers but as enablers of adaptability and growth.

Next came the teams. Sarah encouraged a cultural shift, moving away from rigid frameworks and toward a focus on outcomes. Teams were empowered to align their work with customer needs, and silos were dismantled in favour of cross-functional collaboration. This time, agility wasn't just about surviving disruption – it was about thriving in uncertainty.

Technology played a vital role. Leveraging the book's insights on emerging technologies, Phoenix integrated AI and automation to simplify workflows and free up teams to focus on innovation. But every technological decision was grounded in purpose, ensuring it served both the company's goals and its people.

The hardest part was tackling resistance. Just as in their first transformation, there were those who clung to the comfort of legacy processes. But Sarah knew how to guide them. She used retrospectives not just as a tool for improvement but as a way to connect teams to the 'why' behind every change. Slowly but surely, even the sceptics began to see the value of transformation.

From Phoenix to Beyond

A few years later, Phoenix Corp. stood stronger than ever. It wasn't just Agile – it fully embraced the principles of the post-Agile era. Teams worked with clarity and purpose, leaders empowered their people, and the company responded to market shifts with remarkable ease. It had become a living embodiment of the principles in Sarah's book.

One final challenge came in the form of a new disruptor – NovaTech, a startup armed with cutting-edge technology and aggressive tactics. This time, however, Phoenix didn't falter. It adapted, responded, and outpaced its competitor, turning the challenge into an opportunity.

In a final meeting with her leadership team, Sarah reflected on the journey. 'We've proven that agility is more than a buzzword – it's a mindset. And if we keep learning, growing, and evolving, there's nothing we can't overcome.'

From the ashes of its past, Phoenix Corp. had not only risen but soared to new heights. Its story became a testament to the power of breaking myths, embracing clarity, and transforming for the future.

And at the heart of it all was the lesson Sarah had carried with her: true transformation is a journey without end.

Appendix A – Glossary

This glossary provides clear, concise definitions of the key terms used throughout this book, ensuring clarity and understanding for all readers. The terms cover leadership and Agile principles, methodologies, and emerging concepts crucial for navigating transformation.

Adaptive Leadership: A leadership style that guides organizations through change by fostering innovation, collaboration, and flexibility.

Adaptive Leadership Frameworks: Models and practices designed to guide leaders through the challenges of implementing and sustaining Agile transformations in dynamic environments.

Agile Coach: A mentor who supports individuals and teams in understanding and applying Agile principles.

Agile Maturity Models: Frameworks that assess the depth of Agile adoption, progressing through stages such as Initial, Managed, Defined, Quantitatively Managed, and Optimizing. These models are often tailored, as in the CLEAR Model®, to address evolving organizational needs.

Agile Mindset: A way of thinking that values adaptability, collaboration, customer focus, and continuous improvement.

Agile Rebellion: Instances or case studies highlighting organizations or teams that reject over-commercialized or superficial Agile implementations in favour of a return to its core principles.

Agile Restoration: The process of returning Agile to its foundational principles, focusing on adaptability, simplicity, and collaboration.

Agile-Washing: The superficial adoption of Agile terminology without meaningful practice or cultural change.

Antifragility: When a system, team, or idea improves after shocks or pressure instead of just surviving them.

Autonomy: Empowering teams to make decisions and take ownership of their work, fostering innovation and accountability.

Backlog: A prioritized list of work items or features for a team to address in upcoming sprints.

Blockchain in Agile: Blockchain technology enhances transparency, accountability, and automation in Agile workflows.

Business Agility: An organization's capacity to adapt rapidly to market and environmental changes while maintaining customer focus and innovation. This concept aligns closely with frameworks like the CLEAR Model®.

CLEAR Model®: A model for business agility focusing on Culture, Leadership, Execution, Adaptability, and Responsiveness, designed to align Agile principles with organizational strategy.

Commodification of Agile: The over-commercialization of Agile through excessive certifications and tools that dilute its core principles.

Context-Driven Agility: Tailoring Agile practices to suit specific organizational, cultural, or team contexts, ensuring relevance and effectiveness.

Corporate Theatre: The superficial adoption of Agile practices or ceremonies without embedding the underlying principles, creating the illusion of transformation rather than actual change.

Cross-Functional Team: A team composed of individuals with varied expertise collaborating towards a common goal.

Customer-Centricity: Placing customer needs and feedback at the centre of organizational strategy.

DEAD (Dynamic, Evolving, Adaptable, and Disruptive): A reinterpretation of Agile and Change Management, highlighting their relevance and ongoing evolution.

Disciplined Waterfall: A rigid, plan-driven approach disguised with Agile terminology but lacking iterative and adaptive principles.

Dual Operating Systems: A structure where an organization maintains both a stable hierarchy and an adaptive, Agile network to balance efficiency and innovation.

Ecosystem Coaching: The practice of applying Agile coaching beyond individual teams, focusing on entire organizational ecosystems.

Emerging Technologies: Innovations like AI, blockchain, IoT, and 5G that influence Agile practices and organizational strategies.

Ethics in Agile: Integrating transparency, fairness, and accountability into Agile practices and decision-making.

Extreme Agile: A concept integrating AI into Agile workflows to achieve exponential productivity gains, requiring a balance between technological leverage and human insight.

Framework Fatigue: Overwhelming an organization with numerous Agile frameworks, often leading to confusion and poor implementation.

Frameworks: Structured approaches such as Scrum, SAFe, and Kanban that guide the implementation of Agile principles.

Generational Agility: Tailoring Agile approaches to suit generational differences in work preferences and communication.

Global Agile Practices: Adapting Agile principles to diverse cultural and geographic contexts for effective collaboration.

Human Debt: The accumulation of negative organizational impact caused by neglecting employee well-being, psychological safety, and sustainable work practices.

Human Expertise in Agile: The value of human creativity and critical thinking in Agile workflows, particularly in AI-driven environments.

Hybrid Work Agility: Strategies and practices to adapt Agile principles for hybrid or remote work environments.

IoT in Agile: Leveraging real-time data from interconnected devices to improve decision-making and sprint prioritization.

Iterative Development: A process where work is broken into small, manageable cycles, allowing for continuous feedback and improvement.

Labelling Teams Without Practice Change: Misleadingly calling teams 'Agile' without adopting Agile practices.

Leadership Agility: The ability of leaders to adapt their approach to foster innovation, collaboration, and continuous learning.

Lean Integration: Incorporating Lean principles into Agile workflows to improve value flow and efficiency.

Levels of Maturity: The progressive stages of Agile adoption, ranging from Initial (ad hoc practices) to Optimizing (continuous improvement).

Minimum Viable Product (MVP): The simplest version of a product that delivers value, enabling early user feedback.

Misuse of Agile Terminology: Applying Agile terms incorrectly, leading to confusion and failed implementation.

Model Drift: The phenomenon where a framework or methodology becomes misaligned with the challenges it was intended to address, necessitating evolution or replacement.

Opportunity Flow: A leadership mindset that emphasizes continuous improvement by identifying and leveraging emerging opportunities instead of focusing solely on fixing problems.

Post-Agile: A mindset and approach where agility is embedded as a strategic organizational principle rather than confined to methodologies or frameworks.

Predictive Maintenance: Leveraging IoT data to anticipate and resolve issues proactively, aligning with Agile responsiveness.

Psychological Safety: Creating an environment where individuals feel safe to take risks and express ideas without fear of negative consequences.

Retrospective: A meeting where teams reflect on recent work to identify successes and areas for improvement.

Scaling Agile: Expanding Agile principles across an entire organization to improve collaboration and performance.

Servant Leadership: A leadership style that prioritizes the team's needs and facilitates their success.

Smart Contracts: Self-executing blockchain-based agreements that automate Agile processes, such as milestone approvals and deliverables.

Speed-to-Value: A metric prioritizing delivering customer value as quickly as possible while maintaining quality and sustainability.

Sustainable Agility: The practice of maintaining Agile principles in a way that supports long-term organizational resilience and employee well-being.

Systems Thinking: A holistic approach to organizational agility that considers the interconnected nature of teams, processes, and outcomes.

Team Empowerment: Providing teams with the authority and resources needed to achieve their objectives autonomously.

Transformation: The process of transitioning from traditional practices to Agile ways of working.

Value Delivery: Ensuring that every output aligns with customer needs and organizational goals.

Value Streams: The sequence of steps that deliver value to customers, emphasizing flow efficiency and waste reduction in Agile practices.

VUCA (Volatility, Uncertainty, Complexity, Ambiguity): A framework describing the challenging conditions organizations face, which Agile practices aim to address.

Appendix B – References

Adkins, L. (n.d.). *Coaching agile teams: A companion for scrummasters, agile coaches, and project managers in transition*. Project-Management.com. Available from: https://project-management.com/best-agile-project-management-books/

Agile Academy. (n.d.). *Is agile dead?* Agile Academy. Available from: https://agileacademy.io/blog/is-agile-dead

Agile Delta. (n.d.). *Analysis of the current state of the post-agile world*. Medium. Available from: https://agiledelta.medium.com/analysis-of-the-current-state-of-the-post-agile-world-56317f27c6f4

Agile Delta. (n.d.). *Are we operating in a post-agile world?* Medium. Available from: https://agiledelta.medium.com/are-we-operating-in-a-post-agile-world-6f032874f71a

2.Agile Delta. (n.d.). *Are we operating in a post-agile world?* Part Medium. Available from: https://agiledelta.medium.com/are-we-operating-in-a-post-agile-world-part-2-83f6e2d62f48

3.Agile Delta. (n.d.). *Are we operating in a post-agile world?* Part Medium. Available from: https://agiledelta.medium.com/are-we-operating-in-a-post-agile-world-part-3-f9c83bc6b560

Agile Delta. (n.d.). *Are we operating in a post-agile world? Part 4 – Adapting agile for contemporary organizational challenges*. Medium. Available from: https://agiledelta.medium.com/are-we-operating-in-a-post-agile-world-part-4-bc76b36b6c7a

Agile Delta. (n.d.). *Are we operating in a post-agile world? Part 5 – Embracing strategic agility*. Medium. Available from: https://agiledelta.medium.com/are-we-operating-in-a-post-agile-world-part-5-embracing-strategic-agility-425b329abbb5

Agileful. (n.d.). *Agile in healthcare: Enhancing patient care through iteration*. Agileful. Available from: https://agileful.com/agile-in-healthcare-enhancing-patient-care-through-iteration/

Aha! (n.d.). *Guide to agile development methodologies*. Aha! Available from: www.aha.io/roadmapping/guide/agile/development-methodologies

Ali, J. (2024, August 7). *Agile study backer talks catastrophic software failures*. The Register. Available from: www.theregister.com/2024/08/07/agile_catastrophes_risk_undermining_the/

Ali, J. (2024, December 3). *Agile is rigor mortis as software's state religion*. Hacker Noon. Available from: https://hackernoon.com/agile-is-rigor-mortis-as-softwares-state-religion

Ali, J. (2024, June 4). 268% higher failure rates for agile software projects, study finds. Engprax. Available from: www.engprax.com/post/268-higher-failure-rates-for-agile-software-projects-study-finds/

Amazon. (n.d.). *Future of work simplified: Understand your organization*. Amazon. Available from: www.amazon.co.uk/Future-Work-Simplified-Understand-Organization/dp/B08DSND2L9

Amazon. (n.d.). *Thrive: The future of work – Embracing the organization*. Amazon. Available from: www.amazon.co.uk/Thrive-Future-Work-Embracing-Organization/dp/178 1194556

Ambler, S. (n.d.). *The agile community shat the bed*. LinkedIn Pulse. Available from: www. linkedin.com/pulse/agile-community-shat-bed-scott-ambler-1npwc/

An updated agile manifesto. (2019, March 22). Medium. Available from: https://medium. com/@markbarbs/an-updated-agile-manifesto-6aa5cf168101

Anywhere Club. (n.d.). *Agile trends: The future of agile & new methodologies to watch in 2024*. Anywhere Club. Available from: https://aw.club/global/en/blog/agile-trends

APM Blog. (n.d.). *Agile is dead! Long live agility*. APM Blog. Available from: www.apm.org. uk/blog/agile-is-dead-long-live-agility/

Appelo, J. (n.d.). *Agile is dying: It's dissolving*. LinkedIn Pulse. Available from: www.linkedin. com/pulse/agile-dying-its-dissolving-jurgen-appelo-f9are/

Appelo, J. (n.d.). *Agile undead: A synthesis*. LinkedIn. Available from: www.linkedin.com/ pulse/agile-undead-synthesis-jurgen-appelo-54wne/?trackingId=2G7ehCA5S9i Dpduh9g7jTw%3D%3D

BBC News. (2024, January 18). *Hybrid working: Is it a dream or a nightmare?* BBC. Available from: www.bbc.co.uk/news/articles/c0qww8xdvnwo

Berg, C. (n.d.). *LinkedIn post activity*. LinkedIn. Available from: www.linkedin.com/feed/ update/urn:li:activity:7136443897513160704/

Berg, C. (n.d.). *Post went viral*. LinkedIn Pulse. Available from: www.linkedin.com/pulse/ post-went-viral-cliff-berg-uxkke/

Beyond Budgeting Institute. (n.d.). *Ambition to action: The Equinor Beyond Budgeting journey*. Available from: Happy Ltd. www.happy.co.uk/blogs/ambition-to-action-the-equi nor-beyond-budgeting-journey/

Bluesoft. (n.d.). *Is agile dead? Evolution and the future of agility*. Bluesoft. Available from: https://bluesoft.com/blog/is-agile-dead-evolution-and-the-future-of-agility/

Bogsnes, B. (n.d.). *Beyond Budgeting at Equinor: How to become more adaptive and more human*. Drucker Forum. Available from: www.druckerforum.org/blog/beyond-budgeting-at-equinor-how-to-become-more-adaptive-and-more-humanby-bjarte-bogsnes/

Bogsnes, B. (n.d.). *Beyond Budgeting in Statoil*. YouTube. Available from: www.youtube.com/watch?v=0V4-LzJkI4I

Boostkamp. (n.d.). *Is agile dead?* Boostkamp. Available from: www.boostkamp.com/blog/is-agile-dead

Brathwaite, B., & Schreiber, I. (2009). *Challenges for game designers*. Course Technology.

Brechner, E. (n.d.). *Agile project management with Kanban*. Project-Management.com. Available from: https://project-management.com/best-agile-project-management-books/

Burrows, M. (2025). *Wholehearted: Engaging with complexity in the deliberately adaptive organization*. Agendashift Press. Available from: www.agendashift.com/books/wholehearted

Business Agility Institute. (n.d.). *2024 business agility report*. Business Agility Institute. Available from: https://businessagility.institute/learn/2024-business-agility-report/754

CGI. (n.d.). *The future of agile: Trends and predictions for 2023 and beyond*. CGI. Available from: www.cgi.com/uk/en-gb/article/agile-digital-services/the-future-of-agile

CIO. (n.d.). *5 reasons why agile transformation fails*. CIO. Available from: www.cio.com/article/3549828/5-reasons-why-agile-transformation-fails.html

Cohn, M. (n.d.). *Agile estimating and planning*. The Digital Project Manager. Available from: https://thedigitalprojectmanager.com/personal/personal-growth/agile-project-management-books/

Consultancy ME. (n.d.). *The future of work: From cubicle to tribe*. Consultancy ME. Available from: www.consultancy-me.com/news/8698/agile-dynamics-leaders-pen-the-future-of-work-from-cubicle-to-tribe

Cynefin Company. (n.d.). *SAFe: The infantilism of management*. The Cynefin Company. Available from: https://thecynefin.co/safe-the-infantilism-of-management/

DeGrace, P., & Stahl, L. H. (1990). *Wicked Problems, Righteous Solutions*. Prentice Hall.

Doz, Y., & Wilson, K. (2017). *Ringtone: Exploring the rise and fall of Nokia in mobile phones*. Oxford University Press.

EA Voices. (2014, March 19). *Agile is not dead, it's morphing*. EA Voices. Available from: https://eavoices.com/2014/03/19/agile-is-not-dead-its-morphing/

eloomi. (2023, February 21). *The 5 power skills to engage and enable employee development*. Available from: https://eloomi.com/resource/article/the-5-power-skills-to-engage-and-enable-employee-development/

Engage & Prosper. (n.d.). *Why agile and flexible working outshines hybrid working*. Engage & Prosper. Available from: www.engageandprosper.com/news_and_updates/why-agile-and-flexible-working-outshines-hybrid-working-embracing-the-future-of-work

Engprax. (2024, July 18). *Response to misleading claims by Jon Kern: 'Agile manifesto co-author blasts failure rates report, talks up "reimagining" project'.* Engprax. Available from: www.engprax.com/post/response-to-misleading-claims-by-jon-kern-agile-manifesto-co-author-blasts-failure-rates-report-talks-up-reimagining-project/

Engprax. (2024, June 4). *268% higher failure rates for agile software projects, study finds.* Engprax. Available from: www.engprax.com/post/268-higher-failure-rates-for-agile-software-projects-study-finds/

Engprax. (2024, September 15). *Martin Fowler (agile manifesto co-author) spread misinformation, report finds.* Engprax. Available from: www.engprax.com/post/martin-fowler-agile-manifesto-co-author-spread-misinformation-report-finds/

Engprax. (n.d.). *Impact engineering: Transforming beyond agile project management.* Engprax. Available from: www.engprax.com/work/impact-engineering-transforming-beyond-agile-project-management/

Feathers, M. C. (n.d.). *Working effectively with legacy code.* Goodreads. Available from: www.goodreads.com/list/show/41715.Top_100_Agile_Books

Forbes. (2019, August 23). *The end of agile.* Forbes. Available from: www.forbes.com/sites/cognitiveworld/2019/08/23/the-end-of-agile/

Forrester. (2025, January 27). *Amidst the AI hype, Agile still remains relevant in 2025.* Forrester Blogs. Available from: www.forrester.com/blogs/amidst-the-ai-hype-agile-still-remains-relevant-in-2025/

Fowler, M. (2001, June). *Writing the agile manifesto.* Martinfowler.com. Available from: https://martinfowler.com/articles/agileStory.html

Fowler, M. (2005, December 13). *The new methodology.* Martinfowler.com. Available from: https://martinfowler.com/articles/newMethodology.html

Fowler, M. (2018, August 1). *The state of agile software in 2018.* Martinfowler.com. Available from: https://martinfowler.com/articles/agile-aus-2018.html

Fowler, M. (2019, August 1). *Agile software guide.* Martinfowler.com. Available from: https://martinfowler.com/agile.html

Fowler, M. (2021, October 26). *My foreword to 'The art of Agile development'.* Martinfowler.com. Available from: https://martinfowler.com/articles/art-agile-foreword.html

Fowler, M. (n.d.). *Refactoring: Improving the design of existing code.* Goodreads. Available from: www.goodreads.com/list/show/41715.Top_100_Agile_Books

Gärtner, M. (2024, October 29). *Agile is dead – and I thought I had that conversation.* Shino.de. Available from: www.shino.de/2024/10/29/agile-is-dead-and-i-thought-i-had-that-conversation/

Gärtner, M. (2024, October 30). *Agile is dead.* Shino.de. Available from: www.shino.de/2024/10/30/agile-is-dead/

Gärtner, M. (2024, October 31). *Agile is undead.* Shino.de. Available from: www.shino.de/2024/10/31/agile-is-undead/

Goodwins, R. (2024, June 10). *Fragile agile development model is a symptom, not a source, of project failure.* The Register. Available from: www.theregister.com/2024/06/10/agile_opinion_column/

Highsmith, J. (n.d.). *Reimagining Agile: How agile lost its soul and is seeking to get it back.* Medium. Available from: https://jim-highsmith.medium.com/reimagining-agile-how-agile-lost-its-soul-and-is-seeking-to-get-it-back-90ecb8500444

Highsmith, J. (n.d.). *The agile compass: Prioritising what matters 'over' competing demands.* LinkedIn Pulse. Available from: www.linkedin.com/pulse/agile-compass-prioritizing-what-matters-over-demands-jim-highsmith-w17pc/

History: The Agile Manifesto. (n.d.). Agile Manifesto. Available from: https://agilemanifesto.org/history.html

Hohl, P., Klünder, J., van Bennekum, A., Lockard, R., Gifford, J., Münch, J., Stupperich, M., & Schneider, K. (2018, November 9). 'Back to the future: Origins and directions of the "Agile Manifesto" – views of the originators', *Journal of Software Engineering Research and Development.* https://jserd.springeropen.com/articles/10.1186/s40411-018-0059-z

Hunt, A., & Thomas, D. (n.d.). *The pragmatic programmer: From journeyman to master.* Goodreads. Available from: www.goodreads.com/list/show/41715.Top_100_Agile_Books

HUPS. (n.d.). *Agile in the age of AI.* HUPS. Available from: https://hups.com/blog/agile-in-the-age-of-ai

ICAgile. (n.d.). *Agile is dead or is it?* ICAgile. Available from: www.icagile.com/resources/agile-is-dead-or-is-it

Improving. (n.d.). *Agile mythbusting: Debunking the 'agile is dead' narrative.* Improving. Available from: www.improving.com/thoughts/agile-mythbusting-debunking-the-agile-is-dead-narrative/

Inbound Logistics. (n.d.). *Agile supply chain: What it is, benefits, and applications.* Inbound Logistics. Available from: www.inboundlogistics.com/articles/agile-supply-chain/

Influential Agile Leader. (n.d.). *Agile in education: Fostering adaptive learning environments.* Influential Agile Leader. Available from: www.influentialagileleader.com/agile-in-education/

ITProToday. (n.d.). *Reassessing agile software development: Is it dead, or can it be revived?* ITProToday. Available from: www.itprotoday.com/software-development-techniques/reassessing-agile-software-development-is-it-dead-or-can-it-be-revived-

Kerr, C. (2015). *EA executive discusses challenges of implementing agile in game development.* Gamasutra. Available from: www.gamasutra.com/view/news/243461/EA_executive_discusses_challenges_of_implementing_Agile_in_game_development.php

Kim, G., Behr, K., & Spafford, G. (n.d.). *The Phoenix project: A novel about IT, DevOps, and helping your business win.* Goodreads. Available from: www.goodreads.com/list/show/41715.Top_100_Agile_Books

Kimberly-Clark Professional. (n.d.). *Siemens energy: Decades of manufacturing evolution.* Kimberly-Clark Professional. Available from: www.contenthubext.kimberly-clark.com/Content/Public/202615587.pdf

LeadDev. (n.d.). *If agile isn't dead, why is it still not working?* LeadDev. Available from: https://leaddev.com/velocity/if-agile-isnt-dead-why-it-still-not-working

Lindsay, G. (2024). *Clearly Agile: A Leadership Guide to Business Agility.* Practical Inspiration.

LinkedIn. (n.d.). *Agile reflection.* LinkedIn. Available from: www.linkedin.com/feed/update/urn:li:activity:7186004530109558785/

LinkedIn. (n.d.). *Forget Agile is dead, here's what's really happening.* LinkedIn. Available from: www.linkedin.com/pulse/forget-agile-dead-heres-whats-really-happening-project-upright-giwsc/

LinkedIn. (n.d.). *Future of work and agile: Embracing flexibility & continuous improvement.* LinkedIn. Available from: www.linkedin.com/pulse/future-work-agile-embracing-flexibility-continuous-improvement-dmvqf/

Long, A. (n.d.). *LinkedIn post activity.* LinkedIn. Available from: www.linkedin.com/posts/long-andrew-m_agiletransformation-safe-agile-activity-7118296788087771136--grh/

Managed Agile. (n.d.). *What's the future of agile? Is there something else coming next?* Managed Agile. Available from: https://managedagile.com/future-of-agile/

Manifesto for Agile Software Development. (2001). *Manifesto for Agile software development.* Available from: https://agilemanifesto.org/

Martin Fowler (software engineer). (n.d.). *Wikipedia.* Available from: https://en.wikipedia.org/wiki/Martin_Fowler_%28software_engineer%29

Martin, R. C. (n.d.). *Agile software development, principles, patterns, and practices.* Goodreads. Available from: www.goodreads.com/list/show/41715.Top_100_Agile_Books

Martin, R. C. (n.d.). *Clean code: A handbook of agile software craftsmanship.* Goodreads. Available from: www.goodreads.com/list/show/41715.Top_100_Agile_Books

McKinsey & Company. (n.d.). *How Roche pursues agile and digital transformation.* McKinsey & Company. Available from: www.mckinsey.com/capabilities/people-and-organizational-performance/our-insights/how-a-healthcare-company-is-pursuing-agile-transformation

McKinsey & Company. (n.d.). *The journey to an agile organization.* McKinsey & Company. Available from: www.mckinsey.com/capabilities/people-and-organizational-performance/our-insights/the-journey-to-an-agile-organization

Merapar. (n.d.). *Agile is dead? Complexity isn't!* Merapar. Available from: https://articles.merapar.com/agile-is-dead-complexity-isnt

Mountain Goat Software. (n.d.). *Is scrum dead? Is agile dead?* Mountain Goat Software. Available from: www.mountaingoatsoftware.com/blog/is-scrum-dead-is-agile-dead

NextUp Solutions. (n.d.). *If Agile is dead, who killed it? Suspect #3: The changing world.* NextUp Solutions. Available from: https://nextupsolutions.com/insights/if-agile-is-dead-who-killed-it-suspect-3-the-changing-world

Nonaka, I., & Takeuchi, H. (1986/1987). 'The new new product development game'. *Harvard Business Review.*

Open Leadership Network. (n.d.). *Open Leadership Network.* Available from: https://openleadershipnetwork.com

Pearson. (2023, September 25). *Pearson Skills Outlook: Power skills.* Available from: https://plc.pearson.com/en-GB/news-and-insights/pearson-skills-outlook-powerskills

Project Management Institute. (n.d.). *Navigating the future of work with an agile mindset.* PMI. Available from: www.pmi.org/learning/thought-leadership/navigating-the-future-of-work-with-an-agile-mindset

Project Management Institute. (n.d.). *Power skills.* Disciplined Agile. Available from: www.pmi.org/disciplined-agile/people/powerskills

Rasmusson, J. (n.d.). *The Agile samurai: How agile masters deliver great software.* The Digital Project Manager. Available from: https://thedigitalprojectmanager.com/personal/personal-growth/agile-project-management-books/

Reimagining Agile. (n.d.). *Reimagining agile – Making agility accessible to all.* Reimagining Agile. Available from: www.reimaginingagile.com/

Resonate Blog. (2024). *Leadership in times of 'agile is dead' awakening.* Resonate Blog. Available from: https://blog.resonate.company/2024/02/leadership-in-times-of-agile-is-dead.html

Ries, E. (n.d.). *The lean startup: How today's entrepreneurs use continuous innovation to create radically successful businesses.* Goodreads. Available from: www.goodreads.com/list/show/41715.Top_100_Agile_Books

Rubin, K. S. (n.d.). *Essential scrum: A practical guide to the most popular Agile process.* Shortform. Available from: www.shortform.com/best-books/genre/best-agile-books-of-all-time

Scrum Inc. (n.d.). *Agile unleashed: Scale at John Deere.* Scrum Inc. Available from: www.scruminc.com/agile-unleashed-scale-john-deere-case-study/

Simply Psychology. (n.d.). *Hofstede's cultural dimensions theory & examples.* Simply Psychology. Available from: www.simplypsychology.org/hofstedes-cultural-dimensions-theory.html

Speed, R. (2024, June 5). *Study finds 268% higher failure rates for agile software projects.* The Register. Available from: www.theregister.com/2024/06/05/agile_failure_rates/

Success Engineering. (n.d.). *Agile is not dead, just not kept up with the times.* Success Engineering. Available from: https://successengineering.works/agile-is-not-dead-just-not-kept-up-with-the-times/

Sutherland, J., & Sutherland, J. J. (n.d.). *Scrum: The art of doing twice the work in half the time.* The Digital Project Manager. Available from: https://thedigitalprojectmanager.com/personal/personal-growth/agile-project-management-books/

Taleb, N. N. (2012). *Antifragile: Things that gain from disorder.* Random House.

The Agile Manifesto. (2001, August). United States Naval Academy. Available from: https://usna.edu/Users/cs/needham/courses/ic470/fallAY11/TheAgileManifesto.pdf

The Liberators. (n.d.). *Agile is dead.* Medium. Available from: https://medium.com/the-liberators/agile-is-dead-%EF%B8%8F-5e7590466611

The Liberators. (n.d.). *Agile is not dead, it's evolving.* Medium. Available from: https://medium.com/the-liberators/agile-is-not-dead-its-evolving-bad953fce931

Vastmans, K. (n.d.). *Scaling agile... or why some people think Agile is dead.* LinkedIn Pulse. Available from: www.linkedin.com/pulse/scaling-agile-why-some-people-think-dead-koen-vastmans-mygxe/

Vuori, M., & Huy, Q. N. (2016). 'Distributed attention and shared emotions in the innovation process: How Nokia lost the smartphone battle', *Administrative Science Quarterly,* 61(1), 9–51.

Webber, A. (2024). *Hybrid working: Productivity, promotions, and policies.* Stanford Institute for Economic Policy Research & Shenzhen Finance Institute. Available from: www.personneltoday.com/hr/hybrid-working-stanford-study/

Wikipedia. (n.d.). *Agile software development.* Wikipedia. Available from: https://en.wikipedia.org/wiki/Agile_software_development

Wikipedia. (n.d.). *Disciplined Agile delivery.* Wikipedia. Available from: https://en.wikipedia.org/wiki/Disciplined_agile_delivery

Wikipedia. (n.d.). *High-context and low-context cultures.* Wikipedia. Available from: https://en.wikipedia.org/wiki/High-context_and_low-context_cultures

Wikipedia. (n.d.). *Timeline of project management.* Wikipedia. Available from: https://en.wikipedia.org/wiki/Timeline_of_project_management

Acknowledgements

Writing this second book has been another incredible journey for me, and I am deeply grateful to the many individuals who have supported, inspired, and accompanied me along the way.

First and foremost, my heartfelt gratitude goes out to my wife, Anneke. Your unwavering support, insightful feedback, and constant encouragement have been my guiding light throughout this journey. I couldn't have done it without you.

I am profoundly grateful to the thought leaders whose work has significantly influenced my thinking. This book also reflects conversations with peers, clients, and collaborators. The insights, debates, and feedback shared with me throughout this journey shaped the thinking behind each chapter. My thanks go to everyone who challenged my assumptions and sharpened these ideas.

Dave Snowden: Your pioneering work in knowledge management and complexity science has been instrumental in shaping modern organizational practices.

Nigel Thurlow: Your leadership in integrating Lean and Agile ways of working, particularly through The Flow System, has set new standards for organizational excellence.

Steve Denning: Your insights into leadership and storytelling have transformed how we communicate and lead in the business world.

Geert Hofstede and **Edward T. Hall**: Your groundbreaking research in cultural dimensions has provided invaluable frameworks for understanding cross-cultural communication.

Amy Edmondson: Your concept of psychological safety has redefined team dynamics and organizational learning.

Dr. John Kotter: Your work on change management has been a cornerstone for leaders navigating organizational transformation.

Carol Dweck: Your research on mindset has opened new pathways for personal and professional development.

Patrick Hoverstadt: Your expertise in systems thinking has provided valuable perspectives on organizational strategy.

Dr Jean Twenge: Your research on generational differences has shed light on the evolving workplace dynamics.

Thomas Kuhn: Your work on the structure of scientific revolutions has influenced my approach to paradigm shifts in business.

Edgar Schein: Your studies on organizational culture have been instrumental in understanding corporate environments.

I extend my gratitude to the pioneers and practitioners in the Agile and software development communities:

Jim Highsmith, Alistair Cockburn, Martin Fowler, Jon Kern, Dave Thomas, Mike Cohn, Scott Ambler, Mark Lines, Evan Leybourn, Laura Powers, Mike Burrows, Arie van Bennekum, and **Jeff Sutherland**: Your contributions have been foundational in advancing Agile ways of working and practices.

Special thanks to my friends, collaborators, and colleagues who have been instrumental in various initiatives:

Russ Lewis, TC Gill, and **Femi Odelusi**: Working together on the Business Agility Institute UK launch has been such a rewarding experience for me. Your passion and dedication are truly inspiring.

Paul Smith, Saif Mohammad, and **Mark Bramwell**: Sharing the journey to receive our Global CIO 200 award together in South Africa and then all of us travelling back to London for the UK CIO award the following day was a truly memorable experience. Your continuing camaraderie and support mean a huge amount to me. Thank you all!

Thank you to the amazing review team of **Neil Walker, Amy Luethmers, Russ Lewis, TC Gill, Femi Odelusi, Alkesh Shah, and Melissa Reeve**. Your thoughtful feedback, time, and attention to detail have significantly strengthened this book and helped refine both its structure and message.

Thank you to **Pam Ashby** (Marketing), **Marina Alex** (Sales), **Riina Hellström** (HR/People Team), **Ondřej Dvořák** (Legal), and **Daniela Forsgård** (Finance) for your invaluable contributions to Chapter 9. Your insights have enriched the discussion on Agility across these key business areas.

Thank you, **Sanches Clarke,** for all your amazing support and feedback you gave in reviewing Chapter 12.

Tobias Mayer, Allan Kelly, Chris Charalambous, Philippe Guenet, Nick Perry, James Shore, Diana Larsen, Alize Hofmeester, Adrian Dooley, Markus Gärtner, Sheetal Thaker, Scott Seivwright, Danny Wrigglesworth, Nic Skinner, Alessandro Agratini, Lif3away Inc, Perfect Rebel, Fluxion, James Dwan, Vince Grant, Anthony Anderson, Brian Solis, Tushar Sahoo, and **Venkatesh Mahadevan**: Your shared insights, learnings, feedback given, and friendship from some of you have truly enriched this journey.

To the tribe of CxO friends and colleagues, your shared wisdom, friendship, and inspiration have been a cornerstone of this journey. This book is a testament to the collective knowledge and encouragement I have received. Thank you all for being part of this adventure.

To the entire community of practitioners, scholars, colleagues, friends, and family who have supported me, whether mentioned by name or not, please know that your contributions have been invaluable.

About the Author – Giles Lindsay CITP FIAP FBCS FCMI

Giles Lindsay is an award-winning technology executive renowned for his leadership in business agility and digital transformation. As the CEO of Agile Delta Consulting, a global interim technology leadership and Agile consultancy, and a bestselling author, Giles is dedicated to helping organizations realize their full potential through strategic planning, operational excellence, and a culture of continuous improvement. In April 2024, his first book, *Clearly Agile: A Leadership Guide to Business Agility*, became a #1 best-seller on Amazon, establishing him as a leading voice in Agile and business agility leadership.

With over 25 years of experience in software engineering and technology leadership, Giles has been at the forefront of industry change, leading cross-functional engineering teams to deliver innovative solutions across sectors like finance, telecommunications, travel, and healthcare. His expertise spans both nimble startups and global enterprises, where he has held roles such as CTO and CIO, always focusing on driving growth, aligning technology strategies with organizational goals, and enabling transformation. An advocate for responsible AI and ESG principles, he champions ethical innovation and sustainability as cornerstones of modern digital strategies.

A certified Agile practitioner, coach, instructor, and keynote speaker, Giles has helped teams across the world optimize performance and embrace true agility and Agile ways of working. His passion for talent development is evident in his commitment to mentoring emerging leaders, enabling them to thrive in their careers.

In 2024, along with several colleagues, Giles played a key role in successfully establishing the Business Agility Institute UK, assuming the role of President. He is also a Non-Exec Board Director at the Agile Business Consortium, where he contributes to shaping the future of agility and business transformation. His work in fostering a broader Agile and business agility community has been instrumental in advancing the conversation around Agile transformation in the UK and beyond. Following establishing the Business Agility Institute UK, he helped organize and chair the inaugural Business Agility Conference UK, which was a resounding success.

Giles is proud to have received several prestigious awards recently, including recognition in the World 100 CIO/CTO List 2024, Global CIO 200 2025, and UK CIO 100 2025. He was honoured with the 'Legend Award' at the UK CIO 200 Summit and invited to join the Forbes Technology Council. In 2025, Agile Delta Consulting, under his leadership, was named Business Agility & Digital Transformation Consultancy of the Year and received the Client Service Excellence Award at the UK Enterprise Awards. These accolades reflect his commitment to innovation and the impact he is making within the technology industry.

Giles also has a unique collection of mementoes from his Agile journey, ranging from a pizza-sized cookie decorated with 'Best Agile Coach Ever!' to a promotional video showcasing the transformation at a fintech company and even a T-shirt celebrating a successful Agile transformation. He often quips, *'Now I've got the Book, the Film, and the T-shirt'* – writing his first book felt like the perfect conclusion to this trilogy.

Beyond his coaching and executive leadership roles, Giles has served as a trusted advisor and council member in the Agile space, including as a member of the PMI Disciplined Agile Advisors Group and the Disciplined Agile Consortium Advisory Council.

As a Chartered IT Professional (CITP), a Fellow of BCS, The Chartered Institute for IT (FBCS), the Chartered Management Institute (FCMI), and The Institution of Analysts & Programmers (FIAP), Giles is recognized as a respected figure in his field. He has presented at numerous conferences and seminars worldwide, making complex agility and technology concepts accessible and inspiring others to apply these principles for real business impact.

In *The Adaptive Leader*, Giles continues to draw from his rich experience, offering a practical, insightful guide for leaders seeking to harness the power of agility to create adaptable, inclusive, and value-driven organizations. By focusing on Adaptive Leadership in the post-Agile era, he provides actionable strategies that help leaders navigate the complexities of modern business with confidence and clarity. Whether you're an experienced executive, an aspiring leader, or simply curious about agility, Giles' insights offer an indispensable resource for anyone aiming to thrive in the evolving future of work.

Also by the Author

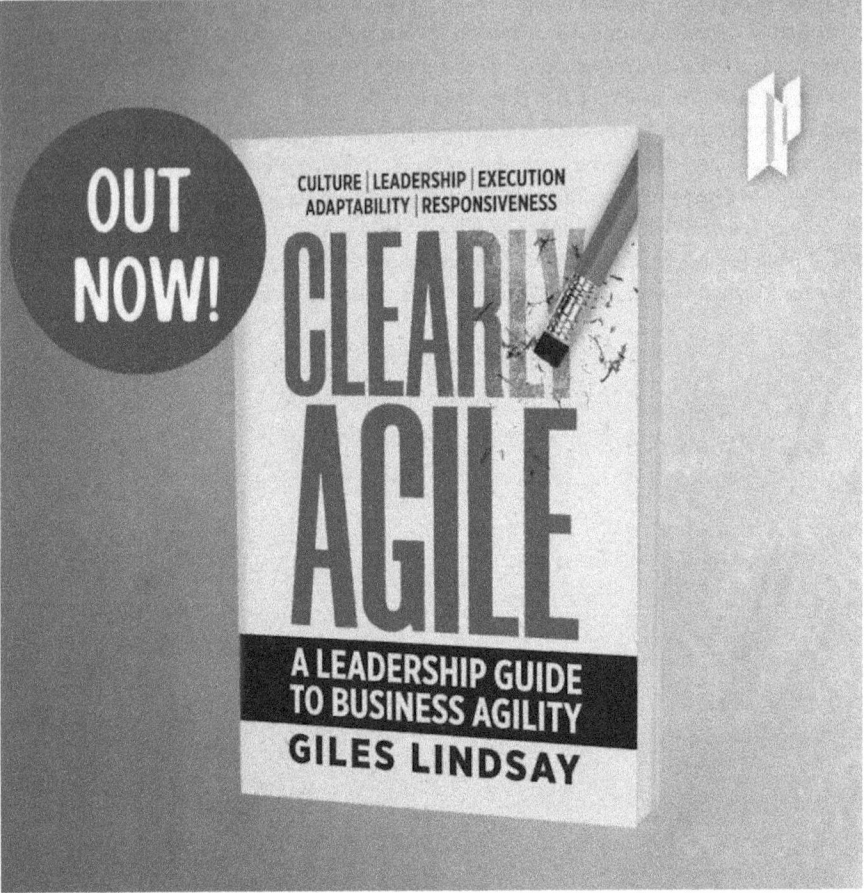

OUT NOW!

CULTURE | LEADERSHIP | EXECUTION
ADAPTABILITY | RESPONSIVENESS

CLEARLY AGILE

A LEADERSHIP GUIDE
TO BUSINESS AGILITY

GILES LINDSAY

Index

Note: Page numbers in *italics* denote figures.

strategies to improve cross-functional agility
241–243
outcome-driven teams 115
over-adaptation without governance, impact of 107

past mistakes, learning from 246
Patagonia 55, 164, 339
People-First Leadership 159, 160–161, 163
Perry, Nick 316
personal agility plan 55
personalization 89
Phoenix Corp 352–353
pilot projects 171
policy implementation 96, 100
politics 186–187
post-Agile era 3, 9, 63–64, 158, 235, 331
  adaptive leadership for success of 77–78
  and Agile, distinction between 66–67
  Agile community and leaders role 80–81
  Agile Rebellion, case Studies of 81–83
  and behavioural agility *see* behavioural agility
  as business agility evolution 79
  and CLEAR Model® implementation 71–73
  culture and embedding of 67–68
  differing from adjacent ideas 64–65
  internalizing and sustaining agility in 69–70
  leadership concept 65–66, 151
  measuring agility in 78–79
  methods 3–4
  reframing the landscape 70
  transition, overcoming challenges in 79–80
Power BI 189, 343
power distance 202
Power Distance Index (PDI) 201
power skill development 292
Predix platform (GE) 278
process overload 21
Product Owners 252, 253
Product-Led Agility 257
progress celebration 343
Project Management Institute (PMI) 292
Project Management Office (PMO) 120
psychological safety 10, 13, 108, 112, 114, 122, 124,
        143, 206, 228, 238, 259, 292, 298, 308, 310,
        317, 328, 337
  and AI 262, 264
  in business agility 161, 164–165, 169, 171
  and emotional intelligence 97, 257, 259
  Google's *Project Aristotle* 91, 121, 245, 298
  and leadership practices 28, 38, 58, 66, 80, 95, 102
  pitfalls of 94–95
  role in resilience 98

role in sustaining agility 299
stages of 299
in team-centric agility 114, 115–116
public dashboards 343
purpose vs profit 55

quantum computing 268, 269, 279–280, 284, 345

RACI matrix (Responsible, Accountable, Consulted,
        Informed) 118–120, *119*, 295
radar charts 233
reading and reflection 55
recombination 173
regulatory compliance 339
Reimagining Agile 311–313
  adaptive leadership for 315–317
  contributors to 319
  embracing context-driven agility 318–319
  emphasizing core values and principles 317–318
  integrating diversity 319–320
  key shifts and strategies for 313–314
  movement 315, 320–321
  redefining Agile's core principles 314–315
  reflecting on Agile's future 321–322
remote and hybrid work 12, 125–127, 263, 264, 294,
        298, 340
resilience building 98, 302–303
resistance management, team-centric agility 117–118,
        124
reskilling 297, 333
responsibility theatre 142
Responsive Customer-Centricity 159, 162
retail, Agile in 182, 186
retrospectives 70, 300
revenue growth, and revenue growth 136–137
reverse mentoring 205
reward systems 297
risk management 26
risk-taking approach 299
ritualism vs real agility 238
rituals, unhelpful 39
Robotic Process Automation (RPA) tools 189
ROI of Agile 237–238

SAFe Consultants 251
sales, Agile in 182
scalability 189
Scaled Agile Framework (SAFe) 7–8, 23–24, 32, 47,
        75, 141, 172, 238, 246, 313, 317
  consultants 251
  as 'fake Agile' 31, 157–158
  Maturity Model 231–232, 233, 307